MW01041921

A course in macroeconomic modelling and forecasting

A course in macroeconomic modelling and forecasting

John D. Whitley
London Business School

HARVESTER
WHEATSHEAF

New York London Toronto Sydney Tokyo Singapore

First published 1994 by
Harvester Wheatsheaf
Campus 400, Maylands Avenue
Hemel Hempstead
Hertfordshire, HP2 7EZ
A division of
Simon & Schuster International Group

© John D. Whitley 1994

All rights reserved. No part of this publication may be reproduced,
stored in a retrieval system, or transmitted, in any form, or by any
means, electronic, mechanical, photocopying, recording or otherwise,
without prior permission, in writing, from the publisher.

Typeset in 10/12 pt Times
by Vision Typesetting, Manchester.
Printed and bound in Great Britain by Redwood Books Ltd,
Trowbridge, Wiltshire

British Library Cataloguing in Publication Data

A catalogue record for this book is available from
the British Library

ISBN 07450 1425 9 (pbk)

---

2 3 4 5 98 97 96 95

To Abi, Francine and Duncan

Contents

Preface

The intention of this book is to make it possible for those wishing to learn about macroeconometric models to acquire the skills needed to understand and evaluate models. It is aimed at third-year undergraduates, postgraduates and professional economists, in either the public or private sector. The book can be used as part of a course in applied macroeconomics or applied econometrics. It assumes some understanding of standard macroeconomic theory, and although an econometrics background is useful, it is not necessary. The treatment is not particularly mathematical for, although a familiarity with matrix algebra is assumed, alternative ways of describing modelling methods are given. The book can also be used as a guide in interpreting models and their results for those who use the products of model-based exercises. Too often users of models are unsure whether the results that they are presented with reflect a particular view of how the economy functions, or are the result of specific (often very technical) assumptions by the modeller. After reading this book the model user should be able to understand why different models or different approaches result in different conclusions.

The motivation for writing this book has come from lecturing to students and professional economists, both in the UK and abroad, about macroeconometric models and their properties. Although the presence of the ESRC Macroeconomic Modelling Bureau at Warwick since 1983 has led to a major improvement in the dissemination of information about UK models and their properties, there is no one source which gives a description of both technical matters and empirical features of macroeconometric models. Furthermore, the Bureau has concentrated on UK models and the material in this book is more international in nature, for it gives the reader an insight into models of different economies, as well as multicountry models.

My debt to many colleagues in the macroeconomic modelling profession is immense, and many of the ideas in this book come as a result of joint work and many conversations. Ken Wallis has been an enormous influence on me, as has Paul Fisher with his tremendous ability to understand technical problems. The list of others to whom I am indebted is extensive, but I should like to mention particularly Mike Artis, Ray Barrell, David Currie, Stephen Hall, Brian Henry, Patrick Minford, Dave Turner, Ron Smith, Rod Whittakker, Alpo Willman and Simon Wren-Lewis. Needless to say, I am responsible for any errors and omissions in this book. Thanks are also due to Katja Huep for tolerant and efficient help with the preparation of the manuscript and for the forbearance of my family while this book was in preparation.

The author and publishers wish to thank the ESRC Macroeconomic Modelling Bureau, University of Warwick, for permission for the use of copyright material. The author acknowledges his intellectual debt to his various colleagues at the Bureau, M J Andrews, D N F Bell, K B Church, P G Fisher, J A Longbottom, P R Mitchell, S K Tanna, D S Turner and K F Wallis, while retaining full responsibility for errors and omissions. The financial support of the Economic and Social Research Council is also gratefully acknowledged.

Permission by Kluwer Academic Publishers to use results from Tables 4.4 - 4.5 and 5.1 - 5.3 of P G Fisher, Rational Expectations in Macroeconomic Models, is gratefully acknowledged.

1 An introduction to macroeconomic modelling

This book is concerned with macroeconomic models. These have been used regularly for the last 30 years or so. They have been used by the private sector, in academic institutions and in government and official agencies to analyse the economy and to evaluate macroeconomic policies, and to make predictions about the likely future behaviour of the economy (forecasts). The tradition of modelling began in North America and in Western Europe, but it has spread increasingly throughout the world. As economic links between nations have increased, so there have been attempts to incorporate the joint dependence of economies, either through linked models or by construction of global (world) models. Despite the fact that macroeconometric modelling is now an established activity, it has not been without its critics. This book is an attempt to describe how macro models have developed, to give a picture of their current level of development, and to examine some of the issues, both economic and technical, that arise in their construction and use. Particular emphasis is placed upon the policy implications arising from different macro models. The book is not about the construction of models through econometric estimation methods: this is well covered elsewhere. Instead we concentrate on the economic issues associated with model building, and the consequences of following alternative approaches. Macroeconomic models in general use have tended to follow a rather aggregate time-series approach, and the book therefore rather inevitably centres on this, but at the same time it compares critically the usefulness of the 'standard' modelling approach with models based on other methods, such as vector autogressive methods (VARs), computable general equilibrium (CGE) models and representative agent models.

Because the book is about empirical models there is some comparative description of actual models, but we do not aim to provide a comprehensive account of all the models in everyday use since this would result in an enormous amount of information and run the risk of becoming confusing rather than helpful. Furthermore, real-world models are likely to change in detail, so any attempt to provide a comprehensive cross-section account of models would inevitably soon become dated. Instead we focus on a subset of models in order to illustrate some of the issues in modelling. In this way it is intended that the reader can assimilate some skills in using and evaluating models which are of general applicability. Although several empirical examples are given that

1

use UK models, the book aims to provide an international flavour since many of the issues that are explored are relevant to modelling in general. This is true of both the technical model-handling methods and the general economic features. The discussion of multicountry models enables us to distinguish between different modelling approaches as well as different structural features of different economies.

The material in the book reflects my experience over 20 or more years with macroeconometric models at the National Institute, the Institute for Employment Research and the Macroeconomic Modelling Bureau (both at Warwick), and the London Business School. This has involved model construction, policy analysis, forecasting and comparative model analysis with a variety of models of differing economies and of the global economy. Some of the material has been published in other places, especially in publications by the Macroeconomic Modelling Bureau, so that the intention of this book is not originality, but rather to assemble a reasonably comprehensive account of modelling methods and findings.

The book begins with a brief history of modelling and then moves into a short account of some of the main models in current use, in the UK and elsewhere. The discussion extends into a description of how institutional arrangements have influenced the nature of models in different countries. We also consider some of the other considerations which influence the form, size and detail of the model. The second chapter sets out a framework which is used in subsequent chapters to describe both technical issues with the models and their relation to economic theory. It begins by setting out a simple linear model which is then developed to describe modelling methodology, introducing non-linearity, simultaneity and dynamics, and distinguishing between the structural and reduced form of the model. The relationship of the macroeconometric model to alternative approaches (vector autoregressive and computable general equilibrium models) is also considered. We then move on to consider how models relate to the standard macroeconomic textbook concepts such as the *IS/LM* curves and aggregate demand and aggregate supply schedules (*AD/AS*). With the extension of the model to that of an open economy this leads into the use of concepts such as the equilibrium exchange rate and the equilibrium rate of unemployment. The relationship to theoretical paradigms is used extensively throughout the book as a framework against which to compare the results of the models. The extensive use of UK models to illustrate various propositions largely reflects the more systematic and regular monitoring of models that has been made possible by the work of the ESRC Macroeconomic Modelling Bureau at the University of Warwick, but many of the results are general in nature, results from models for other countries are also presented, and global models are well represented in the discussion.

In the third chapter of the book we outline the main developments that have taken place in macroeconometric models over the last 25 years, following the monetarist challenge to the rather Keynesian orthodoxy of the 1970s, through the rational expectations revolution of the early 1980s and the supply-side approach also prevalent in the early 1980s, to the approximate consensus that presently exists. Our chronological account describes how the existing models have responded to these new challenges, and how new competitor models have emerged. We emphasise in particular how the changes that have taken place in macro models over this period have influenced macroeconomic policy (and indeed how the models themselves have been influenced by policy considerations). In order to focus the discussion more clearly we set out a stylised representation of the models. We follow this discussion of the changing structure of models by considering how far these changes are reflected in the quantitative estimates of the output and inflation responses to changes in fiscal and monetary policy. We then compare current differences in model-based estimates of policy responses. This tells us how far models differ. The remainder of the book is focused upon explaining how and why these differences occur, and describes various methods which can be used to understand these differences.

Chapter 4 concentrates on the structures of the models rather than on their system properties, and isolates key areas which are crucial to these system properties. Our analysis presents this in terms of the behaviour of different economic agents in various markets within the economy. There is always a danger in discussing macro models that the results appear as a black box, and this makes it particularly difficult to explain why one model produces different results from another. Without losing the appreciation that the economy (and hence models) is a combination of interrelated phenomena where one agent's decisions impinge upon another, we show that a lot can be understood by considering the main structural equations in the models. For example, the modelling of consumer purchases by the personal sector has a great importance for the economy as a whole, if only from the fact that it accounts for such a high proportion of total demand. The consumption decision has been an area where a great deal of effort has been expended by modellers in an attempt to explain the rather dramatic swings that have occurred in the proportion of personal income saved. In turn this has led to the reconsideration of the role of inflation in spending decisions, and more generally the role of wealth and the impact that the financial deregulation and liberalisation of the 1980s have had on consumer behaviour. These developments have a relevance not only for understanding the consumption decision itself, but also for the way in which the economy as a whole responds to shocks.

The behaviour of firms has implications for the way in which investment decisions are made, employment levels set, and price and output levels determined. We outline the ways in which models treat the behaviour of firms, and how changes in the way that firms' behaviour is viewed have consequences for the model as a whole. In an open economy, trade between countries (imports and exports) is an important element both for a single country and for the links between countries. Key issues that have dominated the modelling of trade have been the role of relative prices in correcting trade imbalances and the treatment of non-price competitiveness. One particular concept that has attracted some attention is the notion of an equilibrium real exchange rate which ensures balanced trade for a given level of domestic activity, or external balance. The real exchange rate is typically treated as an endogenous variable, modelled either directly or from the identity linking the real rate to the nominal rate and the price level. Exchange rates (and interest rates) can be considered as determined in the financial market of the economy and they provide yet another key link between economies of different countries. So one way of thinking about macro models is by

3

analysis of markets: the goods market where quantities of goods and services are determined by the interaction of firms and consumers; the labour market where firms and labour interact to set wage levels and employment; and financial markets. This can be a convenient way of summarising the key features of models, but yet another framework which can be adopted is that of analysing models by the demand and supply sides of the key behavioural relations. There are several alternative ways in which the supply side of models can be considered. In Chapter 4 we show how the supply side plays an essential role in determining the long-run response of a given model, and how it can be used to describe the equilibrium level of output and unemployment (internal balance), often known as the natural rate of output (unemployment) or the NAIRU (non-accelerating-inflation rate of unemployment). The chapter sets out a picture of how models operate, based on the experience of the UK, but also considers whether this experience is representative of other countries, notably the USA and the rest of Europe. It contrasts some of the different traditions and how these have influenced practical modelling.

Whereas Chapter 4 concentrates on the structure of models and the economic issues raised, the models themselves are typically a simultaneous account of interrelated developments. Thus, for example, it is only an approximation to assume that the goods market determines the quantity of goods and services produced in an economy, for decisions about the level of employment and the wage at which labour is priced are given in the labour market, and these decisions also impinge upon the final level of output in an economy. Similarly, as in elementary economics texts, the price level can be seen as the outcome of both demand and supply factors. Therefore, although an examination of the key building blocks of a model is crucial to understanding the underpinnings of economic behaviour assumed, to understand fully the model as a whole we need to allow for the interactions which take place between sectors. Chapter 5 is concerned with explaining methods which are used to analyse the complete model, and deals with important questions such as the determination of short- and long-run responses of the economy to a given shock, and the trade-offs between policy objectives. It shows how there are different ways of analysing the supply-side response of the models. The chapter also describes how rational (model-consistent) expectations raise additional problems of experimental design. Whereas most analysis of models is based on the assumption that the model is known and that random elements take their mean value of zero (deterministic analysis), another relevant issue is the impact of uncertainty on forecasts and policy multipliers. These methods are all given practical relevance by examples from exercises with models used regularly for empirical analysis.

Chapters 6 and 7 deal with specific uses of macro models: the production of forecasts and the assessment of the effects of economic policies, respectively. Technical issues are described and the discussion also considers how models might be evaluated on the basis of their forecasts. Chapter 7 draws on several areas: the use of simulation methods to give a set of ready reckoners for policy multipliers; evaluating regime changes; simulating new policies; and the use of optimal control methods. The role of expectations is also considered.

Chapter 8 broadens the discussion to include multicountry models and Chapter 9 examines how models have been used to analyse the European monetary system (EMS) and European monetary union (EMU) and global government deficit-reduction policies. The emphasis is on how different techniques can be used, and the variety of conceptual problems that arise. Finally, Chapter 10 summarises the usefulness of macroeconometric models and attempts to predict the sort of developments that we might see over the next decade in their construction and use.

Table 1.1 gives an outline of the book, indicating in which chapters discussion of key topics takes place.

1.1 A brief history of models

The aim of this section is not to give a full chronological account of the development of macroeconometric modelling, but to give some sense of perspective to present-day models. For a full account of the history of macromodelling the interested reader is referred to the volume by Bodkin *et al.* (1991). The first empirical macro model is usually taken to be that of Tinbergen in 1936, who published a model of the Dutch

Table 1.1 A guide to the book

Chapter	1	2	3	4	5	6	7	8	9	10
Model description	✓	✓	✓	✓				✓		
Simulations		✓	✓		✓		✓	✓	✓	
Expectations			✓	✓	✓	✓	✓	✓	✓	✓
Forecasting		✓				✓		✓		✓
Economic policy		✓	✓		✓		✓	✓	✓	✓
Supply side		✓	✓	✓	✓			✓		✓
Uncertainty					✓	✓	✓		✓	
Alternative approaches		✓				✓	✓			✓
Use of residuals		✓			✓	✓	✓			
Methods		✓			✓	✓	✓		✓	
Model properties		✓	✓		✓				✓	✓
Global models	✓		✓						✓	✓

economy. Although Keynes strongly criticised Tinbergen, it was Keynes himself who stimulated further modelling activity by his efforts in formulating the system of national accounts. This system still provides much of the backbone for current modelling activity. Lawrence Klein was the architect of much of the modelling activity that followed the Second World War. Along with Goldberger he constructed the now famous Klein–Goldberger model of the US economy and then continued to be a major force in the modelling area through his work with Wharton econometrics. The Klein influence has spread world-wide through his students. He was also a major figure in the development of the first UK model, that of Klein, Ball and Vandome in 1961. The Klein–Goldberger model was the source for the classic work by Adelman and Adelman (1959), who sought an explanation of how it could generate business cycles, and whose methods have become standard in current modelling practice. A major effort in macroeconometric modelling in the USA in the 1960s came with the development of the Brookings model, again involving Klein, along with Duesenberry. This was an ambitious project involving a large team of researchers, and the first version of the model contained some 200 equations (later to expand to 400) with the most disaggregation that had then been attempted. The scale of the Brookings project was enormous both then and now, involving some 30 economists, many of them already well known. The Brookings project made huge strides in the areas of model solution techniques and policy analysis, and many current procedures stem from this project. The Brookings exercise also spawned other models, notably the MPS model which was developed by Ando and Modigliani and which extended the role of the financial sector. In the 1970s the Wharton and DRI models (pioneered by Eckstein) were further evidence of the importance of the Brookings work, and these models still survive today in a more commercial forecasting context. Not all the modelling activity in the USA followed from team activities, some models being more idiosyncratic and the work of talented individuals. In this class is the Fair model of the USA and the St Louis Federal Reserve model, which followed a far more monetarist approach than the other US models.

UK modelling activity really began with the Klein, Ball and Vandome model, which was notable for being based on quarterly data. However, with the return of Klein to the USA, the model was not maintained. A parallel effort was also being made at Cambridge under Richard Stone. This model, which later became known as the Cambridge Growth Project model, was initially more of a planning framework than a fully estimated macro model. It was subsequently developed in the 1970s and 1980s so that it became dynamic and based on econometric analysis, but its distinguishing feature has remained its high degree of disaggregation. It survives today as a commercial activity organised by Cambridge Econometrics. Although the Oxford project of Klein, Ball and Vandome did not continue, it did stimulate activity at the London Business School (LBS) which began to produce econometric forecasts in 1966. The National Institute of Economic and Social Research, and Her Majesty's Treasury, had also been producing forecasts of the economy through the 1960s, but these were not the product of a complete macro model (although some econometric relationships were used in the forecasting process). By 1969 the National Institute was using a full model to produce forecasts, and the Treasury followed shortly afterwards. All three models were initially of the Keynesian type and were centred around the income–expenditure approach. The LBS model showed the greatest inclination to adapt. Under the influence of Ball and Burns, and later Budd and Burns, the LBS model in the late 1970s began to favour the international monetarist explanation of economic events, and this led to further changes in the 1980s which were more consistent with the philosophy of the Thatcher government than any of the other existing macro models, including that of the Treasury but with the exception of the Liverpool model. It is therefore probably no great surprise that Terry (now Sir Terry) Burns became the Chief Economic Adviser to the government and was subsequently followed by Alan Budd in that role. As is evident from the model results described later in the book, however, the formal properties of the LBS model are not radically different from those of the other mainstream models, and the difference in policy advice given by the LBS probably reflects more the economic inclinations of its proprietors. Thus the subsequent replacement of Alan Budd by David Currie has resulted in somewhat different, though subtly different, policy advice despite little modification to the formal model. In contrast the National Institute has faced the credibility problem that it tends to be still regarded as very Keynesian despite the fact that its model has changed more radically than that of the LBS in recent years and that its current model can only be regarded as Keynesian in the short run. This contrast emphasises the need to distinguish the policy advice given by model proprietors from the formal properties of their model.

An important factor in the development of macro models has been the greater availability and power of computer hardware. Early models were limited by the constraints on computer power. But there were also other considerations. The National Institute initially planned to use a model developed by Byron (reported in Byron, 1970) but, partly due to its preliminary results and partly due to its complexity, the model was never used and a frantic effort was made to develop a smaller, more tractable model based on only a dozen or so behavioural relationships. Although many have quoted the version reported in Surrey (1971) as being the first NIESR model, the Surrey version never corresponded with the actual model first used in 1969, this model being largely the work of Black and Kidgell. A similar conflict arose in the mid-1970s when, following general criticism of macro models, and specific criticisms of the naïve Keynesian form of the NIESR model, Fane and colleagues set about constructing a more coherent but empirically supported model. But this model was never used, for it was seen to be too radical a change, and instead a more limited adjustment of the existing model was made. As the pressure for change built up (see the discussion in Chapter 3) and following a change in director, the National Institute eventually adopted more radical changes both in econometric methodology, stimulated by Stephen Hall and Brian Henry, and in economic framework, following the efforts of Simon Wren-Lewis.

The Treasury commissioned Ball and Eaton of the London Business School to formalise their existing relationships, and a formal model was used by the Treasury in 1970 to produce forecasts. However, the Treasury model and its forecasts were subject to considerable secrecy, and it took a parliamentary amendment by Jeremy Bray MP to oblige the Treasury to make its model and forecasts publicly available. In the mid-1980s the Treasury model had become more eclectic than Keynesian, but had also become rather large and unwieldy. Thus a major effort was made to 'slim' it down. Latest developments see the Treasury attempting to privatise both modelling and forecasting, but is too early to judge whether this effectively means the end of the 'Treasury model'.

The Bank of England also used the London Business School to start its model building activity in the mid-1970s, and recruited John Bispham, ex-NIESR, to operate it. Subsequently the Bank model developed away from its LBS origins, but it also experienced the slimming operation that the Treasury underwent.

Before we discuss the other UK models which have tended to lie outside the mainstream modelling activity (the Cambridge Economic Policy Group, the Liverpool model and the City University Business School model) it is interesting to note that the mainstream teams (LBS, NIESR, Treasury, Bank of England) have experienced a considerable interchange of personnel, particularly during the last ten years. This reflects a general underlying consensus about macroeconomic modelling between these groups, and it is from the other groups listed above that the main challenges in approach have come.

The Cambridge Economic Policy Group (CEPG) was led by Wyn Godley. It originated in the mid-1970s following dissatisfaction with the treatment of the financial deficits of the main sectors of the economy, and in particular the failure to associate the size of the public sector deficit with that of the balance of payments, on the assumption that the private sector deficit was reasonably stable. There was some doubt about the empirical support for this proposition at the time, but it was certainly proved wrong in the 1980s when the private sector financial deficit fluctuated wildly. The CEPG ceased after 1983 following a cut in funding. Holly (1991) attributes this, at least in part, to the fact that CEPG fell foul of the emerging econometric methodology, and he speculates that it might have survived if it had made some concessions without losing its basic economic message. Godley remains a fierce critic of mainstream modelling methodology (see Treasury and Civil Service Committee, 1991) and he has proved quite prophetic in his projections of the consequences of economic policy in the 1980s and early 1990s.

The 1980s saw the advent of two new modelling groups in the UK, specifically set up to counter the traditional approach to modelling: the City University Business School model (CUBS) and the Liverpool Research Group in Macroeconomics (LPL). The creation of these models was made possible by finance from the Economic and Social Research Council (previously the Social Science Research Council). Previously, modelling was financed on an *ad hoc* basis and had to compete with other academic projects for funding. In 1982, however, the ESRC decided to allocate a specific budget for macroeconomic modelling over a four-year period, to be allocated by a Macroeconomic Modelling Consortium to which the Treasury and the Bank of England contributed. In 1985/86 the Consortium spent just under £1m on academic-based modelling.

The CUBS model was designed to emphasise the supply side of the economy and its distinguishing feature was the absence of an income–expenditure framework. It was designed by Michael Beenstock and was a small annual model with some 130 variables, of which 70 were exogenous. It had some 10 core behavioural equations. The Liverpool model was also a small annual model with fewer than 20 behavioural equations. Its principal features were that it was new classical in nature and was the first UK model to incorporate rational expectations. Its conclusions were highly monetarist, as were those of the CUBS model. The size of these models was in strong contrast to the more mainstream models. In 1983 the LBS model had some 400 variables with over 160 behavioural equations, the NIESR model was a little smaller with some 275 variables and some 90 behavioural equations, and the Treasury was the largest quarterly model with 700 equations and well over 1000 variables (this was later slimmed down to around 500). The Bank of England model, also quarterly, contained some 800 variables, many of which related to the monetary sector. All these models contained little in the way of disaggregation, but in contrast the Cambridge Growth project model distinguished some 39 producing industries and had almost 5000 endogenous variables, 3000 exogenous variables and around 16 000 behavioural parameters and coefficients. Many of these related to the input–output core of the model. A summary account of the main models is given in Table 1.2 and the principal changes in the UK models over the 1980s in Appendix I.

Most technical innovations and empirical developments have come from ESRC-supported modelling projects and have been taken up by forecasters and modellers in the private sector. In contrast, much of the large development work in the USA is commercially funded. In 1983 the Macro Modelling Consortium financed some five models (LBS, NIESR, CUBS, LPL, CGP), the CEPG model having ceased to be funded. At the end of the first four-year period in 1987 the Consortium decided to stop research support for the CGP and CUBS models, and at the end of the second four-year period in 1991 it removed support for the LPL model but began to provide funding for Simon Wren-Lewis (ex-NIESR) to build a new, more theoretically based model at Strathclyde University. Whether it was a sign of academic hostility to big models or a lack of research funds is not clear, but the round of funding over the four-year period 1991–5 represented a major reduction to just £1.8m over the four years for macroeconomic modelling compared with some £4.6m over the previous period. Thus the groups which continued to be supported were also hit quite hard. Whether large-scale modelling will be supported at all from public funds in the future is uncertain.

The decision to cease funding for the CUBS model coincided with the departure of Beenstock, but also reflected the fact that the model had not changed at all during the four years of operation, despite having some 'strange' properties. The LPL model had also changed very little over its eight years of public support, although the research team had built a quarterly version of the model. The decision to drop the CGP model from the Consortium portfolio of models seemed to reflect a feeling against large disaggregated models. Part of the dislike arose from the large resource cost in supporting such a large model, but a more telling factor was probably the feeling that the CGP model was associated with economic planning and hence was seen to be inappropriate in the new world of market-dominated economic policy. The CGP model survives in commercial form, run by Cambridge Econometrics, and the LPL model also continues, but the CUBS model has ceased to exist. Funding decisions in the UK have often been related to academic rather than political prejudice, as in the example of CEPG above. The danger is that there is pressure for academic conformity and this approach has been criticised, among others, by the *Financial Times*: 'The public interest might be served better by a policy that promoted choice and diversity rather than a cosy cartel of like-minded clones' (*Financial Times* editorial, 8 July 1992).

With the demise of many of the publicly funded models there has been a reduction in the amount of modelling work. A possible counter-move has been the introduction of the Oxford Economic Forecasting commercially based model, which was designed around a version of the Treasury model. There is, however, no shortage of forecasters using some formal methods, although not necessarily a full model. The Item group uses the Treasury model, the Henley Centre being another example of a commercial operation. Many forecasts are made by city firms of stockbrokers, such as Phillips and Drew, and the Treasury produces a regular monthly forecast comparison of some 20 different organisations. Large-scale modelling is an activity which is highly resource intensive, and the decision to cease funding some models means the potential loss of human capital, for there has been no example of a model once abandoned becoming active again. The Consortium seems to have taken the view that modelling has potential for support from other sources, particularly commercial funding. However, experience shows that this tends to emphasise forecasting rather than model research activity. A method of commercial support can also inhibit the disclosure of certain types of information and raise obstacles to neutral evaluation. Some argue that the human capital issue is not a problem because modellers do seem able to transfer their skills quite readily to other institutions, as seen by the common transfer of personnel between teams. A more telling argument for the reduction in public funding of models is that there are too many models. An extreme argument is that they are all inadequate. This is a theme that we return to in several places in this book. The nature of macro modelling as an industry and the role of public support is considered by Smith (1993).

As a result of its consideration of the funding of macroeconomic modelling in 1983, the Macroeconomic Modelling Consortium felt that there was a need for an independent body to improve the accessibility of models, to facilitate the general understanding of the properties of the UK models and to allow regular comparisons of the models and their forecasts to be made. As a result, a Macroeconomic Modelling Bureau (MMB) was set up at the University of Warwick under the supervision of Ken Wallis. Much that is now known about macro models and much of the material used in this book is a product of the work carried out by the Bureau. During its first eight years, the Bureau operated an annual cycle of model deposits and comparisons. A survey of the work of the Bureau is given by Smith (1990). The ESRC-supported models, together with the Treasury and (later) Bank of England models, were deposited at the Bureau in the autumn of each year. The OEF model was also included in the Bureau portfolio of models from 1989. These models were set up on the Warwick University mainframe computer, and a special interface programme enabled UK academics to access these models over the university computer network (JANET). This satisfied the need for physical accessibility. Intellectual accessibility and general understanding of the models was promoted by a regular comparison of model properties and forecasts, published initially in a series of books (Wallis *et al.*, 1984–7) and then in regular articles in the *National Institute Economic Review*. Although the Treasury and Bank declined to provide a forecast base to the Bureau, the ESRC teams routinely supplied this a part of their annual deposit, along with any adjustments and exogenous variable projections that were required to reproduce it.

Gradually the work of the Bureau extended beyond the reporting of model properties and the economic features of the models to a combination of model analysis and econometric work designed to understand and resolve differences between the models. Following the observation of strong differences between models in simulation work, it was found that it was often possible to trace these differences to the specifications of particular sectors and equations in the models. In many cases it came down to differences in the value attached to a specific coefficient. It was then possible to use econometric analysis to choose between rival specifications or to suggest an alternative encompassing explanation. The resulting respecified equation could then be introduced into the model(s) and the simulations repeated. This often led to a reduction in the disparity of simulation results, and hence differences were partly or wholly resolved (see Turner, Wallis and Whitley, 1989b, for an example), or the simulation analysis indicated other areas of disagreement that had been hidden by the initial specification difference (see Fisher *et al.*, 1990a, for an example of this). Of course there are some areas where econometric analysis cannot discriminate between rival hypotheses, but the Bureau's analysis then at least indicated where important sources of disagreement lay.

This methodology does not require the models to share a common theoretical foundation, for the encompassing framework emphasises the need to test a model against competing models, and major differences in theoretical approach may make it easy to discriminate empirically between alternatives. One problem is that attention is usually restricted to single-equation comparisons, and techniques for the comparisons of small systems of non-linear equations are as yet not available. In practice, single-equation methods are also used to estimate the original model equations.

Whereas modelling in the UK has principally been publicly funded, and that in the USA commercially funded, much of the activity in the rest of the world has been centred around official models. These have typically been models either of the ministries of finance (equivalent to the UK Treasury) or of the central banks. This tends to lead to a less developed public exposure of models. In most cases there are few competing models in each country. An apparent exception is France where there were nine French models during the 1980s. But although there may be many models, they tend to be differentiated for particular purposes (for example, more than one model is based at INSEE, the French statistical office). Courbis in Bodkin *et al.* (1991, p. 233) states that 'The purpose of the French models was to enlighten government choices'. Such diversity tends to be regarded as confusing rather than informative in the UK policy environment. In Germany there are several institutes which primarily engage in forecasting and which are supported by the state, but they are not so clearly associated with particular models as in the UK.

So far in our account of historical developments in modelling we have concentrated on models of single economies. However, the growing interdependence of economies has emphasised the need to construct multicountry systems. The first major effort was made by the establishment of Project Link in 1968. This aimed to take independent country models and then link them together through merchandise flows and prices. This project had expanded to include almost 100 independent models by the end of the 1980s and the Link 'model' is now the official model of the United Nations. The Link framework is most clearly aimed at forecasting, and much less ambitious approaches are needed for regular simulation analysis. Not surprisingly, models were built by international organisations. Thus the International Monetary Fund (IMF) developed the MULTIMOD model (Masson and Symansky, 1990), which is used for policy analysis but not directly for forecasting.

The OECD followed the Link methodology initially by linking national models through trade flows, but this gradually developed into a complete integrated model (Interlink). The US Federal Reserve developed its Multi-country Model (MCM), which emphasised the modelling of financial linkages. UK efforts began in the Treasury through the work of Beenstock and Minford and then developed into the World Economic Prospects model (Horton, 1984). Two variants of this were developed. The GEM model (Global Econometric Model) was developed at NIESR and is now jointly maintained with LBS. The other variant became the world component of the OEF model. Elsewhere in Europe a multicountry model (MIMOSA) was jointly developed by OFCE (Observatoire Français des Conjonctures Economiques) and CEPII (Centre d'Etudes Prospectives et D'Informations Internationales) in Paris. The EEC has also developed a world model (QUEST) which is operated by the DIW (Deutsches Institut für Wirtschaftsforschung) in Berlin. Features of these models and some of their properties are described in Chapter 8.

1.2 Current macroeconometric models

In this section we list some of the main macroeconomic models in current use, and this very short descriptive list acts as background to a discussion of the considerations governing the size and types of model. This helps to explain why different models of the same economy exist and why different countries have different models.

This list (see Table 1.2) is not intended to be comprehensive, for it does not cover all countries, or all the models within a given country. Some of the models are described in more depth later, but as this book is not intended to be a descriptive account of models, we only pursue detailed analysis where it gives rise to particular points of modelling approach or economic interest. The table includes country models in the UK, the USA and some European countries as well as global models. For the country models, we describe their method of financial support, their approximate size, their periodicity and

Table 1.2 Summary of models

UNITED KINGDOM

Cambridge Econometrics; Cambridge; commercially funded annual model; adaptive expectations; forecasting and simulation 5000 endogenous variables (500 exogenous); 39 industries; neo-Keynesian

London Business School (LBS); independent research; quarterly model; rational/learning expectations; 650 variables; manufacturing/non-manufacturing breakdown; forecasting and simulation; sticky price/imperfect competition

National Institute of Economic and Social Research (NIESR); London; independent research institute; quarterly model; rational expectations; 586 variables (176 endogenous); manufacturing/non-manufacturing breakdown; forecasting and simulation; sticky price/imperfect competition

Oxford Economic Forecasting (OEF); commercially funded quarterly model; adaptive expectations; 325 variables; manufacturing/non-manufacturing breakdown; forecasting and simulation; sticky price/imperfect competition

HM Treasury (HMT); official model of UK Government; quarterly; 509 variables (332 behavioural); manufacturing/non-manufacturing breakdown; forecasting and simulation; eclectic; adaptive expectations

Bank of England (BE); official central bank model; quarterly; 270 endogenous variables; manufacturing/non-manufacturing breakdown; forecasting and simulation; eclectic; adaptive expectations

Liverpool (LPL); Liverpool University; commercially funded; quarterly; new classical; 39 variables (11 endogenous); aggregate model; rational expectations

UNITED STATES

Data Resources Inc. (DRI); commercial; quarterly; forecasting and simulation; 1215 equations

Warton Economic Forecasting (WEFA); commercial; 750 equations (280 stochastic); forecasting; neo-Keynesian

FAIR; independent research; simulation; rational expectations; 128 equations; aggregate model

FRANCE

Metric; INSEE/publicly funded; quarterly; new Keynesian; 950 equations

DMS; INSEE/publicly funded; annual; 2900 equations; 11 industries; Keynesian in short and long run

Table 1.2 (continued)

NETHERLANDS

MORKMON; Central Bank; quarterly; forecasting and simulation; 360 equations (160 behavioural); aggregate

FREIA-KOMPAS; Central Planning Bureau; quarterly; forecasting and simulation; 500 endogenous variables (120 exogenous); aggregate model

---

NORDIC COUNTRIES

Denmark: ADAM; Dept of Budget (Government); annual; adaptive expectations; 927 equations (92 stochastic); 20 industries

Denmark: MONA; Danish National Bank; quarterly; 323 equations (53 behavioural); Keynesian short run; forward-looking expectations in bond markets

Norway: MODAG; Central Bureau of Statistics (official institution); annual; 1225 equations (183 stochastic); adaptive expectations; 31 industries

Norway: KVARTS; Central Bureau of Statistics; 800 equations (80 stochastic); quarterly; 12 production sectors

Sweden: KOSMOS; National Institute of Economic Research (independent); semi-annual; 467 equations (21 stochastic); adaptive expectations; 8 industries

Finland: KESSU; Ministry of Finance (Government); annual; 969 equations (240 stochastic); adaptive expectations; 25 industries

Finland: BOF; Bank of Finland (central bank); quarterly; neo-classical long run; 272 equations (70 stochastic); quasi-rational expectations; 5 industries

Finland: QMED; Bank of Finland; quarterly; 79 variables (20 stochastic); rational expectations; simulation

---

MULTICOUNTRY MODELS

Federal Reserve Board (USA): MCM; quarterly; 5 linked national models (150–250 equations each)

European Commission/DIW: QUEST; quarterly; 2500 equations; 14 countries in detail/5 zones; 60 equations per large country; bilateral trade

National Institute/London Business School (UK): GEM; quarterly; 16 countries/G7 in detail/3 other OECD/6 regions; 750 variables

OECD: INTERLINK; semi-annual; large OECD countries in detail; 4200 equations

Oxford Economic Forecasting (UK); quarterly; 930 variables (780 endogenous); 15 countries/4 blocks

Liverpool (UK); annual; rational expectations; 9 major OECD/3 blocks; 153 equations

OFCE/CEPII (France): MIMOSA; annual; 5000 equations; 6 countries in detail/15 regions

Ministry of Finance (France): ATLAS; 10 regions; 1450 equations (540 stochastic); quarterly

Table 1.2 (*continued*)

IMF: MULTIMOD; annual; simulation; G7 countries/4 regions; 53 equations per country; 1300 variables; new classical

Taylor (USA); commercial; quarterly; simulation; small 6-country models; 98 stochastic equations

McKibben/Sachs (USA): MSG; annual; rational expectations

Wharton (USA); 23 OECD countries; 6 regions

Data Resources Inc. (USA); 3 large country models; regional Europe

Economic Planning Agency (Japan): EPA; Quarterly; 9-country model; 6 regions; 1200 equations

---

any key features. For the multicountry or global models, we give a summary of their disaggregation of the world economy. These descriptions are based on recent versions of the models from various published and unpublished documents with a timing around the end of the 1980s/early 1990s. Details such as exact size may change, or may already have changed. Our textual discussion merely uses the models in the list as examples of issues in modelling approach. We abstract from the estimation procedures used in constructing the models, but note that in most cases equations are estimated by single-equation methods rather than whole system methods. This is partly to avoid the need to re-estimate the entire model when one or more single equations is respecified, but mainly because of the formidable technical problems in estimating very large models as a system. In particular, the identification condition is not usually met (see Stewart and Wallis, 1981).

We illustrate why some of the macro models differ in approach and explain some of the reasons why there may be more than one model for each economy. Models may emphasise different concerns (for example, explaining a particular sector of the economy in more detail); they may be aimed at forecasting rather than at conducting policy simulation exercises; or they may be aimed at the long term rather than the short term. Alternatively, they may reflect different theoretical viewpoints.

 Models may differ because their aim is different or because they have a different theoretical perspective.

In the early days of modelling, the size of models was severely limited by technical problems. Since practical models have tended to be non-linear, simple analytical methods cannot be used and some sort of iterative procedure is needed to solve the essentially simultaneous system. In the late 1960s, the UK National Institute model was solved manually. This task required some skill by the model user in assessing the likely set of solution values, even though the degree of simultaneity was not that high. Developments in both computer software and hardware have made the size limitation constraint almost obsolete.

> Model building invariably faces the conflict between the desire to explain more, and hence to construct a bigger model, and the wish to make the model manageable, both in terms of understanding it and in reducing maintenance costs.

However, the question of model size is not a purely technical matter, depending on computer limitations. It often reflects a methodological viewpoint. Many of the mainstream models have grown significantly since the 1970s as new monetary and financial sectors have been introduced (for example, the UK LBS model almost doubled in size on the introduction of its financial sector). In addition to the wholesale addition of new sectors, the introduction of additional explanatory variables in one or more equations may increase the size of the model if the new variables also need to be determined endogenously in the model. The desire to explain more (i.e. reduce the number of exogenous influences in the model) is another factor leading to greater model size, whereas in a forecasting context there may be pressure to forecast in more detail, and hence to increase the degree of disaggregation in the model. There are several costs associated with larger models, however, and these have led to some teams attempting either to limit further increases or to simplify the existing model (as in the case of the UK Treasury, which developed its 'SLIM' model). These costs relate to the resources required for data management, to the time taken to monitor and modify equations in the model and, perhaps more pertinently, to the added difficulty in 'understanding the model'. Most modellers and forecasters feel the need to be able to explain the results of their model in terms of its underlying mechanisms, in order to counter the common criticism that models are simply black boxes. Many modellers feel that, to gain academic credibility, it is necessary to be able to contrast the properties of their models with the appropriate theoretical paradigm. The larger and more complicated the model, the more difficult this task is. With scarce resources it is not often possible to monitor routinely all the equations of a model, and attention is usually focused on the 'key' behavioural equations, leaving 'less important' equations alone. The work of the Macroeconomic Modelling Bureau has shown, however, that it is often the properties of these relatively neglected sectors that can explain 'unexpected' simulation properties or inadequate forecasting performance.

The 'optimum' size of model is not unique. For some models it may be essential to model some sectors of the economy in detail (for example, the UK Treasury feels the need to model the public sector in detail, and the Bank of England desires similarly to model the monetary sector). There remains a fundamental methodological issue which also accounts for some of the differences in the size of models, particularly in the UK. Some view the economy as basically straightforward and simple, and consequently consider that any macroeconometric model should also be simple. This view is particularly associated with the monetarist/neo-classical view of the world and is represented among the UK models by the Liverpool model. Adjustment to any disequilibrium is quite rapid in the classical models, and hence the economy can be represented by a small set of 'equilibrium' equations.

> Monetarist models typically incorporate the view that the economy can be explained by a small number of equations.

Macroeconometric models that have been developed in the 1980s illustrate the tensions between macroeconomic theory, microeconomic theory and data acceptability. Models such as DRI and Wharton lie closer to the data end of the spectrum than the mainstream, but in contrast MULTIMOD, Liverpool and Taylor are closer to the microeconomic derivation. The MSG model (MSG2) is perhaps the closest to microeconomic foundations, since it has several explicit structural parameters derived from theory and is calibrated to a data set rather than to estimates from a time series of data. MSG2 also has parameter estimates that are imposed in common across different countries in the model.

The mainstream consensus among macro modellers is a blend of macroeconomic theory and data acceptability, and this is reflected in the list of models in Table 1.2. The view represented by most of these models is a short-term world where prices are fairly sticky, so that the results of the model are quite Keynesian, and a longer-run representation where neo-classical tendencies dominate and prices are flexible. The key empirical questions then concern the length of time that it takes for the economy to return to equilibrium following a shock, and the size of the short-run quantity adjustments. Models which assume that the world is neo-classical even in the short term are quite rare; in the list of models they are represented by the Liverpool model in the UK, by the Taylor model in the USA, and by MULTIMOD among the multicountry models. All the remaining models are of the general sticky-price variety. Another form of consensus among models is that the previous distinction between short-run models designed for forecasting and medium-term models aimed at policy has largely disappeared, and the majority of models are used for both. This is not invariably the case, however, and until very recently the French INSEE has supported an annual model designed for medium-term work (DMS) and a quarterly model aimed at short-term forecasting (METRIC). Similar remarks apply to the Norwegian MODAG and KVARTS models.

The mainstream quarterly models in the UK (LBS, NIESR, HMT, BE, etc.) tend, in varying degrees, to view the economy as subject to a degree of nominal inertia. This inertia, coupled with possible structural differences within the economy, requires a more detailed and possibly more disaggregated approach. In this view, disaggregation is used only where necessary to capture empirical and economic differences within the economy, and the quarterly models have remained highly aggregated, with the main distinction typically between manufacturing and non-manufacturing sectors. Even here disaggregation is usually only pursued piecemeal. The development of these models, which in recent years has tended towards attempting to simplify the basic structure, is probably related to the close interplay in the UK between macro-econometric models and the high-level macro policy debate. Macro policy in the UK has been highly non-interventionist over the last 15 years, and consequently has not regarded a knowledge or understanding of more than the basic features of the economy as necessary. This has probably influenced the nature of the macro models.

 Disaggregation tends to be an empirical matter rather than one of principle in the UK mainstream models. This is less true of other European models.

In contrast, disaggregation has been seen to be more important in the rest of Europe where a more strategic planning approach tends to be adopted. Here macroeconometric models tend to be more highly disaggregated, in the belief that the approximations required by the highly aggregate models are misleading both in a forecasting and in a policy context. The highly disaggregated approach is best typified in the UK by the Cambridge Growth Project model (now Cambridge Econometrics), which starts from the view that disaggregation is necessary and builds up the macro aggregates consistently from behaviour at the industry level. In the USA, decisions on disaggregation tend to be determined by commercial considerations. The trade-off between the added information obtained from the disaggregated approach and its cost in resource requirements is an empirical matter, but it also depends on the relevance to the perceived objectives of the model-builders and their 'clientele', who may be policy-makers or the private sector.

As well as differing in the degree of disaggregation and the theoretical perspective, models may differ in the type of data used in their construction. Nearly all existing macroeconometric models (as opposed to calibrated general equilibrium models) use time-series data in the main, but they do differ in the periodicity of the data used. Highly disaggregated models tend to use annual data because of data limitations, but this is not the only reason for difference. The Liverpool model of the UK economy used annual data because it wished to emphasise long-run equilibrium features rather than short-run dynamics. In fact one of the criticisms that was made of the mainstream models was that their concern with the very short run made them negligent of the long-term implications of the policy adjustments that they proposed on the basis of their models. As we discuss below, the quarterly models have given greater emphasis to their long-run features and this source of difference has become less stressed. The recent conversion of the Liverpool model to a quarterly basis shows that models may also need to be able to provide a commentary on the short run if they are to attain credibility for their policy suggestions. This argument is based on the view that only models which forecast well should be treated seriously in the policy debate. However, as we shall see in Chapter 6, judgements on forecasting ability are not easily arrived at; nor are they necessarily an essential requirement for a 'valid' model.

In the majority of multicountry models, the external economic environment is treated as exogenous, and in most cases domestic policy variables are also treated in this way. However, in models such as MSG, MULTIMOD, Liverpool and to some extent GEM, there are various policy feedback rules which ensure that policy is 'sustainable'. Solution of models containing forward expectations requires that these models have a stable long-run path. In the absence of stable behaviour of the underlying model structure some kind of stabilising policy feedback may be necessary. However, these rules tend to be imposed rather than being based on observed behaviour, and there is the danger that they dominate the model based on the empirical behaviour of economic agents.

It is possible that the existence of different models may stimulate innovation by competition between them, and by focusing on the differences between them. Whether this is possible without some outside agency such as the MMB in the UK is debatable. Where models share a common theoretical framework, there is the presumption that the data may be able to provide discriminating evidence to support one or the other, and hence there should be a long-run tendency towards only one such model. In practice, the dynamic nature of macroeconometric modelling due to changes in institutional arrangements, developments in theory, new evidence and changes in policy objectives may prevent this long-run equilibrium outcome from being reached. The way in which modelling is supported is also important to innovation and variety. There is an argument that innovation has been low in the USA given the background of commercial funding, whereas the UK tradition of hands-off public support has encouraged new developments. In Europe, outside of the UK, modelling tends to be concentrated in official or quasi-official institutions. There is a danger that this leads to a greater degree of conservatism and less openness than with funding at arm's length.

Further reading:

Bodkin *et al.* (1991)
Smith (1990)
Smith (1993)

2 | A framework for modelling

In this chapter we set out a framework for the analysis of models. We begin by describing the general framework in which we can discuss the various ways of using models for simulation, policy analysis and forecasting. We then set out a stylised economic structure of the models which can be used as a reference point for some of the common concepts in standard macroeconomic theory. In this way we can develop a broad framework for describing and evaluating the results from macroeconometric models.

We begin by describing a general linear form of model which will help us to fix ideas.

2.1   The general linear model

Let us be clear first by what we mean by a macroeconometric model. A macroeconometric model is a mathematical representation of the quantitative relationships among macroeconomic variables such as employment, output, prices, government expenditure, taxes, interest rates and exchange rates. It is therefore distinct from the textbook style of model which comprises stylised relationships between variables, but which does not attempt to quantify the strengths of these relationships. This is not to denigrate textbook models. They are extremely useful in providing a framework against which to compare macroeconometric models, and in this book we attempt to make this contrast frequently.

The equations of the macroeconometric model comprise technical relationships, accounting identities and behavioural equations. Technical relationships are relationships which do not explain the actions of economic agents, but which may either approximate institutional arrangements (for example, the workings of the tax system) or relate variables which are conceptually similar but which may be measured in different ways (for example, the retail price index and the consumer price index). The parameters of these relations may be derived directly from prior information or may be estimated from data. These relationships are typically subject to error in that they are approximations. Accounting identities are different in that they are exact relationships which hold at all points in time. The identity between national output and components of final expenditure, and between the government borrowing requirement and taxes and government spending, are typical examples of accounting identities in macro-econometric models.

 Models contain technical relationships, accounting identities and behavioural equations.

Behavioural equations are relationships which describe the aggregate actions of economic agents such as consumers, producers, investors and financial institutions. They are usually derived from economic theory, but the feature that distinguishes them from textbook models is that the parameters of the models are quantitative, and are usually based on empirical information. One of the main issues that may separate different models is the exact blend of theory and statistical evidence that goes into their construction. Behavioural relationships are measured with error. The mapping from economic theory to empirical model may be inexact for various reasons. The theoretical concepts may not correspond with economic data available, and theory typically says very little about dynamic adjustment. Another, very important reason is that the relationships often attempt to portray the aggregate actions of economic agents from models of the behaviour of a (typical) representative agent. Such aggregation may be inappropriate, and aggregate relationships may not be stable over time even if the representative economic agent behaves in a fairly consistent manner.

Behavioural equations are relationships which describe the aggregate actions of economic agents such as consumers, producers, investors and financial institutions.

A simple model framework

To fix ideas more specifically we begin with a very simple model system.

$$y_1 = \alpha_0 + \alpha_1 y_2 + \alpha_2 z_1 + u_1$$
$$y_2 = \beta_0 + \beta_1 y_1 + \beta_2 z_2 + u_2 \tag{2.1}$$
$$y_3 = y_2 - y_1$$

The first equation explains variable y_1 as determined by y_2, z_1 and an error term u_1. The second equation describes y_2 by y_1, z_2 and an error term u_2. In estimation, assumptions are made about the distribution of the error terms. In simple ordinary least-squares estimation, these are that the errors follow a normal distribution with zero mean and constant variance, and are serially uncorrelated and independent of the variables on the right-hand side of the equation. However, we are not concerned here with how the equations have been produced and with the nature of the error terms. Indeed, it is possible that the equations do not result from formal statistical analysis.

The y variables are called the *endogenous* variables, since they are determined by the model. The z variables are *exogenous* variables, determined outside the model. The third equation is the identity linking variables y_1 and y_2 to variable y_3. This may be a simple accounting identity which holds exactly at every point in time and hence has no error associated with it.

We have three endogenous variables, and clearly there needs to be one equation for each endogenous variable for the model to be identified. Normally we associate each equation with a particular variable because the right-hand-side variables in the equation are the ones that theory suggests we should associate with the behaviour of the left-hand side variable rather than the right-hand side variables of another equation. Thus we would say that the first equation explains variable y_1. This corresponds with the typical way that the relationship might be estimated from the data. However, this model is simultaneous since y_1 depends on y_2 and vice versa, and we could rewrite the first equation to explain variable y_2. It might then be more difficult to describe the various relationships in a way that related to the underlying theory. The terms α and β are the parameters of the model, and once chosen they usually remain fixed when the model is solved and simulated. The equations represented above are the *structural* equations of the model: that is, they are usually associated with specific economic behaviour. For example, the first equation might be a consumption equation which specifies that consumer spending (y_1) depends on real incomes (y_2). The identity might be interpreted as stating that savings (y_3) are the difference between real incomes and spending.

> Endogenous variables are those explained by the model; exogenous variables are supplied to the model and not explained by it.

The model above can be solved analytically by writing the solutions for the endogenous variables as functions only of the exogenous variables and the error terms. This is the *reduced form* relationship, and the underlying structural parameters can be derived from the reduced form coefficients subject to the usual identification conditions. If y_1 did not depend on y_2 then the model would become recursive and y_1 could be solved independently of y_2 (but the solution for y_2 would still depend on y_1).

> The individual equations in the model are the structural equations. The solution of the model which expresses each endogenous variable purely in terms of exogenous variables is the reduced form of the model.

In practice, macroeconometric models include many more than three equations and it is convenient to express these in matrix notation. (This is purely a simplification and does not require any knowledge of matrix algebra. One can simply think of the vector y being a set of endogenous variables ($y_1 \ldots y_n$), z being a set of exogenous variables ($z_1 \ldots z_n$) and the vector u being a set of error terms).

We begin by using the linear form of equation. The system given by equation 2.1 is the structural equations.

The parameters give the response of each endogenous variable to changes in the other endogenous variables or to the exogenous variables. These will include policy variables as well as other influences outside the scope of the model (world economic developments, natural resource endowments, etc.). However, the full solution of the model allows for all the endogenous variables to affect each other, and this corresponds to the reduced form equation where the parameters (π_i) are now combinations of the original structural coefficients (α_i and β_i).

The solution for y_1 can be written as:

$$y_1 = \pi_0 + \pi_1 z_1 + \pi_2 z_2 + v$$
$$\pi_0 = (\alpha_0 + \alpha_1 \beta_0)/(1 - \alpha_1 \beta_1)$$
$$\pi_1 = \alpha_2/(1 - \alpha_1 \beta_1) \tag{2.2}$$
$$\pi_2 = \alpha_1 \beta_2/(1 - \alpha_1 \beta_1)$$
$$v = u_1 + \alpha_1 u_2$$

with a similar expression for y_2.

2.2 Extensions of the linear model

> In a static model, adjustment is immediate and complete within the time period; in a dynamic model, endogenous variables adjust to changes in the independent variables over several time periods.

In our example, the endogenous variables respond immediately to changes in the exogenous variables. This is called a *static* model. To allow for lagged adjustment of the endogenous variables, a dynamic specification can be achieved in a number of ways, but it principally involves the use of lagged values of the endogenous and exogenous variables appearing on the right-hand side of the equation. In economic terms, the presence of lagged adjustment often makes the model less simultaneous in nature, since each y may no longer depend on current values of the other endogenous variables. This is the *dynamic* model. Various rationales can be used for the presence of lagged adjustment, such as adjustment costs, contracts and inertia. The partial and adaptive expectations mechanisms are often used to introduce lags of the dependent variable into the equation (see Stewart and Wallis, 1981). The model may also incorporate future expected values of variables, in which case adjustment may occur in advance of any change in other variables (see further discussion in Chapters 3, 4 and 5).

The first equation of the system can now be written as:

$$y_{1,t} = \alpha_0 + \alpha_1 y_{2,t} + \alpha_2 z_{1,t} + \alpha_3 y_{1,t-1} + u_{1,t} \tag{2.3}$$

Here the coefficient (α_2) on the current exogenous variable (z_1) gives the 'impact' effect of a change in this variable on the first endogenous variable (the other endogenous variables are assumed to be unchanged), and the long-run effect can be obtained by setting $y_{1,t} = y_{1,t-1}$ and solving the resultant equation. The long-run response of the first endogenous variable y_1 is now given by $\alpha_2/(1 - \alpha_3)$.

In forecasting, the exogenous variables have to be projected into the future, and the forecast for period $t + 1$ will depend not only on these projections, but also on the solution of variable y_1 in period t. Further details of methods of forecasting are given in Chapter 6.

> A linear framework is rare for macroeconometric models; non-linear models have to be solved numerically by iterative techniques on computers.

A further complication is that a purely linear framework is unlikely in empirical work. Many economic relationships are best represented in log-linear form so that elasticities rather than marginal propensities are constant over time. In addition, economic relationships often involve the use of ratios, which also makes the model non-linear. Once a departure from linearity occurs, the model can no longer be solved analytically and non-linear methods have to be used. Early models were small because limitations in computer hardware prevented the numerical analysis of large systems of equations.

Before we discuss non-linearity let us generalise the simple three-equation structural model using matrix notation.

$$By_t + Cz_t = u_t \tag{2.4}$$

where u is a vector of disturbances, reflecting the fact that the equation does not hold exactly at all points in time.

If the equation is estimated then the disturbances can be expected to satisfy certain conditions, such as zero mean, constant variance and normality. These properties only carry over automatically to the model equations when the equation is estimated over exactly the same period on which the model is based. The matrices B and C are the structural parameters of the model and are often expressed as marginal propensities, reaction coefficients, etc. Normally, the diagonal elements of B are set equal to unity so that the ith equation is said to determine the ith variable, but unless B is diagonal the model is really simultaneous.

To solve the model we solve out for all the contemporaneous endogenous variables in terms of their lagged values and exogenous variables. This is the reduced form, and this can be written:

$$y_t = \Pi z_t + v_t \tag{2.5}$$

where

$$\Pi = B^{-1}C \tag{2.6}$$

and

$$v_t = -B^{-1}u_t \tag{2.7}$$

where the π matrix represents policy multipliers or ready reckoners: that is, they measure the effects on the endogenous variables of a one unit change in the exogenous variables. With a linear model we can combine the ready reckoners to give the effects of a policy package: that is, the effect of more than one instrument change.

In forecasting, the disturbances would, in a correctly specified model, be set at their mean value of zero, and the exogenous variables would be projected into the future. The forecast solution for the endogenous variables ($\hat{y}$) would then be given by:

$$\hat{y}_t = \Pi\hat{z}_t \tag{2.8}$$

If the model is log-linear rather than linear then the matrices of parameters B and C represent elasticities rather than marginal response coefficients. Analytic solution methods are then no longer appropriate and iterative methods are used (see Chapter 5).

The non-linear model can be written as:

$$f(y_t, z_t, \alpha) = u_t \tag{2.9}$$

where α is the vector of parameters. Allowing for dynamic responses so that lagged values of the endogenous variables enter into the structural equations, and distinguishing between lagged endogenous variables and exogenous variables (x), we obtain:

$$f(y_t, y_{t-1}, x_t, \alpha) = u_t \tag{2.10}$$

The solution process proceeds as follows:

$$f(\tilde{y}_1, y_0, x_1, \alpha) = 0 \tag{2.11}$$

where the first period is solved conditional on values in the previous period, and current values of the exogenous variables. In period t the solution is:

$$f(\tilde{y}_t, \tilde{y}_{t-1}, x_t, \alpha) = 0 \tag{2.12}$$

In the dynamic model, therefore, the solution for the endogenous variables in period t depends on the solution in previous periods, $t - i$.

Standard simulation analysis proceeds by comparing a base solution of the model with a solution where one of more of the exogenous variables are perturbed. Comparing the base and perturbed solutions then gives an estimate of the policy multiplier(s) if the exogenous variable is a policy instrument. In a non-linear model, the multipliers are potentially base dependent.

2.3   Relation to other approaches

In this section we compare how the standard macroeconometric model representation differs from other modelling approaches. We can consider these as other positions along the spectrum of possible models which range from pure microeconomic theory models through macroeconomic theory to pure reliance on data. An example of the last of these is the VAR (vector autoregressive) approach developed by Sims (1980), where data are given all the weight and theory very little.

Vector autoregressive models (VARs)

Vector autoregressive models have been used as a serious alternative method of economic forecasting (see Chapter 6) and also for policy analysis. VARs are unrestricted reduced forms in which all the variables are endogenous. The simple two-equation VAR system might be written as:

$$y_{1t} = f(y_{1,t-1}, y_{1,t-2} \cdots y_{1,t-m}, y_{2,t-1}, y_{2,t-2} \cdots y_{2,t-m})$$
$$y_{2t} = f(y_{1,t-1}, y_{1,t-2} \cdots, y_{1,t-m}, y_{2,t-1}, y_{2,t-2} \cdots y_{2,t-m})$$

$$(2.13)$$

In this system the variables y_1 and y_2 are explained by their lagged values alone. No current values of one variable enter into the determination of the other.

$$y_{1,t} = f(y_{1,t-1}, x_t, y_{2,t}, y_{2,t-1})$$

$$(2.14)$$

Now compare this with the equation above. The structural reduced form contains current values of both other endogenous and exogenous variables. In the VAR model there is no distinction between these two types of variable. In addition the parameters in the macroeconometric model reduced form are combinations of the structural parameters. In the VAR model there are no restrictions imposed upon the coefficients attached to each variable. In practice, however, with a VAR of more than two to three variables there will be a large number of parameters and this can result in very imprecise estimates. Usually the number of lags in each equation is limited by using Bayesian priors, hence the term 'Bayesian vector autoregressive models' (BVARs).

At the other end of the modelling spectrum are pure theory models, derived from microeconomic optimisation theory based on the individual subject to various constraints. This has led to the computable general equilibrium (CGE) style of model, where the theoretical model is calibrated from data.

Computable general equilibrium models (CGEs)

The aim of these models is to use the 'deep' underlying structural parameters of the system which reflect tastes and technology, rather than reduced form parameters such as the marginal propensity to consume out of current income. This approach descends directly from the work of Arrow and Debreu (1954) and uses the Walrasian general equilibrium framework calibrated by real-world data to ensure consistency with observed empirical facts (for example, the elasticity of substitution in production, given an assumption about the functional form of the production function). Or they may be estimated from cross-section data on households or firms. Since the distribution from which the parameters are chosen is not known, no assessment of statistical significance can be made of them or of the outputs of the model. In some cases the data on which the model is based may have to be adjusted so that they are consistent with the equilibrium of the model (since the real world is typically in disequilibrium, whereas the model is not). With a focus on microeconomic theory CGE models are well suited to the analysis of issues in tax policy and international trade (Shoven and Whalley, 1984).

Early CGE models were used for comparative static analysis of the change between equilibria and hence in predicting the long-run effects of a change in policy. Recent developments have attempted to incorporate dynamic adjustment. Originally they used macroeconomic closures that were regarded as unsatisfactory by many macro-economists, and the omission of an aggregate price level or a role for money was regarded as an important defect. The MSG model which was developed by McKibben and Sachs (1991) is an example of a dynamic CGE model. The dynamic aspects are introduced by the use of intertemporal budget constraints and intertemporal objective functions for agents. Money is introduced by the restriction that households require money to buy goods. In order to explain macro data it is assumed that there are deviations from optimizing behaviour due to myopia or restrictions on the ability of households or firms to borrow at the risk-free bond rate on government debt. This leaves a role for current variables such as income to influence consumption as well as wealth. The MSG model also allows for short-run nominal wage rigidity. These developments make the distinction between macroeconomic models and CGE models more blurred, especially where the macroeconomic models themselves have become more firmly based on optimising behaviour. However, it is often argued by some macro modellers that aggregate behaviour is not necessarily consistent with optimising individual behaviour relationships; there may be constraints or institutional impedi-ments or interactions which lead to aggregate relationships that have empirical regularities not evident from micro behaviour. Or the aggregate data may simply be inconsistent with the theoretical concepts.

2.4 Economic concepts and relation to theory

In this section we describe models in the form of a stylised framework and link this framework to some of the concepts in standard macroeconomic theory. This also enables us to compare different approaches within macroeconometric modelling. Initially we set out a framework which might appear at first sight to be neo-Keynesian, but which can also be used to illustrate the neo-classical and monetarist views. This framework is also useful in describing the main developments in models which are discussed in the following chapter.

Models can be described in three different ways: we can focus on the behaviour of economic agents; on the interaction of markets; or on the interaction of demand and supply. We abstract from problems of dynamics in this exposition, although these can be critical in differentiating between different schools of thought.

Focus on the behaviour of economic agents implies an analysis of the different

A framework for modelling

sectors of the economy: the personal sector, the corporate sector, the public sector and the overseas sector. Analysis of the personal sector means a discussion of spending decisions, the supply of labour and the accumulation of financial assets. The behaviour of firms has implications for the way in which investment decisions are made, employment levels set, and price and output levels determined. The public sector determines government spending and taxation as well as the stance of monetary policy. The overseas sector influences trade and capital flows, and hence influences interest rates and exchange rates.

The market approach describes the behaviour of the goods market where quantities of goods and services traded are determined by the interaction of firms and consumers; the labour market where firms and labour interact to give levels of wages and employment; and financial markets where quantities and prices of financial assets are determined.

The third approach is to distinguish between the demand and supply side of the economy. There may be different ways of describing the supply side of the economy and of disentangling demand from supply influences. This is particularly so when the supply influences are implicit, or when the estimated relationship is in the reduced form of the demand and supply components of a sub-system of the whole model. In our stylised model below, we attempt to be very general. In Chapter 4 we discuss in more detail how different parts of the structure are modelled in practice, and the implications of different treatments.

> Models can be described in a variety of ways: by the interaction of different economic agents; by the behaviour in different markets of the economy; or by the interaction of demand and supply.

We start with the national income accounting identity, which is familiar from basic macroeconomics and which tends to be the form in which macroeconomic statistics are commonly collected in most economies. This simply states that national output or expenditure is the sum of domestic demands plus demand from abroad for domestic goods (exports) less that part of demand which is satisfied from abroad (imports).

Thus we have:

$$DD = C + I + G \tag{2.15}$$

$$Y = DD + X - M \tag{2.16}$$

where DD is total domestic demand, C is consumption spending, I is fixed investment and the addition to stocks by both public and private sectors, and G is government consumption of goods and services. Y is national output and X and M are exports and imports of goods and services respectively. For convenience we ignore the distinction between GDP and GNP, and between GDP at market prices and GDP at factor cost.

Government consumption is usually treated as a policy variable and is predetermined or exogenous. Thus:

$$G = G_0 \tag{2.17}$$

28

Consumption decisions might depend on income, wealth and interest rates (elementary macroeconomic texts usually only determine consumption by income).

$$C = f(Y, W, r) \tag{2.18}$$

Ignoring the public component of investment spending, we might explain private spending by aggregate demand (the accelerator model) and interest rates

$$I = f(Y, r) \tag{2.19}$$

Ignoring the open economy aspects of the model for the present (exports and imports), we have the relationships that represent the familiar IS curve of macro-economics, which describes the locus of points of income and interest rates that give equilibrium in the goods market.

The LM curve is introduced through the money market and is usually represented by a money demand function together with assumptions about the determination of the stock of money (money supply).

The money demand equation might be generally expressed as:

$$M^d = f(Y, P, r, W) \tag{2.20}$$

and for the present we assume that the supply of money is exogenously determined.

$$M^s = M_0 \tag{2.21}$$

Thus we now have the ingredients for the standard IS/LM representation of the closed economy with a fixed price level. We introduce in turn open economy aspects, the relaxation of the fixed price assumption, the labour market and the government budget constraint, which has implications for the relationship between monetary and fiscal policy. We discuss the introduction of a flexible exchange rate and the endogeneity of wealth.

The open economy is initially introduced by adding relationships for exports and imports.

$$X = f(Y^*, ep/p^*) \tag{2.22}$$

$$M = f(Y, ep/p^*) \tag{2.23}$$

where Y^* is foreign income and ep/p^* is the real exchange rate, with p the domestic price, p^* the foreign price and e the nominal exchange rate. We now have all the ingredients for the standard Mundell–Fleming analysis of fiscal and monetary policy, if we add the balance of payments identity and an equation for capital flows.

$$BP = (X - M) + f(r - r^*) \tag{2.24}$$

where the second element in equation (2.24) represents capital flows. Equation (2.24) is sometimes expressed in terms of the nominal exchange rate (further discussion of this takes place in Chapter 4).

We now relax the fixed price assumption by introducing equations for wages and prices. The price equation we present is a simple mark-up equation on wages costs and import prices, and the wage equation is expressed in terms of the real wage $(w - p)$, which depends on unemployment and various push factors (Z).

$$p = f(w - \pi, ep/p^*) \tag{2.25}$$

is the price equation where π is the level of productivity and

$$w - p = f(U, Z) \tag{2.26}$$

The introduction of flexible prices now means that the LM curve shifts as the price level changes. To explain unemployment we need to complete the explanation of the rest of the labour market. First, we use the identity that unemployment is the difference between the labour force and employment.

$$U = l - e \tag{2.27}$$

Employment is given by output and real wages (we discuss alternatives in Chapter 4) and the labour force depends on population trends and real after-tax wages $(w - p - t)$.

If we rewrite the income term in the consumption equation as Ywd, which measures disposable wage income, we have a link between the labour market and the goods markets, since:

$$e = f(Y, w - p) \tag{2.28}$$

$$l = f(POP, w - p - t) \tag{2.29}$$

$$Ywd = e \cdot (w - t) \tag{2.30}$$

(we abstract for the moment that consumers' disposable income also includes net interest, dividend income and current transfers).

The system can now be used to describe the aggregate demand and supply schedules of macroeconomic theory, with the aggregate demand schedule depicting how the IS/LM intersection shifts as the price level changes. The aggregate demand schedule is downward sloping, its steepness reflecting the steepness of the IS schedule, and hence its interest elasticity. In Chapter 5 we show how empirical models can be decomposed into IS/LM and AD/AS curves.

The aggregate supply curve comes from examining how employment/unemployment varies with the price level, and the nature of this relationship is primarily given by the labour market.

An alternative representation which can be given for the aggregate supply curve is simply an inversion of $q^s = f(p)$, and this can be written in the form:

$$p = f(y - y^*) \tag{2.31}$$

where $y - y^*$ represents the deviation of demand from its equilibrium level. This form of the price equation is common in the new classical literature.

The aggregate supply schedule is normally drawn as upward sloping. The debate over whether it is vertical is discussed in Chapter 4 and is examined in practice in the models in Chapter 5. In order to relate aggregate supply to output, and hence trace out possible intersections of aggregate demand and supply, we can use a simple production function.

$$Y = f(K, L, \phi) \qquad (2.32)$$

where ϕ measures technological progress.

The next step is to introduce the public sector more fully, and this links monetary and fiscal policy and provides a link with the determination of wealth. First, we add the government budget constraint.

$$G - T + rB = \Delta M + \Delta B + \Delta O \qquad (2.33)$$

where G is government spending, T tax receipts, B the stock of government debt and O debt held by the overseas sector. The left-hand side of the expression is the government financial balance or deficit and is defined as spending less taxes plus interest payments on outstanding government debt. The right-hand side shows how this is financed: by issuing money or bonds to domestic residents or overseas. Cumulated bond-financed deficits appear in the form of government debt and hence lead to higher debt servicing in the future and hence to increases in the current public sector deficit. Further aspects of the financing issue and the relationship between monetary and fiscal policy in the models are given in Chapter 7.

We define wealth as the sum of money and government debt held by the private sector, deflated by the price level.

$$W = (M + B)/P \qquad (2.34)$$

Thus there are several linkages between policy and private sector behaviour. We define fiscal policy as determining the size of the government deficit and monetary policy as the way in which the deficit is financed. Fiscal policy influences private consumption spending directly by changing disposable incomes through taxation. To the extent to which the government finances a deficit by issuing debt, interest rates may need to rise in order to encourage the personal sector to hold the additional debt. This provides a further link between policy and private spending decisions. In addition, both money and bonds appear as wealth and may also affect spending. An exception would be if bonds were not counted as net wealth since they were interpreted as implying future tax liabilities (so-called Ricardian equivalence). In simple IS/LM terminology, the IS curve will tend to shift as wealth changes, and the LM curve may also move if wealth enters into the demand for money relationship.

The exposition above is in terms of markets. We can now reinterpret it in terms of economic agents or sectors. First, we consider the personal sector. Individuals supply labour for which they receive a wage; aggregate wage income also depends on the numbers employed. Wage income is augmented by current grants, net interest and property income, and disposable income determines consumer spending either directly or through the accumulation of wealth. Thus there are strong interactions between the goods and labour markets in terms of effective demand. Through government taxation decisions and the way that deficits are funded, there are also links between the private sector and the public sector. The private corporate sector appears in the models through investment decisions, by setting prices and/or output levels in the goods market, and by setting employment levels and wages in the labour market. The investment decisions also depend on the financial sector, primarily through interest rates. Thus there are many interactions between agents and markets in the models. One of the key issues in modelling is to what extent different economic agents' decisions are imposed consistently upon the model: for example, whether firms' investment, employment and pricing decisions are modelled in an interrelated way.

Although it may seen attractive to view the determination of expenditures as the demand side of the model, in practice some of the relationships may already include implicit supply-side elements, say in the form of utilisation, so that they are not pure demand equations. Exactly which equations of the model can be considered to form the supply side of the model is a contentious issue and is the focus of discussion in Chapter 4. However, at this stage it is useful to describe some other common concepts which appear in the theoretical literature and which have some counterpart in empirical models.

The first of these is the equilibrium rate of unemployment, which is sometimes referred to as the non-accelerating-inflation rate of unemployment (NAIRU) or the natural rate. These terms are not really interchangeable, as we discuss in Chapter 4. In principle, the equilibrium rates of output and unemployment in the models are determined by the intersection of aggregate demand and supply. In practice, the key questions that arise are whether an equilibrium is reached by the empirical model, and what are the relative slopes of the two schedules, accepting that short-run responses may be quite different from those that emerge after a period of time. However, as we describe in Chapter 4, the intersection of aggregate demand and supply produces not a unique equilibrium, but merely the level of demand/unemployment which satisfies the requirement of internal balance in the economy. For external balance (i.e. with the balance of payments in equilibrium), there may be an equilibrium level of the real exchange rate (often called the fundamental equilibrium exchange rate or FEER). This is the value of the exchange rate which satisfies the balance of payment equilibrium condition for a given equilibrium level or growth of demand. The combination of the internal and external balance conditions therefore produces a unique equilibrium level of the real exchange rate and unemployment.

Much of the debate which has gone on between the monetarist/neo-classical school and the Keynesian approaches has been in the nature of adjustment to equilibrium as well as in the nature of the equilibrium itself. The neo-classical approach tends to assume that prices adjust quite rapidly in response to a shock, and that any persistence of disequilibrium is a result of real rigidities in the economy. The more Keynesian approach, in contrast, sees disequilibrium as a more protracted process with nominal rigidities preventing rapid adjustment. The neo-classical approach also tends to emphasise the importance of stocks such as wealth rather than flows such as current income. The Keynesian approach see households as constrained by current income. The monetarist approach, which shares the neo-classical view, sees expenditures governed by excess money with the line of causation running from money to expenditure and hence to prices, rather than the reverse. This places the demand for money equation at the heart of the system with the interest elasticity relatively low (in the extreme case, velocity is independent of interest rates and the quantity theory of money holds). In the Keynesian view, the demand for money is highly interest elastic and the supply of money may be endogenous rather than exogenous as in the monetarist view. Many empirical models do not have an explicit demand for money function, the demand for financial assets being built up from its components.

This short exposition has attempted to describe how macroeconometric models combine many of the features of standard macroeconomic theory. This framework can be useful in understanding how the models behave, and with which macroeconomic paradigm they can be associated, if any. Lest our discussion oversimplifies the macro background to empirical models, let us at this point note that they also contain some of the more sophisticated features of theory, such as rational expectations and fiscal solvency conditions. These will become clearer when we describe the actual features and properties of the models in the following chapters.

2.5 Comparative model structures

In this section we give a very brief overview of the structures of the main models. The principal characteristics of some of the main multicountry models are discussed in Chapter 8. The aim of this section is not to give the reader an enormous amount of detail to absorb, but to offer enough information for the reader to be able to follow subsequent discussion of model structures and properties. Inevitably, focusing on models at one point in time runs the risk that the descriptions will soon be outdated. However, while details may change, many of the underlying features of the models and the issues that they address remain very much the same.

Disaggregation

With the exception of the Cambridge Growth Project/Cambridge Econometrics model there is an interesting contrast between both time and spatial dimensions of the UK and Nordic models. The former are all quarterly (with the recent transformation of the LPL model) and disaggregation across sectors is very limited (NIESR being the most disaggregated in terms of output). The Nordic models contain only one quarterly example (BOF4), and the least disaggregated model is that of BOF4 with five sectors. Dutch models tend to be closer to the UK models in terms of disaggregation, whereas French models are closer to the Nordic tradition. Disaggregation aspects largely determine the size of the models. The mainstream UK models tend to have fewer than 300 endogenous variables and fewer than 700 in total, similar to the size of Dutch models. The larger Nordic models have around 1000 equations, but less than 200 of these are stochastic, the remainder being associated with input–output or similar relationships. KOSMOS has nearly 500 equations, but only 21 stochastic relationships, making it not much larger than the smallest of the UK models, LPL, which has

Table 2.1 Structural charactertistics of the UK models (all quarterly models)

	LBS	NIESR	LPL	HMT	BE	OEF
Disaggregation	Manufacturing/non-manufacturing split	8 categories of output	None	Manufacturing/non-manufacturing split	Manufacturing/non-manufacturing split	Manufacturing/non-manufacturing split
Main features	Imperfect competition, nominal inertia	Imperfect competition, nominal inertia	New classical	Eclectic	Keynesian short run with nominal inertia; classical tendencies in the long run	Origins in HMT model but has since been modified
Expectations	Exchange rate either forward looking or learning approach	Rational in exchange rate, prices, wages, stockbuilding	Rational	Adaptive or implicit	Adaptive or implicit	Adaptive or implicit
Demand:						
Consumption	Real income, housing and financial wealth, nominal interest rates, demographic factors	Non-credit-financed spending a function of financial wealth, real income and real interest rates	Private sector demand determined by wealth and long-term interest rates	Total wealth, inflation-adjusted income, real interest rates	Financial wealth, housing wealth, real income, mortgage equity withdrawal	Income, total wealth, nominal interest rates, relative price durables/non-durables
Investment	Competitiveness, Tobin's Q (ratio of equity price to investment deflator)	Output, relative factor prices, relative material prices, expected capacity utilisation, diseq. liquidity		Relative factor prices, expected output, liquidity	Output and relative factor prices, real interest rates	Output, relative factor prices
Exports	World trade, relative prices	World trade, relative export prices, stochastic time trend	Net trade: real exchange rate, domestic and foreign income	World trade, relative unit labour costs, time trend	World demand relative unit labour costs/prices	World trade, time trend, relative wage costs

Imports	From identity between demand and output	Import share a function of capacity utilisation, specialisation and price competitiveness		Share of imports depends on specialisation index, relative prices, capacity utilisation	Manufacturing imports a residual between demand and output; domestic output share of demand depends on relative wage costs, time trend and utilisation	Domestic demand, time trend, relative import to domestic price, capacity utilisation
Supply:						
Production technology	Implicit Cobb–Douglas	Vintage capital approach	Implicit	Cobb–Douglas?	Not explicit	Explicit Cobb–Douglas production function
Employment	Real wages, capital stock, domestic and foreign demand	Adjustment to desired level from vintage capital approach; hours buffer	Direct estimation of unemployment rather than employment	Expected output, relative factor prices, time trend	Total hours depend on output, real wage, real cost of capital	Output time trend, hours, capital stock derived from pf, with hours a buffer
Wage formation	Real wages depend on total unemployment, long-term unemployment, productivity	Real wages depend on productivity, import prices, taxes, cost of stockholding, proportion of population not working	Real wages depend on unemployment, benefits and unionisation	Real wages depend on productivity, terms of trade, income taxes, company profitability, unemployment	Real wages depend on productivity, tax wedge, unemployment, real exchange rate	Real wages depend on unemployment, income taxes, productivity
Prices	Costs (labour and imports), capacity utilisation	Unit labour costs, import prices, capacity utilisation, cost of stockholding	Inflation a result of difference between money demand and fixed money supply	Imperfect competition and profit-maximising behaviour prices depend on total costs, utilisation, inflation variance	Implied price of domestic output depends on unit labour costs, capacity utilisation	Import costs, wage costs, capacity utilisation

Table 2.1 (continued)

Explicit NAIRU	No	Yes	Yes	No	In principle	No
Interest rates	Exogenous	Either policy instrument or reaction function for short rates; long rates forward looking	Efficient markets hypothesis	Policy variable; long rates depend on past short rates	Exogenous; long rates depend on past short rates	Reaction function; money growth differential, inflation differential, interest rate differential, exchange rate, current balance
Exchange rate	Learning approach based on UIP	Modified UIP with net assets risk premium	Real UIP	Adjusts to equilibrium rate, which depends on relative money, relative prices, interest differentials, oil prices	Modified UIP with backward-looking exchange rate expectations; risk premium is current balance plus inflation differential	Interest differentials, current balance, relative money, wage costs
Money supply	Endogenous, no explicit money demand equation	Endogenous, money demand equation for M0	In long run determined by PSBR target; policy variable in short run	Endogenous by identity	Endogenous by identity	Endogenous by identity

only 11 behavioural equations. There is considerable variety in the size of the US models, reflecting whether they are aimed at forecasting (DRI and Wharton) or are principally simulation models (FAIR). Comparison of size can be misleading as a guide to the economic complexity of the model. Ideally, we would like to be able to present models in terms of the number of variables broken down into exogenous, technical, identities and behavioural. The definition of stochastic may actually include some technical relationships that have been estimated, and hence is a broader definition than behavioural equations, which describe the economic behaviour of agents in the economy. If we examined the models in terms of main behavioural equations, they would turn out to be very similar in size. In most cases disaggregation is a top-down process and there is not a consistent accounting framework throughout each sectoral level. An exception is the Cambridge Growth Project model where the main macro aggregates are built up from the detailed industrial sectors.

Broad approach

The classification of models by broad approach is also difficult, since models do not often fit easily within simple descriptions such as Keynesian or monetarist. Nevertheless it is useful to attempt such a classification as a first approximation. In making such a classification, a useful distinction is between models that assume rapid adjustment of the economy to any exogenous shock, and those that do not. Where adjustment is not rapid, it is then useful to distinguish between sluggish adjustment due to real rigidities, such as the adjustment of real wages, or due to nominal rigidities. The former class of model would tend to be associated more with the neo-classical approach (where rapid adjustment would make them new classical in nature) and the latter with a more new Keynesian approach. At the extreme, where adjustment may not actually be sufficient to return to full-employment equilibrium, this is the old-fashioned Keynesian equilibrium under-employment model. In practice, most models tend to be sluggish in the short run, but may show neo-classical features in the longer term. The LPL model of the UK economy is clearly a new classical model, as is the FAIR model of the USA. The other models tend to be characterised by nominal inertia, which makes them Keynesian in the short run. However, the definition of the long run remains very much an empirical matter (see Chapter 5), and it is rare for an explicit long-run solution to be made. An exception is the UK NIESR model. Even then there is no firm guidance as to how long it takes to reach a new equilibrium.

Expectations

It remains comparatively rare for expectations to be explicitly treated in macro models. The UK models are rare in that rational, or forward consistent expectations, have been commonly used. In the LPL model expectations appear in several sectors, and the NIESR model uses expected variables in investment, employment and wage equations as well as in the exchange rate equation. Other European models have not incorporated rational expectations on a routine basis, and their use in the USA reflects a methodological stance. Some European models have an explicit treatment of expectations in foreign exchange and bond markets, but these are not usually based on the rational expectations approach (for example, MONA of Denmark and BOF of Finland).

Treatment of demand

As described in Chapter 1, the main endogenous components of demand are private consumption and investment and imports and exports. Many accounts of consumption equations written by the modellers themselves describe the consumption equation as based on the life-cycle hypothesis. This is rather a vague description in practice, since the empirical models include explanations of consumption by real incomes alone, a combination of real incomes and wealth, and wealth alone. Of the single-country models, only LPL has an explanation of consumption by wealth alone, but the measure of wealth used does not include human wealth, in contrast to the treatment in MULTIMOD (which is a multicountry model). Use of income alone is becoming comparatively rare in models (MODAG, the Norwegian model, and KOSMOS, the Swedish model, are examples). The consensus is for a combination of wealth and income, wealth usually defined as the sum of financial and physical assets, in the determination of consumer spending with a role for either real or nominal interest rates in addition. This suggests a life-cycle approach modified by liquidity constraints. KOSMOS has an inflation variable as a proxy for wealth, and this approach is more common among some of the multicountry models discussed in Chapter 8. The NIESR (UK) model is different from the others in that only financial wealth enters the consumption decision, but all new credit is assumed to result in an equal increase in expenditure. MODAG (Norway) also includes a credit availability variable.

Determination of fixed non-housing investment tends to be based on either the neo-classical profit-maximising approach or on Tobin's Q in the models (the LPL model explains total private expenditure by wealth and so does not have a separate investment equation). In most cases output also enters as an explanatory variable, and NIESR, HMT (both UK), MODAG (Norway) and MORKMON (Netherlands) include liquidity effects in some form.

There are some key differences in the treatment of trade. Some of the Nordic models adopt the hypothesis that export prices are determined solely by world prices in the long run, so export volumes are given by their marginal cost (this assumption combined with the hypothesis that export prices match import prices gives the Scandinavian model of inflation, or law of one price). Otherwise the standard paradigm is that exporters have some market power and exports are determined by a combination of world demand and relative prices or competitiveness. Imports are also determined by relative prices or costs together with domestic demand. An exception is the LBS model in the UK, where imports are determined as a residual between demand

and output. In most industrial economies there has been a trend rise in import penetration, and this is often proxied by a time trend or in some cases by a variable which attempts to proxy increased specialisation in international trade. These issues are discussed further in Chapter 4 under the heading of trade.

Supply

Not all the models contain an explicit production function, although one is often implicit in the derivation of factor demands. The use of the vintage approach is traditional in Dutch models, but it is also a feature of the NIESR model of the UK. The MORKMON model of the Dutch economy uses a CES production function to model potential output. This can be used in combination with the demand components of the model to generate measures of disequilibrium. A rationing process then allocates the discrepancy across imports and stockbuilding. This approach is relatively rare, however. In general, estimates of potential output derived from production functions are used to generate measures of overall capacity utilisation, which then enter into behavioural equations such as those for prices or imports. But the key elements in the supply process are the wage and price equations themselves. Prices are typically explained as a mark-up on costs, with capacity pressures occasionally influencing the size of this mark-up. Some models also typically include a role for foreign competing prices. Wages are usually described as being set in a bargaining framework, but the LPL model is an exception as it is based on the competitive paradigm. A major distinction lies between models which use the Phillips curve approach and those which explain the level of real wages by excess demand in the labour market and other labour market push factors. In all the UK models, the wage equation is expressed in terms of the real wage, whereas the Phillips curve approach is widely used in the USA, France and elsewhere in Europe (although not invariably).

Financial assets and the exchange rate

In the UK models, short-term nominal interest rates are usually either an exogenous policy variable or determined by a reaction function. An exception is the LPL model, where the efficient markets hypothesis is used to justify the equalisation of real domestic and foreign interest rates. Long-term rates are given as a function of short-term rates, and where these are forward looking the arbitrage conditions are imposed. Some of the other European models determine interest rates from financial sectors where interest rates equate the demand and supply of money, but the introduction of a monetary sector is a comparatively new addition to many models (and some Nordic models do not have a monetary sector). One of the implications of adding a monetary sector is that the size of the model is typically increased rather sharply. In the non-LPL UK models, the main purpose of the monetary and financial sectors is to derive personal sector wealth and sectoral flows of financial assets.

Exchange rates are given by the UIP approach in some UK models and by more *ad hoc* mechanisms in the others. Exchange rate formation in other European models is more varied, and most Nordic models do not have an endogenous treatment of the exchange rate.

Further reading

Carlin and Soskice (1990)
Levačic and Rebmann (1982)

3 Developments and comparison of models

This chapter reviews how the structures of mainstream models have changed and a new consensus has emerged, and assesses the impact of these developments on the properties of the models. We examine how different estimates of a demand expansion compare, and analyse the main features that determine the nature of full-model responses to demand and interest rate shocks.

3.1 Developments in models

The history of macroeconometric modelling in several countries is described in Bodkin *et al.* (1991) and is briefly described in Chapter 1. It is clear that models which are used for practical forecasting and policy simulation analysis do not remain inviolate from changes going on in the world around them. Chapter 2 illustrates how there is a broad consensus in modelling in the single-country case. In this section we describe how the macroeconometric models of the 1970s have faced up to the monetarist challenge and how this new consensus has emerged; one which is quite distinct from the monetarist view. The developments are illustrated with examples from the UK models, although many similar developments were also occurring in models in other countries. The impact that these developments actually had on the properties of these models, and hence their policy implications, as revealed by simulation analysis is also discussed.

In this section we describe how the mainstream models have faced the monetarist challenge and how a new consensus has emerged, although one still distinct from the monetarist paradigm.

The mainstream models

There was a considerable degree of consensus among the UK models of the mid-1970s, the main challenge coming from the New Cambridge approach, as developed by the Cambridge Economic Policy Group (CEPG) led by Godley. Even this was based on Keynesian origins, however. The mainstream models at the time were those of the National Institute for Economic and Social Research, the London Business School and HM Treasury. The Cambridge Growth Project model was at this time still very much peripheral to broad macroeconomic modelling.

> The mainstream models were centred round the income–expenditure national accounts identity.

The mainstream models were based on the income–expenditure approach with the level of output and employment principally determined by the level of demand. The demand side of these models can be set out in a very stylised way as shown in equations 3.1–3.6, these equations corresponding to the framework developed in Chapter 2.

$$Y = C + I + G + \Delta S + X - M \tag{3.1}$$

$$C = c(Y - HP) \tag{3.2}$$

$$I = i(Y, r) \tag{3.3}$$

$$\Delta S = s(Y) \tag{3.4}$$

$$M = m(Y, ep/p^*) \tag{3.5}$$

$$X = x(Y^*, ep/p^*) \tag{3.6}$$

Equation 3.1 is the standard national income accounting identity, which sums the expenditure components of GDP (consumers' expenditure, fixed investment, government spending, stockbuilding, exports and imports). Equation 3.2 is the consumption equation, which explains personal consumption by real incomes (Y) and credit restrictions (HP). It is of a Keynesian form with consumers assumed to be constrained by real incomes and credit conditions. Equations 3.3 and 3.4 explain fixed investment and stockbuilding by simple accelerator models (changes in output) with some allowance for interest rate effects on fixed investment. Finally, equations 3.5 and 3.6 explain trade, exports and imports, by domestic and foreign income (y, y^*) and by competitiveness (ep/p^*) where e is the exchange rate measured as the foreign price of domestic currency, p the domestic price level and p^* the foreign price level. A rise in this term is associated with a worsening of competitiveness. Most of the models did not at this time have an endogenous explanation of exchange rates (e) so that most of the variation in competitiveness in model simulations came from changes in relative prices (p/p^*), whose effects were rather small on imports and exports. Monetary influences were largely absent, their main role being the role of credit conditions on personal consumption and a small interest rate influence on fixed investment. This implies that the IS schedule implicit in these models was relatively steep. In the absence of money demand functions (where money demand functions were included they were often found to be unstable), the implied LM schedule is highly elastic, and thus the properties of these two schedules suggested a powerful role for fiscal policy and a weak one for monetary policy.

> The early models had a combination of a steep *IS* curve and a flat *LM* curve, implying a powerful role for fiscal policy relative to monetary policy.

The determination of aggregate supply was rudimentary. It came not from an explicit output supply relationship or constraint, but from increasing inflation through the mechanism of the Phillips curve treatment of wages.

$$\dot{w} = w(u, \dot{P}^e) \tag{3.7}$$

with price expectations ($\dot{P}^e$) given by past inflation

$$\dot{P}^e = \dot{P}_{t-1} \tag{3.8}$$

and the price level in turn given by a constant mark-up on costs

$$P = \beta(w - \pi) + (1 - \beta)P_m \tag{3.9}$$

where $(w - \pi)$ represents unit labour costs (wages less productivity) and P_m is the price of imports. The typical size of the coefficient on price expectations in the augmented Phillips curve (3.7) was less than unity, implying a long-run trade-off between unemployment and inflation. An important practical problem was that empirical estimates of the wage equation (3.7) proved unstable, and in particular it was difficult to find a statistically significant and robust role for excess demand (unemployment) on wages, the wage equation usually being overwritten in forecasting exercises. Unemployment itself was determined by a simple identity between employment and the labour force (3.10).

> The influence of aggregate supply came largely from the Phillips curve mechanism.

$$U = L - N \tag{3.10}$$

The labour force (L) was treated as predetermined apart from demographic trends, and employment (N) was based on an inverted production function where employment lagged behind output.

$$E = f(Y) \tag{3.11}$$

Figure 3.1 shows a simple representation of the implied aggregate demand and aggregate supply schedules of these early models. The aggregate demand schedule is steep, reflecting the steep *IS* and shallow *LM* schedules. The aggregate supply schedule can be described as fairly flat up to some 'full-employment' level of unemployment and then becomes quite steep, reflecting resource constraints rather than inflationary pressures. Although capacity pressures could also appear elsewhere in the model, as in

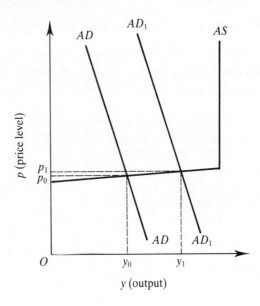

Figure 3.1 The 1970s models

the determination of imports, the main source of supply-side influence was through the wage equation. In some of the models, the *AS* schedule actually sloped downwards in the short run, as higher output reduced unit labour costs and hence prices.

The policy implications which emerge are that demand policies could have powerful effects on output and employment with little role or need for supply-side policies. In Figure 3.1 the initial equilibrium is at income level y_0 and price level p_0 where the aggregate demand schedule (*AD*) intersects the aggregate supply schedule (*AS*). If there is a fiscal expansion which shifts the aggregate schedule from *AD* to AD_1 the equilibrium shifts to y_1, p_1, giving a higher level of output for only a small increase in the price level. Only if the aggregate demand schedule were to intersect the aggregate supply schedule on its vertical part (denoting full employment of resources) would a demand expansion lead to higher prices (inflation) with no increase in output.

 The early models had a steep aggregate demand schedule and a flat, sometimes downward-sloping, aggregate supply schedule.

The monetarist challenge

The mainstream models came under heavy attack in the late 1970s. They had long been criticised for inadequate theoretical foundations, but when they began to exhibit serious forecasting failures their whole *raison d'être* became somewhat fragile. Their main failure was to predict the inflationary consequences of the Barber boom of 1973–4 and the juxtaposition of output recession and high inflation (stagflation) following the quadrupling of oil prices around the same time. The initial challenge came from monetarists who did not claim to have an alternative macroeconomic model, but who based their predictions of inflation on simple quantity theory (examples being Gordon Pepper of Greenwells and Alan Walters, then at the London School of Economics). These monetarists were scathing of the need to have fully elaborated mechanisms for predicting the economy, arguing that the 1970s could be explained by a simple relationship between money supply growth and inflation. Academic support came from work by Friedman (1968) in the USA, who showed that there was no long-run trade off between unemployment and inflation, and that unemployment would converge to some 'natural' equilibrium rate which could not be altered by demand management policies.

> The monetarist challenge came at a time when the mainstream models were experiencing frequent forecast failures and were finding the combination of a rising level of unemployment and rising rate of inflation difficult to explain.

In the Friedman view any attempt to lower unemployment would simply lead to accelerating inflation, and temporary reductions in unemployment were illusory since these were merely the result of incorrect price expectations.

> The so-called Lucas critique argued that models could not cope with policy changes.

A second line of attack came from the argument that the structure of macro-economic models was influenced by regime changes, such as changes in policy approach – the Lucas critique. Lucas and Sargent (1978) argued that 'macroeconomic models are of no value in guiding policy and this condition will not be remedied in modifications along any line which is currently being pursued'. It was soon recognised, however, that the Lucas critique applied not to the behaviour of economic agents, but to their expectations of future policy (which influenced current behaviour). The advent of the new classical model which combined both the key elements of monetarism and explicit treatment of expectations (forward expectations) emphasised the attack. In the UK, the Liverpool model based on this approach became operational around 1980. The mainstream models needed to respond to these challenges, but the reaction was one of general adjustment – not a wholesale rejection of existing models, but a process of adaptation. The models continued to be in use in the policy process simply because there was no alternative capable of providing internally consistent quantitative advice: 'Even had policy advisers fully understood the Lucas critique it would not have immobilized them. By the time they understood it, it was in any event subject to significant watering down in the profession' (Higgins, 1987). This is particularly true of the UK, where it was recognised that the new classical predictions came from the joint assumptions of market clearing and rational expectations – in the USA this distinction did not appear to be made. Thus the UK models did begin to incorporate rational expectations, but not with the monetarist result.

 The response to the Lucas critique was that it was overstated and, in any case, could be accommodated by the use of rational expectations

The mainstream response

Changes to the mainstream models are associated with greater emphasis on the supply side and on medium-term considerations. There are a variety of interrelated motivations for these developments. First, supply-side shocks appeared to be more prevalent in the economy during the 1970s, and the models were thought to be ill-equipped to deal with the impact of oil price rises, productivity slow-downs and so forth. Second, there was an independent desire for greater theoretical consistency in the models, both in respect of a better-articulated macroeconomic framework incorporating both demand and supply factors, and also in terms of internal consistency: for example, in the joint determination of output, prices and the demand for factors of production. In these respects, empirical models resemble the textbook models. In the UK, modelling was regarded as very much a second-rate activity. In France it might be argued, in contrast, that models were quite sophisticated theoretically, but not very sound empirically. Thus the trade off between performance and 'attractiveness' was applied in different ways.

 Motivations for change came not only from the monetarist challenge, but from the frequency of supply shocks, the need to relate to the new economic policies of the 1980s, and the desire for greater theoretical consistency.

Finally, policy itself can be said to be responsible for model changes in than it was felt important that the models should be capable of analysing and evaluating a macroeconomic policy which was increasingly supply-side based. This followed the election of a new government committed to a supply-side approach, in the UK, under Mrs Thatcher, and of the Reagan administration in the USA.

Attributing the relative importance of these three motivations is not possible, since they all result in the same shift in general emphasis, but it is evident that the change in policy approach did precede and possibly hasten the main supply-side developments in the mainstream quarterly models.

Changes in the mainstream UK models have been evolutionary rather than revolutionary.

A move away from the Keynesian position had started in the second half of the 1970s, with the London Business School tending towards a view described as 'international monetarism', in which changes in relative money supplies affect prices via changes in the exchange rate, given long-run purchasing power parity (Ball, Burns and Laury, 1977). The Treasury and NIESR models had begun to develop financial systems in order to link the financial sector, exchange rates and the operation of monetary policy, but these developments had less impact on the overall properties of the models than those of the LBS. The main practical element in this approach was the influence on exchange rate behaviour of relative money movements. Combined with the view that fiscal expansion had important monetary effects, this established an additional role for crowding out via inflation, other than simply through the behaviour of the nominal interest rate. The full implications of the international monetarist approach could only be guaranteed, however, if higher price inflation was fully transmitted into higher wages, which was not a feature of the early models.

> Early signs of change came in the LBS model in the late 1970s, which adopted an 'international monetarist' position. Key to this was the determination of the exchange rate by monetary factors.

The models adapted in the 1980s. They used ideas from the new classical school in several ways, but differed in several critical respects. In this section we note the broad developments in the models and then proceed to set out the resultant changes in the simulation properties of the models and hence their implications for policy.

> The mainstream models have adopted the new classical emphasis on stock rather than flow adjustment, but have not accepted the market-clearing paradigm.

The new classical approach, which is represented by the LPL model, can be characterised as a combination of market clearing and rational expectations, and it emphasises the role of stocks rather than flows. The mainstream models have moved in this direction, notably by the introduction of wealth effects in consumption equations. New classicism also stresses the supply side of the economy, not through the inclusion of an explicit production function, but rather through a representation of the labour market which is responsive to changes in benefits and taxes, but not to the level of demand. The approach adopted by the mainstream models has not been to follow the competitive paradigm of the classical school; instead developments have centred around a framework of imperfect competition in goods and labour markets, and the adoption of a bargaining approach to wage determination, following the work of Layard and Nickell (1985).

> There is now more general acceptance that there is no long-run trade-off between inflation and unemployment, but this is not yet a property of all the models.

The general acceptance of this framework has meant that wage equations are now specified in terms of the level of real wages, which is in principle affected by any factors which influence the bargaining strengths of employers and employees, including supply-side variables such as tax rates, unemployment benefits and labour market mismatch. Here the desire to model the 'incentive' effects of the new macroeconomic policy is evident, although the tax coefficients are typically ill-defined in empirical work. An additional feature of the Layard–Nickell approach is the incorporation of demand pressure variables in price setting, although the specification remains largely cost based. Layard and Nickell emphasises that the long-run solution to the wage and price equations delivers the non-accelerating-inflation rate of unemployment (NAIRU), and Joyce and Wren-Lewis (1991) show how this analysis, suitably extended for open-economy effects, can be applied to the NIESR model. The other UK quarterly models do not yet satisfy all the necessary conditions whereby the long-run supply side can be determined by analysis of these equations, but they do represent a considerable advance on simple Phillips curve inflation mechanisms in both theoretical and empirical terms. Although both new classical and mainstream models coincide in the principle that there is no long-run trade-off between inflation and unemployment, the concept of the unemployment equilibrium differs. The natural rate of the new classical school relates to a competitive solution given the existence of market imperfections, whereas the Layard–Nickell framework and its NAIRU is based on a bargaining process under imperfect competition (see Carlin and Soskice, 1990, for further discussion of this). In addition, whereas the Liverpool model differs from its theoretical counterpart in that it exhibits real-wage rigidity, the mainstream models have nominal-wage rigidity through the presence of wage contracts, and other inertia factors. Although the supply-side approach used by Layard and Nickell now appears to be generally accepted in the UK models, there still appears to be a considerable divide on this issue between the UK on the one hand and the USA and the rest of Europe on the other hand. The USA and many other European models still adopt the Phillips curve approach, which explains real-wage inflation in terms of excess demand, rather than the Layard–Nickell framework, which describes the dependence of the real wage level on unemployment. Implications of this difference for full-model properties are described in the further discussion of the supply-side approach below.

> The potential for inflation crowding out of demand has been increased by the inclusion of wealth in consumption equations, but revaluation of physical assets can produce 'crowding in'.

The new classical approach views inflation as determined wholly by excess money, but the mainstream models have not followed this route, for it has proved empirically inadequate. Instead inflation is generated by excess demand in goods and labour markets and by the inconsistency of wage claims by the unionised sector with the wage that employers are prepared to concede (the 'affordable wage'). A necessary feature of the supply-side approach is not only that inflation is generated by additional demand, but that higher inflation itself reduces demand so that in the long run output is supply determined. Although investment expenditures are now more sensitive to inflation than hitherto, often through liquidity effects, the key demand elements which are sensitive to inflation are net trade and consumption. Empirical estimates of competitiveness effects on trade have tended to be revised downwards as more recent data have been incorporated, so that inflation crowding out through this route has decreased. However, many models have introduced capacity utilisation effects on imports, so that short-run increases in demand are associated with high import leakages, so reducing the domestic output boost. At the same time, estimates of long-run activity effects on imports are lower than hitherto.

It is in the area of consumers' expenditure that quantitatively the most important inflation effects on demand occur, and developments here relate to changes in the macroeconomic policy regime. In particular, the failure of the existing models to predict the growth of consumer spending in the late 1980s has been associated with the process of financial deregulation and liberalisation in many economies. Based on the view that financial deregulation has increased the liquidity of physical assets held by the personal sector has led to the extension of the wealth variables in consumer expenditure equations to include physical wealth, of which housing is the principal component. This development increases the role of the housing market in the models, an area which has previously been largely neglected. In current versions of the models, changes in demand may lead to large revaluations of wealth through changes in house prices. In addition, the estimated wealth elasticities of consumption have increased, so that the overall inflation effects on aggregate demand have become substantially higher.

The open-economy dimension focuses attention on the determination of the exchange rate, which is a key ingredient in the inflation mechanism. The increasing degree of information on the floating rate regime together with the removal of constraints on capital mobility have enabled more satisfactory empirical formulations of exchange rate behaviour to be constructed. In particular, there has been a movement towards the use of uncovered interest parity conditions modified by a variable risk premium, typically proxied by the current account. Although this implies greater consensus between the models in respect of exchange rate determination, it increases the sensitivity of the models to interest rates and the current account. Attention is then more sharply focused on how these are determined in the rest of the model structure, where considerable differences remain in empirical characteristics, if not in theoretical design.

Endogenous exchange rate behaviour has become common with the UIP approach (modified for risk) often used in models

Following the advent of the Liverpool model at the beginning of the 1980s, complete with rational expectations, the LBS and NIESR models began to incorporate a model-consistent treatment of expectations in the mid-1980s. This approach requires the use of solution algorithms which ensure that the values of the future expectations variables which influence current behaviour coincide with the model's forecasts for that future period. In policy analysis the impact of forward consistent expectations is generally to speed up the model's adjustment to any given perturbation. In the LBS and NIESR models, the result was an increase in the short-run response of output and employment following a demand shock, since wages and prices remained sluggish, so that these models appear even more Keynesian in the short run. This increased short-term sensitivity is principally due to the reaction of the exchange rate, which under rational expectations 'jumps' in response to an anticipated exogenous shock. It is this non-linearity more than anything else which distinguishes standard model simulations, conducted under forward expectations, from the backward-looking mode, where adjustment is typically smooth. The UK HM Treasury has followed this trend in internal work, but not in the public version of its model, despite the importance of expectations experiments on the model, reported by Spencer (1984). In common with other models, its treatment of the exchange rate begins with uncovered interest parity, but the expected rate is then modelled in a backward-looking manner. The main impact that the incorporation of rational expectations has had on the models has been the need to ensure that the model satisfies the saddlepoint conditions (that is, it has a unique stable solution). This implication was probably unforeseen originally. This requirement has helped to focus attention on the long-run properties of the models.

> Rational expectations have been included in the mainstream UK models, but without producing new classical-style results.

Simulations conducted on the 1970s models tended to pay little attention to the overall setting of monetary and fiscal policy. This was understandable, since exchange rate equations were in their infancy and were little trusted, and the models had little to say about the monetary implications of fiscal changes, either in terms of deriving monetary aggregates or in the effects of higher monetary expansion on demand. Subsequent developments have seen greater attention paid to the overall stance of policy in simulation analysis, particularly to the government budget constraint and to the issue of sustainability. Whereas the 1970s models could generate expanding current account deficits or cumulative increases in the government's financial position with no apparent consequences, these issues are now more carefully considered. In some cases there are formal mechanisms within the models (policy reaction functions) which explicitly adjust interest rates, say, to changes in domestic and foreign economic conditions.

> Greater attention has been paid to financing issues and the sustainability of any given policy stance.

The growing acceptance of the modified UIP approach to exchange rate modelling has, in turn, given the current account a direct role in exchange rate adjustment, although in practice this mechanism is often too weak to ensure correction of current account deficits within a reasonably long simulation horizon. Policy reaction functions assume greater importance if the exchange rate is part of a managed system such as the European exchange rate mechanism (ERM). If the exchange rate is to remain within a given target zone, adjustment of monetary and/or fiscal policy may be necessary, and it is increasingly inappropriate to treat monetary and fiscal policy instruments as predetermined and independent. The operation of the ERM admits the possibility of realignment, which introduces greater scope for credibility and reputation effects.

We can very broadly summarise the developments in the mainstream models by the following set of stylised equations. Equations 3.12–3.17 give the demand side.

> The *IS* schedule of current models is steeper than in the early models, and the power of monetary policy enhanced.

Income–expenditure identity	$Y = C + I + G + \Delta S + X - M$	(3.12)
Consumption	$C = c(Y, r, W)$	(3.13)
Investment	$I = i(Y, w/ck)$	(3.14)
Stockbuilding	$\Delta S = s(Y, cs)$	(3.15)
Imports	$M = m(Y, cu, ep/p^*)$	(3.16)
Exports	$X = x(Y^*, cu, ep/p^*)$	(3.17)

The consumption equation now includes a role for interest rates (r) and real wealth (W). Investment is influenced by relative factor prices (w/ck) or simply the real cost of capital depending on the precise derivation used, and stockbuilding is influenced by the cost of stockholding (cs). Exports and imports are additionally determined by capacity utilisation (cu). The implication of the revisions to the demand side is that the *IS* schedule and hence the aggregate demand schedule are both more interest elastic than before. Monetary factors are more important through their influence directly on consumption, investment and stockbuilding, but also through their effect on wealth in respect of finance of the government deficit (for example, through changes in the holding of public sector debt by the personal sector). Aggregate supply can be described by the wage, price and exchange rate equations.

$$w - p = w(U, t, z, ep/p^*) \tag{3.18}$$

$$p = p(cu, (w - \pi), ep/p^*) \tag{3.19}$$

$$e = e(e^e, r - r^*, \gamma) \tag{3.20}$$

> The aggregate schedule is less steep and the aggregate supply schedule steeper in modern models.

Wages now respond to excess demand, a vector of tax rates (t), the real exchange rate and wage-push variables (z). The price mark-up is sensitive to demand pressure (cu) and prices charged abroad (ep/p^*). The exchange rate is a modified UIP equation, where future expectations of the exchange rate (e^e), relative interest differentials ($r - r^*$) and a risk premium (γ) are included. Expectations may appear additionally in wage equations (expected prices) or in the demand equations (expected output). The implications of these revisions are to make the aggregate supply schedule less elastic in the short run and, in principle, vertical in the long run (Figure 3.2), implying that a demand shock can only attain y_1 temporarily.

The real-world models do not correspond exactly to this framework. They are

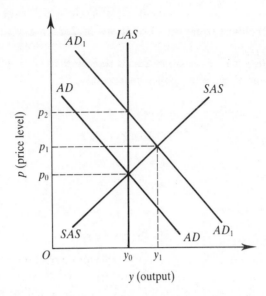

Figure 3.2 The 1980s models

non-linear, containing both dynamics and other influences not reported here. Nevertheless this framework does capture the basic spirit behind the models and provides a useful background to the discussion of the simulation properties of the models. As a first introduction to these we describe the main changes in the properties of the UK models over the last decade in the following chapter.

Comparison with other models

> Developments in the UK models have been more widespread than in models of other economies.

Finally, we make a brief comparison of the UK models against models of other economies, notably those of the USA, Europe and the Nordic economies. It appears that the UK models have been quicker to adopt new theory and innovations such as rational expectations than elsewhere. Modelling in the USA has been dominated by commercial concerns in the last few years, with an emphasis on forecasting rather than policy analysis or model development. Rational expectations tends to be associated with new classicism in the USA. Rational expectations is not widely adopted in Europe, but then neither is an endogenous treatment of the exchange rate. The exchange rate is an important part of the transmission mechanism in the supply response to demand shocks (see the discussion below), and hence treating the exchange rate as exogenous is an important gap. It also raises problems in policy analysis, since the models can no longer be regarded as realistic illustrations of policy scenarios in which exchange rate pressures arise; in such cases the models would clearly require some off-model assumptions and interventions.

Another area where the UK models have become more explicit has been the treatment of the supply side and particularly the role of taxes. This is made possible by use of the Layard and Nickell framework, which expresses the wage bargain in levels, and relates real wages to a set of exogenous factors that include taxes. The standard approach elsewhere is still the Phillips curve, which only expresses wages in terms of a first difference with equilibrium unemployment usually constant.

European models, outside the UK, do focus more on the modelling of technology, especially through explicit production functions, but given that these models rarely have well-determined long-run solutions, this may be a dubious advantage. However, it must be accepted that there are some models (for example, the BOF4 model of the Finnish economy) where model development is equivalent to best-practice UK development, and equally there are some models in the UK which fall below best practice elsewhere.

3.2 Comparative differences among models

In this section we describe some of the properties of macroeconomic models as observed in simulation experiments. We review how far the model developments described in the previous chapter have been reflected in the full-model simulation properties of the models. We do this first by looking at changes in model properties over successive deposits of the main UK models. We then look at the current properties of the UK models, and compare these with estimates from models of other economies and from the multicountry models. In order to give a fuller flavour to the mechanisms operating in the models, we then describe in more detail some standard simulations of the UK models. Although the description relates to the models as at 1990 (the 1991 versions were almost identical) and so is particular to a given vintage of the models, many of the features discussed are of general relevance and can be used as a framework for the discussion of other models (as has been done for the Nordic models, for example).

The methodology of simulation methods and the use of other techniques to investigate the properties of models are described in subsequent chapters, and more detailed discussion of some of the key building blocks in terms of understanding model properties is set out in Chapter 4. The reader is asked at this stage to take the results very much at face value.

Changes over time

Demand shock

In this section we describe the main changes in the full-model properties that have taken place (full details are given in Appendix II). If the models have truly moved towards a more supply-oriented position then we would expect to observe a reduction in the estimated impact on output and unemployment from a demand shock, at least in the medium term. We would also expect to observe an increase in inflation. As an illustration we take an increase in government expenditure under money finance for three of the UK mainstream models: LBS, NIESR and HMT. The choice of simulation and models reflects the availability of published simulation results for these models. It would be interesting to conduct an equivalent exercise under the assumption of bond finance. (Chapter 7 reviews alternative financing assumptions that are possible). However, the fact that equivalent results are not fully available and also the absence of an explicit demand for money equation in some versions of the models make this simulation difficult to conduct. However, the discussion of interest rate simulations below goes some way to filling this gap since the reaction of the models to interest rate changes is a key part of the differential expenditure response under bond finance.

We express the output responses of the models in terms of the government expenditure multiplier: that is, the absolute change in GDP arising from a unit change in government current expenditure on goods and services. The use of the concept of the multiplier helps to standardise the model responses in a form which is independent of the initiating shock. It is also useful in that it is the concept used in elementary macroeconomic theory. Standard elementary theory starts from the idea that the multiplier is the reciprocal of the marginal propensity to save, and then introduces additional leakages into the multiplier process, such as imports and taxes (an empirical decomposition of the multiplier is given in Chapter 5).

The multiplier in the simplest theoretical model is the reciprocal of the marginal propensity to save $(1/s)$, and on plausible estimates of this propensity of 0.25–0.20 (a marginal propensity to consume of 0.75–0.80) turns out to be of the order of 4–5. Once leakages are introduced this tends to fall to a value of around 2, on plausible assumptions of the size of the marginal propensity to import and the marginal tax leakage. Empirical macroeconometric model estimates are usually below 2, and are often around unity. A multiplier of this magnitude implies that the initial injection of government spending is just sufficient to increase total GDP by the same absolute amount, so that private sector spending is unchanged: that is, neither crowded in nor crowded out. A multiplier value greater than unity measures the degree to which a public sector spending increase stimulates additional expenditure in the rest of the economy, whereas a value less than unity measures the extent to which private expenditure is crowded out. A multiplier of zero therefore indicates that an equal amount of private spending is crowded out by the increase in public spending, and a negative multiplier implies that GDP falls in aggregate as more private spending is crowded out than the initial injection of public spending.

> Crowding out can take various forms: financial, physical and inflation are the main ones.

Before we proceed further it is useful to be more precise about what is meant by 'crowding out'. In general we mean the tendency of an injection of exogenous public spending to reduce spending by the private sector. This can happen through several different mechanisms. The first is through *physical* crowding out. Here public resources pre-empt those of the private sector; this might occur through a labour supply or production constraint, but is not a common form of crowding out in empirical models. The second is through *financial* crowding out, which is perhaps the most familiar form of crowding out. It occurs as a result of the rise in interest rates required to finance the increase in the government budget deficit. It therefore arises when the increase in the deficit is financed by sales of government bonds rather than accommodated by an increase in the supply of money. The strict definition of this form of crowding out is the difference between the government expenditure multiplier under money finance and that under bond finance.

$$\Theta_f = \phi_{\bar{r}} - \phi_{\bar{m}} \tag{3.21}$$

where Θ_f is the financial crowding out coefficient, $\phi_{\bar{r}}$ is the multiplier under money finance (constant interest rates) and $\phi_{\bar{m}}$ is the corresponding multiplier under bond finance (fixed money supply). Normally this coefficient of crowding out is expressed as a proportion of the multiplier under money finance. Then a coefficient of unity indicates complete financial crowding out, and a multiplier of zero no crowding out. In the model results reported here, the financing assumption is that of money finance and hence there is no financial crowding out. The third form of crowding out is *inflation* crowding out. This occurs as higher demand generates an increase in inflation, which subsequently reduces private sector demand. It is the main source of crowding out in the simulations reported here.

Estimates of government expenditure multipliers published in Laury, Lewis and Ormerod (1978) are just over unity for the HMT and LBS models, and a little below unity for the NIESR model. The estimates for the LBS and NIESR models show little evidence of increasing crowding out over the simulation horizon (i.e. a falling multiplier). By 1983 little seems to have changed: the impact (first-year) multipliers for both LBS and HMT models were very close to unity, with the NIESR model giving a value of 1.2. The impact multipliers for the HMT model have remained remarkably constant since then. Using the time-series evidence from the annual deposits with the Macroeconomic Modelling Bureau, we also see little evidence of the value of the multiplier falling over the simulation horizon for this model. In fact, the post-1988 versions of the model show an increasing multiplier. In particular, the 1990 version of the HMT model gives a government expenditure multiplier of 1.3 after five years.

The introduction of the financial sector into the LBS model in 1984 and the determination of asset prices under forward-consistent expectations did not change the value of the impact multiplier for the LBS model, but the multiplier had a tendency to rise over the simulation period, reaching a value close to 1.5 after five years in the 1984–6 versions. In contrast, the introduction of forward-consistent expectations in the NIESR model in 1985 does not appear to have markedly changed the value of the medium-term multiplier response. However, the time-series interpretation of the impact of rational expectations in these two models is misleading, for the decomposition of multiplier responses reported in Wallis *et al.* (1986, p. 46) reveals that forward expectations in fact raised the medium-term multiplier in the NIESR model above the level that would have occurred under exogenous expectations, whereas the impact is one of time switching in the LBS model (that is, the multiplier response is advanced in time). However, this decomposition uses exogenous expectations as the alternative to forward expectations of the exchange rate and this prevents any adjustment of the exchange rate, and biases the results towards finding a higher multiplier under forward expectations. The analysis of rational expectations in Chapter 5 shows that, in principle, long-run responses should not be affected by the inclusion of forward-consistent expectations.

The multiplier for the LBS model for the first year of a government spending simulation has shown little deviation over successive versions of the model, but the medium-term multiplier has tended to rise until the removal of the financial model in the 1990 version, whereupon the multiplier fell back to unity after five years. The most recent form of the model (1992), which contains a learning mechanism for expectations formation in the exchange rate equation in place of the rational approach, has a first-year multiplier of over 0.8, and this increases to just under unity after seven to eight years. The NIESR model showed evidence of quite large expenditure multipliers throughout the simulation horizon until 1988 when a major restructuring of the model occurred. Then, although the impact multiplier remained high (recording a value of 1.8 in the 1989 version), the medium-term multiplier response declined sharply to around one half. The subsequent increase in the multiplier after the fifth year of the simulation in the 1990 release of the NIESR model is more difficult to describe in terms of structural model changes, for there were none. Instead the higher multiplier and hence weaker degree of crowding out arise from a more technical change, a change to the terminal condition for the exchange rate and convergence criteria for the model. We discuss the role of terminal conditions in Chapter 5. The conclusion to be drawn here is that the results prior to 1990 may have overestimated the speed of crowding out in this model, and although the multiplier still shows a strong tendency to fall towards zero over a long simulation base, this fall is not as rapid as previously indicated. Multipliers for the BE model have stayed around unity on impact, but the medium-term responses increased sharply to over 1.5 after the 1988 release.

What conclusions can be draw from this comparison of multipliers over time? There is little evidence of any increased crowding out in the HMT model over time. In contrast, the medium-term multipliers have increased in recent years – this is associated with wealth effects as described below. Similar conclusions can be drawn for the BE model. In this respect, at least, there is no sign of a radical or even evolutionary change in the full-model properties of these models. As we describe below, this may reflect the absence of forward-looking behaviour and the sluggishness of price adjustment to a demand shock (the two features are interrelated).

Nor do the reduced-form properties of the LBS multiplier suggest that the model has shifted radically towards the dominance of the supply side (especially compared with the reactions of the LPL model). There is greater sign of this in the NIESR model, where the available evidence does suggest that the long-run value of the multiplier tends towards zero, but there is also the suggestion that this adjustment to the long run could be very long, certainly well beyond the normal simulation horizon for macroeconomic model simulation experiments.

However, focus upon the output response of the models alone may be an imperfect indicator of model changes, especially in respect of greater supply-side influences. We therefore also look at the impact on inflation and unemployment. We would expect the inflation response to any demand change to be higher and the unemployment response to be weaker if the role of the supply side had increased in recent years.

The unemployment responses are standardised across the different vintages of the models to be equivalent to a £2bn increase in government current expenditure on goods and services at 1990 prices, balanced proportionally between procurement and employment spending. Estimates from the HMT model reveal that this reduces total unemployment by around 100 000 consistently over the various vintages of the model. The unemployment response is also fairly similar after the fifth year of the simulation to the impact (first-year) effect. Variations both over different model vintages and over the simulation period are more marked for the LBS and NIESR models. Earlier versions of the LBS model (*circa* 1983) produced unemployment responses of around 125 000 in the first year of the simulation, rising to 150 000–200 000 after five years. Later vintages of the model show a reduction in the first-year unemployment response of around one-third, despite virtually no change in the output response. Medium-term responses have also been lowered, and the most recent versions of this model show no tendency for the response after five years of the simulation to exceed the impact response. The NIESR responses have undergone fairly dramatic change over the successive versions of the model since 1983. The 1984 version of the model produced very large impact and medium-term responses (160 000 and 200 000 respectively). In the following year these had been revised down to 52 000 and 27 000. The main reason for this change was the introduction of new relationships between unemployment and employment which gave a very low weight to changes in non-manufacturing employment. These equations were subsequently revised. In 1988 there were major changes to the structure of the NIESR model. The first-year effect on unemployment now emerges at under 50 000, with similar estimates for the response after five years.

We would conclude that the pattern of unemployment response in the HMT and NIESR models has largely followed the pattern of revisions to output response, but that the successive unemployment estimates from the LBS model show weaker demand responses than do the corresponding effects on GDP.

Finally, we turn to inflation. One possibility is that a demand shock may still generate a sustained increase in output and a reduction in unemployment, but result in greater inflationary pressure. There is not a lot of evidence to support this suggestion from the model simulation results compared over successive vintages. The main impact comes from the NIESR model following the changes introduced in 1988.

> Multipliers across the models have remained around unity, and are clearly positive, and so do not support the claim that fiscal policy is totally ineffective

Interest rate shock

The demand change considered above is an example of a fiscal shock. The changes to the models made over the last decade have given a greater role to financial considerations in expenditure decisions and in the determination of the exchange rate. An interest rate shock simulation gives some quantitative measure of how far these changes are reflected in full-model simulation properties. It also reflects the power of monetary policy captured by the models.

The simulation results summarised in Appendix II are the GDP responses to a 1 percentage point reduction in short-term interest rates (the results for the LBS and NIESR models for the 1988 version are for a five-year shock, and hence are not comparable with the results for other vintages of these models). This is assumed to persist for three years in models with forward-consistent expectations and to be permanent in other cases. The duration of the shock is a key assumption in the effect of interest rates on models with a UIP formulation of the exchange rate, as considered in Chapter 4.

The results for the HMT model consistently give an estimate of an impact effect on GDP of 0.3–0.4 per cent, but there is the suggestion of an increase in the medium-term impact from 0.7–1.0 to around 1.5 per cent in later versions of the model. Some of this increase is due to the role of wealth in the model, and this is described below. The LBS model gives a similar impact estimate to that of HMT, but the medium-term impact of interest rates is weaker, and the more recent versions of the model give an adverse effect on the level of GDP by the fifth year of the simulation. This feature is largely due to the assumption that interest rate cuts are permanent. The effect after three years in the most recent LBS model is an increase in GDP of around 0.9 per cent. Apart from the 1987 vintage, where interest rates were particularly powerful, the NIESR model has moved from being a model which was very interest insensitive to one where interest rates are more powerful, but where they nonetheless play a weaker role than in the other models. The BE model has powerful interest rate effects in the medium term of three to five years, in common with the HMT model, but the impact effects are weaker than in the other models.

> Responses of output and inflation to changes in interest rates have increased in more recent versions of the models, but not always.

The main conclusion is that the models do not appear to have shifted their positions in terms of a demand shock very radically over the period. This is especially true of the HMT and BE models. The NIESR model has more clearly shifted towards a model where the long-run effects of a demand shock on output are negligible, but the length of this adjustment period could be very protracted and is unlikely to be apparent in model simulations over periods less than ten years. Inflationary pressures have also increased in this model, but much less so in the other models. The LBS model appears to have shifted slightly towards greater crowding out of unemployment following a demand shock, but this is not reflected in the GDP responses. The power of monetary policy, as reflected in changes in interest rates, is higher in the HMT and BE models in the medium term than in earlier versions of these models, and although there is some evidence that the direct sensitivity of expenditure to interest rates in the other two models has increased, the adoption of a UIP framework virtually rules out by assumption the possibility of permanent output effects, since under UIP interest rates cannot be permanently different. The adoption of rational expectations has often led to the unexpected result (by those who associated rational expectations with the new classical approach) that the short-run multiplier responses are higher, and this has sometimes carried over to the medium run. However, the analysis of Chapter 5 shows that the inclusion of rational (or forward-consistent) expectations should not change the long-run properties of the model in principle. The addition of rational expectations has had some effect in increasing the price sensitivity of a demand shock in the models, but otherwise there is no great evidence of increased price sensitivity. As we show below, the sluggish price response in the models is a key issue in the determinants of the adjustment to a new equilibrium following a demand shock. Changes in the unemployment responses that have occurred in the model have at times been dominated by the treatment of the relationship between unemployment, employment and the size of the working population, and owe more to this change than to revisions to the output consequences of a demand shock. Consequently, shifts in the reduced-form trade-off between unemployment and inflation owe more to the downward shift in estimates of the unemployment response than to greater inflation sensitivity in the models. Moreover, this shift, where it has occurred, does not correspond with a shift in the equivalent output–inflation trade-off.

One aspect of the models not so far featured in our comparative discussion has been the treatment of supply-side instruments. As our discussion of the application of the Layard–Nickell supply-side approach to the models in Chapter 4 makes clear, there still remains an absence of supply-side policy instruments in the models. Unemployment benefits do not figure to any great extent, and union power variables do not feature at all, apart from in the LPL model. The main supply-side instruments in the models are taxes, and Chapter 4 shows that the supply-side role of these variables principally depends upon the specification of the wage equation. The main change that has occurred in relation to these policy instruments is that their role in the models now appears to be more clearly understood, although there exist statistical problems in identifying tax responses at the structural level, and different theoretical priors are often used to justify different choices in the absence of firm statistical support.

The broad conclusion – that, excepting the NIESR model, the properties of the main UK models have not changed radically over the last decade for a demand shock – appears somewhat disappointing at face value, given the structural changes that have taken place in the models and which are described in Chapter 2. However, many of these changes appear to have been dominated by other, possibly unexpected, changes, notably in respect of the treatment of wealth. Although the models have been moving in the same direction in terms of structural developments, the full-model implications often remain at variance and reflect the modelling of interactions within the model as well as some apparently innocuous modelling decisions. Much of the remainder of this chapter is concerned with how these differences may arise. One difficulty with interpreting model simulation results, whether comparing reduced-form properties over successive model vintages, or comparing different models at a given point in time, is that it is hard to judge whether the model responses are different (or have changed) in respect of dynamic adjustment or in respect of equilibrium properties. Often this is because the simulation horizon is too short to judge. Full analysis of models and their properties requires other techniques and a deeper understanding of the way that the models work. The aim of subsequent chapters is to show how additional techniques can be used to understand the properties of the models better, and to show that many model properties, or differences between model properties, can be related to key parts of the underlying structure. In this way we hope to dispel the notion that models are black boxes whose properties can either be accepted or discarded.

> Structural changes to the UK models have not resulted in a radical change in some of their main full-model properties. The exception is the NIESR model.

Comparative multipliers

> Government expenditure multipliers tend to be around unity across different countries, but there is considerably more variation in the US models.

In this section we compare the demand multipliers from the UK models with multipliers from other countries. We compare the government expenditure multipliers from models of the Nordic economies as reported in Whitley (1992c), from models of the USA as reported in Klein (1991) and from the UK sectors of the multicountry models as reported in Whitley (1992a) and published results from other European models. The results from the UK models are available in the form of a simple PC ready reckoner programme (see Macdonald and Turner, 1989, 1991). The multipliers are reported as the impact during the first year and the longer-term impact. The simulation horizon varies between five and ten years depending on the source of the shock.

It would be useful to compare all the models for a variety of shocks and under a variety of assumptions concerning monetary aggregates, interest rates and exchange rates. However, the government expenditure shock presents itself as the only common denominator (monetary shocks are not possible across all the models). Rules about exchange rates and interest rates also differ. The results for the UK models assume fixed nominal interest rates (with the exception of LBS which uses fixed real interest rates and LPL where balance money and bond financing are assumed); alternative money and bond-financed shocks are reported for the US models; the Nordic results generally assume fixed nominal interest rates and exchange rates; some multicountry results assume fixed monetary aggregates, whereas others assume fixed real interest rates. We present results for some of the multicountry models under both fixed and endogenous

Table 3.1 Government expenditure multipliers compared: government spending increased by 1% of GDP

(a) UK models

	Year 1	Year 2	Year 3	Year 5
LBS	0.82	0.88	0.79	0.76
NIESR	1.49	1.74	1.24	0.97
HMT	1.06	1.19	1.28	1.25
BE	0.99	1.22	1.37	1.54
LPL	2.08		1.19	0.15

Note: Fixed nominal interest rates except LPL, where the expenditure increase is financed by balanced money/bonds, endogenous exchange rates; and LBS, where fixed real interest rates are assumed.

(b) Other European models

	Year 1	Year 2	Year 3	Year 5	Year 10
MONA	0.5 (0.5)	1.0 (0.88)	1.35 (1.25)	1.2 (1.1)	0.25 (0)
KVARTS	0.95	1.20	1.45	1.40	1.40
ADAM	1.02	1.12	1.19	1.01	0.50
MODAG	1.19	1.32	1.36	1.47	1.71
KOSMOS	0.93	1.01	0.96	0.64	0.32
KESSU	1.14	1.32	1.41	1.34	
BOF4	1.00	1.03	1.10	0.96	−0.18

Note: Fixed nominal interest rates and exchange rates for the Nordic models; figures in brackets for MONA are under bond finance.

(c) US models

	Year 1	End-year 9
BEA	2.02 (1.97)	−3.24 (−2.43)
DRI	1.75 (1.71)	4.37 (0.80)
FAIR	1.29 (1.26)	1.88 (1.56)
IND	1.41 (1.18)	1.35 (−0.11)
LM & A	1.98 (1.59)	0.15 (−0.42)
MICH	1.14 (1.12)	1.63 (1.31)
WEFA	1.36 (1.36)	1.94 (−0.73)

Note: Figures in brackets assume monetary aggregates are unchanged; those without brackets assume monetary accommodation.

BEA: Bureau of Economic Analysis
DRI: Data Resources Inc.
IND: Indiana University Center for Econometric Research

LM & A: Washington University Macro Model
MICH: Michigan Quarterly Model
WEFA: Wharton Economic Forecasting

Table 3.1   (continued)

(d) Multicountry models

	Year 1	Year 2	Year 3	Year 5
TAYLOR	(0.6)	(0.8)	(0.5)	(0.2)
EPA	1.2 (1.4)	1.1 (1.4)	0.8 (1.3)	0.5 (1.0)
ATLAS	0.2 (1.7)	0.18 (2.71)	0.51 (3.49)	0.96 (4.41)
FRB (MCM)	0.6 (2.0)	0.6 (1.7)	0.6 (1.2)	0.4 (0.5)
MSG2	(0.56)	(0.43)	(0.30)	(0.06)
IMF/MULTIMOD	0.54 (0.74)	0.28 (0.32)	0 (−0.10)	−0.36 (−0.66)
DIW/QUEST (EC)	1.41 (2.0)		1.17 (1.19)	1.03 (1.17)
	0.51*	0.98*	1.11*	0.49*
GEM	0.50 (0.81)		0.34 (0.61)	0.27 (0.51)
	0.42*	0.37*	0.31*	0.24*
OECD/INTERLINK	0.55 (0.90)		0.73 (0.60)	0.47 (0.53)
	0.49*	0.62*	0.44*	0.24*
OEF	0.98 (1.41)		1.24 (1.78)	1.18 (1.6)
	0.65*	0.76*	0.77*	0.45*
MIMOSA	0.79 (2.49)		0.73 (2.29)	0.57 (2.50)

Note: MULTIMOD and MSG2 include a tax reaction function: DIW, GEM, OECD, OEF and MIMOSA assume fixed real interest rates and fixed exchange rates; floating rate estimates are denoted by *; TAYLOR, EPA and MCM assume fixed monetary aggregates; ATLAS has fixed nominal interest rates and exchange rates. Figures in brackets are US responses, otherwise they relate to a UK fiscal expansion.

Table 3.2   Price-level responses compared: government expenditure shock of 1% of GDP

(a) UK models

	Year 1	Year 3	Year 5
LBS	0	1.7	2.7
NIESR	0.9	3.2	2.6
HMT	0.1	0.8	2.0
BE	0	0.5	1.0
LPL	3.6	10.6	14.0

Note: See Table 3.1.

Table *3.2* (*continued*)

(b) Other European models

	Year 1	Year 2	Year 3	Year 5	Year 10
ADAM	0.49	1.07	1.65	2.73	3.85
MODAG	0.01	0.09	0.25	0.70	2.21
KOSMOS	0.01	0.33	1.01	1.90	1.79
KESSU	0.08	0.01	0.01	−0.01	
BOF4	0.07	0.26	0.40	0.88	1.12

Notes: Fixed nominal interest rates and exchange rates for the Nordic models.

(c) US models

	Year 1	End-year 9
BEA	−0.11	1.60
DRI	0.05	1.26
FAIR	0.05	0.58
IND	−0.03	1.64
LM & A	0.29	2.76
MICH	−0.03	0.41
WEFA	0.04	1.67

(d) Multicountry models

	Year 1		Year 2		Year 3		Year 5		Year 10
TAYLOR	(0.39)								(5.1)
EPA	0	(0.1)	0	(0.2)	0.2	(0.7)	1.4	(1.9)	
ATLAS	−0.15	(−0.07)	−0.10	(0.76)	0	(1.53)	0.36	(2.47)	
FRB (MCM)	−0.1	(0.2)	0	(0.6)	0.1	(1.1)	1.0	(2.0)	
MSG2	(−0.11)		(−0.08)		(0.02)		(0.31)		
MULTIMOD/IMF	0.1	(0.12)	0.26	(0.32)	0.42	(0.54)	0.6	(0.7)	
DIW/QUEST (EC)	−0.08	(0.02)			1.03	(1.29)	1.58	(2.05)	
	0*		0.15*		0.75*		3.02*		
GEM	0.09	(0.26)			0.68	(0.86)	0.89	(1.31)	
	−0.17*		0.11*		0.51*		1.79*		
OECD/INTERLINK	0.16	(0.41)			1.04	(1.42)	1.94	(1.62)	
	−0.16*		0.11*		0.68*		2.22*		
OEF	0.29				1.72	(0.31)	3.01	(0.78)	
	−0.06*	(0)	0.14*		0.59*		2.18*		
MIMOSA	0.28	(0.11)			0.84	(1.78)	1.30	(4.61)	

Notes: See Table 3.1.

exchange rate formation. In the single country models, the shocks relate to an increase in domestic public expenditure; and for the multicountry models, we give estimates for both a UK and a US shock. Discussion of potential spillover effects from one economy to another are discussed in Chapter 8. In some cases, the choice of one type of policy rule is a deliberate view of a sustainable policy stance (for example, MULTIMOD and MSG2 also include a tax rule which prevents the ratio of government bonds to GNP rising indefinitely). In others, it represents an institutional feature (for a long time, exchange rates have been fixed in the Nordic economies). For other models, it is the rule which enables greatest comparability, between them. This raises the general problem of comparability and we have to accept that this cannot always be achieved. What is important is to isolate the contributions that differences in approach make to the overall results. Although tax simulations are not discussed here, the analysis presented in Chapter 4 shows how these results can be anticipated from simple analysis of wage and price equations in the models.

Comparison is also complicated by the fact that results are often only available for a relatively short time period (five years). In general, multipliers appear to be quite low, and despite the variety of results there does appear to be quite a strong consensus towards the finding of a multiplier around unity across the different models from different sources. There is a greater variety in estimates from the US models than for the other models. Short-run multipliers tend to be higher than the UK models (closer to a value of 2 rather than 1), and the results for the multicountry models suggest that a US fiscal expansion is more powerful than the corresponding increase for the UK. The fact that the USA is a relatively closed economy may account for this result. With the exception of the BEA (which appears to be unstable) and LM & A models, multipliers remain high even to the ninth year of the simulation under monetary accommodation. Changing the monetary policy rule leads to greater crowding out in some of the models, but this is not a feature of the response in the first year of the simulation.

The UK models with the exception of NIESR and LPL have first-year multipliers of around unity or less, and these remain fairly constant over time (increasing in the case of BE). The LPL model is new classical by design and does generate a gradual crowding out of output from higher inflation (through wealth), but this crowding out is not immediate as might be expected from the theoretical paradigm. Rather, real-wage rigidities imply that it takes almost five years before there is a return to the initial level of output and unemployment. Although NIESR, also has an explicit NAIRU, the period of adjustment is very protracted, as revealed by this simulation, and there is only a weak tendency for output to return to its base level within a five-year horizon.

The Nordic models exhibit crowding out in the longer term in some cases, but also tend to show an increasing value of the multiplier in the medium term (up to three years). In the absence of interest rate and exchange rate changes, any crowding out must arise from domestic inflation (the results for MONA suggest that interest crowding out is very weak in this model).

The evidence from the multicountry models is quite varied, but in general it tends to suggest quite low government expenditure multipliers. We can consider three cases: where multipliers are around unity and there is little crowding out over time; where multipliers are low, but relatively constant; and where multipliers are initially low and there is strong crowding out in the medium term. In the first group we would include EPA, DIW and OEF models, the last two under fixed exchange rates. ATLAS has a rising multiplier as there is a strong investment accelerator effect under fixed interest rate and exchange rates. In the second group are the Taylor model, MCM, GEM, OECD, MIMOSA, DIW and OEF, the last two under floating exchange rates. In MCM the very modest crowding out arises from higher interest rates and an appreciation of the exchange rate. In the other models, inflation is the prime source of the modest fall in the multiplier over time. The difference between fixed and endogenous exchange rates is to lower the multiplier in the endogenous case without leading to any marked change in the path of the multiplier over time. In the third group we have MSG2 and MULTIMOD. Both have first-year multipliers of around 0.5, similar to those of GEM and the OECD model but crowding out is very rapid in MULTIMOD with output back to its base level after three years and falling below this subsequently. Crowding out is more gradual in MSG2. In MSG2 nominal rigidities slow down this process, whereas in MULTIMOD wages depend on future prices. In both cases, important features are a forward-looking treatment of wealth and exchange rates, these being key sources of crowding out. However, a further crucial feature is the tax rule, which raises the tax rate to prevent the government deficit from increasing. Consequently, some of the crowding out in these two models is a result of an imposed equation in the model which is not based on empirical observation. This may have validity in a general theoretical sense of sustainability (see Chapter 7), but it also tends to dominate the other features of the models (remembering also that MSG2 is not an estimated model). We return to the issue of model closure in Chapter 10.

The general conclusion from the comparison of multipliers is one of relatively small impact effects with little, if any, crowding out at least in the medium term. Where this does occur, it appears to be the result as much of assumed policy reaction as of the fundamental features of the model. However, the LPL, MULTIMOD and MSG2 models do stand apart from the other models in the weakness of their response to a fiscal shock, and this reflects their more classical underpinnings.

The inflation response in the models to the fiscal shock is shown in Table 3.2. Most of the models have negligible first-year inflation effects from a fiscal expansion. Prices fall in some of the US models initially, and the price responses appear extremely weak even after nine years. Apart from the LPL model, inflation effects remain very weak across the range of models, and this is a reason for the lack of any substantial crowding out of the fiscal shock. Due to the exchange rate appreciation in the MULTIMOD and MSG simulations, the rise in domestic prices is weak, but here crowding out arises directly from the exchange rate and from wealth effects rather than from inflation.

The overall impression is of a fairly flat aggregate supply schedule in both the short and medium term for many of the models, with the main exceptions being LPL, MULTIMOD and MSG2, where the supply curve is closer to vertical over the medium term. Even here, however, fiscal expansion can have a positive effect on the level of output in the short term.

> Most of the models exhibit very weak inflationary effects from a demand
> expansion, implying a fairly flat aggregate supply schedule in both the
> short and medium term.

The examination of the UK models below suggests that this feature may arise from
both a weak excess demand influence on wages and a sluggish dynamic adjustment of
prices. There also appears to be some indication that models which have wage
behaviour specified in terms of the level of real wages, rather than the Phillips curve
type of wage inflation explanation, may possess a more clearly defined long run (this
applies to some of the UK models as well as to some of the Nordic and multicountry
estimates, but not in general to the US models).

3.3   Understanding the supply-side response

> Describing the main current simulation properties of the UK models helps us
> understand how these and other models work.

In this section we use current versions of the UK models in order to illustrate the
mechanisms present under a demand shock. This helps us understand how the
supply-side operates in practice in such models. We contrast the properties of the UK
mainstream models with those of the new classical LPL model. Although our
description is necessarily specific to these models, the mode of analysis is general and
can be applied to other models, whether of the UK or of different economies.

The models analysed in this section are the 1990 versions of the UK models, and
full simulation properties are set out in Church *et al.* (1991). The basic multiplier,
inflation and unemployment responses are also summarised in Appendix II. By the end
of 1992, the models had not changed to any significant degree from the versions
described here.

We concentrate on the implications for output, inflation and unemployment of a
demand shock and of a change in interest rates. The impact of tax changes in the models
is discussed in section 4.4.

Demand shock

> Crowding out of a demand shock under fixed nominal interest rates requires
> inflation to increase and this to have an adverse impact on demand.

The demand shock is an increase in government current expenditure of £2bn at 1990
prices. Government expenditure is an exogenous component of aggregate demand, and
hence the initial effect of higher government spending is to raise total demand by the
amount of the shock. Given savings, import and tax leakages, this then translates into

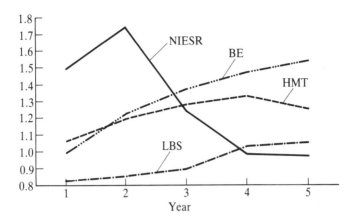

Figure 3.3 Government expenditure multipliers

higher domestic output and employment, which raises personal sector incomes. However, higher demand also creates inflationary pressure through higher wages in the labour market as unemployment falls, and through an increased price mark-up in the goods market. Inflationary pressures then reduce demand through several mechanisms. The reaction of the exchange rate to higher demand can also play an important part in the transmission of inflation. Higher inflation may offset some of the initial increase in demand through a variety of means. First, there will be a deterioration in competitiveness and a reduction in net export demand to the extent that the real exchange rate changes as a result of the demand shock (i.e. the extent to which the nominal exchange rate does not vary to offset exactly any change in the domestic price level). Second, higher inflation can reduce consumption through wealth effects. If nominal interest rates are constant, real interest rates fall as inflation rises, so private sector expenditure (consumption and investment) may increase if it is sensitive to the level of real interest rates.

The resultant change in output therefore depends on the balance between two opposing forces: the positive effect of higher demand and the negative influence of higher inflation. There are two key feedbacks: the impact of higher demand pressure on inflation, and in turn the effect of higher inflation on demand. If either of these feedbacks is weak, a fiscal boost is likely to result in a permanent rise in the level of output and a reduction in the level of unemployment. (Under bond finance, interest rates may rise and result in output crowding out, either directly or through an appreciation of the exchange rate.)

Figure 3.3 shows the government expenditure multipliers for four of the UK models. Results for two further models (OEF and LPL) are described below. This is our starting point for analysis. We shall show how differences in the level and profile of these multipliers can be explained by certain features of the models. The first thing to note is that the range of multipliers is very small compared with that found in the USA, even when we include the OEF and LPL models, which are outliers.

The NIESR multiplier is much higher in the short run than the other models, but subsequently declines to lie below them all by the fifth year of the simulation. The LBS multiplier remains fairly flat (this is an earlier version of the model reported in section 3.2), but in contrast the multipliers for HMT and BE rise over time. The HMT multiplier falls back a little over the last year of the simulation. The OEF multiplier, which is not shown in the figure, is unstable under the assumption of fixed nominal interest rates; it reaches a value of over 5 after five years. The LPL multiplier, which is calculated under an assumption of balanced finance, is higher in the short run than the other models, but declines to close to zero after five years.

> Where there is a clear long-run solution for the model, the implications for the change in the NAIRU can be assessed. Thus the results of a demand expansion for the LPL model follow directly from its long-run new classical nature.

The LPL results clearly arise from its new classical tendencies. A rise in demand which is financed at least in part by money causes inflation. This is because inflation is the result of the difference between money demand and the exogenous money supply. In turn, higher inflation reduces real financial wealth and hence real private expenditure. In the LPL model, the long-run solutions to the equations for unemployment, real wages, equilibrium GDP and the real exchange rate determine the long-run simulation properties of the model. This is then conditional on tax rates, unionisation, real unemployment benefits and world trade. These do not change under a domestic demand expansion, so unemployment and GDP return to their base level, inflation being the adjustment mechanism, and the price level increases permanently (14 per cent after five years).

> The NIESR model has well-defined long-run properties which are consistent with a permanent fall in unemployment (NAIRU) following a demand shock.

The instability observed for the OEF model arises for several reasons, but primarily from the treatment of the housing sector. We discuss this below. The features of the GDP response in simulation results on the UK quarterly models can be analysed by looking first at the behaviour of the exchange rate, and then at the determinants of expenditure. Following the inclusion of physical wealth in consumer expenditure equations, the housing sector plays a key role in understanding these responses.

> Where there is no clear indication that the simulation will converge on a new equilibrium, analysis of demand components is a useful guide. Many of the model differences over output arise from the features of the housing sector and the exchange rate equation.

The role of the exchange rate

Developments in the modelling of exchange rates are described in Chapter 4. There is a key difference between models which have forward expectations of the exchange rate and those that do not. Where the exchange rate is forward looking, as in the NIESR model, the nominal exchange rate 'jumps' immediately in reaction to an exogenous shock, the size of the jump reflecting the long-run change. The change is determined by the change required to bring about a correction of any change in the current account (or more specifically, the change in net overseas assets induced by the shock). Given a degree of nominal inertia whereby domestic prices do not respond immediately to higher demand, this nominal exchange rate fall is also associated with a decline in the real exchange rate. The resultant improvement in competitiveness then stimulates export demand and lowers imports relative to the level they would otherwise have recorded. So the real exchange rate fall is directly associated with a higher short-run multiplier. As domestic inflation rises, the real competitive gain is eroded so that the multiplier falls back. In the NIESR case, however, the real exchange rate does not return to its base level (Figure 3.4), however, and therefore there is a permanent improvement in competitiveness, and a permanent reduction in the level of unemployment (see the discussion of the NAIRU in Chapter 4). This arises because government expenditure is less import intensive than other elements of demand. Other types of demand expansion which do not have this property would result in the real exchange rate, unemployment and the level of GDP returning to base in the long run. This is exactly the result that occurs for the LPL model, where a UIP model of the exchange rate is used. The crowding out of output in the NIESR model is not completely apparent from the simulation results over a five-year horizon.

Earlier versions of the LBS model also exhibited the property that the exchange rate jumped down in reaction to a demand shock, and one might expect the version described here, which differs by having an explicit UIP treatment rather than the market-clearing approach to asset prices, to do likewise. However, the weakness of the import leakage in this version of the model (see Chapter 5 for further discussion) means that the exchange rate hardly has to jump in order to clear the current account. In fact, the exchange rate actually jumps the 'wrong' way and this lowers the impact multiplier

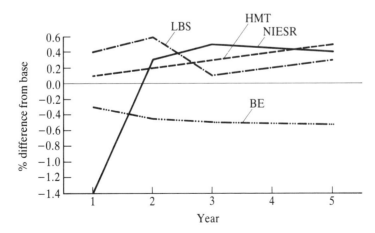

Figure 3.4   Real exchange rate changes

for this model relative to that of NIESR. Under a learning assumption for the exchange rate in the latest version of the model, the nominal exchange rate depreciates steadily over the simulation, and the real exchange rate rises.

> Forward-looking expectations in the exchange rate equation in principle cause the exchange rate to jump down following a demand shock. With nominal price inertia this also raises the impact multiplier

In the BE and HMT models, the exchange rate is backward looking and hence does not jump in reaction to an exogenous shock. Furthermore, although the specification of the exchange rate is designed to produce a result where nominal exchange rates move in line with prices, so that the real exchange rate is constant, there are other factors (see Fisher *et al.*, 1990b) which cause the real exchange rate to appreciate steadily in the HMT simulation and to do the opposite in the case of BE, thus helping to explain the gradual divergence in their estimates of the output multiplier. Similar considerations apply to the OEF model, but here there is some dynamic instability that is reflected in overshooting of the real exchange rate, and which contributes to the general instability in the output multiplier.

Expenditure responses

The long-run responses of the LPL model can be derived from knowledge of its structure, as can those of the NIESR model. The role of simulation analysis is to reveal some of the dynamic adjustment path to this new equilibrium. It is also important to check that dynamic features do not prevent the equilibrium from being attained. Where the model does not have a structure which ensures that a new long-run equilibrium can be reached, an analysis of demand contributions to the change in output and unemployment can aid our understanding of the key mechanisms in the model. Thus understanding the real exchange rate response helps to show how the behaviour of exports and imports changes the multiplier. The other main elements of expenditure are fixed investment and stockbuilding, and private consumers' expenditure. Although the former are the more sensitive items of expenditure, they are not as quantitatively important as consumers' expenditure. In addition, wealth effects have tended to increase the sensitivity of consumption in relation to a demand shock, but not in the expected direction of increased crowding out. The treatment of consumers' expenditure and the implications arising from the inclusion of physical wealth are discussed in section 4.1. We can summarise the results briefly as follows. Higher house prices that arise from an increase in demand can result in a revaluation of the real stock of wealth, which dominates any inflation crowding out of financial wealth. Hence wealth effects can stimulate consumer spending. The possibility of this revaluation effect depends as much on the sensitivity of the house price equations in the model as on differing estimates of the effect of wealth on consumption.

This revaluation effect is particularly large for the OEF model, and is enhanced by the exchange rate instability noted above. Output instability does not arise under endogenous interest rates in the OEF model, since higher interest rates dampen the rise

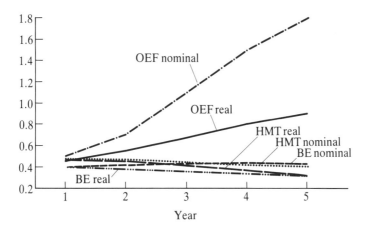

Figure 3.5 Influence of house prices on the multiplier

in house prices. The HMT and BE models also have strong revaluation effects, and Figure 3.5 shows the GDP response which arises in these models if house prices do not increase by more than general prices. In all cases the multiplier is reduced. In terms of the government expenditure multiplier, the effect is to reduce the multiplier to 2.75 after five years for OEF (against the standard simulation response of over 5), and to reduce the HMT and BE multipliers to 0.83 and 1.25 (against 1.25 and 1.54 respectively). There are negligible effects on the multipliers for LBS and NIESR. This has the effect of bringing the government expenditure multipliers closer together.

Weak accelerator effects on investment in the LBS model limit the size of the increase in the multiplier, whereas the real exchange rate fall in the NIESR (and to some extent in the BE model) induces an accompanying accelerator response which further increases the multiplier (a decomposition of multiplier effects is given in Chapter 5).

In the absence of changes in the real exchange rate and in real house prices, the multipliers for the LPL model would be around unity. This shows the importance of the exchange rate and housing sector feedbacks, but it does not necessarily imply that there is complete consensus elsewhere, for there are certain offsetting influences to be found by further examination (Chapter 5).

> When adjusted for changes in real exchange rates and the influence of the housing market expenditure multipliers tend to be about unity after five years, with the exception of LPL. Although the NIESR model suggests a greater degree of crowding out in the long term, this is not evident from simulations over five-year horizons.

Generation of inflation

The discussion of output responses to a demand shock reveals that the crowding-out effects are fairly weak or prolonged unless something like the new classical approach is used. In some models there is the suggestion of overshooting of the nominal exchange rate in the classic Dornbusch–Fisher manner, and the behaviour of the housing sector may actually reverse some of the expected adverse effects of inflation on demand by reducing real exchange rates and increasing real wealth. The other element that we need to consider in understanding the supply-side response of the models is whether the generation of inflation itself is consistent with the crowding-out view.

> **We would expect inflation to settle down close to its base level if the model is returning to equilibrium.**

The monetarist view of the inflation process is embodied in the LPL model. Inflation is caused by an increase in the rate of growth of the money supply relative to the demand for real balances. Thus inflation continues to increase until demand, output and unemployment settle down to a new equilibrium (this is the classic case of a long-run Phillips curve mechanism).

In the non-monetarist models, the inflationary mechanism differs and can be analysed in terms of three major sources: increases in real wages (earnings) that occur as a result of lower unemployment or labour market pressure; increases in producers' prices relative to input costs (i.e. an increase in the mark-up) that arises from demand pressure in the goods market; and increases in import prices relative to domestic prices which arise as the real exchange rate falls.

> **In monetarist models, higher inflation results from excess money. In non-monetarist models, inflation is generated through three sources: increased goods market pressure; increased labour market pressure; and import price pressure.**

We have already discussed the behaviour of the real exchange rate and it is clear that this plays a key role in the transmission of inflation in the NIESR model. This is shown in Figure 3.6 where we plot the total inflation response following a demand shock. The tendency of inflation to settle down to its base level after about seven years is an indication that the model is returning to equilibrium. The short-run inflation response in the NIESR model is far larger than in the other quarterly models, where the responses are comparatively weak, and often trending.

We now turn to the role of labour market pressure. This is the traditional source of inflation in macro models, and the strength of inflationary push is usually gauged by the size of the coefficient on unemployment in the wage equation. Our analysis shows that a simple analytical treatment can be misleading, for in real-world models other elements in the wage equation can be at least as important, or may even dominate the unemployment effect. If we begin with an inspection of the typical size of unemployment response in UK wage equations embodied in macroeconometric models, we find that an increase in unemployment of around 100 000 from a base level of two million increases real wages by around 0.4 per cent in the long run the (BE model has a slightly

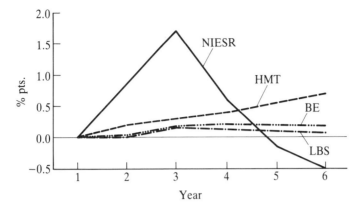

Figure 3.6 Inflation responses

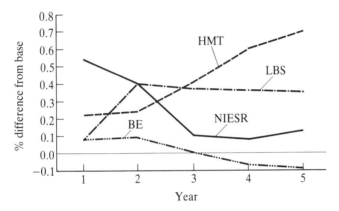

Figure 3.7 Real-wage responses

weaker response). However, this broad consensus does not translate into the changes in real wages that we observe under a demand shock (Figure 3.7).

In the NIESR case, the presence of a labour market mismatch proxy variable (the ratio of manufacturing employment to total employment) causes an increase in real earnings in the short run, whereas the inclusion of a role for company profitability in the HMT wage equation generates an upward trend in wage pressure.

The third source of inflationary pressure arises from the goods market and is captured by the influence of demand on profit margins. For this we need to inspect the properties of the price equations in the models. Most UK models contain a role for demand pressure in the form of capacity utilisation, and although the single-equation responses are quite similar across the models, the determination of capacity utilisation elsewhere in the models can result in differences between them. The determination of capacity utilisation is discussed further in section 4.5. The main difference is between approaches which model capacity utilisation in such a way that investment adjusts to eliminate any unintended change in utilisation, and approaches which allow capacity utilisation to change permanently following a demand shock. (A third possibility included in the LBS price equation is where the capacity utilisation variable does not respond to other influences in the model.) The inflationary impact of increased goods market pressure is strongest in the NIESR model.

We can summarise findings for the UK mainstream models as follows. The NIESR model generates a substantial increase in inflationary pressure in the short run from a combination of all three elements: labour market pressure, goods market pressure, and a fall in the real exchange rate. All three sources diminish in strength over the simulation period, so the inflation surge is fairly short lived. In the LBS and HMT models, labour market pressure is the main source of higher inflation, although this is moderated by an appreciating exchange rate in the HMT model. It is the latter which provides most of the inflation in the BE model, since both goods and labour market pressures are weak.

> In the non-monetarist UK models, the sources of inflationary pressure differ across the models.

The NIESR and LPL models aside, there must be strong doubts about whether the inflationary mechanisms are powerful enough in the UK models to satisfy the requirements of a relatively inelastic long-run aggregate supply schedule. One possible explanation might be that the transmission of shocks to higher prices is too sluggish, even given plausible assumptions about inertia in price setting.

> In many of the UK models, inflationary pressures are weak and adjust very slowly to demand shocks.

Balance of payments and PSBR implications

Finally, we consider the impact of a fiscal expansion on the balance of payments and public sector deficit. The financing assumption is critical to the results for the balance of payments because under money finance the exchange rate can be expected to depreciate in nominal terms, whereas under bond finance an appreciation is expected. A fiscal expansion which increases domestic demand can be expected to weaken the balance of payments for two reasons: higher imports, and the effect of higher inflation on competitiveness. In models with forward expectations of the exchange rate, we would expect the jump in the exchange rate under money finance to be such that the current account of the balance of payments settles back to balance in the long run. No such automatic mechanism exists in models with backward-looking expectations, although the exchange rate equation may include a specific influence from the current account.

We have already noted the weakness of the import leakage in the LBS model as a reason why the exchange rate fails to jump in this model. The current balance actually improves in the first year of the simulation, and this is followed by a

Table 3.3 Balance of payments and PSBR effects of a fiscal expansion: differences from base (£bn)

	Year 1	Year 2	Year 3	Year 4	Year 5
Current a/c:					
LBS	0.1	−0.1	−0.5	−0.3	−0.2
NIESR	−1.5	−1.7	−1.1	−0.8	−0.9
HMT	−0.5	−0.8	−1.0	−1.4	−1.9
PSBR:					
LBS	0.9	0.5	0.7	0.7	0.6
NIESR	1.8	1.4	0.6	0.3	0.4
HMT	1.1	0.9	0.6	0.3	−0.1

small decline in the current account. In contrast, there is marked deterioration in the NIESR model in the short term, but the balance then adjusts back towards equilibrium. This does not actually occur during the five-year simulation horizon of this model, but evidence from longer-run simulations shows that it is a long run property of the model. The deficit in the HMT model increases over time as the real exchange rate appreciates.

A fiscal expansion will initially increase the fiscal deficit. In the present example, an increase of £2bn should result in an equivalent impact effect on the public sector deficit. However, higher economic activity will increase tax revenue and lower unemployment benefits, so there is an offsetting influence to this initial increase in the deficit. On the other hand, higher inflation following a demand shock will increase both public expenditure and taxation receipts, the prevailing wisdom being that this will lead to a net deterioration in the deficit. The overall impact on the public sector deficit of an expenditure increase would normally be expected to be adverse, otherwise expenditure increases could be said to be self-financing.

The evidence from the models gives a variety of estimates. The LBS results suggest that a considerable amount of the extra expenditure flows back in the form of higher receipts so that the PSBR only worsens by £1bn in the first year of the shock, with some further improvement in later years. The flowback is considerably less in the short term for the NIESR model, but is very substantial in the medium term, where the deficit is only marginally higher despite the permanently higher level of expenditure. A similar improvement in time is observed from the HMT model, but from a greater impact position. Here the deficit has settled back to balance after five years.

It should be noted that these models do not have mechanisms which ensure that the outstanding stock of public sector debt cannot rise indefinitely, but the evidence from these simulations does not indicate that this is a major defect under a money-financed expansion. A bond-financed expansion would be expected to incur greater deficit costs on two grounds: first, the expansion in economic activity is likely to be less under bond finance (see Chapter 7); and second, higher interest payments on new debt will increase the deficit, with the possibility that the secondary financing will lead to an accumulation of debt liabilities. There is the suspicion that the flowback effects are rather optimistic under a money expansion.

> Under a demand expansion with fixed interest rates, the current account tends to worsen in the models, but not always, and not necessarily permanently. The impact on the public sector deficit shows a considerable flowback in the form of higher revenue.

Interest rate shock

> Interest rate changes operate in a variety of ways: directly on expenditure; indirectly through revaluation effects; directly on income flows; and directly on exchange rates.

The simulation of a government expenditure increase is an example of a fiscal shock. We now consider the role of monetary policy in the UK models. In monetarist models, high-powered money is usually taken to be exogenous, and increases in broad money are then endogenously determined through the money multiplier, which reflects both bank and non-bank portfolio behaviour. In non-monetarist models, monetary policy usually operates most transparently through control over short-term interest rates. Changes in monetary aggregates are then endogenously determined. The use of money targets either as an approximation to bond finance or as part of a policy simulation is then achieved by assigning an instrument (usually interest rates) to control the monetary target. Methods of doing this are discussed in Chapter 7. Evaluating the impact of changes in interest rates in the models therefore gives some indication of the potency of monetary policy irrespective of whether the treatment of interest rates as strictly exogenous is appropriate or not.

The transmission routes of interest rates to output, employment and inflation are several. First, there is the possibility that interest rates influence private final expenditures such as investment, stockbuilding and consumption either directly or indirectly as part of a cost of capital. Given that interest rates usually represent the opportunity cost, their expected effect on expenditure is negative. The interest rate variables might be nominal or real interest rates, or alternatively short-term or long-term rates.

The second possible route is indirectly as interest rate changes cause a revaluation of assets or directly through income flows of interest payments or receipts. The net effect of interest rates on interest flows depend on whether the sector is a net debtor or a net creditor. Third, interest rates can lead to changes in exchange rates, especially where the UIP, or capital-oriented, approach is used. Here a rise in interest rates would lead to a rise in the exchange rate, so that its future expected depreciation would exactly offset the increased interest rate margin. In UIP models this appreciation depends on

Table 3.4 Direct long-run effects of a 1 percentage point reduction
in interest rates in the UK models (% increase in expenditures)

	LBS	NIESR	HMT	BE
Consumption:				
Non-durables	1.6	0.47	0.43	0.62
Durables	–	0.53	0.87	0.89
Total	1.4	0.48	0.47	0.65
Fixed investment:				
Manufacturing	–	0.6	1.1	0.8
Non-manufacturing	–	0.14	–	0.2
Housing	–	2.8	2.81	1.60
Total	–	0.57	0.48	0.44
Total final expenditure	0.88	0.41	0.38	0.49

the length of the period over which interest rates are increased. A permanent rise in
interest rates would result in an infinite appreciation; hence with forward-looking
models of the exchange rate, the interest rate shock can only be temporary.

Table 3.4 can be interpreted as indicating the magnitude of the slope of the familiar
IS schedule. It gives the responses of each expenditure item calculated by size of the
long-run coefficient on interest rates. These effects are then the impact effects on
expenditure and take no account of other feedbacks. Most of the models contain
interest rate influences on fixed investment, but the LBS model contains no direct
interest rate effects on investment. However, it has strong consumption effects, so it is
more interest sensitive overall than the other models. These other models show a high
degree of consensus over the total, but not the composition of direct interest rate effects.

> The models have direct influences of interest rates on expenditure, but
> these are dominated by other influences in full-model simulations.

However, the overall GDP response to a change in interest rates is weaker in the LBS
model than in either the HMT or the BE model, and not much larger than that in
NIESR.

We therefore need to consider the role of other influences. Under UIP the exchange
rate will jump down by the size of the interest rate rise multiplied by the number of years
that this rise persists. This is so that the expected future depreciation of the exchange
rate exactly offsets the additional interest gain from holding the currency. In practice,
the jump will be modified by the risk premium element in the UIP formulation. In this
example, the interest rate shock persists for three years, so we expect to observe a 3 per
cent immediate fall in the nominal exchange rate in the forward-looking models such as
LBS and NIESR. This is indeed approximated by the NIESR model, where there is an
initial real exchange rate depreciation of 2.4 per cent which is subsequently reversed as
prices rise. Nevertheless the initial improvement in competitiveness roughly doubles
the GDP response and is therefore higher than the BE and HMT models in the first

year of the simulation, despite NIESR having smaller direct interest rate effects on expenditure than these two models. The step fall in both the nominal and real exchange rate in the LBS model is larger than for NIESR and hence produces a larger GDP response, although the peak is lagged until the second year of the simulation. In the BE and HMT models, the exchange rate equation is backward looking and implies a much weaker fall in the nominal exchange rate. In full-model simulations this direct effect is considerably modified by feedbacks elsewhere in the model, and the HMT model produces a steadily depreciating nominal exchange rate which adds to the GDP response. The main reason why the BE and HMT models produce larger output responses than the other models by the second year of the shock is related to the behaviour of real housing wealth.

In these two models interest rates have, directly or indirectly, a large influence on house prices, and this combines with the boost to prices given by higher real incomes so that real house prices rise by 6–7 per cent after three years for the HMT model, and by 11–12 per cent for the BE model. The increase in real house prices leads to a revaluation of private sector wealth which then raises consumer spending. The total effect is to double the GDP response. This feature of the BE and HMT models therefore reinforces the importance of the housing sector when physical wealth is included in the consumption equation. Although the LBS and NIESR models also contain a model of the housing sector, the NIESR model has no role for housing wealth directly in consumption, whereas the LBS house price equation is less sensitive to income and interest rates than either the BE or the HMT model. In addition, the version described here has a lower wealth elasticity on consumption (see section 4.1).

The inflationary impact of lower interest rates

> The inflationary effect of lower interest rates depends on the choice of price index.

Usually models contain several price variables, such as import prices, producer prices and consumer prices, as well as a set of implicit deflators for components of final demand. These will typically be related to each other by a series of technical equations or identities, but there will be one or maybe two key behavioural price equations. The more important issue in respect of interest rate shocks is the choice of which price variable is used in the wage equation. Usually a consumer price measure is used, but this then leaves the decision of whether to use the retail price index or the implicit deflator of consumers' expenditure. For most shocks this is not a particularly important decision, but in the UK statistics, the retail price index includes a mortgage interest component which is obviously sensitive to the prevailing level of interest rates, whereas the consumer price deflator excludes mortgage interest payments.

If the retail price index (RPI) is used in the wage equation – that is, if workers are concerned with being compensated for changes in the RPI rather than the CPI – then a cut in interest rates reduces the RPI on impact and hence lowers wage costs and prices.

Thus models which use the RPI in wage equations (such as BE and HMT) tend to exhibit very low inflationary costs of a reduction in interest rates and may also produce a fall in the price level. In the HMT simulation, the use of the RPI more than halves the inflationary cost of reducing unemployment.

The choice of price variable in the wage equation is clearly important, but there is little evidence that this is given much weight in model construction.

3.4 Summary

In this chapter we have used properties of the empirical models to illustrate the changes in properties that have taken place in the UK models in recent years, their current properties in relation to those of models in the USA and elsewhere in Europe, and the features determining the current reduced-form responses of the UK models. There appears to be considerably more variation among the US models, in respect of a demand shock on output, than in the UK or Nordic models. On the other hand, the inflationary responses in the US models appear to be particularly weak.

The changes that have occurred in the structures of the UK models do not appear to have changed the medium-term estimates of the government expenditure multiplier much. Impact estimates are often higher due to the incorporation of forward-consistent expectations, but there is little sign that the long-run effects of a demand expansion on output are zero. An exception is in the NIESR model where this is a feature, but where adjustment is protracted. The sluggish reaction of inflation in some of the models appears to inhibit adjustment to the long run. Monetary policy influences do appear to have increased in strength in the UK models, but some of the reduced-form responses observed are a direct result of the treatment of the housing sector in the models.

There does seem a tendency for government expenditure multipliers across models of differing economies to be around unity in the early periods following a demand shock, with multicountry models giving an even smaller response (and those for a US expansion a larger impact). A unit response is rather low compared with estimates that are obtained from elementary multiplier analysis, but this does not show the crowding-out effects predicted from more sophisticated theoretical approaches. It is only in models such as LPL, MULTIMOD and MSG2 that crowding out occurs fully within a period of up to five years. MSG2 is a calibrated model and it also includes a specific tax adjustment rule (as does MULTIMOD), which is important in generating this crowding out. The general sensitivity of many of the results to the precise assumptions made about interest rates and exchange rates (and taxes) illustrates the general qualification that must be placed on the interpretation of simulation evidence from macroeconometric models.

> The overall impression is that some of the UK models have not really changed that much in their properties, despite their more acceptable theoretical underpinnings and their use of currently fashionable econometric techniques.

Further reading

Church *et al.* (1991)
Whitley (1992a)
Whitley (1992c)
Bryant *et al.* (1988)

4 | The key components of macroeconometric models

Whereas the previous chapter has described the nature of the models and their development over the last 20 years, this chapter concentrates on the details of some of the more important areas which have influenced changes in the properties of the models over the years. We begin by discussing the treatment of consumption and the role of financial deregulation.

 In this chapter we focus on key areas of model structure: consumption; the exchange rate; trade; wages and prices; and employment.

4.1 Consumption and financial deregulation

The consumption equation has always been at the heart of macroeconometric models based on the national income accounting tradition. The most common approach in the late 1970s was to treat consumers as constrained in their purchase decisions by current income, very much in the spirit of Keynes. The early models tended to imply a marginal propensity to consume of around 0.8. Other influences on consumption were largely absent except for the effect of changes in hire-purchase regulations.

The mid-1970s saw a breakdown of this form of equation which with its implied constancy of the saving ratio, could not explain the ratio's rise (Figure 4.1). This forecast failure resulted in the familiar paradox of thrift and caused the models to overpredict the level of overall economic activity and to miss the 1975 recession. This sequence of events created fresh academic interest in the consumption equation in the UK, and Davidson *et al.* (1978) found econometric support for the presence of an inflation term in the equation, and also concluded that the rise in inflation in the 1970s was the factor behind the rising savings ratio. This article was not only important in reviving the consumption equation, but also highly influential in introducing the error correction approach to econometrics. This was part of the 'Hendrification' of UK econometrics, after David Hendry who popularised it (Gilbert, 1989). It emphasised the importance of long-run equilibrium, and it appears to have been an essential accompaniment to the economic emphasis on long-run properties.

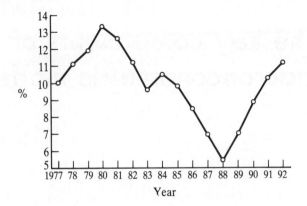

Year

Figure 4.1   UK Savings ratio: 1977–1992

> The combination of problems of forecasting the savings ratio in the 1970s
> helped to develop lasting advances in econometric methodology.

The traditional simple consumption function took the form (with variables in logs):

$$C_t = a + bY_t + cC_{t-1} \tag{4.1}$$

The new form was:

$$\Delta_4 C_t = \alpha_0 + \alpha_1 \Delta_4 Y_t + \alpha_2 \Delta P_t + \alpha_3 (C_{t-4} - Y_{t-4}) \tag{4.2}$$

This 'error correction' model was derived as a 'parsimonious' reparameterisation and restriction from a general dynamic model of the form:

$$C_t = \beta_0 + \sum_{i=1}^{n} \beta_i C_{t-i} + \sum_{i=0}^{n} \delta_i P_{t-i} \tag{4.3}$$

If the model is stable, the general dynamic model has a long-run solution in steady-static state when $y_t = y_{t-i}$ for all i, $C = k + y$ where k is a constant, i.e. $C = kY$ in linear form, a proportional relationship as in Friedman's permanent income theory. The economic rationale for the inclusion of inflation was as a proxy for the inflation loss on liquid assets, although Deaton (1977) suggested an alternative explanation whereby variable inflation created uncertainty and hence a decision to postpone consumption. Subsequent work by Hendry and von Ungern-Sternberg (1981) specifically included a liquid assets term and argued that the inflation loss on this variable should be deducted from measured income. The existing treatment had often provided a positive effect on consumption from higher inflation, since higher nominal interest rates (which adjusted to the higher level of inflation) increased nominal interest receipts by the personal sector nominal incomes. Deflation of nominal receipts by the (higher) price index could not actually reduce consumption. Hendry and von Ungern-Sternberg argued that the income variable itself needed to be adjusted, and a similar approach was proposed by

Pesaran and Evans (1984). The UK Treasury and the Bank of England did actually adopt this inflation-adjusted measure of real income, and the Treasury has persisted with it throughout the second half of the 1980s and into the 1990s. The empirical evidence suggested that inflation effects had been present in the period prior to the mid-1970s, but the data had not been informative enough. It was only when inflation rose sharply in the early 1970s that its influence on consumption could be detected.

> Failures of the consumption equation in the 1980s developed the treatment of physical wealth in models.

The second main challenge to the consumption equation came a decade later in the mid-1980s, when this time the models failed to explain the sharp fall in the savings ratio. This proved to be a key reason for the failure to forecast the boom of 1988.

By this time the mainstream models had begun to incorporate a wealth variable into their consumption equations (the Liverpool model with its emphasis on stocks rather than flows had included a wealth variable from its inception in 1980). This wealth variable was, however, confined to financial wealth. Its inclusion instead of an inflation variable has important implications for the simulation properties of macroeconometric models. Where an inflation term is included as a proxy for wealth, a price shock will tend to have only a temporary effect on consumption unless it permanently raises the rate of inflation, whereas wealth variables will produce a permanent effect from a price-level change. An example of how wealth is integrated into a life-cycle model is given in Chapter 8.

Modellers reacted to the impact of the forecast failures in the late 1980s by assuming that financial deregulation had increased the liquidity of physical assets held by the personal sector. Deregulation resulted in the personal sector increasing the ratio of its debt to income ratios. At the same time this boost to demand stimulated a rise in asset prices (especially house prices), but the ratio of debt to assets rose in spite of the asset appreciation. Various approaches were taken to deal with the problem of under-forecasting consumption. Some like NIESR assumed that the removal of credit controls (which had started in mid-1982 with the abolition of hire-purchase controls) meant that the additional flow of credit flowed straight into consumption. Others assumed that the increased liquidity of physical wealth implied that physical as well as financial wealth was now a relevant explanatory factor in the determination of consumption behaviour. Thus physical wealth began to appear in their consumption equations. The equations then began to appear more like the life-cycle models of consumption rather than the original Keynesian form. This change is important for macroeconometric models for two main reasons. First, the change radically altered the simulation properties of the models, and often in an unexpected way. Second, the introduction of wealth meant that attention had to be paid to its determinants, and particularly to the housing sector, which accounted for the major element of physical assets.

One might expect, a priori, that the introduction of wealth into consumption equations would increase the extent of crowding out, as higher demand would result in higher inflation, which would then reduce the real value of assets (as had been the case where financial assets were included). However, in some cases an increase in demand caused real house prices to rise, which then resulted in an upward revaluation of physical wealth and hence an additional boost to consumption. Whether this occurred in practice depended on the role attributed to wealth in the consumption equation and to the specification of the housing sectors in the models.

Table 4.1 shows the treatment of wealth in the principal UK models in the early 1990s. It can be seen that the models differed in the size of the overall wealth elasticities as well as in the relative size of the elasticities on financial and physical wealth. Some like the LBS and the Bank of England gave twice as much weight to financial wealth as to physical wealth, but the BE elasticities were twice as large as those of LBS on both forms of wealth. In contrast, the HMT model attributed a (relatively large) common elasticity of financial and physical wealth.

Not only was there a lack of consensus over the empirical importance of wealth effects, but this was compounded by the treatment of the housing sector in the models. Previously this had been a small but sensitive part of the models, its main importance being in determining the level of housing investment (a small part of total investment). The equations determining the price of housing had little impact on the models, save for influencing the aggregate price level via the cost of housing services. However, some models, particularly OEF and BE, had quite large elasticities for real house prices with respect to changes in real income. This resulted in large revaluations of wealth following a demand shock, and the output multipliers actually increased quite sharply. This change also increased the output response to an interest rate change and hence enhanced the power of monetary policy. Some details of the effects of these changes were described in Chapter 3, where we reviewed changes in simulation properties. The results from the OEF model are particularly striking. Under an assumption of fixed nominal interest rates, the government expenditure multiplier is unstable. The OEF interpretation is that the presence of mortgage rationing had previously prevented any instability in the economy arising from the housing sector, and that to prevent

Table 4.1 The treatment of wealth in UK model consumption equations

Model	Consumption variable	Wealth variable	Long-run wealth elasticity
LPL	Non-durables	Total wealth	0.43
HMT	Non-durables	Total wealth	0.32
	Durables	Total wealth	0.35
OEF	Non-durables	Total wealth	0.16
	Durables	Total wealth	0.27
BE	Non-durables	Financial wealth	0.30
		Housing wealth	0.14
LBS	Total	Financial wealth	0.14
		Housing wealth	0.07
NIESR	Total	Financial wealth	0.19

instability under a financially deregulated regime requires active use of interest rates. In principle, this argument could explain the collapse of consumption in 1990–1 following a rise in interest rates. However, there is clear evidence that a large part of the failure to predict the economic down-turn was due to the failure of the consumption equation itself, and not to the interactions with the remainder of the model. That is, if we calculate the forecasts for consumption over the 1990–1 period using the now known values of wealth, interest rates and income, the models would produce a consistent over-estimate, even if conventional two-sided prediction tests failed to find this statistically significant.

> There are still unresolved issues over the breakdown of consumption equations in the late 1980s/early 1990s.

The modelling issue that arises, then, is whether the original interpretation of the breakdown of the consumption equations in the mid-1980s is correct, given that forecast failure has reoccurred (in the opposite direction). It had been hypothesised that financial deregulation enabled the personal sector to adjust to a new equilibrium, which involved a higher proportion of debt in their portfolios. The debt adjustment that took place in 1990–1 has cast doubt on this proposition. Modelling attention has now turned to the role of income expectations rather than the structural changes due to financial deregulation. It is suggested that the consumer boom of 1988 was based on over-optimistic income expectations by the personal sector, and that the depression of 1990–1 was the result of the revision of these expectations. However, the modelling of erroneous expectations rather than fully consistent expectations is a difficult area for macroeconometric models in the absence of a direct measure of expectations.

While the debate over the nature of the consumption equation has yet to be resolved, there are other issues that arise from the inclusion of wealth terms. The first point to note is that, although one might expect the inclusion of wealth in consumption equations to reduce the size of the income elasticities (as the interpretation moves to a life-cycle account), this has not happened. Most of the models which contain wealth variables also have income elasticities of close to unity. An appropriate long-run condition for the wealth–consumption ratio to be constant would be that the income and wealth elasticities sum to unity. (In practice, this constraint is a little more complicated, since the consumer expenditure equations are typically expressed in a log-linear form, whereas income is itself related to wealth in a linear way.)

4.2 The exchange rate and financial assets

> The exchange rate plays a key role in the transmission of shocks in macroeconometric models.

The exchange rate often plays an important role in the transmission of inflation in open-economy models. It has also been a source of some of the differences between the properties of models. In the late 1970s and early 1980s there was a lack of data on the exchange rate in a floating regime, especially since capital controls were present for part of this period. Increasing liberalisation of financial markets has made capital more mobile internationally in recent years, so that capital flow considerations, rather than those of the current account, dominate exchange rate movements. Initial attempts to model exchange rates centred on the purchasing power parity (PPP) approach, which stated that the value of currencies would adjust to equalise price levels across economies. However, empirical evidence in favour of this proposition was extremely weak (Isard, 1988), certainly in respect of anything other than the very long run. The PPP hypothesis was embodied into the monetary theory of the balance of payments approach, and this resulted in an empirical formulation which expresses exchange rate movements in terms of relative money supplies. The LBS model adopted this approach in the late 1970s. However, whether because the underlying assumption of PPP was inappropriate or because the whole monetary approach was inadequate, this formulation fared poorly in empirical terms. One particular feature of the monetary approach that conflicted with the capital movements approach to the exchange rate was the reaction of exchange rates to changes in the interest rate. Whereas the traditional asset markets approach would expect higher interest rates to be associated with an appreciating currency, the monetary approach asserted the opposite, on the grounds that a higher nominal interest rate implied higher inflationary expectations rather than an expected fall in the currency.

> Exchange rates can be modelled directly, or indirectly, as the result of capital flows. Direct modelling with emphasis on the UIP approach has become more widespread.

Other attempts to include the exchange rates in macroeconometric models have used two broad approaches: direct modelling, and derivation of the exchange rate from models of capital flows. The HMT model used the latter approach for some time, but empirical estimation of a capital flows system proved difficult and tended to produce very low interest rate elasticities of capital flows (i.e. capital is relatively immobile). The LBS also adopted the indirect approach, but by embodying the exchange rate within a large financial sector. The financial sector was based on market clearing under rational expectations with three key prices: gilts, equities and the exchange rate (strictly, the price of overseas assets). The model was criticised strongly on both theoretical and empirical grounds (Courakis, 1988), and it proved difficult to use in forecasting and simulation analysis since the exchange rate often reacted in unexpected ways. In a market-clearing approach it was then difficult to account for this exchange rate response. By the end of the 1980s, the LBS had almost completely abandoned the original financial model and resorted to direct modelling of the exchange rate.

The direct modelling approach was initially fairly *ad hoc* bearing little relation, if any, to theory. There has emerged a growing consensus around the uncovered interest rate parity paradigm (UIP). This relates the exchange rate to its expected future level, interest differentials and a risk premium. Proper implementation of UIP requires that the exchange rate is forward looking. In the UK models this was equivalent to using rational or model-consistent expectations.

In rational expectations models, it is necessary to choose a terminal condition to tie down the expectations at the end of the period, and the particular choice of a condition for the exchange rate has fundamental implications for the properties of the model as a whole. Some of these more technical issues are covered in Chapter 5.

> Embedding the UIP approach in a forward-looking model depends on the properties of the rest of the model.

In a UIP model, where the coefficient on the interest differential is unity, the exchange rate contains a unit root unless other conditions are present to provide a unique solution for nominal magnitudes. In many cases this feature may not be present and the unit root property becomes translated to the rest of the model, producing indeterminacy. A multitude of solutions would exist, depending only on initial conditions. Hence in order for a full-model solution to exist, the rest of the model must modify this unit root. This is usually achieved by including a risk premium term in the exchange rate equation. The most successful empirical implementation of this term has been the use of a current balance condition (see Fisher *et al.*, 1990a). In a full-model simulation, and requires that the exchange rate adjusts to clear the current balance and this is a necessary condition for stability of net overseas assets. For this to happen under a demand shock, say, the demand expansion should normally weaken the current account and an exchange rate fall should return the balance to its base level. However, Fisher *et al.* find that these two conditions are not always met in the UK models, and hence a UIP model cannot be fully implemented. Fisher (1992) shows how the required properties of the rest of the system relate to the exchange rate jump under rational expectations. A forward-looking exchange rate can have quite strong implications for simulations with macroeconometric models. The LPL model has always embodied a UIP formulation, but the earlier versions of the LBS and NIESR models in the mid-1980s contained forward looking exchange rates without using the standard UIP treatment. Under a fiscal simulation, the exchange rate fell in the first period of the simulation, reflecting the future loss of competitiveness (i.e. to induce the expectation of an appreciation in the future).

At this stage we need to draw the distinction between nominal and real exchange rate changes. One interpretation of the results from the LBS and NIESR models is that the exchange rate was forward looking and hence sensitive to future changes in economic variables, whereas domestic prices were backward looking and sticky. Hence the fall in the nominal exchange rate at the beginning of the simulation was also a fall in the real rate, but as domestic prices adjusted, the real exchange rate would return to base, leaving the long-run result that competitiveness was unchanged. This is the familiar Dornbusch overshooting result (Dornbusch, 1976). In practice, the simulation period was too short to verify whether this long run was ever attained. Up until 1990–1 the exchange rate in the LBS model was the product of the financial model, but the LBS then adopted a direct UIP determination, coinciding in spirit with the NIESR approach. However, whether because of the properties of the rest of the model, or because of technical issues, the ESRC Macroeconomic Modelling Bureau was never able to produce the expected exchange rate jump with the LBS model in fiscal simulations.

 The UIP approach has important implications for monetary policy simulations.

The UIP model also has important implications for monetary policy simulations. In particular, the interest parity condition states that any interest rate differential should correspond to an equal and opposite expected exchange rate change. That is, if there is a positive interest differential of 3 per cent, say, then arbitrage in foreign exchange markets will induce an expected capital loss of 3 per cent to offset this interest gain. This is achieved by a 3 per cent rise in the exchange rate now, so that the required expected depreciation is induced. This implies that the size of the exchange rate jump depends on the length of time that any interest rate differential is maintained. A 2 per cent differential maintained for three years will require an expected exchange rate change of 6 per cent. Therefore a permanent interest rate shock would produce an infinite exchange rate jump under UIP. Monetary policy simulations can only be conducted under a temporary interest rate shift. In practice, monetary policy simulations do tend to produce exchange rate jumps very close to those predicted by the UIP approach. Some differences can arise because of the risk premium element in the exchange rate equation.

Empirical support for the UIP paradigm is reasonably good on UK data, and the proposition of Meese and Rogoff (1983) that the random walk explanation of the exchange rate is preferred to UIP is rejected by Fisher *et al.* (1990a).

The adoption of UIP into the UK models has become quite commonplace, especially in contrast to other European models, which tend to continue to treat the exchange rate as exogenous. The UIP approach has also been successfully implemented in a multicountry model, GEM (see Gurney, 1990). However, there have been some problems in incorporating UIP into UK models (see Chapter 5), and rational expectations models have not been used in practical model-based forecasting. Moreover, rational expectations makes some strong assumptions about an economic agent's knowledge of the true model and credibility of future policy actions. An alternative expectations approach which has been adopted at the LBS is a learning model, where agents adjust towards the solution (see Currie and Hall, 1993). An expectations rule is specified which has parameters that are initially uncertain, but which are sequentially updated as economic agents increase their knowledge of the true parameters of the system. This approach is discussed in Chapter 5. The learning approach still makes some strong assumptions, as does the rational expectations approach.

Another issue pertaining to exchange rates is the treatment of regimes where exchange rates are fixed, or targeted, as in the operation of the European monetary system (EMS), and this is discussed further in Chapter 9.

> The determination of the term structure of interest rates in
> macroeconometric models can also introduce an element of forward-looking
> behaviour.

In most of the models, the short-term interest rate is an exogenous policy variable
(but see Chapter 7 for alternative approaches). However, long-term interest rates are
also usually part of the model, and may be more appropriate to the modelling of
investment decisions than short-term rates. The standard approach in the literature is
the arbitrage process, whereby long rates are the average of future expected short rates.
If future short rates are rationally determined, the long rate is also a jumping variable.
Initially, models had more *ad hoc* treatments of the term structure, which included a
role for market segmentation as a justification for deviations from the competitive
paradigm, so that long rates adjusted more slowly to short rates. This has become less
defensible with the greater degree of financial liberalisation, and the main stumbling
block in practice has been the implementation of forward-looking interest rate
equations. Forward-looking long-term rates are one way that forward-looking
behaviour can be introduced into share price behaviour, since, rather than estimate a
forward-looking model of share prices directly (as happened in the LBS model when it
contained its financial sector), share prices which depend on long rates will also be
indirectly forward looking.

4.3 Modelling of trade

> Properties of the trade equations are key elements in determining the
> nature of any balance of payments constraint.

The issue of whether the balance of payments has been a constraint upon economic
policy has been the focus of considerable attention in post-war UK economic history.
In this section we review the approach to modelling the balance of payments in national
models (a slightly different treatment is adopted in the multicountry models and is set
out in Chapter 8). It has long been recognised that the leakage from any given demand
shock in the form of imports can be an important source of crowding out, whereas if the
trends in import penetration and export shares are not matched, there will be a trend
change in the balance of payments for any balanced growth in the domestic and world
economies (Thirlwall, 1980). In particular, it has been feared that this trend change will
be adverse, so that either competitiveness will have to be continually improved or else
the domestic economy will be forced to grow at a slower rate than other economies.

The balance of payments consists of the current account and the capital account.

$$BAL = CUR + CAP \tag{4.4}$$

The capital account in turn consists of long-term and short-term capital inflows and
outflows. These will be based on portfolio and speculative factors, and hence will be

related to interest rates both at home and abroad, and on expected changes in the exchange rate. If both current and capital accounts are modelled, the exchange rate (which is the price of foreign exchange) is implied as the clearing price in the market. If, alternatively, the exchange rate is modelled as a structural relationship, the capital account is in turn implied by the model for any given level of the current account. Approaches adopted for the capital account are described in the section on the exchange rate, and here we concentrate on the modelling of the current account.

The current account is in turn divided into the trade balance, net flows of interest, profits and dividends, and net transfers. The trade balance consists of imports and exports of goods and services. Almost invariably, imports and exports are separately determined. Often the total is broken down into goods and services separately, and sometimes goods are differentiated by manufactures and non-manufactures (the latter are mainly basic materials and food, drink and tobacco). In the UK, trade in oil is usually described separately given the role of the UK as an oil producer (the models often have a specific North Sea oil account, but it has only a limited feedback effect on the rest of the model: see Wallis et al., 1985, chapter 5). Trade volumes help to determine the share of domestic output in total demand through the in-come–expenditure identity. Trade prices are a key component in the measure of international competitiveness, and import prices are an important link in the transmission of inflation. Trade in goods is often referred to as 'visible trade' and is measured as it flows across international boundaries. Various adjustments are required to convert the data from a trade basis to a balance of payments basis. One major element of this conversion is the need to subtract the freight and insurance elements from imports and to allocate this to the services account. Trade in services (often termed 'invisible trade') largely consists of financial services such as banking and insurance (which has become more important as the ease of financial transactions has increased) and transport and travel (including holidays abroad by UK citizens, and by foreign citizens in the UK). As part of the removal of border controls in Europe in 1993, trade between European countries is no longer recorded by customs and excise declarations, but by VAT returns by importers. This has introduced a discontinuity into the time-series data on exports and imports.

Flows of interest, profits and dividends arise mainly as a result of changes in capital flows. For example, higher interest rates in the UK will imply a future flow of interest payments to foreigners who purchase UK government securities. Foreign capital investment in the UK may also imply some future repatriation of profits and dividends, which will appear as a negative item in the interest, profits and dividends (IPD) account. Where capital flows are not themselves explicitly modelled, items of the IPD account have to be explained by fairly simple relationships. Most macroeconometric models do not have very thorough models of the process of location of plant (foreign direct investment), but this is currently receiving greater attention as a key mechanism in the transmission of growth (as in endogenous growth theories). The fact that growing internationalisation of production means that multinational firms can switch production between countries does bring into doubt the fairly rigid distinction between exporting and importing behaviour in the models. Finally, transfers are those payments made overseas (and correspondingly to the UK) which are not a payment for factor services. Examples are contributions to the EEC budget.

A stylised form of trade volume equations is given below.

$$X = \gamma_0 + \gamma_1 C_x + \gamma_2 S + \gamma_3 T$$

$$M = \theta_0 + \theta_1 C_m + \theta_2 Y + \theta_3 SP + \theta_4 T \tag{4.5}$$

where X is exports; M is imports; S is foreign demand; Y is home demand; SP is a specialisation term; C is competitiveness (x for exports and m for imports); and T is a time trend. These are the long-run versions of the equations. Dynamic features may include a measure of capacity utilisation. A brief statement of the stylised equations such as these hides some of the issues that separate empirical formulations. We deal with these in turn.

 Explaining trend shares of imports and exports poses important modelling issues.

Trends and demand elasticities

First, we discuss an important variation from this system. The identity between demand, output and imports is $D = M + Y$, where D is demand, M is imports and Y is output. If we think of the rest of the model determining the level of total demand, we need a relationship to determine whether this demand is met from imports or domestic output. The traditional approach is to model imports explicitly, so that output is the residual from the identity. In principle, the import share equation could be rewritten as an output share equation with suitably transformed parameters. Thus instead of writing:

$$M/D = f(\ldots) \tag{4.6}$$

we could rearrange this as:

$$Y/D = g(\ldots) \tag{4.7}$$

where the $g(\ldots)$ parameters are simply equal and opposite to those of $f(\ldots)$. If the standard log-linear representation of imports is used, however, such that:

$$\log M = h(\ldots \log D)$$

this simple rearrangement is not possible.

An alternative system, which was used by the LBS for a time, derived output directly and then derived the level of imports as a residual, given final demand. The implied properties of the import equation were not totally plausible, and Chapter 5 discusses how the implied propensity to import appears to be understated.

The interpretation of the import equation is not unambiguous (we discuss that of the export equation below). Many derivations assume that it represents a demand function, but when domestic capacity utilisation measures are included, this suggests that the equation is more in the spirit of a reduced form.

A time trend often appears in the trade equations, and this is usually a proxy for the unexplained trend in import or export share. In import equations, the time trend has a positive coefficient, implying that import penetration has grown secularly faster than is accounted for by the other variables in the relationship; whereas in the export equation, the time trend usually has a negative coefficient, indicating a trend loss of export share (although this discussion is largely based on UK experience, many of the same problems are present in the trade sectors of other economies). The inclusion of a time trend is linked with the size of the estimated elasticity on the demand variable. It has been a common feature of UK import equations that freely estimated demand elasticities are high (between 2 and 3), but if a time trend is added to the equation, the restriction that the elasticity is unity can be imposed and accepted. Similarly, in the export equation, the elasticity of world trade usually turns out to be lower than unity where there is no time trend in the equation, the imposition of a unit elasticity again being valid once a time trend is included. Although the statistical fit of the respective equations is equally good and it is difficult to distinguish statistically between the variants, the choice has important implications for the simulation properties of the models. For if domestic demand is increased, the version of the import equation without the time trend (and hence a large demand elasticity) would imply a large marginal import increase and therefore a small increase in output. The variant with the unit elasticity would give a far smaller rise in import penetration and hence would produce, *ceteris paribus*, a higher domestic demand increase for any given boost in domestic demand. Taken together, the import and export equations, without the time trends to pick up secular changes in share, imply that a balanced expansion in demand both at home and abroad will result in a deterioration in the current balance of the economy. This is emphasised in discussion of the nature of the balance of payments constraint.

Some modellers have attempted to capture the unexplained trend increase in import share (this is a European phenomenon) by including specific factors. One popular view is that import shares have increased as a result of growing specialisation in international trade and the easing of trade restrictions. For example, NIESR has included the ratio of world trade to output as a proxy for this effect. The inclusion of such a variable enables the unit elasticity restriction on imports to be imposed in a valid fashion. The main problem with this variable is that it is required to be forecast itself. Import share equations with elasticities greater than unity do not quite have the same implication in the multicountry model as in the single country model. The multicountry model will merely generate higher import growth, which gets shared out in higher exports for everyone, so that trade is higher but total output in the world economy is unaffected.

The position on modelling export shares is a little more complicated, for there is recent evidence of a flattening out of the trend fall in the UK export share, and even a suggestion that it may have begun to rise. The traditional view had been that the trend fall in the export share since the Second World War reflected non-price competition factors such as quality and delivery dates. Models of exports using data only from the 1980s onwards can therefore produce a unit elasticity on world demand without recourse to a time trend. Models estimated using data from a longer period have to be modified in the forecasting process, and Whitley *et al.* (1992a) describes the impact that different assumptions about the nature of the upward adjustment to exports have on forecasts of economic activity and the current balance in the main UK models (including the Treasury). Usually the export equations have been interpreted as demand equations. However, some interpret the recent shift in the UK volume of exports of goods as a supply-side shift. Holly and Wade (1989) use a model of demand and supply to test whether supply-side changes have improved UK export perform-ance. Their results suggest that this has happened post-1979 by UK firms pricing more competitively in response to an increase in world demand. This is in contrast to the suggestion by Landesman and Snell (1989) that this change has been due to a shift in the income elasticity of demand. However, there is as yet no accepted empirical explanation of the recent changes in export share performance, and hence we cannot be sure whether the recent improvement in export performance is permanent. NIESR has formalised the changing trend share by using a stochastic time trend, allowing the slope of the time trend to change period by period (Anderton, 1991). Most of the hypotheses put forward to account for the recent export improvement are based on the view that supply-side factors have improved non-price competitiveness, but they are difficult to substantiate.

If the export relationships are to be interpreted as demand equations, it should be the price equations which reflect a supply-side change. Alternatively, if both volume and price equations are reduced forms, both should be affected by a supply-side change. Assuming that the volume equation is affected by an exogenous shift could lead to bias if the true cause were a shift in the effect of price competitiveness on the demand for exports. We discuss below reasons why price elasticities may have been under-estimated.

 There are some reasons to suspect that the price elasticities in trade equations are too low.

Competitiveness

 Properties of the trade equations can be used to calculate the underlying equilibrium real exchange rate (FEER).

If trends in import and export equations are deleterious, in the sense that sustained domestic growth is not possible without incurring a balance of payments deficit, then one possibility is to allow the exchange rate to depreciate in order to improve competitiveness. We discuss below whether this is a feasible alternative in the context of the full model, but for the moment we focus upon whether the necessary conditions for an exchange rate devaluation to improve the current account do in fact exist. Some attention was given to this issue by Thirlwall (1980) and was subsequently applied to UK models by Turner (1990). The basis is whether the familiar Marshall–Lerner static condition on export and import price elasticities is satisfied. It has led to the idea of a fundamental equilibrium exchange rate (FEER). This is the real exchange rate which gives balance in the current account, given internal balance. It was originally developed by Williamson (1983) and applied to the components of the multicountry model by Barrell and Wren-Lewis (1989). It has also been applied to UK models by Church (1992). The FEER approach has been criticised and we review some of these criticisms in section 4.6.

Measures of competitiveness differ between models in trade equations. Some modellers prefer to use relative prices, whereas others use relative labour costs (possibly smoothed in some way) or even relative total costs. The empirical evidence does not seem to offer convincing support for one alternative against the others. Simulation properties of the full models may be sensitive to the different specifications, however. For example, relative prices may change as a result of changes in the price mark-up, whereas relative labour costs will be invariant to such a change.

One repeated concern with empirical estimates of competitiveness elasticities is that they are 'too low' and do not always satisfy the static Marshall–Lerner condition. The Marshall–Lerner condition states that, from an initial position of trade balance, for a devaluation to improve the trade balance the sum of the price elasticities of imports and exports must exceed unity. However, this condition is derived on the assumption that, following a devaluation, exporters reduce their foreign currency prices in line with the devaluation. In both practice and empirical formulations, this does not hold. The condition for a balance of payments improvement can be rewritten as:

$$\frac{e}{p_x^f} \cdot \frac{\delta p_x^f}{\delta e} \cdot (\eta_x - 1) + \eta_m > 0 \tag{4.9}$$

where p_x^f is the foreign currency price of exports, e is the exchange rate and η_x and η_m are the (absolute) price elasticities of exports and imports. The partial elasticity $\delta p_x^f / \delta e$ gives the reaction of the foreign currency price of exports to the exchange rate change. The standard Marshall–Lerner condition assumes this to be unity. Now it is possible for the trade balance to be improved even if the price elasticities sum to less than unity, as long as foreign prices change less than the exchange rate. Once we allow for exporters to adjust foreign currency prices by less than the full extent of any exchange rate change, the way is left open for the resultant changes in profitability to influence the supply of exports and the demand for investment. The UK models have at times attempted to include profitability effects in their export equations, but the results have not been very encouraging. There are at least three ways of measuring profitability: in absolute terms; relative to overseas competitors; and relative to the profitability of home sales. Absolute measures have tended to feature more frequently in UK export equations.

Where relative unit labour cost measures are used, this needs to be further modified

Table 4.2 Long-run competitiveness
elasticities (manufactures)

	BE	HMT	NIESR
Exports	0.4	0.28	0.34
Imports	0.5	0.55	0.7

to take into account pricing behaviour. Table 4.2 gives estimates of long-run competitiveness elasticities from the main UK models of 1990 vintage.

The sums of the respective import and export elasticities are either just under or around unity. Successive re-estimation of competitiveness elasticities as the estimation period is extended to include more recent observations has tended to produce smaller point estimates of competitiveness elasticities. This is in contrast to prior expectations which are based on the view that increasingly open trade should result in higher price elasticities. The advent of a single market in Europe in 1993 is one example of more open trade. Part of the single market programme is common standards for goods, leading to a more homogeneous product, a greater degree of substitutability and hence the implication that competitiveness elasticities will be higher. One explanation for the low point estimates is that the data on relative prices or costs are subject to excessive noise due to the extent of short-run fluctuations in exchange rates. Attempts have been made either to separate changes in relative prices due to change in exchange rates from other changes, or to estimate some idea of a 'permanent' concept of relative prices (mainly by smoothing the relative prices series). However, there have been no major empirical breakthroughs in this area.

An alternative explanation is that the export volume equation is misspecified. This could be due to standard identification issues. If we assume that the export volume equation is a demand equation, it should not include any supply-side influences and the export price equation then represents the supply side; again it should exclude factors which cause the demand side to shift. The resultant price elasticity in the export demand equation should therefore be a demand elasticity. If, however, both export volume and price equations are reduced forms, the price elasticity in the volume equation cannot be interpreted as a demand elasticity, but is a combination of both demand and supply elasticities and has no particular behavioural interpretation. Inclusion of profitability effects in export volume equations would rule out a demand explanation.

Further suggestions of possible inconsistency come from an examination of the treatment of trade in some of the models of the Finnish economy. There a typical empirical result is that the data support the idea that long-run export prices are determined solely by world prices in the export price equation (purchasing power parity, or the law of one price), whereas the price elasticity of export volumes is typically quite small when freely estimated. If the first result were the true one (i.e. PPP holds), the estimated price elasticity in the volume equation should approach infinity for consistency with the underlying hypothesis about the nature of competition in world markets. This is that Finnish exporters are price-takers, at least in the long run, and therefore that the long-run export demand schedule is horizontal. The Finnish modellers (e.g. the BOF4 model) impose consistency. Given that the PPP hypothesis is not rejected in the export price equation, the restriction on the export volume that prices do not appear is then imposed, tested and accepted.

While accepting that UK exporters may enjoy some market power, so that PPP may not be the long-run tendency, the consistency point still arises. The standard UK export price result is that the elasticity on world prices is around one-half. It is not clear that consideration has been given to whether the price elasticities in the volume equation are consistent with this view: in other words, volume and price equations tend to be derived separately. In this respect at least, modellers elsewhere appear to be more advanced than in the UK.

FEER

Considerable attention has been given in economic policy circles to the level of the exchange rate consistent with macroeconomic equilibrium, especially in relation to the ERM entry rate selected by the UK in 1990 and whether this represented an overvaluation. The issue of whether the depreciation of the UK exchange rate in September 1992 was necessary for equilibrium is also highly relevant.

An indicator which has been used is the concept of the exchange rate which delivers a 'sustainable' current account balance while the economy is growing at its natural rate (see the NAIRU discussion below). This is equivalent to the idea of external balance in the economy following on from the Salter/Swan analysis. External balance is defined as occurring when the real exchange rate is such that the current account of the balance of payments is offset by structural capital flows. The relationship of FEER to PPP is discussed more fully in section 4.6, where we integrate NAIRU and FEER analysis. In this section we explain how the FEER can be calculated. The FEER is a medium-term concept and is derived from the steady-state implications of the trade equations in the models. It can be interpreted as a short-hand way of deriving the partial properties of the trade system.

We start by writing the identity for the balance of trade in goods and services.

$$BGS = X.PX - M.PM \tag{4.10}$$

where X and M are the volume of exports and imports respectively, and PX and PM are the corresponding prices. If we then substitute the determinants of the components of the identity, allowing for IPD flows, and express competitiveness variables in terms of the real exchange rate (R) we get:

$$CBT = f(R, Y, S, IPD, T) \tag{4.11}$$

where CBT is the trend current account balance; Y is equilibrium domestic demand; S is equilibrium or trend world demand; IPD are trend IPD flows; and T is a time trend.

The FEER is then simply the value of R, the real exchange rate, which ensures that the current balance is equal to structural capital flows. On the simplifying assumption that these are zero, we solve for the FEER in:

$$0 = f(FEER, Y, S, IPD, T) \tag{4.12}$$

This expression can be solved using past historical values of the demand variables, or can be a projection into the future. Different models will give different estimates of the FEER if they have different trade parameters. The methodology can also be used to gauge the sensitivity of the FEER to alternative estimates of the activity and competitiveness elasticities. The results of Church (1992) show that there is not much quantitative difference between the UK models in respect of their trade equations. Starting from an initial point of balance of payments deficit and low competitiveness elasticities, the FEER lies some way below the exchange rate on ERM entry in 1990. Moreover, the estimates suggest that quite substantial changes are required (a fall in the real exchange rate) to eliminate the current disequilibrium.

What the FEER analysis cannot tell us is how we can get back to the equilibrium. There may be a variety of routes. One is to grow more slowly, but this may mean forgoing internal balance. The estimates of Church suggest that sustainable economic growth might be as little as 1 per cent a year, but allowing for the recent improvement in export performance to be permanent raises the 'equilibrium' growth rate at which current balance can be sustained to closer to 2 per cent. Doubling the size of the trade elasticities could change the FEER by 10–15 per cent.

4.4 Wages and prices

> The wage and price sector is at the heart of the new supply-side macroeconomics.

The wage and price sectors have always been a key part of macroeconometric models, largely responsible for the generation of inflation. Historically, the Phillips curve was the standard mechanism for explaining wage inflation, notwithstanding its poor empirical performance. Price equations were usually of the cost mark-up variety, although there was some difference of opinion as to whether costs were measured on an actual or normal cost basis, this distinction being crucial to whether demand had an influence on the mark-up.

The work of Layard and Nickell (1985, 1986; Nickell, 1988) has had a substantial impact on the modelling of unemployment and inflation, both nationally and internationally. They use the imperfect competition approach, concentrating on labour market/goods market interactions. Their approach uses the wage–price system of the model to determine its supply side, which is seen to arise as the long-run (equilibrium) solution to the wage and price equations. However, the term 'supply side' in this context has a quite different meaning to what was previously meant by the supply side in economic modelling. This was most often interpreted as involving the production function, the accumulation of capital, growth of the labour force and technical progress. In this section we review the developments in modelling the 'supply side' with particular emphasis on the role of the Layard–Nickell approach, showing how this can be used to derive a NAIRU for the model, given conditions such as static homogeneity. The role of taxes on the supply side is made explicit in this approach, and we show how the long-run impact of taxes can be predicted quite closely by simple inspection of the wage equation.

At this point it is useful to note that the term 'NAIRU' is strictly incorrect in models with rational expectations. The original concept derives from the solution for unemployment where actual and expected inflation coincide. In a rational expectations model, there is consistency between actual and expected inflation, and the equilibrium level of unemployment does not depend on these magnitudes being equal. In what follows we merely use the term 'NAIRU' to denote equilibrium unemployment.

The determination of wages is intrinsically tied up with the modelling of the labour market. This remained fairly *ad hoc* even up to the mid-1980s in the majority of UK models. Nickell (1984a, p. 13) was most critical:

> The standard practice in the construction of economy-wide econometric
> models is to ignore the existence of markets. Nowhere is this made more clear
> than in the sub-sector of the model devoted to employment and wages ... The
> notion of a labour market obviously lies somewhere in the background of
> these models but it seems to have moved so far back that it has disappeared
> from view ...

Nickell goes on to describe the employment equations in the main macroeconometric models of the UK economy as a simple function of the level of activity, with wages being determined by a string of variables that 'appear to have been selected more or less randomly.' In an analysis of the labour markets of the UK models at about the same time (Wallis *et al.*, 1984), it was shown that it was not possible in many of the models to infer the structure of the labour market from the estimated (reduced-form) relationships.

 Labour market analysis has shifted away from the issue of whether labour markets clear to a framework of bargaining under imperfect competition.

Recent developments in the treatment of the labour market

One of the major developments in the approach to the labour market has been the shift away from a framework where the main issue is whether the labour market clears or not, modifying the competitive paradigm by the inclusion of market imperfections in a fairly *ad hoc* way, towards an approach which explicitly incorporates imperfect competition in goods markets and recognises the role of unions in wage setting. A standard approach to the specification of the labour market is to define a labour demand schedule, a labour supply schedule, and a wage adjustment equation.

The demand schedule is written:

$$N_t^d = f_1(w_t^p, Z_t^d) \tag{4.13}$$

where w^p is the real wage defined in terms of the product price, and Z^d is a vector of exogenous variables affecting the demand for labour. These might include the real prices of other factors of production, the capital stock and output.

The labour supply schedule is:

$$N_t^s = f_2(w_t^c, Z_t^s) \tag{4.14}$$

where w^c is the real wage defined in terms of the consumption price, and Z^s is a vector of exogenous determinants of labour supply such as the labour force, unemployment benefits and real interest rates.

Under market-clearing the real wage (w^*) is obtained by solving the demand and supply equations, by setting demand equal to supply.

$$w^* = f_3(T, Z^d, Z^s) \tag{4.15}$$

where T is a set of tax variables causing a 'wedge' between the real product wage and the real consumption wage. Market-clearing employment (N^*) is given by:

$$N^* = f_4(T, Z^d, Z^s) \tag{4.16}$$

In a disequilibrium framework, actual employment is typically determined as the minimum of demand and supply, and a wage adjustment $N_t = \min(N_t^s - N_t^d)$ mechanism is specified:

$$w_t - w_{t-1} = f_5[(N_t^d - N_t^s), Z_t^w] \tag{4.17}$$

where Z^w is a vector of factors causing wages to deviate from their equilibrium values.

A reduced-form for the market-clearing model is:

$$w_t = f_6(Z_t^d, Z_t^s, Z_t^w, T, W_{t-1}) \tag{4.18}$$

This is distinguished from the market-clearing case (equation 4.15) by the absence of Z^w and w_{t-1}.

The reduced-form representation of employment in the non-market-clearing case is:

$$N_t = f_7(Z_t^d, Z_t^s, Z_t^w, T, W_{t-1}) \tag{4.19}$$

When the underlying demand schedules contain terms in lagged wages, it is only the presence or otherwise of exogenous wage factors that enables inference of the underlying market structure from inspection of the reduced-form equations.

The labour force may be treated as exogenous in this framework, in which case changes in employment can be directly associated with those in unemployment,

$$U_t = L_t - N_t \tag{4.20}$$

or there may be a participation equation to explain L. In practice, the excess demand for labour is proxied by the level of unemployment (U), giving:

$$w_t - w_{t-1} = f_8(U, Z_t^w) \tag{4.21}$$

which closely resembles the augmented Phillips curve:

$$w_t - w_{t-1} = f_9(U_t, P_t^e/P_{t-1}, Z_t^w) \tag{4.22}$$

where P^e is the expected price level.

Use of the Phillips curve relationship enables the equilibrium level of unemployment to be determined from this equation alone, without recourse to the other behavioural relationships in the model. Nickell (1988) argues that this is an unlikely proposition. It is the Z^w variables that determine the equilibrium level of unemployment, and these tend to be largely absent from empirical specifications, leaving the equilibrium level of unemployment as a constant. Where these variables do appear, they tend to be very *ad hoc*, leaving the wage equation with little theoretical justification.

The NAIRU approach

> The derivation of long-run solutions for the wage and price equations can be used to give an expression for equilibrium unemployment (NAIRU), conditional on the real exchange rate.

The approach developed by Layard and Nickell uses a bargaining approach to wages and employment (see Layard, Nickell and Jackman, 1991). This usually consists of a framework where the firm and the union bargain about the wage and the firm sets employment (the 'right-to-manage' model). Nickell (1984a) shows that the introduction of unions as part of the bargaining process has no effect on the labour demand function, but the supply of labour schedule is augmented by union coverage and mark-up measures. In turn, the latter variable must be replaced by all exogenous variables directly relevant to the labour market as well as the direct measures of union power. The wage equation is now a reduced form and includes all the variables exogenous to the labour market. This poses a problem for identification if the wage equation contains all the variables appearing in the demand function (we come back to the interpretation of the demand equation later).

For example, the labour demand and wage equations can be written as follows:

$$\begin{aligned} n &= \alpha_1 w^p + \alpha_2 z_1 + \alpha_3 z_2 \\ w^c &= \beta_1 n + \beta_2 z_1 + \beta_3 z_3 \end{aligned} \tag{4.23}$$

Normally we would think of estimating this system by using z_2 as instruments for the endogenous variables in the wage-setting equation and z_3 as instruments for the endogenous variables in the labour demand equation. We can think of z_2 as containing variables like capital stock, technical progress, etc., and z_3 as unemployment benefits, union power, etc. However, since all exogenous variables in the labour demand equation also appear in the wage equation, the vector z_2 is empty and the wage equation cannot be identified. This is a problem which has not really been tackled in the models. One possibility, introduced by Layard and Nickell (1985) is to drop the assumption that firms are price-takers in goods markets, and hence to allow labour demand to be additionally influenced by aggregate demand.

> The Phillips curve is embodied as the adjustment mechanism within the Layard and Nickell approach to wages and prices.

An excellent account of the economics of the labour market models, including the Layard–Nickell approach, is given in Carlin and Soskice (1990). The model is set out in Figure 4.2 and shows wage- and price-setting schedules in real wage–employment space. The wage-setting curve slopes upwards, showing that unions are able to bargain for a higher real wage when unemployment is low (employment is high). The price-determined real wage under competitive conditions is given by the profit-maximising condition that the real wage equals the marginal product of labour, and given that the marginal product falls as employment rises, the price-setting schedule slopes downwards to the right. In the imperfectly competitive case, there is some evidence that prices do not respond much to demand (Coutts, Godley and Nordhaus,

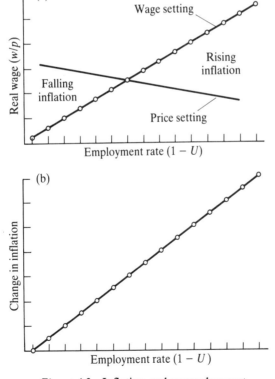

Figure 4.2 Inflation and unemployment

1978), in which case the price-determined real-wage schedule is fairly flat. We now discuss how these schedules can be used to describe the process of equilibrium.

Workers are assumed to seek a given real wage that satisfies their aspirations, whereas firms are seeking to maintain or achieve a given real profit per worker. These competing claims may not be consistent. Only at u^* are these claims mutually consistent. At unemployment levels below this, the bargained real wage exceeds that which firms are prepared to concede. This leads to inflation as the attempts of both sides to maintain their targets pushes up nominal wages and prices. When unemployment is above u^* then inflation is falling. It is only when unemployment is at u^* that the competing claims are reconciled and inflation is stable. Any exogenous factor that causes wage push, and hence raises the wage-setting schedule, raises the equilibrium unemployment rate. The lower part of the figure shows the change in inflation. We can see that, as unemployment rises above its equilibrium rate, inflation is accelerating, and when it falls below, inflation is decelerating. Only at the equilibrium point is inflation constant. Hence the equilibrium is called the NAIRU, or non-accelerating-inflation rate of unemployment. This is the familiar Phillips curve. The equilibrium unemployment rate is not a market-clearing rate. In general there is involuntary unemployment at the NAIRU, in the sense that there are workers prepared to work at the existing real wage who cannot get a job. Levels of actual employment and output are then determined by the level of aggregate demand that is consistent with this NAIRU. The NAIRU is distinct from the notion of the natural rate of unemployment, which emerges from the competitive model where there is no market power whereby unions can achieve a higher bargained real wage than that at which individual workers would be prepared to take a job.

> In practice, conditions to derive the NAIRU may not be met. The set of exogenous supply-side variables implied by the NAIRU expression tends to be small.

Derivation of the NAIRU

Having set out the basic ideas behind the NAIRU and seen how these depend upon the wage- and price-setting equations, we now illustrate how the long-run versions of these equations can be combined.

We write the wage equation as follows, eliminating all dynamic terms:

$$w = p + \pi - \alpha_1 u + \alpha_2 \rho - \alpha_3 t^e - \alpha_4 t^i + \alpha_5 t^d + \alpha_6 z^w \tag{4.24}$$

where π is productivity, ρ is the real exchange rate and the t variables are tax rates, e being employer taxes, i being indirect taxes and d being direct taxes on workers. u is the unemployment rate and p the consumer price index.

The price equation is a mark-up on wage costs and import costs, with an allowance for the possibility that the mark-up rises with demand.

$$p^p = (1 - \beta)(w + t^e - \pi) + \beta m - \gamma u \tag{4.25}$$

we can rewrite this as:

$$p^p(1 - \beta) = (1 - \beta)[w + t^e - \pi] + \beta(m - p) + \gamma u \tag{4.26}$$

where $(m - p)$ is the real exchange rate. This gives:

$$p^p - w = t^e - \pi + \theta(m - p) + \phi u$$
$$\theta = \beta/(1 - \beta) \tag{4.27}$$
$$\phi = \gamma/(1 - \beta)$$

Using the identity between producer prices and consumer prices, we can rewrite equation 4.27 as:

$$p = p^p + t^i$$
$$p = w - \pi + t^e + t^i + \theta(m - p) + \phi u \tag{4.28}$$

Assuming that the dynamic terms can be eliminated, we then obtain the equilibrium unemployment condition by equating the real-wage claims of unions and firms by rewriting equations 4.24 and 4.28 in terms of the real wage and equating both sides of the equations. Thus:

$$(\phi + \alpha_1)u = (\theta + \alpha_2)\rho + (1 - \alpha_3)t^e + (1 - \alpha_4)t^i + \alpha_5 t^d + \alpha_6 Z^w \tag{4.29}$$

The left-hand side of this expression is the NAIRU. It is seen to depend on the real exchange rate, tax terms and the exogenous wage-push factors. Productivity does not appear.

The real exchange rate and the NAIRU

The real exchange rate is defined as implying that a rise in the rate is equivalent to a fall in competitiveness. The real exchange rate is an endogenous variable in the system, and we show in the rest of this chapter how the determinants of the real exchange rate can be combined with the NAIRU to give full equilibrium of the model. If the coefficient on the real exchange rate in the wage equation is zero, this implies that there is real-wage resistance with respect to changes in the terms of trade. In this case, the parameter on the real exchange rate in the NAIRU equation is positive, implying that a rise in the real exchange rate increases the NAIRU. If there is not full wage resistance, the real exchange rate impact on the NAIRU is weaker to the extent that unions adjust their wage claims as terms of trade become adverse. There is then less need for a rise in equilibrium unemployment to reconcile competing claims. Few of the UK models include a real exchange rate term in their wage equations.

The impact of exogenous wage shocks on the NAIRU depends on the size of the coefficients on the unemployment variable. The smaller these coefficients, the greater is the degree of real-wage rigidity and hence the greater is the change in the NAIRU for any shock. Where demand pressures on price setting are absent, the NAIRU will exhibit greater variation of this sort.

 Historical data suggest that neither productivity nor taxes have a permanent influence on the NAIRU.

Productivity and the NAIRU

One possible surprising feature of the NAIRU analysis is that productivity does not enter, so that it is neutral in its effect upon unemployment. This is justified by historical analysis. For example:

> if one looks at the past 100 years, productivity has gone up more or less steadily, and unemployment has shown little trend. Thus I believe that models should be constructed in such a way that large productivity shocks affect unemployment for a while but not forever. (Blanchard, 1988, p. 218).

Some argue that this may be an extreme position based on casual observation of variables that might be indirectly related in this way by means of mechanisms in the models other than the wage and price equations. Nonetheless Blanchard is surely correct in demanding that the role of productivity on the NAIRU should correspond to some prior theoretical view. The restriction required for neutrality is that the long-run coefficient on productivity in the wage equation should be unity. Where the UK models include such a variable in the wage equation, the constraint required for neutrality is not always satisfied. Productivity neutrality implies that, if there is a shift towards higher productivity growth, the equilibrium level of demand and output also increase in line, leaving the level of unemployment unchanged.

Exogenous wage-push factors

Although the theoretical literature tends to stress the potential role of variables such as real unemployment benefits and trade union power in the determination of wages, these are typically absent in the large-scale macroeconometric models. Much of the empirical debate is summarised in Nickell (1984b) and Minford (1984), and concerns the measurement of the benefit variable and the choice of a suitable proxy for union power. These variables only appear in the wage equation of the LPL model in the UK, so there remain very few exogenous variables that can be said to shift the position of the NAIRU, and hence operate on the supply-side of the economy.

Conditions for labour force neutrality of the NAIRU tend to be met in the UK models at best by accident.

The labour force and the NAIRU

The arguments for trend neutrality of unemployment with respect to changes in the labour force are the same as those for productivity: that is, the stylised fact that historical changes in the size of the labour force have not been accompanied by trend changes in unemployment. Layard and Nickell (1985) argue that long-run neutrality of unemployment with respect to the labour force (and capital stock) can be ensured by including a capital–labour ratio in the wage equation with an impact equal to the inverse of the long-run wage elasticity of the demand for labour. However, the capital–labour ratio is not currently included in the wage equations of any of the UK models, and the only neutrality that is imposed is that changes in the labour force move in line with those in the population of working age. Joyce and Wren-Lewis (1991) argue against imposing this constraint in the presence of an endogenous capital stock.

In practice, the UK models exclude labour force variables from their wage equations but still manage to produce neutrality. This arises since the NAIRU is uniquely determined from the solution of the long-run wage and price equations, and hence the NAIRU is invariant to changes in the labour force. However, although this result seems plausible, the implications for real wages are not, since equilibrium real wages (which also come out of the wage–price solution) are also unchanged. Standard labour market analysis would lead us to expect real wages to fall sufficiently to induce an increase in employment exactly equal to the increase in the labour force. Since this adjustment cannot occur within the labour market in this case, it must take place elsewhere, from an increase in aggregate demand, a rise in productivity, or an increase in the capital stock. Whether this occurs is debatable, and in particular there appear to be no restrictions in the models which ensure that the neutrality result emerges. It also seems rather implausible that all the burden of adjustment should take place outside the labour market. In practice, the NIESR model produces unemployment neutrality (as a result of the omission of the labour force variable from the wage equation) while the HMT, BE and OEF models give the result that between one-third to one-half of the increase in the labour force appears as higher unemployment.

Dynamic adjustment

The speed of adjustment of wages to any new shock is an important element in how quickly the NAIRU is reached, if indeed it is reached at all. In relatively decentralised economies such as the USA and the UK, wage decisions are not synchronised, unlike Japan where there is a *shunto* or simultaneous wage adjustment for the larger companies. Where wage contracts are made at different points, whether within an annual cycle as in the UK or a biennial one as in the USA, staggered wage setting gives rise to an overlapping of wage decisions, and aggregation of wages gives the appearance of inertia (Taylor, 1979a). However, a potential offset to this inertia is if each group of workers bargains over wages in a forward-looking way. The NIESR model includes both elements in its wage equation (Moghadam and Wren-Lewis, 1991), but the staggered contracts model used is based on a fixed number of workers settling in each period of the year. This is equivalent to assuming an annual wage round, but there is no firm support for this phenomenon in the UK.

The UK models differ in whether an aggregate wage equation is specified, or whether wages are disaggregated. An intermediate case is where manufacturing wages are modelled and total wages or earnings are related to those in manufacturing in a fairly simple fashion. For a while, the Bank of England model had a three-sector treatment of wages where there was interaction between the sectors, but this approach has not been generally followed.

The role of taxes in the NAIRU

Views about the effect on the NAIRU of taxes which form a wedge between producer and consumer prices appear to have fluctuated over the last decade. Nickell (1988) argues that 'it is essential to include the elements of the wedge in the wage equation, for not doing so is tantamount to imposing some arbitrary degree of real wage resistance (or lack of it) on the model' (p. 217). The view of Layard, Nickell and Jackson (1991) is that taxes should only have a short-term effect on wages and consequently should not affect the NAIRU. We show how the tax effect operates, and in doing so reveal the answer to a question that has puzzled macro modellers for some years: namely, why simulations involving changes in employer taxes have such a beneficial impact on the unemployment–inflation trade-off in the UK models.

> Inspection of the coefficient on tax variables in wage equations provides a good guide to their supply-side influence.

We show how the coefficients on the tax wedge variable in the wage equation influence full-model simulations, by considering the direct incidence of any tax cut on employers' real wage costs and workers' real consumption wages. A tax cut which increases the real consumption wage will lead to higher aggregate demand via higher real disposable income, whereas if the tax cut reduces employers' real wage costs, it will operate as a supply-side shock, lowering the NAIRU by reducing pressure from the forces that drive the inflationary process.

We start from the wage equation 4.24, neglecting the terms other than prices and taxes. The tax variables are represented as proportional taxes for ease of exposition.

$$w - p = \alpha_3 t^e - \alpha_4 t^i + \alpha_3 t^d + \ldots \tag{4.30}$$

By manipulating this equation we can rewrite it in terms of the real consumption wage, and alternatively in terms of the real producer wage. In the first case, this involves taking across both the price term and the direct tax variable to the left-hand side of the equation, and in the second case we subtract prices and indirect taxes to get the real producer wage.

$$w - p - t^d = -\alpha_3 t^e - \alpha_4 t^i + (\alpha_5 t^d - 1) + \ldots$$

$$w - p^p + t^e = w - (p - t^i) + t^e = \alpha_5 t^d + (1 - \alpha_3)t^e + -(1 - \alpha_4)t^i \tag{4.31}$$

The tax parameters in the wage equation then reflect the incidence of taxation. If we take the limiting case of $\alpha_1 = 0$, for example, and $\alpha_2 = \alpha_3 = 1$, then a tax cut will operate through higher demand and will be equivalent to any other demand shock. If, on the other hand, $\alpha_1 = 1$ and the other tax terms have zero coefficients in the wage equation, a tax cut will lower employers' real wage costs and act like a pure supply-side shock.

Let us consider an income tax cut first. If the coefficient on direct taxes in the wage equation is zero, employees take all the benefit of the cut in the form of higher take-home pay. If, however, the coefficient is unity, employees reduce their wage demand in line with the tax cut, so their take-home pay is constant. The reduction in wages reduces employers' real wage costs and hence inflationary pressure. Thus a permanent reduction in unemployment is possible consistent with a stable rate of inflation. Now consider a cut in employers' payroll taxes. If this variable does not appear in the wage equation (i.e. the coefficient is imposed as zero), there is no change in wage demands and the entire impact of the tax falls upon real wage costs, a pure supply-side shift. This explains the results consistently obtained from macroeconometric models, whereby a change in employers' taxes appears to deliver a fall in inflation and a rise in output, and is far more advantageous in this respect than most other policy measures. The analysis shown here confirms that this result emerges as a direct consequence of the absence of the tax term from the wage equation (similar considerations apply to indirect taxes).

If the restriction that the taxes have equal effect on unemployment is desired, this requires that the long-run coefficients on employer taxes and indirect taxes are equal, and in turn that these are equal to one minus the coefficient on the direct tax variable. Empirical investigation finds it difficult to obtain well-determined coefficients on the tax terms. This may reflect aggregation problems. In the absence of well-defined statistical evidence, some prior view is necessary.

Before discussing these prior views, we show how inspection of the tax coefficient in wage equations of the UK models provides a very good guide to the full-model implications. Table 4.3 gives the long-run tax coefficients in the wage equations of the main UK models of 1990 vintage. BE and NIESR impose the restriction that the tax coefficients are equal, but the other UK modellers do not.

Figures 4.3 and 4.4 show the results from full-model simulations involving taxes in the NIESR and HMT models. The results are expressed in terms of the inflation–unemployment trade-off, plotting deviations over the first five years of the simulation. If there is a new equilibrium, we would expect the simulation to settle down

Table 4.3 Tax incidence in the UK models: the long-run coefficients on tax variables in the wage equations

	Direct tax	Indirect tax	Employer taxes
LBS	0	0	0
NIESR	0.47	−0.53	−0.53
HMT	0.6	0	0
BE	0.47	−0.53	−0.53
OEF	0.18	0	0

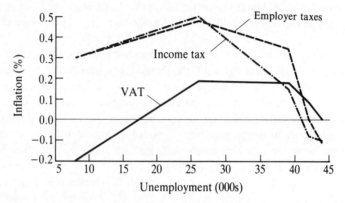

Figure 4.3   Tax effects in the NIESR model

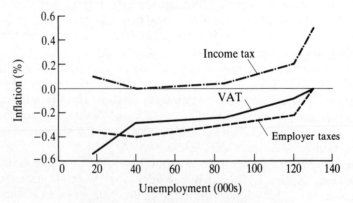

Figure 4.4   Tax effects in the HMT model

to the original rate of inflation. A fall in unemployment at this point implies a supply-side shift, or change in the NAIRU.

Tax equality is imposed in the wage equation in the NIESR model. The NIESR simulation results show that the simulation does settle down to a stable inflation equilibrium, consistent with a reduction of around 40 000 in unemployment, all the taxes having similar long-term unemployment effects.

In the HMT wage equation there are no long-run effects from indirect taxes and employer taxes, so changes in these taxes would be expected to have a pure supply-side effect. In contrast, direct taxes have a long-run coefficient between zero and unity, indicating some supply-side effect. The full-model simulations for HMT show a similarity between the indirect taxes and employer taxes in the long-term, both producing a reduction in unemployment of around 140 000 consistent with stable inflation. This effect is far larger than for the NIESR model, which we expect given the difference in the single-equation elasticities. In contrast, the income tax shock in the HMT model has a demand-side aspect and has not settled down to a stable inflation equilibrium after 5 years. One further contrast between the two models is in the dynamic response, where tax cuts in HMT tend to lower inflation in the short-term whereas the opposite occurs for NIESR; this reflects the jump of the exchange rate in the NIESR model.

Thus we can conclude that apparently innocuous choices about tax coefficients in wage equations can have dominating influences on the full-model simulation results. As indicated above, an earlier view was that the tax wedge should have a long-run effect. Opposing views have existed, however. For example, Blanchard (1988) argued that the tax wedge should be neutral in the same way as productivity. Thus:

> To a worker who can get only a 3 percent rather than a 5 percent increase this year, it makes no difference whether that lower increase comes from a slowdown in productivity growth or from an increase in the tax wedge ... It seems to me that the same logic that compels us to constrain a model in such a way that productivity growth has no effect on long-run equilibrium unemployment implies that changes in the tax wedge also have no effect on unemployment. (p. 218).

This neutrality property would require imposing the restriction that the long-run tax coefficients on indirect taxes and employer taxes in the wage equation should be equal to minus unity and that on direct taxes zero. Layard *et al.* (1991) have now also adopted the view that the tax wedge should have no long-run effect. This is based on the idea that labour supply decisions are based on the opportunity cost of leisure relative to the wage, and this is not affected by the tax wedge.

Relationship to the Phillips curve

Figure 4.2 above shows how the Layard–Nickell approach to wage bargaining produces implications for the relationship between inflation and unemployment as part of the dynamic adjustment to equilibrium. The Phillips curve is therefore encompassed by a more general approach. The latter by itself may have an equilibrium unemployment implication, but because it does not contain any level terms in wages and prices, it cannot be said to determine the equilibrium real wage. This has to be determined elsewhere in the model, usually by the price equation. The Layard–Nickell bargaining approach gives an equilibrium solution to the real wage (obtained by substituting out for the unemployment terms in the wage and price equations) and can be said to determine real wages within the labour market. Although the levels approach to wage determination is included in models of some other economies (notably Finnish models), it has not yet been received with much attention outside the UK, and the Phillips curve paradigm persists.

Practical issues

There are several practical issues which complicate the NAIRU methodology. In order to derive the NAIRU, static homogeneity is required (so that the wage and price equations can be renormalised in terms of the real wage with no wage or price terms left over). This does not always hold, so it is impossible to derive the NAIRU for the majority of UK models (NIESR excluded). Second, there is the issue of adjustment to the NAIRU, which depends on the dynamics of the model. This can prevent adjustment taking place. Turner (1991a) sets out the elements in the HMT model which prevent the NAIRU being reached, and these relate both to the absence of static homogeneity in some of the price equations and to problems of dynamic adjustment.

A particular problem arises if there is unemployment hysteresis in the model, for then the equilibrium level of unemployment depends upon the previous history of unemployment, in which case there is no unique unemployment equilibrium. Hysteresis may occur when it is the change in unemployment which affects wages rather than its level. However, in the UK models there are, in general, unemployment-level effects with little evidence of hysteresis. An exception is in the LBS model, where the wage equation contains a role for long-term unemployment. However, Turner and Whitley (1991) show that the functional form that is used in the LBS model, produces implausible wage responses in certain situations, and furthermore that the statistical support for a separate influence for long-term unemployment is weak.

Hysteresis can also arise through capital scrapping. Carlin and Soskice (1990) show how this can affect pricing decisions. Some elements of this are captured in the vintage capital approach, which is embodied in the NIESR model. Yet a third possibility arises from the behaviour of exporters. In times of low profitability, exporters might be forced to retire from overseas markets. Subsequent return may prove more difficult than exit, possibly due to barriers to entry, hence an improvement in competitiveness may not return the economy to its original equilibrium. Such considerations may also make exporters less inclined to relinquish their export markets in the first place, so a possible feature of this analysis is that unemployment does not rise as much following a deterioration in competitiveness. In general, the models, both in the UK and elsewhere, do not capture this treatment of exports, exporters being assumed to substitute freely between domestic and export goods.

Another practical problem is that the demand variable in the price equation is more likely to be a measure of capacity utilisation (that is, a measure of goods market pressure) than unemployment, so this has to be combined with unemployment in some meaningful way in order to calculate the NAIRU. Furthermore, the modelling of capacity utilisation itself may not be consistent with the concepts of resource equilibrium.

Finally, we note that the capital stock is often absent from the wage equations, and from UK models. In this respect, the NAIRU would appear to be more of a medium-term equilibrium than a long-term concept.

4.5 Production, factors of production and prices

If emphasis on wages and prices, together with the real exchange rate, is the 'new' approach to the supply side, then the 'old' approach is to focus upon the production function, treatment of technology, and the demand and supply of factors of production. If the treatment of the firm is internally consistent in models, we would expect factor demands, price setting and decisions about the supply of output to be derived jointly. Nickell (1988) argues that if this consistency is not present, the equilibrium level of employment consistent with the NAIRU may not correspond with that given by the labour demand function conditioned on equilibrium real wages. One possible reconciliation is through changes in aggregate demand, which influences labour demand, but this does not guarantee consistency, which can only be fully satisfied if the price and factor demand schedules are derived from the same theoretical assumptions, and also if the appropriate cross-equation parameter constraints are satisfied. This is not always the case, as we shall see, although increased attention has been given to this issue.

> The production function is not always explicit in UK models; this contrasts with the experience in the rest of Europe.

Although the production function might be thought to be at the heart of the supply side of macroeconometric models, the approach of Layard and Nickell has emphasised that the production function is essentially a technical relationship, and that it is the background to the economic decisions made by firms that concern their pricing and factor demand decisions.

Alone among the UK models, the CUBS model used a production function to determine the supply of output. The other models have a more implicit determination of output supply.

> Factor demands can be derived from a production function approach or from use of a cost function. Although in principle the two can be identical, practical issues often lead to differences in treatment.

Two common approaches to deriving factor demands are used in the UK models: the explicit use of a production function, and the cost function approach. They can be derived under assumptions of perfect competition or imperfect competition. These are distinguished from approaches derived from the work of Brechling (1965) and Ball and St Cyr (1966), where the production function is simply inverted, and desired employment is related to output and lags of employment, capital being proxied by a time trend. Under this interpretation it is important that the long-run coefficient on output be greater than unity, implying decreasing returns to scale.

The first approach can be summarised as follows. Assuming a production function of the general form:

$$y = y(n,k,t) \tag{4.32}$$

where y is output, n is employment, k capital stock and t is technology, then the labour demand function can be derived by rearranging the marginal productivity condition for labour under profit maximising. The marginal productivity condition is then simply that the firm equates the real wage to the marginal product of labour:

$$w/p = y_n(n,k,t) \tag{4.33}$$

If we use the production function to eliminate the capital stock, we then obtain:

$$n^d = n^d(w/p,y,t) \tag{4.34}$$

Log-linear estimation then gives:

$$\ln n = a_1 \ln y - b_1 \ln(w/p) \tag{4.35}$$

If the technology is assumed to be Cobb–Douglas, certain restrictions are imposed on the production function, and hence on the labour demand function. The more general constant elasticity of substitution (CES) assumption implies that:

$$a_1 = \frac{(1+b)/v}{1+b} \quad b_1 = \frac{1}{1+b} \tag{4.36}$$

where $1/(1+b)$ is the elasticity of substitution, and v returns to scale. Now under the Cobb–Douglas assumption there are constant returns to scale and unit elasticity of substitution. Hence these restrictions imply that:

$$\ln n = \ln y - \ln(w/p) \tag{4.37}$$

Often lagged employment appears in the employment equation, the justification for this inclusion being typically rather *ad hoc*, although sometimes arguments provided by Tinsley (1971) and Sargent (1978) are employed. If the environment is one of imperfect competition rather than perfect competition, the firm then faces a downward-sloping demand curve and the marginal productivity condition becomes:

$$w/p = \frac{y_n}{1 + \varepsilon} \tag{4.38}$$

where ε is the elasticity of demand. The price level now becomes endogenous but otherwise there are no differences from the perfectly competitive approach if the elasticity of demand is constant.

Several practical problems arise with this approach, of which we mention three. First, there is the problem that the estimated long-run coefficients on real wages and hence the implied elasticity of substitution may conflict with the assumptions made about the production technology. In particular, real-wage elasticities with respect to employment tend to be well below unity (usually below $\frac{1}{2}$), which clearly conflicts with the Cobb–Douglas approach and implies a very low elasticity of substitution. Second, output is an endogenous variable and should be treated this way in estimation. Third, it is difficult to ensure consistency between factor demands and price-setting decisions using this approach, since the underlying cost function is implicit.

This last disadvantage is avoided by the alternative to the profit maximisation assumption, namely that of cost minimisation. Before we explain factor demand formation under cost minimisation, we outline the extension of the profit-maximising approach to include raw materials and energy in the production function. The production function can then be written as:

$$y = y(n,m,e,k,t) \tag{4.39}$$

where m represents raw materials and e energy. Solving the marginal productivity conditions gives a labour demand function of the form:

$$n^d = n^d(w/p, p_m/p, p_e/p, k, t) \tag{4.40}$$

where p_m and p_e are the prices of raw materials and energy respectively. If this approach is adopted, the output variable has to be defined in gross terms, as does the output price (p).

The cost minimisation approach basically involves minimising a cost function of the form:

$$C_t = w_t L_t + c_t K_t \tag{4.41}$$

where w is the wage rate and c is the cost of capital, subject to the production function. The cost function can be easily extended to include raw materials and energy.

Cost minimisation produces a labour demand function which contains relative factor prices, rather than the real wage, and output can now be taken as given to the firm. Thus:

$$n^d = n^d(y, w/c, t) \tag{4.42}$$

In order to be more flexible, the cost function is often expressed in the translog form, and this can then be shown to be consistent with a variety of underlying technology assumptions. This also makes it more amenable to incorporation of dynamic adjustment factors than approaches based on the production function, but more importantly, it also enables the price equation to be derived in a consistent framework along with factor demands, a feature that the production function approach does not include. Where a production function is explicitly estimated, it can be used to derive estimates of capacity utilisation, but the cost function approach typically has to resort to indirect measures or independent equations to determine capacity utilisation. Different methods and their implications are discussed below. In principle, there need be no conflict between the production function and cost function approaches, but in application, various simplifying assumptions such as functional form are adopted.

The discussion has taken place in terms of the labour input defined as persons, whereas person-hours is a more appropriate concept in terms of the underlying production function. Many macroeconometric models ignore the hours dimension (an exception in the UK is the BE model). One reason for this neglect is the lack of hours of work data for other than the manufacturing sector. It does lead to problems for the models when the effects of varying the standard length of the working week are the topic of analysis (see Whitley and Wilson, 1988). The lack of the hours dimension is also noted in the treatment of labour supply.

> Consistency of pricing decisions with factor demands is difficult under the production function approach, whereas the cost function approach is usually explicit about the treatment of technology.

Comparative analysis of the employment equations in the models

Our starting point for a comparative discussion of the employment equations is the labour demand equation presented in Layard and Nickell (1985), but slightly modified. This provides a useful benchmark and can be written as:

$$\ln n_t = \alpha_0 + \alpha_1 \ln n_{t-1} + \alpha_2 \ln(w/p)_t + \alpha_3 \ln(w/c)_t + \alpha_4 \ln AD_t + \alpha_5 \ln K_t \qquad (4.43)$$

The variable AD is a measure of aggregate demand and the other variables are as defined above.

We have presented an aggregate equation. In practice, the UK models tend to adopt disaggregation into two main sectors (manufacturing and non-manufacturing) with the NIESR model having a wider disaggregation, but this does not raise any additional issues of interpretation.

In most cases, the capital stock does not appear in employment equations; an exception is the LBS model. The other UK models tend to include both output and relative factor prices, suggesting a cost minimisation interpretation (although the HMT model does not impose the restriction that both factor prices have identical influence). However, in the absence of a capital stock variable, the acceptance of a unit output elasticity appears odd. Nickell (1984a) goes further to argue that output should not appear at all in the employment equation. Under profit maximisation, output only appears if the capital stock has been substituted out, and the output variable should then be endogenous. In the case of imperfect competition, aggregate demand may then play a role, being the exogenous factor which shifts the labour demand curve, but Nickell argues that output is endogenous even under imperfect competition unless there is evidence that firms are constrained in the goods market. This hypothesis is not usually tested. The use of output in the employment equation makes it difficult to distinguish between a labour demand function and an inverted production function, and it is only the presence of a relative factor price variable that precludes the inverted production function interpretation.

Among the UK models, it is currently the case that only in the LBS and NIESR models is an explicit and consistent treatment of factor demands implemented. The approaches of the other models are more *ad hoc*. For example, the HMT employment equation is derived from a Cobb–Douglas production function, which is not consistent with the empirical estimate of the elasticity of substitution. The LBS model uses cost functions under a profit-maximising assumption to derive factor demand and price equations. Employment then depends on real wages, output and capital stock.

The NIESR model adopts a putty–clay vintage approach. The putty–clay assumption allows the firm to choose the labour requirement for new capital equipment, but once the equipment is installed the number of workers per machine is fixed. In contrast the putty–putty approach allows forms to change the labour requirement on new equipment both before and after installation. Relative factor prices influence employment in the model through the choice of the capital–labour ratio embodied in each vintage. This makes productivity dependent on past levels of investment. One motivation for this innovation was the potential for explaining changes in productivity in the 1980s, and in particular the role of capital scrapping during the 1979–81 recession. However, Oulton (1989) shows that the vintage model is no better at explaining this period than the traditional putty–putty approach. Furthermore, the estimates of scrapping from the vintage approach often turn out to be implausible. In the NIESR vintage approach, consistency between price and employment decisions cannot be tested since the cost function is implicit. However, there is a form of consistency in that the measure of capacity utilisation resulting directly from the production technology enters into the price equation.

> The vintage approach has the advantage that it provides a link between investment decisions and productivity growth, but in practice this mechanism is relatively weak.

The vintage approach works as follows. Capital is assumed to be putty–clay. This means that firms can choose new technology involving a cost-minimising capital-labour ratio, but that once it is installed the technological characteristics cannot be altered and the ratio of labour to capital is fixed. The existing capital stock will therefore comprise investment of different vintages, all with different labour-capital ratios, with the assumption that older machines require more labour input. New investment therefore has labour-embodied technical progress and consequently raises average labour productivity. This then has implications for prices and competitiveness. Although it incorporates a link between investment and productivity, the practice with the NIESR model does not appear to produce results very different from the other mainstream UK non-vintage models. This may reflect sluggish adjustment of investment or assumptions about the scrapping of old capital equipment.

In the other UK models, technical progress is usually assumed to be labour-augmenting and is proxied by time trends. This makes the models somewhat less interesting for analysis of long-term trends and the interaction of investment, capacity and technical progress.

The introduction of relative factor prices into the UK models has been a relatively recent phenomenon and makes them look more like factor demand equations than inverted production functions. The recent discovery of factor price effects in employment equations is not a reflection of previously uninformative data, for these influences can be found in equations estimated using data only up to 1978. In other words, the effects were there earlier if only they had been looked for. The size of elasticities in the UK models is very small, however, typically being less than 0.5. This is lower than the cross-country evidence presented in Bean, Layard and Nickell (1986), which finds a typical elasticity of unity. The influence of factor prices is also small in full-model simulations, and they tend to be dominated by demand variables.

> Relative factor price influences on employment tend to be small in the UK models.

The HMT and NIESR models also include a role for profitability or company liquidity, both using the concept of disequilibrium liquidity. In the NIESR case this is a temporary influence, whereas it has a permanent role in the HMT simulations.

In principle one might expect firms' employment decisions to be based on expected demand or output. The HMT model uses a backward-looking model to derive expectations of manufacturing output, whereas NIESR use explicit forward-consistent expectations of output in deriving expected labour requirements. However, previous work by the Bureau (Wallis *et al.*, 1987) has found little support for the use of expected output in place of actual output in employment equations.

> Models of the Nordic economies tend to show greater variety in their employment equations than do the UK models, but they have not yet adopted an integrated treatment of factor demands and prices.

We now compare the UK employment equation with those in Nordic models. The Nordic models contain a greater variety of approach to labour demand than do the UK models. They also contain a greater degree of disaggregation, but although some of the UK models have moved towards a consistent treatment of firms' price and employment decisions, none of the Nordic models examined appears to have moved in this direction. The KESSU model of the Finnish economy uses a profit-maximising approach, whereby only real wages and not output or demand enter the employment equation. Two of the Nordic models contain explicitly estimated production functions: in the ADAM model of Denmark a putty–clay vintage model, and in the BOF4 model of Finland, a CES production function. The latter model also has an hours dimension. The elasticity of substitution is around 0.9. MODAG, a model of the Norwegian economy, uses the inverted production function approach.

Finally, we emphasise the point that the price equation can be seen as the dual of the labour demand function. In the bargaining framework both reflect the 'right-to-manage' approach, whereby firms negotiate with unions over the wage but then choose employment levels. If both price and labour demand equations are included, therefore, they should be completely consistent. Otherwise the employment function should be an inverted production function whose role is simply to calculate the employment implications given output; it is no longer a labour demand equation.

Investment

By 'investment' in macroeconometric models we usually refer to fixed physical investment rather than financial investment. In this discussion we neglect the modelling of investment in stocks. Fixed investment can take various forms. It can relate to investment by sector (for example, manufacturing) or by type of investment good (plant and machinery, or buildings and works). It can also take the form of residential investment. These decisions are usually based on criteria different from those for other forms of fixed investment, partly since they tend to be made as a result of personal sector rather than company sector behaviour. We therefore focus on non-residential investment in our discussion.

Investment decisions can, in principle, provide an important link between technology, productivity and growth, although we argue that these links are not particularly well developed in macroeconometric models.

Many of the issues surrounding the determination of employment also apply to investment, where it is also considered a factor of production. Thus the profit-maximising approach determines the desired capital stock in terms of the real price of capital, whereas the cost-minimising approach gives an explanation of capital stock in terms of relative factor prices.

Profit-maximising approach $\quad K^* = f(c/p)$ $\qquad\qquad$ (4.44)

Cost-minimising approach $\quad K^* = f(w/c)$ $\qquad\qquad$ (4.45)

These are analogous to the expressions for employment shown above, so the demand for factors of production is determined in a consistent fashion. However, once adjustment lags are introduced, and other variables included, the empirical relationships do not usually maintain the principle of interrelated factor demands, and formal attempts to estimate interrelated factor demand functions have not met with great success. In Wallis et al. (1987) it is shown that independence of dynamic adjustment of the factor demand equations in the UK models is a reasonable assumption. Interrelatedness can also be lost if the accelerator theory of investment is introduced. This is based on the simple case where factors are combined in fixed proportion.

Accelerator $$K^* = \alpha Y \qquad (4.46)$$

There are several additional factors of relevance to the modelling of investment. First, theory tends to derive an expression for the desired *capital stock* rather than the level of investment. Second, there are additional problems in measuring the price of capital, and in measuring capital stock itself. Third, there is the issue of how investment is to be financed, since decisions to invest may depend on the form of finance.

> Modelling investment has added complications: theory tends to derive expressions for the desired capital stock; measurement problems of the capital stock and the price of capital exist; and the decision to invest may depend on the form of finance.

Adjustment to the desired capital stock

The theory of investment starts with the derivation of the determinants of the desired capital stock as above. In the simple neo-classical models, it is assumed that the capital stock can be adjusted instantaneously, and investment is then given by:

$$I_t = K_t^* - (1-\delta)K_{t-1} \qquad (4.47)$$

In the presence of adjustment costs, however, adjustment is not instantaneous but is spread over a number of periods. Early model-based explanations tended to adopt the accelerator approach to investment with the adjustment process determined by empirical factors. More recent attention to optimising models has led to explicit incorporation of costs of adjustment into the firm's cost or net revenue function, and the constrained optimisation then implicitly gives both the desired capital stock and the adjustment profile simultaneously. One of the key factors that distinguishes investment decisions is the dependence on future costs and revenues, and this element of uncertainty can be incorporated into the analysis by assuming that the firm maximises an objective function which is the expected present value of current and future costs or net revenues. If the cost function is quadratic the investment decision is of the form:

$$I_t = \lambda_1 K_{t-1} + \lambda_2 K_{t-2} + \sum_{i=0}^{\infty} \mu_i X_{t+i}^e \qquad (4.48)$$

where X_{t+i}^e is a sequence of expectations of the determinants of the desired capital stock and the μ coefficients are functions of the parameters λ_1 and λ_2, thus ensuring that the forward and backward representations are treated symmetrically. This approach was used by Hall and Henry (1985) in an earlier version of the NIESR model.

The more common approach is where the optimisation is made in two stages. In the first stage, the desired capital stock is determined, and in the second stage, the speed of adjustment is determined. Delays relate to time-to-build considerations, placing of contracts, etc. In any period, investment will depends on a variety of projects, each started at different times, and hence forward and backward features are combined. In the light of this, empirical models tend to be based on econometric rather than theoretical considerations. This general form may be written:

$$I_t = w(L)(K_t^e - K_{t-1}) \qquad (4.49)$$

where $w(L)$ is some general distributed lag process and X^e is a vector of influences on the desired capital stock. The vector X^e may include expectations of future variables, and if these are substituted out, there may be a confounding of $w(L)$ with the dynamics of the expectations scheme.

Measurement problems

With the exception of the accelerator model, most of the models of investment, once lagged adjustment is allowed, leave an equation which includes the lagged capital stock. Many empirical formulations either substitute out this variable or ignore it, mainly because of the well-known problems in measuring the capital stock. There are no quarterly time-series data. Common methods are to use past investment to derive a measure of the existing capital stock on a perpetual inventory method, but this can be a very poor approximation when relative factor prices are changing. It may then be no longer profitable to use parts of the existing capital stock, leading to an increase in the rate of scrapping, but the perpetual inventory method assumes a fixed depreciation rate based on average capital lifetimes.

Earlier models had tended to approximate the price of capital by the interest rate, but empirical studies found it hard to detect a well-determined influence from interest rates on investment. Recent attention to the measurement problems have led to more useful measures of the cost of capital (for example, Kelly and Owen, 1985). The cost of capital can be written as:

$$c = q(r + \delta) - \mathring{q} \qquad (4.50)$$

where q is the price of capital goods, r is the discount rate (usually approximated by the market rate of interest), and δ is the rate of depreciation. A major problem in constructing a measure of the cost of capital, c, is the treatment of taxes, where a variety of different rules have applied in the past. The cost of capital can become forward looking when the term in capital gains, $\mathring{q}$, is based on the expected future price of the capital good. Following the measures developed by Kelly and Owen, many of the UK models now contain a term in the user cost of capital. This enables them to discuss the implications not only of changes in interest rates, but also of changes in the tax treatment of investment. The complicated nature of the construction of the cost of capital measure has, however, encouraged some modellers to resort to a simple interest rate variable in their investment equations.

An alternative treatment which is used in several models (including LBS) is a formulation based on Tobin's Q. The Q model is essentially a version of the neo-classical approach (Hayashi, 1982), but one where all the relevant information about expectations is incorporated into the Q index. Tobin's Q is defined as the ratio of the market value of an additional unit of capital to its replacement cost. The market value is simply the expected present value of future returns, so the firm will increase its profits or market value by investing when the value of the Q ratio exceeds unity. Empirical exercises using Tobin's Q have not been very successful. One reason may be that the theory specifies Q in marginal terms, yet measurement is of the average Q. Furthermore, the market value component of the ratio tends to be dominated by equity prices, which can be quite volatile. Where the Q approach has been adopted, as in the LBS model, it is important that Q varies in response to shocks. For example, the equity price should be determined in a forward-looking way. The absence of such a treatment in the LBS model explains why investment is relatively insensitive to shocks, since output does not feature in the equation.

> The explanation of investment by Tobin's Q has the advantage that it incorporates expectations, but in model simulations it is important that the key components of the ratio react in a forward-looking way if the spirit of the Q approach is to be maintained.

Empirical results tend to show consistently that output plays an important role in the determination of fixed investment, and that the use of the real capital cost or relative factor prices, alone, is insufficient.

> Neo-classical explanations of investment behaviour tend to be inadequate, and investment is dominated by output.

There is a tendency to look for the restriction that the long-run elasticity of investment with respect to output is unity in investment equations that are included in macroeconometric models, and most models satisfy this requirement. Occasionally, the freely estimated elasticity exceeds unity (see Turner, Wallis and Whitley, 1989a, for an illustration). If the unit elasticity restriction is then invalidly imposed, the result may be a very sluggish adjustment of investment to any shock. Whether the unit restriction is theoretically valid depends upon the interpretation of the equation. The view that it should be unity derives from the constant returns to scale argument, but if the investment equation is regarded as conditional on the labour force, we would expect to observe diminishing returns and hence an elasticity greater than unity, exactly analogous to the employment example described above.

The use of a single cost of finance in the definition of the cost of capital assumes that this cost is the same whatever the source of finance available to the firm: for example, retained profits or borrowed funds. In practice, a different tax treatment of dividends and capital gains may require different measures of the cost of capital. Taxes may also be relevant where a firm is tax exhausted (i.e. not paying taxes either because it is not making profits or because it has allowances which use up all its tax liabilities). Firms may then 'sell' their unusable tax allowances by encouraging other firms to lease assets. The leasing phenomenon has increased greatly in the UK, and it poses considerable problems in estimating investment equations where a distinction between sectoral investment decisions is made.

Finally, we consider some of the other variables which often appear in investment equations in macroeconometric models. The main factors that we consider are profits, liquidity and intentions variables.

A direct role for profits can be justified on neo-classical lines where they represent the quasi-rents on the existing capital stock and hence the incentive to invest. Alternatively, they can represent failures in the capital market, which might be caused by informational asymmetries between borrowers and lenders. Profits then reflect a cash-flow constraint on investment decisions. Although profit or cash-flow models have been found to perform no worse, and often better, than standard investment functions (see Ford and Poret, 1990), they have not proved an enduring feature of macroeconometric models. There are probably two explanations for this. First, profits are not modelled with any great confidence in the models, and hence there is a desire to avoid introducing such a variable into the investment equation lest it should unduly distort the results in simulation exercises and in forecasting. Second, there is some concern about the flow of causation: whether investment causes profits or vice versa. Both the NIESR and HMT models have used measures of 'disequilibrium liquidity' in their investment equations. In the NIESR model (which also includes equity prices) this is constructed from the difference between, on the one hand, a desired measure of liquidity determined from equations for the long-run desired level of gross liquid assets and bank borrowing, and, on the other, actual net liquidity given by the sector's budget constraint. In the case of HMT, the disequilibrium liquidity influence is an imposed system which only operates in simulation mode. Here changes in company liquidity from its base level influence investment, employment, dividends and stockbuilding.

Investment equations tend not to include specific investment intentions variables, although these often influence forecasts of investment made with the models. Future developments may see these variables formally incorporated into investment equations. It had previously been assumed that forward-looking behaviour could be introduced by the use of model-consistent expectations variables. However, recent experience has suggested that expectations may not be model consistent in the short run, at least, and hence there is a use for survey intentions data. These variables have not been included hitherto partly on the grounds that they could not be forecast, but a compromise might be to allow them to be 'forecast' on a model-consistent basis beyond the period for which they provide information.

Price equations

> Price equations in the model tend to be a mark-up on costs, with the mark-up being sensitive to demand influences.

In all the UK non-monetarist models, prices are determined largely as a mark-up on costs, with a percentage increase in labour and import costs (capital costs are usually neglected) eventually leading to an equal percentage increase in prices. This is the static homogeneity property. In some models, however, static homogeneity does not hold (see Turner, 1991a, for a discussion of the HMT model in this respect) and this dampens the transmission of inflation following a demand shock, and hence inhibits adjustment to the long run. Lack of static homogeneity is more likely to occur when the price system is disaggregated in the models, for then institutional features may dominate individual sectors and imply non-homogeneous behaviour. A view then has to be taken whether to impose the more theoretically appealing homogeneity property or to allow sample experience to dominate the properties of the equation(s). The LBS and NIESR models tend to have less disaggregated price systems than HMT, BE or OEF, and this enables static homogeneity to be more easily tested, accepted and imposed, but they do share a common problem of slow adjustment. All the models tend to have a key pivotal equation, and this is usually the manufacturing wholesale price equation. It typically takes over one year before 90 per cent of higher costs are transmitted into higher prices in most of the UK models, and some are considerably more sluggish. Despite the importance of price rigidity in most macroeconometric models, there has been relatively little formal modelling of the underlying factors causing it. Rather the dynamics are 'data determined' with little theoretical structure. An exception is provided by Joyce and Wren-Lewis (1989), which is integrated into the NIESR model. Here prices are estimated in a framework where a combination of reputation costs (based on the idea that large price changes are most easily perceived) and asynchronised pricing leads to nominal inertia. This framework embodies the idea that prices adjust gradually, but also that firms anticipate changes in costs and demand, so that prices depend not only on lagged prices, but also on expected wages, productivity and import prices.

> Absence of static homogeneity in price equations may result in weak inflationary pressure and prevent adjustment to the NAIRU.

Another explanation for the empirical inertia found in price equations is that researchers have found it difficult to find evidence of a co-integrating relationship. The aggregate profit share in the UK has trended downwards over the last two decades; price equations typically contain no explicit variable to explain this decline. The classic result of omitted variables is to generate very sluggish adjustment. Other models outside the UK also seem to share this problem.

> Sluggish adjustment of prices may reflect theoretical ideas of reputation costs or may indicate misspecification.

The usual macroeconometric approach to modelling prices often has an asymmetry between domestic and import pricing decisions. Domestic prices are determined by cost factors but are independent of competitor import prices, whereas import prices usually depend at least in part on domestic pricing considerations (the so-called pricing-to-market hypothesis). It is important to distinguish import costs that relate to the cost of raw materials, etc., and which appear as part of total costs, from the competing prices of final goods. Some models allow for the influence of competitor prices on domestic prices, but this is not yet a widespread approach. Finally, we note that in many models (and generally in the UK) the size of the mark-up on costs is sensitive to the pressure of demand.

The treatment of capacity utilisation

 An *ad hoc* treatment of capacity utilisation may imply either permanent or temporary effects on the price mark-up.

Where the price mark-up is sensitive to demand conditions, it is usually some measure of demand pressure in the goods market that is appropriate. In this section we are concerned with how the model generates estimates of this demand pressure. Where a production function is explicit in the model, this can be used to generate estimates of capacity utilisation. What happens to capacity utilisation in a simulation is of key importance. If, for example, there is a permanent increase in utilisation, the price level is also shifted permanently, whereas if the utilisation effect is transitory, so is the price effect. Whether this is appropriate depends on whether the return to normal levels of capacity utilisation corresponds with a return of the model to equilibrium output and demand levels. If not, the absence of any further inflationary push from capacity utilisation may prevent the necessary adjustment from occurring.

The use of a production function also implies the idea of a normal level of capacity utilisation, although this normal level may change in response to factor prices or other economic factors. In principle, investment operates as an adjustment mechanism which ensures that normal capacity is regained (this mechanism is employed in the NIESR vintage capital framework). Other models, such as HMT, do explain capacity utilisation on the basis of a Cobb–Douglas production function, but there is no feedback from capacity utilisation to investment and hence back to capacity output. The BE model uses a third option, which estimates capacity utilisation as a distributed lag on manufacturing output. This formulation has the property that once output stabilises so does capacity utilisation. The LBS model uses yet another method, whereby capacity utilisation is proxied by the ratio of output to capital stock. However, capital stock adjusts very sluggishly to any shock, so the net result is a sustained change in capacity utilisation over simulation periods up to five years. At least, however, investment feedbacks are present which is more than can be said for another way of treating capacity utilisation also included in the LBS model. Here a direct measure of utilisation is employed in estimation, the CBI survey measure of spare capacity, but this is treated as exogenous in simulation.

Our conclusion is that the links between investment, prices and capacity output are not always well developed in the models. In some cases, the modelling of capacity utilisation has proceeded in an *ad hoc* way that may lead to unintended or implausible model properties. Lest this section should appear over-critical of the UK models, there is no evidence that models elsewhere have adopted a superior treatment.

4.6   The FEER and the NAIRU

The expressions for the FEER and the NAIRU can be combined to give equilibrium for the whole economy.

In earlier sections of this chapter we have set out how analysis of the wage and price system of the model can, in some circumstances, be solved to derive an estimate of the NAIRU, or equilibrium level of output conditional on an estimate of the real exchange rate, and how the trade equations can also be solved to give an estimate of the equilibrium real exchange rate, given equilibrium output. The NAIRU is the estimate of internal balance and the FEER that of external balance. They can therefore both be represented within a general framework which gives full equilibrium in the economy.

This follows the Salter–Swan diagram (Salter, 1959; Swan, 1960) and is shown in Figure 4.5. It should be emphasised that although, in discussing wage and price equations on the one hand, and trade equations on the other, we have referred to estimates of the NAIRU and the FEER as if they were single point estimates, the diagram makes clear that they are actually estimates of the respective schedules. Full equilibrium in the economy is given by the intersection of the two schedules.

The NAIRU schedule is the combination of values of unemployment or output at which inflation is stationary, so that competing claims are mutually consistent for each value of the real exchange rate. A high real exchange rate lowers import prices and hence reduces inflationary pressures in the economy. As a result, the equilibrium level of activity consistent with stable inflation rises. The NAIRU schedule therefore slopes downwards in real exchange rate/unemployment space.

The FEER schedule is the combination of points of the real exchange rate at which the current account is balanced while domestic demand exerts no pressure for change on the current account. A high value of the real exchange rate causes the current

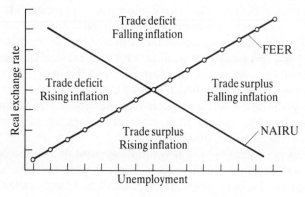

Figure 4.5   Internal and external balance

account to move into deficit, and this requires an increase in unemployment (decrease in demand) to bring the current account back into balance. Hence the FEER schedule slopes upwards to the right in the diagram.

We can now describe the diagram in terms of four quadrants which depict alternative disequilibrium positions. Positions above the FEER schedule are equated with a trade (or current account) deficit, for here the real exchange is too high in relation to the level of demand (unemployment) to give trade balance. Correspondingly, points below the FEER line are points of trade surplus. Points to the right of the NAIRU are positions where the level of unemployment is higher than that needed to ensure stable inflation, given the level of the exchange rate. Hence inflation is falling.

The quadrant to the left (below) the NAIRU and above the FEER schedule represents a combination of a trade deficit and rising inflation. It therefore requires higher unemployment to reduce inflation and this will also generate a movement towards trade balance, but may also require a real exchange rate adjustment. The position of the FEER and NAIRU schedules depends on all the exogenous influences that go into their derivation. These include the level of structural capital flows, which influences the sustainable current account, world economic activity, and exogenous wage-push and trade-account variables such as union power and trade specialisation. If tax rates determine the NAIRU, they also influence the final equilibrium of the economy.

This framework can be viewed as a useful way of summarising the properties of macroeconometric models. It does, however, require a substantial amount of model analysis, and there is also the possibility described in the earlier section of this chapter that it may not be possible to derive an expression for the NAIRU from the models.

 The FEER/NAIRU approach has its limitations and may be more suitable for medium-term rather than long-run analysis.

The methodologies of both the FEER and the NAIRU have been criticised. Some of the objections are reflections on possible shortcomings of the models themselves, while others are more in the spirit of criticisms of the basic approach.

We begin, however, with one positive benefit that such analyses have had on macroeconomic modelling. The inspection of the models necessary to produce the FEER and NAIRU estimates has in many cases shed light on existing inadequacies in the models, and helped to focus on some of the key issues.

One major issue that relates more specifically to the NAIRU is that of dynamic adjustment. If this is very sluggish, the long-run equilibrium may take some considerable time to be reached. If there is hysteresis in the wage equation, the long run may not be unique. Although the Layard–Nickell approach was developed to make the supply side of models more transparent, their explanations of changes in the supply side relate mainly to variables such as tax rates, skill mismatch, benefits and unionisation. There is relatively little role for factors such as North Sea oil, and the approach does not have much to say about long-term trends in productivity and technology. Critics of the approach argue that to call the Layard–Nickell approach a treatment of the supply side is a misnomer, since most of the interesting potential features are hidden away in trends and constant terms. The new endogenous growth literature (e.g. Romer, 1986) emphasises the possibility of international convergence in the rates of growth of technical progress, and also suggests that the traditional distinction between trend and cycle is inappropriate for temporary disturbances for cycles may well end up having permanent effects. Recent work by Allen and Whitley (1994) suggests that investment may influence export performance, and although this mechanism is not yet routinely incorporated in empirical macroeconomic models, it could provide a link between technology and economic growth.

The Layard–Nickell approach may also be criticised in that it results in a reduced-form explanation, and this may be consistent with several alternative structures. The wage and price equations are not therefore true structural relationships, but quasi-reduced forms. A major omission from the Layard–Nickell approach is the determination of the long-run level of the inflation rate (or core rate). This arises if the domestic money stock is endogenous and if the model possesses static homogeneity in nominal variables. In such a system there may be no equilibrium inflation rate unless there are nominal–real interactions, due perhaps to nominal inertia. Otherwise the system has at least one unit root on the nominal side. This situation can be avoided if real wealth is influenced by inflation operating on financial assets fixed in nominal terms. A fixed money base may also provide sufficient information to tie down the inflation rate to a unique value. If this is true, the assumption of fixed nominal interest rates commonly adopted by the models is inappropriate, for a fixed money base requires endogenous interest rates.

Empirical estimates of the NAIRU (see Joyce and Wren-Lewis,1991) tend to show that the NAIRU tracks actual unemployment quite closely. This may actually be due to the statistical procedures adopted in estimation of the wage and price equations. These are often estimated in a form that ensures that the residuals from the equations are stationary and have zero mean. We would therefore expect the difference between the NAIRU and actual unemployment also to be stationary, since this is merely the combination of stationary sets of residuals. Furthermore, this approach ensures that the explanatory variables explain all the systematic changes in the NAIRU.

Discussion of whether exchange rates are overvalued begs the question as to how this is measured. Economists tend to use two main indicators. The first is purchasing power parity (PPP) and the second is that of fundamental exchange rates (FEER). Neither is uncontroversial. PPP essentially tries to compare the price of the same basket of goods in different countries. It is based on the idea that competition will tend to drive prices of identical goods together. One major problem with this approach is that it tends to concentrate on prices of traded goods and ignores elements of non-price competition. On the one hand, it is more difficult to justify the PPP approach in a world of differentiated products and imperfect competition, but on the other hand, it is argued that PPP is a reliable long-run tendency, since the ability of companies to move their location from one country to another may well generate a long-run tendency to restore price relativities.

In contrast, the FEER approach can deliver real exchange rates that can move significantly against each other in the long run, driven by considerations of current account balance. The calculation of the FEER is quite a complex task. It requires projections of equilibrium paths for domestic income, world commodity prices and the accumulation of overseas assets. It is often argued that the calculation of the FEER schedule is fraught with difficulties and uncertainties. One of the main uncertainties is the wide range of current account deficits that are sustainable, in the sense that they can continue to be financed without undue pressure on interest rates. An even more basic problem, referred to above, is that import and export price elasticities in the models are often surprisingly low, and it is reasonable to argue that these elasticities are biased downwards, especially with removal of trade barriers and movements towards freer trade opportunities. Downward bias of price elasticities may not matter unduly for forecasting trade volumes, but it matters considerably when calculating the price changes required to effect a given change in the current account: the effect is that the FEER calculations will exaggerate the degree of disequilibrium in the current exchange rate.

The conclusion is that one cannot rely overmuch on current estimates of the real overvaluation of the exchange rate at the time of ERM entry, and there are grounds for believing that estimates of the fundamental divergence of the actual from the equilibrium exchange rate are biased towards finding excessive disequilibrium. The case for a substantial depreciation is therefore weakened. Supporting evidence can be based on the observation that the UK has succeeded in attracting a significant proportion of international, mainly Japanese, direct investment. It is unlikely that this would have happened if the pound had been considered substantially overvalued. Wren-Lewis (1992) argues that the calculation of the FEER depends upon a view of structural capital flows, since these determine the required trend size of the current balance. Yet structural capital flows are really endogenous, since they also depend on the equilibrium exchange rate, which determines the opportunities for successful investment. The FEER might then be regarded as a medium-term rather than a long-term equilibrium concept.

 Despite its limitations, the FEER/NAIRU analysis does produce useful insights into the models and make them more transparent.

This section has shown how the NAIRU and FEER analysis can be brought together in a way that explains the full equilibrium of the model. The spirit of the approach sees these more as medium-term than long-term equilibrium concepts. The analysis, although difficult to produce, does offer some quite useful insights, having some modelling benefits as well as going some way towards making the workings of the models more transparent.

Further reading:

Cuthbertson, Hall and Taylor (1992), chapter 6
Layard, Nickell and Jackman (1991)
Carlin and Soskice (1990)
Hall (1994)

5 │ Methods of analysis

This chapter is concerned with methods of analysing models. It discusses rational expectations, stochastic simulations, optimal control and other methods commonly used. Real empirical exercises are used as illustrations.

This chapter is concerned not with the actual properties of models, but with methods that can be used to derive them. It is therefore a bit more technical in nature than the preceding chapters. It is aimed principally at the model-user, but also attempts to make some of the methods, and their shortcomings, more transparent to those more generally interested in the models. The chapter begins with a framework against which the various ideas can be discussed. It then describes simulation and analytical methods of deriving model properties. It deals with the handling of rational expectations and the treatment of uncertainty through stochastic simulations.

Why is there this issue of deriving model properties in the first place? It arises because models tend not to be constructed as whole systems whose properties are known in advance. In most cases, the model is estimated equation by equation, or sector by sector, and despite an overall conceptual and theoretical framework, there is no guarantee that the system properties actually correspond with those intended. Even in models such as LPL, which follows a tight theoretical specification, properties may not always correspond in practice with those expected. In addition, theoretical considerations often apply to qualitative priors, and quantitative results cannot always be derived a priori.

However this does not mean that analytical investigation of a model is not the most useful way of deriving a model's properties, and in this chapter we describe ways in which such analysis may not only help in setting out model properties, but also indicate conditions that may need to be imposed on the model in order to ensure that the desired properties arise.

By referring to 'desired' properties we indicate that modellers do have priors about what is a plausible or acceptable property of their model. The usual criteria are theoretical consistency and empirical validity, but different modellers may differ in the relative weights that they place on these two criteria. Theoretical considerations often relate more to long-run implications than to short-run responses.

128

If model properties are not defined *ex ante*, what methods are available for deducing them? Let us start with the basic linear framework.

5.1   Standard simulation methods

This section develops further the model framework set out in Chapter 2 to illustrate simulation methods in model handling.

The structural linear model contains relationships between current endogenous variables (y) and predetermined variables (z). These predetermined variables can include both exogenous variables and lagged endogenous variables. This can be set out in matrix notation as:

$$By_t + Cz_t = u_t \tag{5.1}$$

where u is a vector of disturbances, reflecting the fact that the equation does not hold exactly at all points in time.

If the equation is estimated by single-equation methods, the disturbances can be expected to satisfy certain conditions (e.g. zero mean, constant variance and normality). These properties only carry over automatically to the model equations when the equation is estimated over exactly the same period on which the model is based. The matrices B and C are the structural parameters of the model (marginal propensities, reaction coefficients, etc). Normalising on the diagonal elements of B implies that the ith equation can be said to determine the ith variable, but unless B is diagonal the model is really simultaneous.

To solve the model, we solve out for all the contemporaneous endogenous variables in terms of their lagged values and exogenous variables. This is the reduced form, and can be written:

$$y_t = \Pi z_t + y_t \tag{5.2}$$

where

$$\Pi = B^{-1}C \tag{5.3}$$

and

$$v_t = B^{-1}u_t \tag{5.4}$$

where the π matrix represents policy multipliers or ready reckoners. In other words, they measure the effects on the endogenous variables of a one unit change in the exogenous variables. With a linear model we can combine the ready reckoners to give the effects of a policy package: that is, the effect of more than one instrument change.

In forecasting, the disturbances would, in a correctly specified model, be set at their mean value of zero and the exogenous variables would be projected into the future. The forecast solution for the endogenous variables ($\hat{y}$) would then be given by:

$$\hat{y}_t = \Pi \hat{z}_t \tag{5.5}$$

Model solution becomes more complicated when we recognise that there are non-linear (e.g. log-linear) equations. Analytic solution methods are then no longer appropriate and iterative methods are used. There are several of these (see Fisher and Hughes-Hallett, 1987, for a comparison), but the most common method used in model solution in practice is the Gauss–Seidel method. This basically consists of taking an initial solution for the y variables, often their value in the last period, and solving for the model period by period using iterations which adjust the starting point for the next round by some proportion of the difference between the current value of the endogenous variables and their value in the previous iteration round. When this difference falls within a prescribed limit, we say that the model has converged. Solution then proceeds to the next period, using this period's solution as the starting point. This method proves robust over quite a variety of models, hence its popularity. In addition, it is very easy to program.

The non-linear model can be written as:

$$f(t_t, z_t, \alpha) = u_t \tag{5.6}$$

where α is the vector of parameters. An additional complication is to allow dynamic responses so that lagged values of the endogenous variables enter into the structural equations. We then distinguish between predetermined variables that are lagged endogenous variables, and exogenous variables (x). Thus:

$$f(y_t, y_{t-1}, x_t, \alpha) = u_t \tag{5.7}$$

The solution process proceeds as follows:

$$f(\tilde{y}_1, y_0, x_1, \alpha) = 0 \tag{5.8}$$

where the first period is solved conditional on values in the previous period, and current values of the exogenous variables. In period t the solution is:

$$f(\tilde{y}_t, \tilde{y}_{t-1}, x_t, \alpha) = 0 \tag{5.9}$$

In the dynamic model, therefore, the solution for the endogenous variables in period t depends on the solution in previous periods, $t - i$.

> Standard simulation methods consist of comparing a base solution of the model with one where one or more of the exogenous variables are perturbed.

Standard simulation analysis proceeds by comparing a base solution of the model with a solution where one or more of the exogenous variables are perturbed. Comparing the base and perturbed solutions then gives an estimate of the policy multiplier(s) if the exogenous variable is a policy instrument. In a non-linear model, the multipliers are potentially base dependent.

Reverting back to the linear form we have:

The base solution $\quad By_t + Cz_t = u_t \tag{5.10}$

The perturbed solution $By_t + C(\delta + Z_t) = u_t$ (5.11)

In this example the perturbation, δ, is constant, but there is no reason why it should not vary over time. If δ has only one non-zero element, the simulation corresponds to a single policy instrument response.

The normal mode of simulation is the dynamic one where, as noted above, the solutions for the current endogenous variables are computed using the calculated values of the endogenous variables in previous periods. This is the method used to describe most of the properties of models. When the simulation is carried out over a period of history where data on the current endogenous variables are available, the alternative static method of simulation is often used. This employs the actual values of the lagged endogenous variables, and corresponds in spirit with the OLS estimation approach. The role of dynamic versus static simulation in the tracking performance of models is discussed in Chapter 6.

> Static simulation uses actual values of the lagged variables in solution, whereas dynamic simulation uses calculated values.

5.2   Long-run properties

> An interest in the long-run properties of a model is associated with an interest in its supply side, since the two are intrinsically connected. The model must often have a well-defined long run if it is to be solved under rational expectations.

One of the key issues in model analysis is the derivation of the long-run properties of a given model. As described in Chapter 3, these are often equivalent to determining the supply-side of the model. In rational expectations models, discussed in this chapter, it is often necessary for a model to have a stable well-defined long run, or saddlepath, if a solution to the model is to be obtained. In some cases, the steady-state properties of the model can be used to choose its terminal conditions. It is, in any case, of interest to know if the model settles down to a new equilibrium following a shock.

In discussing long-run properties of models, we need to distinguish between short- and long-run equilibrium. Short-run equilibrium can be identified with flow equilibrium where stock adjustment may be incomplete, whereas the long-run equilibrium is where stocks of assets adjust fully. Determining the long run requires that the model is stable, and this may be a focus of interest in its own right.

> The concept of the long run in macroeconometric models is not unique, depending on whether flow or stock adjustment is assumed to be complete.

Relevant economic theory is typically of an equilibrium or comparative static kind and has relatively little to say about dynamic adjustment. In dynamic single-equation models, such comparisons are commonplace. Procedures for carrying out the same analysis in dynamic linear simultaneous models are also well established. However, practical models are non-linear and alternative methods have to be applied. There are several which are relevant:

1. Direct inspection/linearisation.
2. Use of an extended solution path.
3. Constructing a steady-state version of the model.
4. Analytical investigation of sub-sectors.
5. Decomposition of the reduced form.

> There are several methods available for deriving the 'long-run' properties of models: direct inspection; extended solution path; steady-state models; sub-sector analysis; and decomposition of the reduced form. There is no one preferred method.

They all have advantages and disadvantages in use, and there is no one preferred method. However, experience at the Warwick Bureau has shown that some methods may be more appropriate to certain types of model than others.

Direct inspection

> Linearisation of the model can enable its roots to be explicitly calculated.

In this method, long-run properties can be derived from inspection of the model. For this to be possible, the model has to be small and expressed in a way closely related to economic theory. The problem with this method is that inspection does not guarantee that the long-run solution actually corresponds with this. However, method 4, which uses direct analytical inspection of sub-sectors, can be quite informative. A more fruitful approach can be local linearisation of the model. This uses analytical linear techniques to determine the roots of the model. The nature of these roots can determine not only if there is a long-run solution to the model, but also the nature of adjustment to it. In particular, we may be interested in whether the model is unstable or not (i.e. whether the roots lie inside the unit circle). However, many linearisation techniques require the model to be initially stable. This may require the initial model to be reformulated. An example of the linearisation method is the study by Barrell *et al.* (1992), which was applied to the GEM multicountry model.

Unfortunately, many 'linearised' versions of non-linear models have properties that are different from the original non-linear model. If these differences are due to the non-linearity itself, an important element of the original model has been discarded. Although linearisation techniques are regularly applied to large models, there are several different methods available and there is a lack of comparative evidence on which to base the sensitivity of the results to the method applied. Most of the methods rely on using the simulation responses of the non-linear model to generate the information set on which the linear model is formed.

When dealing with a system of linear equations, we can calculate single-equation roots to determine the properties of single-equation solutions, and the roots of the characteristic polynomial to determine the properties of the system. In general, one cannot use the roots of individual equations to infer the properties of the dynamic system; nor can one attribute system roots to individual equations. However, in principle, the system set of roots are functions of the coefficients of the system. It is often found that individual roots can be associated with particular coefficients (e.g. Kuh, Neese and Hollinger, 1985).

In a non-linear system the roots are not defined, except for a linearisation which is state dependent. By considering a linearisation, we may be able to inspect local stability from a first-order approximation to the system. But there is an inherent weakness. It is conventional to linearise around a stable base trajectory. If this is not done, the base itself may generate unstable roots. If any stable trajectory can be obtained for the linearisation procedure, the system must have at least one stable solution. Stability also depends on the form in which the model is expressed. For example, the price level might not be stationary, whereas its first difference, the rate of inflation, might.

Extended solution path

 The extended solution path of a model involves solving the model over longer and longer periods until it appears to have stabilised.

Models tend to be simulated only over relatively short time horizons, often only up to five years for a quarterly model. The length of this period is typically too short to determine whether the model has settled down to its long-run steady state, especially if a stock equilibrium is to be reached. Extending the simulation over a longer time period may allow this steady state to be observed. This approach assumes that the model has a steady state to which it will settle down, and if it does not, no amount of extension of the solution periods will find one. In the case of a model expressed only in terms of first differences, for example, there is no long-run solution (i.e. the roots lie on the unit circle). Alternatively, it might appear that the model has settled down to a new solution, but this might not be the case. The incentive to explore the simulation path further will then be removed and wrong inferences may be drawn. Even if the model possesses a steady state, it may require a very extended sample period to derive it. This is particularly true if the process of stock adjustment is very protracted. The main problem here is often the construction of the base simulation itself, since it may result in non-admissible solution values, such as negative unemployment, as the model is taken some way outside its sample experience.

This approach is most useful where the model exhibits highly unstable behaviour, since this can be readily identified. It is, however, another matter to be able to specify the source of the observed model instability. The main problem with this approach is

133

that, unless there is a clear a priori view of what the new equilibrium or steady state should be, conclusions are highly judgemental. They rely on simple inspection of the simulation path (or differences), probably for a small subset of variables. There are no objective criteria, although it is possible to use rules of thumb, such as the fact that change in endogenous variables from the base path in successive periods is less than the convergence criteria applied to the model solution.

The construction of an extended base takes some care. The exogenous variables in models of national economies usually fall into three main groups: domestic economic policy variables, various external trends such as demographic variables, and variables describing the environment in the rest of the world economy. These must all be projected forward at chosen growth rates in an internally consistent manner, obeying relevant identities and restrictions on the range of variables. In a relatively open model, with a large number of exogenous variables, it is necessary to ensure that any implicit relations among these variables are satisfied in projected data; these are automatically satisfied, in principle, in the historical data, but they are not usually included specifically in the model equations. Consistent assumptions about fiscal and monetary policy stance are required, noting theoretical results such as the intrinsic potential dynamic instability under bond finance.

Steady-state approach

> The steady-state approach involves collapsing the dynamics of the model to give a formulation in terms of either levels or growth rates.

This approach involves constructing a steady-state version of the model, equation by equation, and then solving this model directly using standard non-linear techniques.

The long-run implications of a single-equation dynamic model are usually summarised by the corresponding static equilibrium model, bearing in mind that this is of little interest unless the dynamic model is stable. For the simple autogressive-distributed lag model,

$$y_t = a + \sum_{j=1}^{r} b_j * y_{t-j} + \sum_{j=0}^{s} c_j * x_{t-j} + u_t \tag{5.12}$$

the deterministic static equilibrium is:

$$y^* = \frac{\sum c_j}{1 - \sum b_j} x^* \tag{5.13}$$

An alternative way of expressing this is to define polynomials in the lag operator, $b(L)$ and $c(L)$, where:

$$b(L) = 1 - \sum_{j=1}^{r} b_j L^j \tag{5.14}$$

and

$$c(L) = \sum_{j=0}^{s} c_j L^j \tag{5.15}$$

The model may then be written as:

$$b(L)y_t = a + c(L)x_t + u_t \tag{5.16}$$

The stability condition is then that the roots of the equation $b(z) = 0$ satisfy $|z| > 1$ and the long-run multiplier is $c(1)/b(1)$.

A model containing current and lagged values of variables can be rearranged into a model in terms of first differences, and the remaining levels terms can be handled in a variety of ways. Bewley (1979) suggests the following transformation:

$$1 - \sum b_j y_t = a + \sum_{j=0}^{r} - 1b_j^* \Delta y_{t-j} + \sum c_j x_t + \sum_{j=0}^{s} - 1c_j^* \Delta x_{t-j} + u_t \tag{5.17}$$

$$b_j^* = -(h_{j\mid 1} + \cdots + b_T) \tag{5.18}$$

and

$$c_j^* = -(c_{j+1} + \cdots + c_s) \tag{5.19}$$

so that, on renormalising the equation, a direct estimate of the long-run coefficient and its standard error can be obtained by regressing y on x and current and lagged first differences of x and y (using an instrumental variable estimator). Alternatively, we can write:

$$\Delta y_t = a + \sum_{j=1}^{r-1} b_j \Delta y_{t-j} + b_t y_{t-r} + \sum_{j=0}^{s-1} c_j \Delta_{t-j} + c_s x_{t-s} + u_t \tag{5.20}$$

where

$$b_j = (1 - b_1 - \cdots - b_j)$$
$$c_j = (c_0 + \cdots + c_j) \tag{5.21}$$

so that the remaining levels variables appear with the maximum lag in the model. Then the long-run coefficient is simply given by the ratio of the coefficients on these levels terms (with the sign reversed on the b coefficient); thus an equation only containing first difference terms would have no long-run static equilibrium.

Care has to be taken in interpreting dynamic relations if there are implicit expectations terms. A common justification for dynamic models is that economic agents react to forecasts of a variable, or estimates of an unobserved component of a variable, as an extrapolation of past observations.

$$b(L)y_t = a + \Theta \hat{x}_{t+1,t} + u_t \tag{5.22}$$

‖ Care has to be taken where the dynamics reflect expectations mechanisms.

where x_{t+1}^e is the one-step-ahead forecast of x in $t+1$, formed in period t. If x follows the autoregressive process:

$$x_t = \phi_1 x_{t-1} + \cdots + \phi_p x_{t-p} + \varepsilon_t \tag{5.23}$$

then the forecast of x, based on current and lagged values of x alone, is:

$$x_{t+1,t}^e = \phi_1 x_t + \cdots + \phi_p x_{t-p+1} \tag{5.28}$$

Substituting this into the original model gives a series of terms in lagged values of x and the long-run coefficient is then calculated as $c(1)/b(1)$. This does not correspond with the long-run implied by the original model, which is:

$$\Theta/b(1)$$
$$\phi_1 + \cdots + \phi_p = 1 \tag{5.25}$$

and only corresponds if the above condition is met: that is, the autoregression has a unit root, representing a difference stationary process, as Kelly (1985) notes.

A dynamic equilibrium in which variables have common constant growth rates is often of interest, corresponding to constant inflation or steady-state growth, for example. When the dynamic equation is in log-linear form, which is often the case, it can be rewritten in growth rate form. If the theory suggests that in equilibrium y and x are in constant proportions to each other (say, $y = kx$) then in a log-linear equation there is a long-run coefficient of 1. This can be imposed by writing the dynamic model (with $r = s$) as:

$$\Delta \ln y_t = a + \sum b_j \Delta \ln y_{t-j} + \sum \dot{c}_j \Delta \ln x_{t-j} - \dot{c}_s(\ln y_{t-s} - \ln x_{t-s}) + u_t \tag{5.26}$$

which is a model of the form used by Sargan (1964) and Davidson et al. (1978), subsequently known as the error correction model. In dynamic equilibrium, the coefficient of proportionality, k, depends on the growth rate, g.

The connection between these models and commonly observed features of time-series models is associated with the concept of an integrated series, as is explained by Granger (1981). If y and x are integrated or difference stationary, there exists a constant A such that

$$w_t = y_t - A x_t \tag{5.27}$$

and y and x are said to be co-integrated. The concept that y and x move together corresponds with a long-run equilibrium relation.

In the direct solution method, the dynamics of the individual equations are collapsed to give a steady-state version of the model, implicit expectations being ignored as above. Converting the model to a steady state in this way increases the degree of dependence among the endogenous variables, since what might have been a lagged relationship in the original dynamic model now becomes a contemporaneous one in the steady-state model.

Several issues have to be tackled before the steady-state exercise can be completed.

A static long-run equilibrium presents difficulties for the typical dynamic model, which contains various stock-flow identities. For example, the PSBR may be financed by a mixture of bonds and money. A static equilibrium would require that the stocks of bonds and money are constant, which would in turn require that the PSBR is zero. Unless the tax rate is to be varied to satisfy this condition, this would in turn require that government expenditure itself is stationary. A more realistic approach is to specify a steady-state growth path. Here government spending can grow, the only requirement then being that it is financed in such a way that the ratio of bonds to money is constant (the general issue of fiscal solvency and the possibility of debt explosion is discussed below and in Chapter 8). The steady-state growth path is one where there is constant growth in real variables, constant inflation and a constant unemployment rate.

In a relatively closed model, some variables treated as exogenous in the original dynamic model may now be treated endogenously. A particular example is the use of a policy reaction function to achieve closure of the model: for example, to ensure that the public sector deficit remains a constant proportion of GDP. Other variables outside the policy domain might also be endogenised by using simple rules that ensure consistency between them. Emphasis on the steady state focuses attention on issues of policy closure, features which might be neglected in standard simulation exercises.

In the direct solution approach, an exogenous variable data set at a single point of time is all that is required for solution. The solution of the model itself is not of great interest, since the growth solution is largely imposed upon the model. The features that are of interest might be the steady-state unemployment rate, and other key ratios such as the wealth–income ratio.

> The steady-state method requires internally consistent projections of the
> exogenous variables.

An example of this approach is a study on the CUBS model by Wallis and Whitley (1987), and this is briefly summarised here. It was motivated by the finding that the dynamic version of the CUBS model was unstable, and by the desire to trace the source of this instability. The results of the exercise were also contrasted with the extended simulation path approach. Although this is a particular example some general modelling issues emerge.

The exercise with the CUBS model first used the extended simulation base approach, with exogenous variables projected smoothly over the period 1984–2039. The key assumptions were that real variables grew at 3 per cent p.a., with 3 per cent inflation. The instability of inflation in the model was immediately apparent (see Figure 5.1). The inspection of the price equation in the model suggested that the source of the problem was the size of the elasticity of the money stock. When this was reduced by one-half, the long-run base of the CUBS model appeared stable.

However, additional problems were soon apparent when the steady-state model was considered. In particular, the steady-state version of the CUBS model was not consistent with balanced growth. Four areas of the model required amendment.

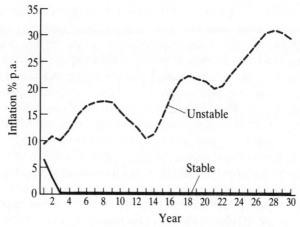

Figure 5.1 CUBS model: dynamic features
Source: Wallis and Whitley (1987)

Production function

The use of a KLEM production function of the form:

$$Y = F(K, L, E, M) \qquad (5.28)$$

where Y is output, K is capital stock, L is labour force, E is energy and M is raw materials, requires the output variable to be defined as gross. However, the CUBS model used the net output definition, and although the model possessed constant returns to scale in respect of capital and labour, the presence of a term in energy results in increasing returns to scale overall, which prevents balance in net output, capital and labour. The solution adopted by Wallis and Whitley was to drop the energy term from the production function.

Time trend in the capital stock equation

The structural equations for labour demand and capital in the CUBS model contained terms in both factors, the presence of a time trend in the capital stock equation reflecting embodied technical progress. However, in order for the model to produce balanced growth in labour and capital, the size of the coefficient on the time trend had to be reduced.

Price equation

In steady-state growth, we require that the growth rate of prices is identically equal to the growth of money less the rate of growth of output (money neutrality). This condition required the calculation of the appropriate coefficient on money in the price equation.

Financing of the PSBR

The relationship between the PSBR and money and bond finance was rewritten by Wallis and Whitley to ensure that money and bonds grew at the same rate, to maintain a constant ratio of money to bonds (portfolio balance). This illustrates a difficulty in completely eliminating all dynamic relationships in a steady-state model, since the PSBR determines the change in the money stock but it is the *proportionate* change in money that determines the inflation rate.

The steady-state model was then solved using a set of (1984) values of the exogenous variables. It produced the following steady-state results:

Output growth	0.95% p.a.
Inflation	6.7% p.a.
Money growth	7.7% p.a.
Unemployment rate	13%
Ratio of PSBR/GDP	3.9%

Solving the steady-state model over a sequence of periods rather than at one point in time verifies that the steady-state solution does in fact produce balanced growth. Having constructed a steady-state model, it is then possible to derive its properties by perturbing exogenous variables. The steady-state responses reveal that demand expansion has no effect on output, but the implied equilibrium rate of unemployment can be shifted by supply-side instruments such as the rate of unemployment benefit. Although the dynamic responses from the amended CUBS model are similar to the steady-state properties, some differences remained, suggesting that dynamic features can prevent or distort the path to the longer-run equilibrium.

Analytical investigation of sub-sectors

 This involves examining the properties of the model, sector by sector.

In some ways this method of examining model properties is very similar to the steady-state method. In essence it is based on the assumption that, while the model may be simultaneous, there is a greater degree of simultaneity within certain blocks of equations than between different equation blocks. This often corresponds to the approach adopted in estimation, where some explanatory variables will be treated as endogenous but others as predetermined. An obvious example would be factor demand functions. Clearly, economic theory has a strong role to play in choosing the appropriate blocks. There is always the trade-off that selection of too large a block may not lead to any great gains compared with analysis of the complete model. On the other hand, the selection of too small a block may eliminate too much of the simultaneous interaction between equations to provide an adequate guide to understanding the full model. Once the relevant block has been selected, there are a variety of ways of analysing its contribution to the model.

One possible approach is to construct a static long-run or steady-state growth version of the sector as described above. Two examples of this are given below, and relate to the determination of the implied NAIRU and FEER. Equally, it is possible to analyse the dynamic responses of the equations within the block, perhaps with a view to seeing whether adjustment to the long run is relatively rapid or sluggish.

An alternative is to linearise the relevant equations and then compute the roots of the equations treated as a block. An example of this is given in Wallis *et al.* (1984), where the focus of interest was the CUBS model of the labour market.

A third possibility is to use partial simulation to 'block out' the rest of the model, leaving only the sector of interest to be solved endogenously. Partial simulation involves exogenising feedbacks to the rest of the model from the chosen block of equations. It is important to distinguish between exogenisation as a tool of model analysis and exogenisation techniques as part of policy analysis. This is described more fully in Chapter 7. The partial simulation approach was used in the study by Wallis *et al.* (1984) as a check upon the linear analysis. We describe two other applications here. One is the use of partial simulation analysis to identify the implied *IS/LM* schedules in US models, as used in Klein (1991). The second is partial simulation analysis to decompose the government expenditure multiplier in the UK models.

The usefulness of the 'block' approach lies in its ability to predict the full-model implications of changes to exogenous variables. The NAIRU method described in Chapter 4 appears particularly useful, but it depends upon homogeneity being present in order to rewrite the equations in the relevant manner. Another interesting example is where the analysis of just one equation, and moreover the inspection of one coefficient, can enable useful insights to be gained into the supply-side properties of the model. The coefficient on tax terms in the wage equation proves of enormous value in predicting the nature of the supply-side response of the model, as shown in Chapter 3.

Decomposition of the government expenditure multiplier using partial simulation analysis

 In this example, we show how partial simulation analysis can be used to highlight the relative importance of different structural features of models.

Partial simulation involves exogenising particular variables in the model to prevent feedbacks. The role of exogenisation is considered more formally in Chapter 7. Knowing which variables to exogenise requires some prior understanding of the basic transmission mechanisms in the models. The particular example that we discuss is based on a government expenditure simulation on the UK models of autumn 1990 vintage.

As we have emphasised throughout the book, it is far easier, and also more useful, to have some sort of framework in mind when attempting to interpret model

Table 5.1 Decomposition of the government expenditure multiplier

	Year 1	Year 2	Year 3	Year 4	Year 5
HMT:					
Basic multiplier	0.87	0.81	0.86	0.88	0.91
Multiplier and accelerator	0.92	0.91	0.92	0.94	0.90
Constant competitiveness	0.96	1.07	1.19	1.29	1.38
Full model	0.99	1.06	1.12	1.11	1.02
NIESR:					
Basic multiplier	0.91	1.02	1.10	1.16	1.20
Multiplier and accelerator	1.01	1.17	1.26	1.33	1.38
Constant competitiveness	1.29	1.71	1.66	1.47	1.11
Full model	1.84	2.21	1.32	0.62	0.40
LBS:					
Basic multiplier	0.82	0.92	0.94	0.97	1.00
Multiplier and accelerator	0.86	0.96	0.98	1.01	1.03
Constant competitiveness	0.91	1.10	1.17	1.11	1.00
Full model	1.08	1.64	1.69	1.63	1.63

properties. In this case we use standard textbook analysis of the government expenditure multiplier.

This analysis starts by looking at the simple multiplier of the form:

$$\frac{\Delta Y}{\Delta G} = \frac{1}{1 - c(1 - t) + m} \tag{5.29}$$

where Y is output, G is government expenditure, c is the marginal propensity to consume, t is the marginal tax rate and m is the marginal propensity to import. This multiplier is shown as the first row of the table for each model. Simple textbook analysis would suggest that this multiplier is above unity. The numbers in the table are derived from simulating a government expenditure shock, holding wages, prices, exchange rates, investment and stockbuilding fixed. The multiplier values for HMT are all below unity, those for NIESR above, and those for LBS around unity. In the case of HMT, the low basic multiplier is associated with a low marginal propensity to consume and very sluggish adjustment. In turn, the LBS multiplier is low relative to NIESR because much of the change in income is in the form of company undistributed profits, which do not feed through to personal income and to consumption. Two offsetting features hide other important differences for LBS: first, there is a very high marginal indirect tax content of government expenditure; and second, there is a negative(!) marginal import content.

The next stage is to start from the first simulation, but in addition to allow investment and stockbuilding equations to be reintroduced. This simulation can then be described as giving the combined multiplier and accelerator response of the model.

We would expect the total multiplier to increase, since the accelerator effects should augment the basic multiplier. This expectation is fulfilled, but the accelerator effects are clearly quite weak in the HMT and LBS models. The reason why the accelerator is so low in the HMT model is that most of the higher demand arises in the public sector and so does not generate additional investment. Moreover, the marginal import content of the higher level of private investment and stockbuilding that does arise is relatively high. The LBS accelerator effects are very weak because output does not appear in the investment equations. In contrast, there are quite powerful accelerator effects in the NIESR model. Some of this arises from the relatively large increase in private sector output from the basic multiplier response.

We now allow for inflation effects in the model. Consequently, the wage and price equations in the models are re-endogenised and the simulation rerun.

However, the exchange rate is assumed to be fixed in real terms. This is in order to isolate the role of the exchange rate and to distinguish general inflation effects from those arising from changes in competitiveness. We would expect, a priori, the impact of higher inflation to dampen the multiplier, but this does not occur for the HMT model at all. In the case of LBS and NIESR, the negative impact on the multiplier occurs only after several years. In the case of HMT, this rather surprising result arises because of increases in housing wealth that raise consumption (see Chapter 3 for further explanation of this particular mechanism). If house prices only rose in line with general prices in the economy, however, the multiplier would remain around unity, very similar to its value in the previous variant simulation. This suggests that there is very little inflation crowding out in the HMT model. Inflation effects might be somewhat greater if we adopted an alternative monetary policy assumption. Since we have assumed constant nominal interest rates, inflation will tend to reduce real interest rates and raise private expenditure, where real interest rate effects are present. Inflation tends to raise the multiplier for most of the simulation period in the LBS model, since it shifts the distribution of income towards wage-earners and hence raises personal income and expenditure. Finally, we can observe that the introduction of inflation effects into the NIESR model significantly raises the multiplier over the first three to four years of the simulation. This again reflects the monetary policy assumption. Lower real interest rates induce the fairly large accelerator response of fixed investment and stockbuilding in the model. As the price level rises, however, the real value of wealth diminishes and reduces consumer demand permanently, whereas when inflation settles down the impact on real interest rates and investment wears off.

The final step in calculating the multiplier response is to reintroduce the exchange rate equation. We now have a full-model simulation with complete interaction between the model variables. This lowers the multiplier response in the HMT and (particularly) NIESR models, but raises it substantially in the LBS model. The sensitivity of the models to the introduction of the exchange rate equation shows the key role that this equation plays in the models, and how differences in the exchange rate can lead to differences in full-model properties. We do not attempt to describe the differences in exchange rate equations here, for they have been discussed in Chapters 3 and 4. What we do emphasise is how a simple description of the models from their full-model simulation properties can be misleading. For example, one might be tempted to classify the LBS model as Keynesian from its model simulation results and to regard the NIESR model as much less so. But the decomposition of the multiplier actually shows far more Keynesian influence in the NIESR model than in that of LBS; it is the role of the exchange rate which disguises these differences in structure.

Derivation of the slopes of the IS/LM schedules

In this example, Green *et al.* in the volume of comparative essays on US models edited by Klein (1991), attempt to derive partial slopes of the *IS/LM* schedules and *AD/AS* schedules of the US models. In many respects, there are strong similarities with the example above. One important point to note is that, unlike textbook models, dynamic adjustment means that the schedules may shift over time, so that there is no such thing as *the IS* slope, etc. Here we concentrate on their findings on *IS/LM* schedules, with emphasis on the methodological approach. The approach is illustrated in Figures 5.2 and 5.3.

Consider an expansionary shift in the *IS* schedule (i.e. a move to the right). This raises output and interest rates in the standard static model from the initial position of y_0, r_0 to y_1, r_1. The slope of the *LM* schedule as given by AB/BE is then traced out. However, with endogenous prices, the *LM* schedule is likely to shift to the left so that the simulation response will actually measure AF/DF, which is clearly a biased measure of the *LM* slope.

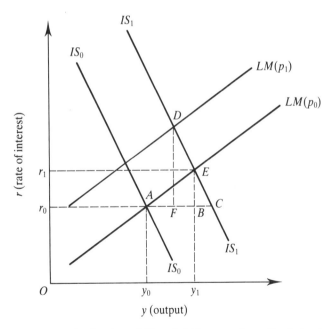

Figure 5.2 Derivation of *IS* and *LM* curves for a fiscal shock

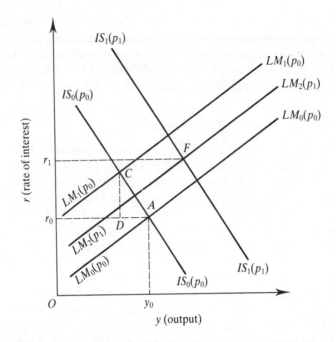

Figure 5.3   Derivation of *IS* and *LM* curves for a monetary shock

To eliminate the shift in the *LM* schedule, the fiscal shock simulation can be carried out under a fixed-price-level assumption which approximates point *E*. Alternatively, the fiscal shock can be used to trace out the slope of the *IS* curve, by calculating the shock with base-level interest rates (r_0) and price level (p_0) with the slope given by *BC/BE* (this is similar to the decomposition of the multiplier in the example above). Green *et al.* conduct the experiment by calculating the shock around the initial *IS* schedule, recomputing the simulation under the base level of government spending and the value of interest rates from the original full-model simulation of the fiscal shock.

Now imagine a (negative) monetary shock which moves the *LM* schedule from LM_0 to LM_1 and hence moves the equilibrium from point *A* to point *C*. The slope of the *IS* schedule is given as *AD/CD* (Figure 5.3). However, following changes in the price level, both *IS* and *LM* schedules may shift further, resulting in a final equilibrium F and hence a biased measure of the shift in the *IS* schedule. This is resolved by solving the simulation under a fixed price level. The slope of the *LM* schedule may also be calculated from this simulation by fixing the money supply at its initial position and solving the system, given the value of income from the full-model simulation.

Thus we have three different ways of isolating each schedule (two of which relate to whether the direct estimate of the schedule is computed around the initial or perturbed schedule). In principle, all three methods should give the same result. If not, interdependencies exist which have not been eliminated. One example of this is where a change in the stock of money through the shift in the *LM* schedule may change wealth, and hence consumption and the *IS* schedule. In general, Green *et al.* find that such interdependencies are quite small, given that results are similar for different methods of isolating the slopes of the curves (although they do not consider evaluating the slope of the perturbed schedules directly). However, they also find that the *IS* schedules are typically quite steep and the *LM* schedules quite flat. This would tend to imply that biases of the estimate of the *IS* schedule due to shifts in the *LM* schedule would be small if the *LM* schedule was itself flat. One problem with the application of the method of Green *et al.* to UK models is in the ability to simulate a shift in the *LM* schedule. This is because the supply of money is not often an exogenous variable. Hence work tends to follow the method described in the multiplier decomposition example.

 US results tend to suggest that the *IS* schedule is steep and the *LM* schedule relatively flat.

Decomposition of the reduced form

 This uses relationships, such as ratios, between endogenous variables in the reduced form to analyse the model.

In some cases, the model-user may not have the structural information to analyse model blocks, or may not have access to the model to conduct partial simulations. The only available information might be the results of full-model simulation experiments with the model: that is, the reduced-form properties. Alternatively, the model-user may explicitly wish to concentrate on the full-system properties of the model, in order to estimate the nature of any trade-off between endogenous variables. We give two examples of this approach. The first was used to analyse the supply side of the Nordic models in a comparative exercise, and also in comparing the supply-side response of multicountry models. This example is also useful in the insights that it gives into the state of modelling in these areas. The second example concerns the evaluation of trade-offs, in this case the trade-off between unemployment and inflation. This is an obvious issue of policy concern, and can be interpreted as yet another way of examining the implicit supply curve of the model. There are some important differences between the two examples. Whereas the decomposition of reduced-form responses requires only one full-model simulation, the trade-off approach requires several simulation experiments.

 This approach is useful when further simulation analysis is not possible; it can then give a rough approximation to the contribution of various relationships in the model to the overall supply response.

An example of decomposition of the reduced form is based on the study by Whitley (1992a) on multicountry models, and it was earlier applied to models of the Nordic economies in Wallis and Whitley (1991a). It is aimed at understanding the aggregate supply response. It starts from the idea that a demand shock to the model will trace out the aggregate supply schedule. The main problem is that we need to assume that the position of the aggregate supply schedule remains unchanged. The change in the slope of the aggregate supply schedule is given by the ratio of the price response to that of output (i.e. the inverse of the aggregate supply elasticity). Given that the short-run schedule may be different from the long-run schedule, we need to allow that this response may vary over time. Under a demand shock, the main reason why the aggregate supply schedule may itself shift is a change in the real exchange rate (see the discussion of the supply side in Chapters 3 and 4). This is largely neglected in the examples, but the scale of the change in the real exchange rate can be observed and used as a guide to the validity of the approximation. Hickman (1988) in the Brookings study of multicountry models showed that the price–output response could be decomposed into various ratios of key endogenous variables, which themselves bore a close relation to structural relationships in the model. Thus we can write:

$$\Delta P / \Delta Y = (\Delta P / \Delta W) . (\Delta W / \Delta U) . (\Delta U / \Delta N) . (\Delta N / \Delta Y) \tag{5.30}$$

where Δ denotes percentage deviations from the baseline simulation, P is the price level, Y is the level of output, W is the level of wages, U is the unemployment rate and N is employment. If the models were block recursive, each component of this expression could be identified with part of the structure. Thus the first term, the ratio of prices to wages, would be associated principally with the size of the cost mark-up in price equations; the second term, the ratio of wages to unemployment, with the demand effect on wages (the wage equation); the third term, the ratio of unemployment to employment, with labour force participation; and the final term, the ratio of employment to output, with productivity changes (the employment equation). We would expect the first and final terms to be positive: that is, prices rise as wages rise, and employment rises as output rises. The expectation is that the middle two terms are negatively signed: lower unemployment raises wages, and higher employment reduces unemployment.

In practice, of course, each of the variables is endogenous and jointly determined, implying that the various ratios are not independent of each other. Interpretation of the ratios as structural features is valid only if the feedbacks from the rest of the model are minor. This is not always the case. For example, productivity may enter directly into the determination of real wages, so that the first and last ratios on the right-hand side of the expression above are interdependent.

The identification of this as a supply-side framework is also dependent on the supply schedule itself being invariant to the shock, and this is invalidated if the real exchange rate changes. This may occur in models which have a NAIRU under a demand shock, as described in Chapter 4. The Hickman decomposition method is only a very crude approximation, but used with care, it has been found to be useful in interpreting model responses. It has the advantage that the outside user of the model only requires some basic model simulation results. It can also throw light on dynamic adjustment, which is neglected by the methods that use static or steady-state model properties.

Table 5.2 Contributions to the aggregate supply elasticity: multicountry models (year 6)

		$\Delta P/\Delta W$ (1)	$\Delta W/\Delta U$ (2)	$\Delta U/\Delta N$ (3)	$\Delta N/\Delta Y$ (4)	$\Delta P/\Delta Y$ (5)	AS (6)
DIW	GE	0.88	−6.85	−0.80	0.55	2.64	0.38
	FR	0.08	−1.10	−0.76	0.56	0.04	25.00[a]
	IT	0.98	−8.34	−0.63	0.71	3.67	0.22
	UK	0.88	−4.55	−0.78	0.44	1.38	0.72
GEM	GE	0.95	−1.61	−0.88	0.77	1.04	0.96
	FR	0.93	−8.50	−0.15	0.90	1.03	0.97
	IT	0.63	−3.80	−1.00	0.47	1.13	0.89
	UK	0.99	−8.90	−0.43	0.79	3.03	0.33
OECD	GE	1.05	25.88[a]	−0.80	−2.00[a]	43.40[a]	0.02
	FR	1.15	−8.12	−0.57	0.42	2.24	0.45
	IT	0.93	−5.45	−0.96	0.48	2.33	0.43
	UK	1.10	−7.44	−1.17	0.51	4.91	0.21
OEF	GE	0.78	−2.28	−0.86	0.97	1.49	0.67
	FR	0.68	−2.46	−0.78	1.03	1.35	0.74
	IT	1.12	−3.86	−0.65	1.28	3.61	0.28
	UK	1.11	−4.31	−0.47	1.17	2.63	0.38
MIMOSA	GE	0.76	−6.81	−0.86	0.70	3.15	0.32
	FR	0.19	−1.49	−0.70	0.64	0.13	7.88[a]
	IT	0.64	−5.66	−0.87	0.55	1.73	0.58
	UK	1.13	−5.24	−0.63	0.87	3.22	0.31
Average		0.85	−5.09	−0.74	0.73	2.15	0.47

Notes:
[a] Excluded from total
$\Delta P/\Delta W$: ratio of prices to wages
$\Delta W/\Delta U$: ratio of wages to unemployment rate
$\Delta U/\Delta N$: ratio of unemployment rate to employment
$\Delta N/\Delta Y$: ratio of employment to GDP
$\Delta P/\Delta Y$: ratio of prices (GDP deflator) to GDP
AS: aggregate suppy elasticity = $1/(\Delta P/\Delta Y)$
All variables measured as percentage difference from base (except unemployment rate: absolute difference from base).
Columns (1) × (2) × (3) × (4) = (5) subject to rounding.

Source: Whitley (1992a)

In the example using multicountry models (Table 5.2), the contributions to the aggregate supply elasticity are set out. Here we concentrate on results after the sixth year of a government expenditure shock simulation. If the supply schedule is vertical, we would expect to observe a value of the *AS* elasticity close to zero. The finding that in two cases, DIW and MIMOSA, both for France, the *AS* elasticity is well above unity suggests that the *AS* schedule is very flat. The other simulations suggest a relatively inelastic supply schedule, but one which is not vertical. The first column of the table, which shows the ratio between price and wage responses, gives values close to unity, suggesting that wage costs are fully transmitted to prices. However, the two outliers identified above, have very low values for this elasticity, and this explains the weak transmission of inflationary pressures in these models. Similarly, the third column, which shows the relative response of employment to unemployment, tends to show some consensus towards values of -1; implying that changes in employment are fully reflected in (opposite) changes in unemployment. Once more, there are some outliers (e.g. GEM) where responses are far weaker than the average. If there is a low coefficient between employment and unemployment, increases in demand will not tend to be reflected in tighter labour market pressure (as measured by unemployment) and this reduces the inflationary pressures in the model. This is critical in producing the inelastic supply response, as discussed in chapter 4. In general, it is the wage response that is crucial in determining the reduced-form ratio of prices to output in the models. In the majority of cases, small aggregate supply elasticities are associated with strong wage–unemployment response ratios. Finally, the employment–output response ratios might be associated with the behaviour of productivity in the models. These ratios tend to lie between values of one-half and two-thirds. Once more, inspection of models that tend to be outliers from the mainstream often explains why the aggregate supply response is also different. For example, the strong productivity response in the DIW simulation for the UK is an important factor in why the aggregate supply schedule is flatter in this case.

In some cases, outliers for some of the responses suggest that there are some unusual factors at work in these models, and the decomposition method provides some guidance to the impact that these differences play in the overall solution of the model. The method is far less useful if the models have settled down to long-run equilibrium where output has returned to base, for then most of the ratios will take values of zero or infinity.

The trade-off method

 Reduced-form results can be used to calculate trade-offs between endogenous variables, as in the Phillips curve.

When different policy objectives cannot be simultaneously achieved, and one objective can be achieved only at the expense of another, it is conventional to speak of the trade-off between them. For the last 20 years, the trade-off that has occupied the centre of macroeconomic policy debate has been that between inflation and unemployment. The following example describes methods which attempt to derive this trade-off. We begin by outlining the simulation method. First, we need to distinguish between two distinct uses of the term 'Phillips curve'. The term has been applied to relationships in which unemployment is treated as an explanatory variable used to predict wage changes. Wage equations are a key part of macro models as much of the content of this book has emphasised. In the complete model, however, various other feedbacks and interrelations are specified, and unemployment and rates of change of wages are jointly dependent, endogenous variables.

Simulation analysis makes it possible to study the joint variation of inflation and unemployment. For example, by perturbing an appropriate policy instrument, the rate of inflation associated with different levels of unemployment can be calculated. This relationship has also been called a Phillips curve. Much of the attention has focused on whether the long-run Phillips curve is vertical, this being equivalent to a natural rate of unemployment or NAIRU.

Considering unemployment and inflation as endogenous variables of a model which has k policy instruments, we first ask what inflation–unemployment combinations are possible. If there is only one policy instrument, $k = 1$, then the solutions as this instrument is varied lie on a trade-off curve in inflation–unemployment space. The theory of economic policy set by Tinbergen (1952) suggests that two instruments are necessary to achieve desired values of the two target variables, then any combination of inflation and unemployment is possible.

In practice, constraints on the set of feasible solutions arise from non-linear and dynamic features of the model and possible limitations on the range of policy instruments. The requirement that certain variables assume positive values may be introduced by log transforms, and floors and ceilings may be introduced by variables such as capacity utilisation. Likewise, the dynamic specification of the model may limit the speed at which particular target values can be attained. Thus solutions may lie within a restricted area of the inflation–unemployment space. Of principal interest is the fact that this area has a fixed south-western boundary, representing a limit to which both inflation and unemployment can be reduced.

In the simulation method, the policy instruments in the models are perturbed one by one, progressively changing the size of the policy shock until it reaches its upper range of permissible values (e.g. income tax rates of 100 per cent), or until the model no longer gives an admissible solution (e.g. negative unemployment). Plotting the resultant solution values for each instrument gives an estimate of the inflation–unemployment trade-off. Extreme values of the policy instrument may be more unreliable, since the model is being used well outside its sample experience.

Each trade-off is specific to a policy instrument. One obvious question is how the trade-off differs according to the policy instrument. The trade-offs also vary over time as dynamic adjustment to a step change in the policy instrument takes place.

This technique was applied to earlier versions of the main UK models by the ESRC Macroeconomic Modelling Bureau, reported in Wallis et al. (1987) using the autumn 1986 versions of the models. Figures 5.4 and 5.5 show the computed trade-off curves for two of the models (LBS and HMT), computed after one and five years. Implicitly, money finance of any change to the PSBR is assumed, by using constant nominal interest rates.

The results for the HMT model (Figures 5.4(a) and (b)) show negatively sloped trade-offs for all the instruments except for VAT in the short term. The trade-offs appear to be non-linear; this is most marked when unemployment falls below two million. There is considerable divergence between the short-run slopes, but after five years the trade-offs tend to converge, with the exception of the corporation tax case. The trade-offs become steeper over time, which is consistent with the long-run aggregate supply schedule being steeper than the corresponding short-run curve. The

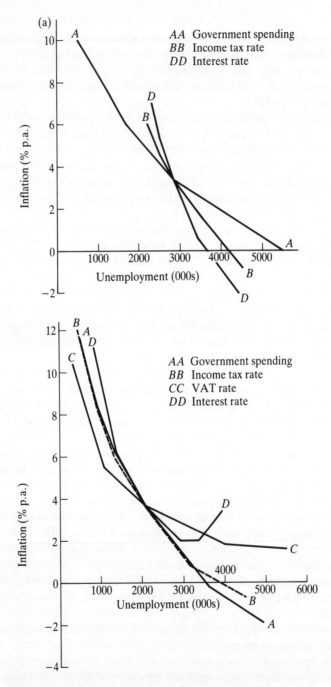

Figure 5.4 Inflation–unemployment trade-offs: HMT model:
(a) after one year; (b) after five years

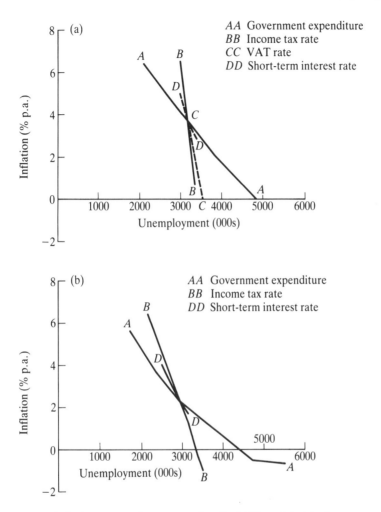

Figure 5.5 Inflation–unemployment trade-offs: LBS model: (a) after one year; (b) after five years

feasible solution space – that is, the lowest combination of unemployment and inflation that can be reached – would be the envelope obtained by connecting the most south-westerly trade-off curves.

The LBS model used contained forward-consistent expectations. The computed trade-offs occupy a smaller solution space than the HMT model, and this may be a consequence of stability conditions required for solution of this model under rational expectations. There is also less evidence of non-linearity (Figure 5.5), although this may in turn reflect the smaller solution space. The trade-offs become less steep over time, but do not converge to the same extent as they do for HMT. The minimum rate of unemployment that could be achieved would seem to be around 1.8 million.

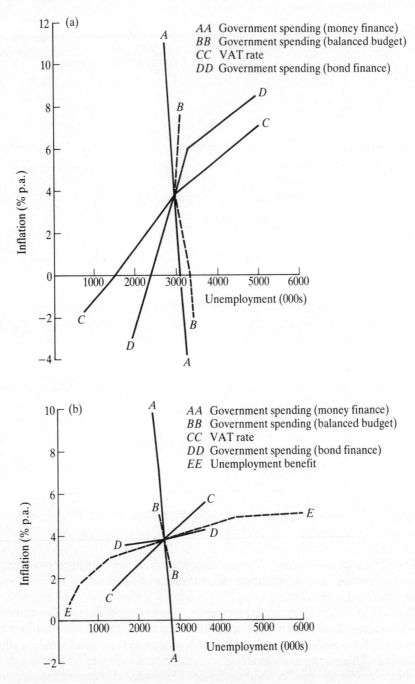

Figure 5.6 Inflation–unemployment trade-offs: LPL model: (a) after one year; (b) after five years

These results show no indication of a long-run trade-off between inflation and unemployment. In contrast, we can see the results of the same analysis on the LPL model (Figure 5.6). The empirical analysis shows considerable support for the theoretical expectations from this model. After five years, money-financed, balance-financed and tax-financed government expenditure changes show negligible unemployment effects, giving a steep, almost vertical trade-off. This is not true of the bond-financed case, bond finance having no effect on the money stock, and hence inflation. Changes in VAT and unemployment benefits tend to yield positive trade-offs as these variables have a supply-side interpretation in the model. The results of the analysis with the LPL model tend to imply a natural rate of unemployment of some 2.7m, although this is dependent on the values of the supply-side instruments in the model.

An alternative technique which can be used to derive policy trade-offs is the optimal control approach. We discuss this method in connection with policy analysis in Chapter 7.

5.3 Rational expectations and macroeconometric models

The discussion of developments in macro models in Chapter 3, and the description of exchange rate modelling in Chapter 4, have already outlined the principles behind the rational expectations approach, and some of its main impact upon macro models. A survey of the treatment of expectations in models is given by Currie and Hall (1994). This chapter is concerned more with technical issues, ranging from solution methods for macroeconometric models with forward-consistent expectations to simulation design. Rational expectations have now become a standard part of many macro-econometric models. Holly and Corker (1984) reported on the introduction of model-consistent expectations in the London Business School model, and Hall and Henry (1985, 1986) on its impact on the NIESR model, while experiments on the HMT model were reported by Spencer (1985). Rational expectations has also found its way into models of other economies: for example, Murphy (1988) in a model of the Australian economy. It has also been included in global (multicountry models): Masson, Symansky and Meredith (1990) discuss its introduction into MULTIMOD, and Gurney (1990) its inclusion in the GEM model.

We begin by outlining the adaptive expectations models, which were the typical explicit expectations mechanism before the advent of rational expectations. We then describe the definition of rational expectations, and distinguish these from model-consistent expectations. Solution methods for rational expectations models are then briefly described (we use rational expectations as a convenient shorthand for model-consistent expectations). The role of terminal conditions in these models is then explored, and we examine the impact of rational expectations on simulation design, giving examples from the macroeconometric models. Finally, we summarise the impact that rational expectations have had on macroeconometric modelling (policy aspects having been considered in Chapter 3).

Adaptive to rational expectations

The traditional adaptive expectations mechanism can be written as:

$$y_t^e = (1 - \lambda)(y_{t-1}^e) \tag{5.31}$$

which makes expectations adjust by some fraction of the error made in the previous period. Because the adjustment parameter is less than 1, expectations do not fully adjust in the current time period. Therefore, if y is growing over time, a consistent (under) prediction error will be made. Of course, it is possible to generalise the adaptive expectations rule so that this specific problem is avoided (see Flemming, 1976), but the main problem is that the rule will break down if the behaviour of y changes over time. Such a change in behaviour is likely if the policy regime changes (hence the force of the Lucas critique). Rules such as that given above will not be structurally stable. We would need to be able to respecify the expectations mechanism each time there was a change in policy. The problem is accentuated by the fact that, in practice, the unobservable expectations in the equation are eliminated by substituting them out, so that only lagged values of y appear in the equation (see Stewart and Wallis, 1981). The expectations parameters are therefore mixed up with the structural parameters of the model.

> Rational expectations, when applied to macroeconometric models, is more correctly termed model-consistent expectations.

The rational expectations literature is usually assumed to have started with Muth (1961), although Grunberg and Modigliani (1954) had already shown that, where agents react to forecasts and thereby alter the course of events, this reaction can be taken into account to give a correct, self-fulfilling forecast. Muth's definition stated a rational expectation to be 'essentially the same as the predictions of the relevant economic theory' (1961, p. 46). The same kind of internal consistency is imposed by the rational expectations algorithms used to solve the model, in that each period's future expectations coincide with the model's solution for the future period. In mathematical terms, the rational expectation is the conditional expectation. The approach is more accurately termed model-consistent expectations. It assumes that agents do not make consistent errors, but it also operates on the stronger assumption that they act as if they had complete knowledge of the economic system, together with all its parameters. When applied to any given model, the parameters of that model are assumed to be the true parameters of the system.

In non-linear models, the deterministic solution to the model will not be the mathematical expectation of the probability distribution of the stochastic model (see Section 5.4). This means that in a deterministic solution of a non-linear model, when all the error terms are set to zero, the result will not give the expected value for the endogenous variables. The deterministic solution will therefore be biased and will not correspond with the full rational expectations solution. It is in this sense that we call the solution model consistent rather than rational.

$$f(y_{t+1}^{e}, y_{t-1}, x_t, \alpha) = u_t \tag{5.32}$$

This is equivalent to solving the system given above. Note that we have to be clear about the dating of the information set on which expectations are formed; this is usually assumed to be $t - 1$. Also note that the presence of lagged variables can no longer be justified by expectations, but must depend on costs of adjustment, etc.

Solution methods for rational expectations models

‖ Solution methods for non-linear large-scale models work by approximating the (stable) saddlepoint path of the model.

Blanchard and Kahn (1980) developed a solution method for the linear model under rational expectations which allowed explicit derivation of the properties of the system. In particular, the method considers the uniqueness and stability of the system. A solution satisfying uniqueness and stability is generally called a saddlepoint path. In order for this saddlepoint path to be reached, Blanchard and Kahn showed that there must be as many unstable roots of the system as there are forward expectation terms. In a linear system, this involves inspecting the eigenvalues or roots.

The solution of this system is different from the traditional solution method for non-linear models. The system with non-rational expectations works on the principle that the solution for the current period, t, depends only on current and lagged variables, so that the solution sequence can be carried out one period at a time. In model-consistent methods, current variables depend on expectations of future variables as well, which in principle involves an infinite progression into the future. Solution of the model can no longer proceed one period at a time, since the model is no longer recursive over time.

‖ The main non-linear methods are the extended solution path, multiple shooting and the penalty function approach.

There are three methods of solution that can be applied to the non-linear system with forward expectations. An excellent technical exposition is given by Fisher (1992). The most widely used is the *extended path* method of Fair and Taylor (1983). This was developed from the method first used by Fair (1979) and applied by Minford *et al.* (1979) to the LPL model of the UK economy. The second method is the *multiple shooting* method of Lipton *et al.* (1982), and modified by Spencer (1985). This method is as common in the solution of large-scale models, but can be useful in solving models with a forward unit root, as in the UIP exchange rate case. Finally, there is the *penalty function* method of Holly and Zarrop (1983).

The extended path method of Fair and Taylor is relatively easy to understand and to implement in large-scale models. It is based on iterative methods. First, values for the expectations variables are assumed, and then conventional Gauss–Seidel solution methods are used to solve the model, conditional on these values. Then the expectations variables are set equal to the solution values from the first stage. The process is repeated until the expectations variables are consistent with the solution values of the relevant model variables: that is, until

$$y_t^e = y_{t+1} \tag{5.33}$$

Hall (1985) argues that a more computationally efficient method is to stack the time periods together to generate one huge equation system. Fisher, Holly and Hughes-Hallett (1986) develop a complete family of first-order methods which include the Fair–Taylor and Hall approaches as special cases. The simplest way to understand this method is to think of the solution of the model as comprising two parts: the solution of the model given exogenous variables and fixed expectations (the so-called inner loop), and the updating sequence for expectations as the solution values of the endogenous variables change (the 'outer' loop). Hall's method involves just one inner loop iteration before expectations are updated. The process is then repeated until expectations have converged on the model solution values. Alternatively, we could continue to iterate on the inner loop until the model has converged, given fixed expectations, and then solve for expectations values, repeating the whole process until the solution is fully consistent. Intermediate cases where the inner loop is not solved to convergence are also possible. Another variation on the solution procedure is the extent to which expectations are updated: it is possible to make expectations adjust fully to the change in the endogenous variables, or only incompletely. Which precise variation is used will depend on the particular nature of the model, but Fisher, Holly and Hughes-Hallett (1986) show that experiments on the UK models found the most efficient method to be where a fixed number of inner-loop iterations are made. The Hall method, with one single inner loop, treats expectational variables like other endogenous variables and is often less efficient, while full convergence of the inner loop fails to exploit the fact that there are usually some variables within the model that are slow to converge.

The penalty method also uses a two-part scheme, but it is derivative-based and updates the expectations by Newton's method rather than by simple updating as in the Fair–Taylor method. The analogy is with optimal control methods (see Chapter 7 for a discussion of these), treating the consistent expectations condition as a target, and the expectations variables as instruments. The function $\Sigma(Y - Y^e)^2$ is minimised using standard optimal control methods with Y^e as the instrument. The function has a minimum when $Y = Y^e$.

Fisher (1992) argues that the penalty function method might be more efficient by requiring less outer-loop iterations, but this only holds if the number of expectational terms is small. In addition, there is the fixed cost of evaluating the derivatives required and storing these for future use. Most efficient use of the penalty function method would involve the updating of derivatives between iterations, but this is very costly in computational resources. The iterative methods described above have the advantage of simplicity over the penalty function approach, and also have the advantage that they can be tailored to the specific features of a model, while remaining relatively robust over a wide range of models.

The basis of the shooting method as a procedure is equivalent to the Blanchard–Kahn solution for a linear model. The method separates the forward terms from the backward terms in the model. Taking an initial guess for the forward elements, the model is solved forward until period $t+1$ is reached. If x_{t+1} satisfies the terminal condition, the solution is computed. If not, a Newton algorithm is used to update the initial guess as a function of the terminal condition error. For example, if we have an equation

$$X_t = X_{t+1} + \gamma Z_t \qquad (5.34)$$

we can renormalise this to give:

$$X_{t+1} = X_t - \gamma Z_t \qquad (5.35)$$

starting from an initial estimate of the first period through the path of X_t until the solution for X at the terminal date (X_T) equals the pre-set terminal condition.

The problem is that solving a rational expectations model in backward mode only must generate a system which is unstable, since we know that there are as many unstable roots as there are expectational variables. Thus the single shooting method has to be extended to multiple shooting, where the period is sub-divided. The terminal conditions are set for each sub-period, all the solutions are stacked together, and they are then solved simultaneously. The main problem with this method is that it is unreliable and difficult to apply to large-scale non-linear models. A particular case where forward shooting can be useful, however, is in the solution of models which contain a UIP exchange rate relationship. Often the terminal condition for this relationship is explicit (such as when the level or change of the current balance or net overseas assets ratio must return to base), and the deviation from this condition in the terminal period can be used to calculate the initial jump of the exchange rate.

The steps in this procedure are as follows. First, solve the model in normal mode. Then check the divergence of the assumed terminal condition from its calculated value at the terminal date. This divergence is then used to compute the necessary jump in the exchange rate in the first period of the simulation. Successive period values up to the terminal date are calculated by the simple UIP condition (see Chapter 9 for an illustration). The model is solved again and the terminal condition is rechecked. If the condition is satisfied, the model is solved for the standard convergence conditions on the endogenous variables; otherwise the initial exchange rate jump is recalculated and the process continued.

Uniqueness, stability and terminal conditions

> Terminal conditions are used to tie down the solution path of the model to approximate the unique stable path.

The Blanchard–Kahn solution of linear models shows that they only have a unique stable solution if there are as many unstable roots as there are expectations variables. A view has emerged that multiple solutions are not a problem as long as only one is stable.

If economic systems are designed to have the saddlepoint property by construction, the only problem in solving a large-scale model is the location of the saddlepoint solution. Terminal conditions are used to help choose the saddlepoint path. Since behaviour today depends on expectations of what happens in the future, the principle of forward consistent expectations involves an infinite progression over the future. Model solution methods seek to truncate this by approximating the path of the solution of the model beyond the period of interest. This is done by specifying a terminal condition which projects the variables of which expectations are formed beyond the end of the simulation horizon.

There are two alternative ways of choosing the terminal condition. The first, which has been adopted by the LPL model, is to impose the equilibrium conditions of the model as the terminal condition. Clearly, this is possible only where the nature of the equilibrium is known a priori, and few models satisfy this criterion. The other method is simply to impose a terminal condition that the variables settle down to either a constant level or a constant growth rate at the terminal date (thus attempting to approximate the stable path after the end of the simulation horizon). In both cases, the length of the solution period before the terminal date should not affect the solution values over the period of interest. This might happen if the equilibrium condition were imposed via the terminal condition well in advance of the model actually settling down to an equilibrium. The solution values would then be distorted.

In order to check whether the results are sensitive to the terminal condition (whether the type of condition or the terminal date), the usual practice is to test the numerical sensitivity of the solution to alternative choices of the terminal date or condition. The sensitivity of the solution to alternative terminal conditions can also indicate whether a unique stable solution does in fact exist. Since the solution should be independent of the terminal condition (as long as it is imposed sufficiently far out in the simulation), the choice of terminal condition should not matter. If it does, it suggests that there is more than one stable solution trajectory.

To give a bit more insight into these issues, we now present some examples from the UK models which have forward-consistent expectations. We begin by describing explicitly the types of terminal condition:

Equilibrium condition $\qquad \hat{p}_{t+1} = \bar{p}_{t+1}$ $\qquad\qquad\qquad\qquad$ (5.36)

where $\bar{p}_{t+1}$ is given by off-model analysis.

Constant level condition $\quad \hat{p}_{t+1} = \hat{p}_t$ $\qquad\qquad\qquad\qquad\qquad$ (5.37)

where the solution for $t+1$ is the same as in period t.

Growth rate condition $\qquad \hat{p}_{t+1} = \hat{p}_t \cdot (\hat{p}_t/\hat{p}_{t-1})$ $\qquad\qquad\qquad$ (5.38)

so that the variable is projected to growth at the same rate as in the last period of the solution. In a quarterly model, this growth rate condition might be alternatively expressed in quarterly or annual terms.

The analysis of Fisher (1992) suggests that, if the model jumps very quickly to the steady state, then equilibrium values, if they are known, are the best choice. Otherwise constant level conditions are appropriate. If the model is sluggish in moving to a new equilibrium, or returning to the original equilibrium, then constant growth conditions become the best choice. Furthermore, the constant growth conditions are likely to be more robust when the system is one of steady-state growth, rather than steady-state level, equilibrium. Where a level equilibrium is involved, the solution period may need to be very long; this is a feature of the NIESR model, where the exchange rate equation includes a condition that the stock of net overseas assets return to base following a shock. Of particular interest is the case when the model contains a unit root: for example, when an equation is a random walk specified as a forward difference (as in the UIP exchange rate formulation). Then there are an infinite number of possible solutions depending on the choice of terminal value, which must then be a fixed point value in order to obtain a unique solution path. This is why the terminal condition chosen for an exchange rate equation is often that either the current balance returns to base, or the stock of net overseas assets does likewise.

Otherwise there is nothing to tie down the long-run solution of the exchange rate: any value is consistent with a stable solution, the actual value being given by initial conditions. In a sense this can be regarded as a failure of the model to satisfy the conditions for a stable equilibrium. The forward shooting method of solution is then appropriate in many cases. There is the suggestion that if the model is stable then the extended-path method of Fair–Taylor should be capable of providing a solution of the model. In the unit-root case, instability may be prevented by an appropriate choice of monetary policy. An example of this is the determination of interest rates by expected inflation. It is unlikely that models with a unit root in the exchange rate (such as in the UIP case) will be stable under the assumption of either fixed nominal or fixed real interest rates. If the modified UIP treatment of exchange rates is adopted, the risk premium element may be sufficient to modify the unit root and provide a stable solution.

Terminal conditions in the Liverpool model

The LPL model uses the equilibrium method of selecting terminal values. Of particular interest in the LPL model is the fact that no dependent variable in the structural form has its own expectations as an explanatory variable. This implies that it is not possible to examine the dynamic properties of the model, equation by equation. Furthermore, the terminal conditions do not constrain the model to pass smoothly through the terminal point, or imply that the solution would remain at terminal values if the time horizon were extended. Hence equilibrium conditions do not actually constrain the model to reach a stable equilibrium.

Four variables have expectations that appear in the model (Table 5.3): capacity utilisation (deviation from trend), inflation, real debt interest, and the real exchange rate. The terminal conditions for inflation and capacity utilisation are set exogenously, whereas the other two are determined endogenously. Figure 5.7 shows how the solution changes as the terminal date is varied. As the solution period is increased, the model does appear to give a good approximation to the unique long-run path, but the

Table 5.3 Terminal conditions in the LPL model

(a) Expectational variables

Expectational variables	Equation in which expectation appears
Capacity utilisation	Non-durable consumption
Real debt interest	Equilibrium government spending
Real exchange rate:	
1 year ahead	Real short interest rate
5 years ahead	Real long rate
Inflation:	
1 year ahead	Nominal short rate
5 years ahead	Nominal long rate

(b) Terminal conditions
   (T denotes the last period of the solution.)

Capacity utilisation	Deviation from trend output, projected at zero
Real debt interest	Projected by value in T times the growth of equilibrium GDP at T
Real exchange rate	Projected at constant value 5 periods after T by level of equilibrium
	Exchange rate at T times its growth rate at T
Inflation	Projected 5 periods ahead at constant value given by the exogenous PSBR/GDP ratio at T

Source: Fisher (1992), Tables 4.4-4.5

last five periods of each solution show consistent and marked deviations from this path. This implies that use of the last five years of the solution (this version of the LPL model was annual) would provide a poor approximation to the long-run path of the model, and the model-user would have little confidence in the results for this period.

These results are strongly influenced by the behaviour of the real exchange rate, for the actual real rate shows a persistent deviation from its 'equilibrium' level. The expected real exchange rate has to 'jump' to get back to its equilibrium level, and this distorts the behaviour of the other endogenous variables in the earlier part of the simulation. The jump in the expected exchange rate can be traced back to the high first-order serial correlation coefficient in the exchange rate equation. Later versions of the LPL model corrected this.

The next issue is to look at alternative terminal conditions applied to the LPL model. Figure 5.8 shows the difference that constant level and constant growth terminal conditions make to the solution of the LPL model. The equilibrium terminal conditions used in the LPL model clearly distort the solution when the model is only solved for 13 years. The constant level and growth conditions do much better at approximating the long-run path. However, the distortions become much less marked

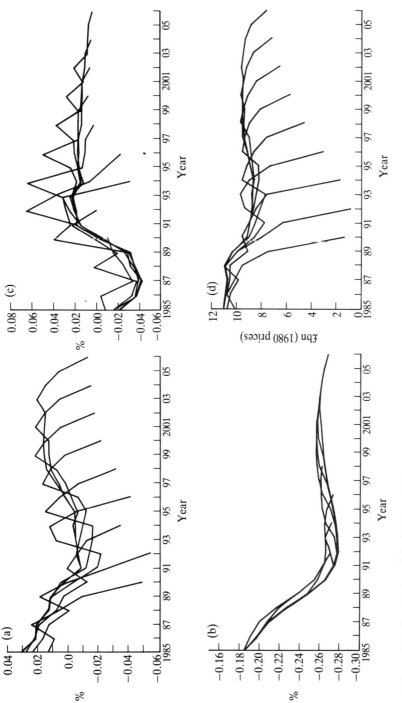

Figure 5.7 Sensitivity of the LPL model to terminal dates: (a) inflation rate; (b) real exchange rate; (c) real debt interest; (d) capacity utilisation (deviation from equilibrium output)

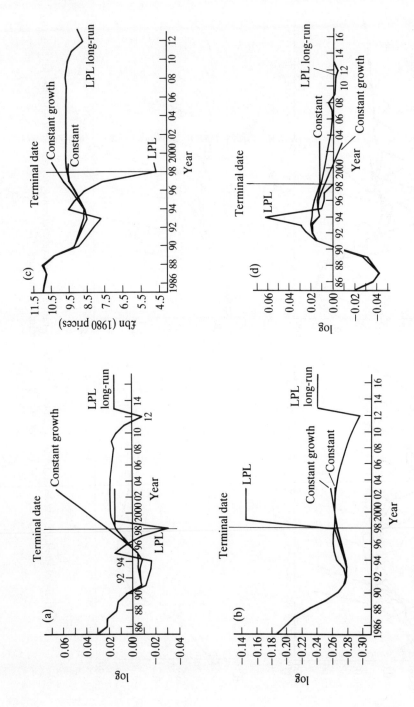

Figure 5.8 Sensitivity of the LPL model to terminal conditions: (a) inflation; (b) real exchange rate; (c) capacity utilisation (deviation from equilibrium output); (d) real debt interest

if the model is solved over a much longer time horizon. These results show that, even where the equilibrium of the model is fairly tightly defined, the use of fixed (equilibrium) terminal conditions can distort the solution of the model if they are imposed too early in the solution. In essence, the model is being forced back to equilibrium far too early. The general lesson is that long solution periods are preferable for rational expectations models, since the solution is less likely to be distorted by inappropriate terminal conditions. However, the precise length of solution period can only be determined by empirical investigation. As we shall see later, the evidence from some models suggests that the time horizon has to be extremely long before the model has settled down. This has costs in the sense that a very long base is required.

Additional light is shed on the use of terminal conditions when we look at responses in simulation. Again we use the LPL model with its equilibrium, or fixed-value, terminal conditions. One particular terminal value is of interest, that for inflation, which is set by an exogenous projection of the PSBR/GDP ratio. Basically, there is a problem when we try to conduct a simulation in which the long-run inflation rate is changed, for unless the exogenous terminal condition is also changed in an appropriate manner, the model will force inflation back to base in the final period of the solution, thus distorting the results. This potential distortion is avoided if we use a constant growth terminal condition instead, for this allows the inflation rate to change and allows the model to choose any stable inflation rate rather than a particular rate.

Terminal conditions in the LBS model

Our second example is that of the LBS model of the 1985–9 era, when forward-consistent expectations appeared in the financial sector of the model. Three expectational variables were used: the price of gilts, the price of equities, and the price of overseas assets (the inverse of the exchange rate). The solution has a seasonal sensitivity: that is, it differs according to which quarter of the year the simulation ends. The differences in the solution for the price of gilts feeds back through the model, and GDP itself become seasonally sensitive. In this model, the seasonality could be traced back to the annual uprating of tax allowances for the effects of inflation. If the saddlepoint path exhibits seasonality, the terminal conditions need to allow for this fact. When the terminal condition is expressed in a constant level or growth condition in annual (or fourth-difference) form, the sensitivity of the solution largely disappears.

Terminal conditions in the NIESR model

The NIESR model has tended to include several forward-looking variables since forward expectations were introduced into the model in the mid-1980s. However, the most important of these variables is the real exchange rate. Recent versions of the model used the UIP-style formulation. A unit root implies that there is no unique stable solution, and such a model will tend to fail to solve under constant growth terminal conditions. It is then necessary to use a terminal condition which contains enough date. The 1988 version of the NIESR model included the change in net overseas assets in the exchange rate equation (this is very approximately equivalent to use of a current account term). This feedback element may now be sufficient to move the root of the complete model away from unity. The equation now specifies that the long-run solution of the exchange rate must move to offset any change in net assets from their base level. It may then be possible to revert to a standard growth rate terminal condition, but if the system root is still close to unity, the time horizon required for solution may be very long.

Fisher (1992) illustrates the impact that a UIP-style equation, such as that used in the NIESR model, can have on the full model, and how it is possible to use a small linear system to predict the size of the initial jump in the exchange rate to an exogenous shock. The UIP equation can be written as:

$$\varepsilon_t = \varepsilon_{t+1}^e + (r_t - r_t^f) + \beta N_t \tag{5.39}$$

where N is net overseas assets, ε is the nominal exchange rate, r is interest rates, the superscript ^{e} refers to expected value and f to the foreign rate. Thus the exchange rate depends on its expected future value, interest differentials and the stock of net overseas assets. In a full-model context, this equation will fail to provide a unique solution without exogenously set terminal conditions. However, a way out is to make either interest rates (r) or the stock of net overseas assets (N) endogenous. In many large-scale models, short-term interest rates are assumed fixed (but see Chapter 7), and hence the appropriate solution is to allow N to be endogenous. Since stability analysis is difficult using simulation methods, Fisher (1992) analyses the model by reducing the rest of the system to a single linear feedback equation for net assets and then solving the two-equation model using linear methods. A stochastic simulation method is used to estimate the feedback equation for net assets from the full NIESR model, and this feedback equation is then expressed in the form of a distributed lag.

The feedback equation is specified in terms of the first difference of net assets, since a permanent shock in the NIESR model suggests that net assets do not settle down at a new long-run level, but to a new long-run rate of change. The two-equation dynamic model can be expressed as:

$$[(1-F) \quad -0.011] \; \varepsilon_t = 0$$
$$\tag{5.40}$$
$$[-\delta(L) \quad (1\text{-}L)][N_t] = [X_t]$$

where

$$\Delta N_t = X_t + \delta(L)\varepsilon_t \tag{5.41}$$

In equation 5.41, X is an exogenous component, and $\delta(L)$ is the polynomial feedback equation. $\delta(1) = -0.082$, suggesting that a 1 per cent step in the exchange rate leads to a trend decrease in N of 0.082 percentage points per quarter.

This system has five non-zero roots, and with one forward expectation term, one of these should be unstable (greater than unity). The roots are 1.03, 0.96, 0.87, 0.54 and these should be unstable (greater than unity). The roots are 1.03, 0.96, 0.87, 0.54 and 0.05, suggesting that there is a saddlepoint solution to the model, but as the unstable root is close to unity, it implies a large initial jump in the exchange rate in response to any shock. Since the largest of the stable roots is also close to unity, this suggests that the model is slow to adjust to equilibrium. Fisher shows that this system is a good approximation to the full model, but that the simulation period needs to be quite extensive for the full model to attain the analytical results. These imply that a shock of half a percentage point to X implies a long-run change of 6.1 per cent in the exchange rate.

The development of this simple system is very informative in predicting how the other main UK models would respond to the inclusion of a UIP equation. In order to do this, the UIP exchange rate equation is written in a more general form which encompasses the treatment in the other models. Thus:

$$\varepsilon_t = \alpha \varepsilon_t + (1 - \alpha)\hat{\varepsilon}_{t+1} + 0.44B_t \tag{5.42}$$

This equation follows the model developed by Fisher et al. (1990a), where B is the ratio of the current balance to GDP. If $\alpha = 0$ then we have the forward-looking equation as described above with the replacement of the current balance term for net assets. Increasing the weight on α reduces the forward element in the equation. If a polynomial feedback equation is fitted, this has the property that half a percentage point improvement in the current balance ratio implies a long-run increase of 5.5 per cent in the exchange rate. The roots of the system for the purely forward-looking version of the equation $\alpha = 0$ are 1.03, 0.67, 0.37 and 0.03, indicating that an exogenous shock causes quite a large initial jump in the exchange rate, but quite rapid adjustment to the new equilibrium. The entirely backward version has roots of 0.91, 0.88 and 0.37, which implies slow monotonic adjustment. The intermediate case with $\alpha = 0.5$, which gives equal weight to the forward and backward elements, has two real roots, 1.33 and 0.37, and a complex pair. So the initial jump is less than in the pure forward case, but adjustment is oscillatory. What is perhaps not fully appreciated is that all three forms of equation tend to the same long-run equilibrium. Thus forward expectations do not alter the nature of the long run, but they do radically change the path of adjustment to it. In a large-scale model, dynamic adjustment in the rest of the model may mean that convergence to the new long-run equilibrium does not take place.

Two other conclusions can be drawn. First, the size of the coefficient on the current balance term (B) determines the size of the initial jump relative to the equilibrium change. The larger the coefficient, the greater is the initial overshoot. There is the possibility that a large initial overshoot can cause solution problems using iterative methods. Second, we can draw some conclusions about the use of a current balance rather than a net assets term in the exchange rate equation. Fisher et al. (1990a) argue that the time-series properties of the data would support the use of the current balance ratio (which is I(0) or stationary) as opposed to net assets, which is I(1) or trended. In terms of model properties, the use of current balance rather than net assets causes a larger initial overshoot, although both tend towards the same equilibrium. This can be rationalised by the fact that step changes cause a revaluation effect on assets in the short run, but in the longer run changes in net assets are dominated by changes in the current balance, revaluation effects being negligible.

Focus upon the simple two-equation model helps to reveal the importance of the rest of the model (encapsulated in the feedback equation) for the stability of the model. If there is only a weak feedback from the exchange rate to the current balance (or net assets term), then (for an exogenous interest rate) the unit root of the exchange rate equation is not modified sufficiently to produce a stable model solution. At best the system may be just stable, which means that the feedback is so weak that it requires a very large jump in the exchange rate to correct the current balance. Even worse is if the feedback to the current balance is of the wrong sign: that is, a fall in the exchange rate worsens the current account. Then the unit root is modified in the wrong direction and no solution is possible for the model; it is inherently explosive. The nature of the feedback is given by the rest of the model. All the factors that determine the current account are relevant: domestic demand, relative prices, and so on. This explains why Fisher *et al.* (1990) found it impossible to derive a solution to the BE model using a UIP exchange rate equation of the above form with fully forward expectations. The feedback in the BE model is unstable, and incorrectly signed at times; this can be traced back to the behaviour of the housing sector.

We might question why the nominal exchange rate should be expected to clear the current account, since homogeneity requirements (originally stated by Ball, Burns and Laury, 1977) suggest that nominal exchange rate changes tend to be fully reflected in domestic prices and output returns to base. In the HMT model an exchange rate solution is possible, since there are some departures from static price homogeneity. In the case of the NIESR model, there are revaluation changes to personal wealth which cause the current balance to change in response to an exchange rate shock. However, as Fisher (1992) argues, these revaluation effects are in parts of the model where the empirical foundations are particularly weak. This suggests that there must be some other anchor to the system, maybe through a fixed money stock as in the case of LPL, where there is no instability despite the presence of a UIP equation with no risk premium element. Then the endogeneity of the interest rate ensures a stable model solution. There has to be some nominal anchor in the system to ensure stability if the forward-looking system is fully homogeneous.

> Solution of models under forward-consistent expectations requires the model to satisfy certain conditions in order to rule out unstable solutions. This may rule out some simulation experiments.

Simulation design with rational expectations models

> Simulations with rational expectations models have to be explicit about whether policy changes are permanent or temporary, anticipated or unanticipated.

In standard simulations with backward-looking models, it is usually assumed that all changes to policy instruments are permanent and unanticipated. In order to make a distinction, it is necessary to distinguish between permanent and temporary influences, and between anticipated and unanticipated effects with structural equations. In rational expectations there is a difference between these alternative assumptions, which arise from the system solution of the model, rather than from any structural components.

Anticipated and unanticipated shocks

Conventional backward-looking models react no differently to an anticipated or unanticipated shock – there are not usually any mechanisms whereby income changes might be perceived to be temporary or permanent. However, forward-looking models can react differently to an anticipated or unanticipated shock. If agents anticipate a future policy change, they may change their behaviour in advance of the actual change occurring. A classic example of this is an announcement that the rate of VAT will increase in the next budget, which may bring forward spending in advance of the VAT rise. Effects of this kind have been quite common in recent UK macroeconomic history.

We assume for the moment that agents' anticipations are correct. If the model has a unique long-run solution, the anticipated shock example should give the same long-run solution as the unanticipated case. Results for the LBS, NIESR and LPL models are presented for a government expenditure shock of 3.25 per cent. In order to calculate the impact of an anticipated shock in a forward-looking model, the simulation period should start before the shock is introduced. In our example, we start the simulation some eight periods before the shock is introduced. In both the LBS and

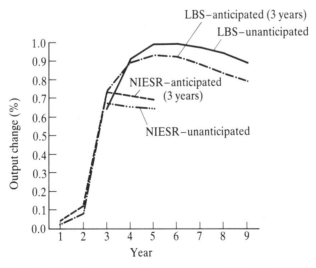

Figure 5.9 Anticipated and unanticipated shocks: LBS and NIESR models

NIESR models (Figure 5.9) there is only a small difference between the effect of the different shocks over the period for which the shock is in force. There is, however, a small reaction in the anticipated case in the period before the shock actually occurs, so that some effects may be observed in advance. The pre-shock effect is most marked on the exchange rate, where the initial jump now takes place at the beginning of the simulation period rather than at the beginning of the shock period. Thereafter the exchange rate depreciates steadily to meet up with the path under the unanticipated shock.

The LPL model also gives the results that the two alternative cases give very much the same result in the long run, but the anticipated shock has a larger pre-impact effect than for the other models, leading to lower output (this reflects the property discussed below, that higher government spending increases inflation and reduces current real wealth in this model).

Permanent and temporary shocks:

In a conventional model with backward-looking expectations, a temporary shock is defined as one which is operative during only part of the simulation period, whereas a permanent shock is one where an exogenous variable is perturbed throughout the simulation period. Once a temporary shock is removed, the model tends back to its original steady state (as long as it is stable). With forward-consistent expectations, however, the solution to the model under a temporary shock is calculated on the assumption that economic agents know that it will be removed at some future date. This may affect their current behaviour. The current response to a temporary shock will depend also on the dynamic adjustment of the model, since this determines how

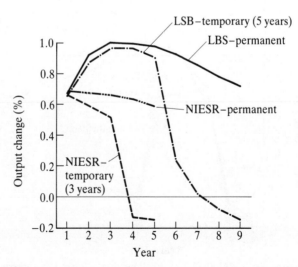

Figure 5.10 Permanent and temporary shocks: LBS and NIESR models

quickly lagged adjustment effects wear off once the temporary shock has been removed.

How important the permanent/temporary distinction is in forward-looking models can be illustrated by some examples from the 1985 vintage of the LBS, NIESR and LPL models. Another example of a pre-announced rise in taxes to reduce the budget deficit in a multicountry model is discussed in Chapter 8. The common shock to all the models is a government expenditure increase of 3.25 per cent. The temporary shock lasts for five years in the LBS model, for six years in the LPL model and for three years in the NIESR model (the total simulation period was far shorter for this model).

The results for the LBS and NIESR model (see Figure 5.10) show that the simulation responses over the common period for which both temporary and permanent shocks are in force, are smaller for the temporary shock (although the differences are not great for the LBS model). This implies that agents have adjusted for the fact that the shock is temporary, but that they do not completely discount it. If this were the case, they would not change their current behaviour in the face of a temporary shock. One reason why there is a current effect from a temporary shock is that the price level is permanently changed, thus altering all nominal values, including the exchange rate.

We now turn to the LPL model. Here the monetary assumption accompanying the fiscal shock is critical. The standard assumption in the LPL model is that fiscal changes are financed by a balanced mix of money and bonds, and this automatically adjusts the terminal condition of the model to produce a different terminal value for inflation. The LPL model does in fact have a variable called 'temporary money' and another called 'permanent money'. The permanent method adjusts the terminal value for inflation as above, but use of the temporary change means that the terminal condition for inflation must be rewritten as a constant growth rule so that the correct long-run steady state can be calculated. It is, however, an empirical matter whether the model is stable under a prolonged 'temporary money' shock.

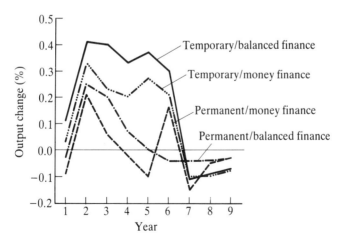

Figure 5.11 Permanent and temporary shocks: LPL model

Results for the LPL model are shown both for balanced finance and for money finance (Figure 5.11). The differences on GDP as between a permanent and a temporary shock are more marked than for the other two models. The rather strange feature of the results is that a temporary shock raises current output by more than a permanent shock. This effect is due to the intrinsic structural characteristics of the model. A permanent shock in the model has strong inflation effects, and these reduce current expenditure through wealth effects. A temporary shock has weaker inflation effects, and hence the impact on current wealth and output is correspondingly lower. Since the empirical evidence for the size of the wealth coefficient in the durable spending equation in the LPL model is questionable, one might also question the general conclusion drawn from the LPL results.

We have already alluded to the consistency problems that might arise for permanent shocks. It is, of course, a basic result that, if the simulation experiment is itself expected to generate an unstable result, it cannot be solved in forward-looking mode. For example, Blinder and Solow (1973) show that a bond-financed fiscal expansion may produce instability by generating an accelerating stock of debt. Considerable care has therefore to be taken in selecting shocks in a forward-looking model. The fiscal solvency issue is treated in Chapter 8.

Credibility

One of the key issues that is associated with forward expectations models is that of credibility. Standard simulations with forward-consistent models assume that the policy is fully credible, whether temporary or permanent. To enable variations on this, it is necessary to make some specific assumptions about the information set of economic agents. We can extend our examples to illustrate the use of this approach by unanticipated and anticipated shocks (other ways of examining credibility effects will also be discussed).

In this example, we assume that we have a permanent and a temporary government expenditure shock as before, using the LBS model. We complicate the analysis, however, by allowing that a shock which was thought to be permanent turns out to be only temporary, and that a shock which was expected to be temporary turns out to be permanent (Figure 5.12). These additional variants can be classed as unanticipated policy reversal. In order to compute these simulations, it is necessary to proceed in two stages. In the case of the original expected temporary shock, we take the expectations generated from this solution, which were based on a model-consistent solution where the shock was indeed temporary, and then treat these as fixed in a second simulation which has a permanent rather than a temporary shock. In other words, the expectations become inconsistent once the shock persists. In the case where an original permanent shock becomes temporary, we take expectations from a model-consistent permanent shock simulation, and then impose them on the temporary shock simulation over the period of the temporary shock. In both cases, we allow agents to adjust expectations once the policy reversal is known (that is, when the

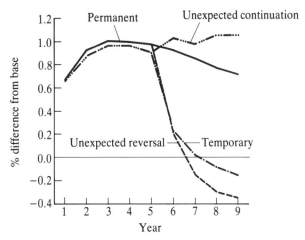

Figure 5.12 Policy reversals: output in the LBS model

Source: Fisher (1992)

previously expected temporary shock continues and when the previously expected permanent shock ends). The results show that, on policy reversal, the solution moves towards the alternative trajectory. Thus where the temporary shock becomes unexpectedly permanent, expectations immediately adjust to the new regime, and the GDP solution path jumps to the solution for the permanent shock.

We can generalise these methods to deal with the general issue of incomplete credibility or incomplete knowledge, although there appear to have been few examples of this in large-scale models (exceptions are Keating, 1985a, and Westaway, 1992). In order to do this we need to adopt a sequential approach. We first simulate the model in full forward-looking mode with a specific assumption about the information set of economic agents. For example, to simulate an unexpected change in regime, we could use the rule that they expect the tax rate to be constant in the face of a given shock. We then retrieve the expectational values from this simulation (the outcomes for the other endogenous variables are no longer of interest) and use these as exogenous inputs in a second simulation which might include a specific rule that taxes are used to balance the budget. This is clearly not a model-consistent solution, since the expectations of economic agents do not coincide with the forecasts of the model. We can relax the assumption to allow agents to observe the new rule after some period of time, by endogenising expectations after a given period in the solution (this is very similar to the policy reversal simulations above). There are many other alternative experiments which could be carried out in this fashion; the key to them all is that some explicit assumption about how expectations are formed is necessary.

The general problem with this approach is that either expectations remain non-rational, in the sense of not being consistent with model outcomes, or they suddenly become rational. An intrinsically more appealing approach has been developed which allows agents to learn about the economic model. Agents are allowed to make mistakes in the short run in the learning approach, although they may well not make systematic mistakes over an extended period. The learning approach uses the Kalman filter method to update the expectations-generating mechanism by past errors. The initial expectations-generating mechanism relates expectations to key variables in the reduced form of the model. This approach has been used in the LBS model to replace the fully forward treatment of the exchange rate (Hall and Garratt, 1992). It has also been used within the GEM model to investigate wage behaviour (Barrell *et al.*, 1993).

The learning approach

A simple representation of the learning approach is the model:

$$y_t = \beta x_t + u_t \tag{5.43}$$

where agents update sequentially their estimate of the true parameter β as more information on y and x becomes available. The usual assumption is that there is some prior estimate of β, β_0, which is varied stochastically using time-varying parameters by least squares learning. Cuthbertson, Hall and Taylor (1992, chapter 7) spell out the formal framework. Updating the parameters by a Kalman filtering procedure assumes that agents use the assumed information set optimally. This approach also deals with the signal extraction problem, as in the case where, say, the economic agent only has information on his measured current income when trying to estimate his permanent income. In practical model applications, the information set is usually restricted to lagged data. This enables the expectations mechanism to be solved pre-recursively to the simultaneous part of the model. It is too early to draw many conclusions about the learning approach, but it has the advantage of avoiding the full-information assumption of rational expectations and does not require the use of special features in model solution such as terminal conditions.

5.4   Stochastic methods

||| Stochastic simulation methods are used to measure uncertainty in models.

Macroeconometric models are subject to inherent random variation, and standard solution and simulation methods typically ignore these random elements and produce a point estimate. We might legitimately be concerned with the measure of uncertainty surrounding a model. In other words, we are interested in the probability distribution of outcomes. There are different types of uncertainty in which we might be interested:

1. The uncertainty surrounding a forecast from a model, perhaps the derivation of a confidence interval around the forecast.
2. Uncertainty about the size of policy multipliers.
3. Questions of the robustness of alternative policy rules to random disturbances.
4. Uncertainty as a measure of the non-linearity of a model

> Uncertainty can be about forecast errors, the size of policy multipliers and the robustness of policy rules, or a measure of non-linearity.

We can distinguish between two main sources of error in models. First, there is the element of randomness in the error terms of the structural equations. In estimation, the distributional assumption is that these errors are normally distributed. In a linear multivariate model, the distribution of the endogenous variables of the system would also be normally distributed, but in a non-linear model, the distribution of the endogenous variables is not known and must be obtained by stochastic simulation methods. These involve repeated drawings of artificial pseudo-random numbers to represent repeated samples of the equation disturbances. The model is then solved for each of these drawings of the random disturbances, giving an empirical distribution of endogenous variable values, whose mean, variance and other moments can be calculated. The measures of dispersion of this distribution then provide an indication of the uncertainty that surrounds the model's solution and forecasts.

A second source of error is the estimation error of the model's coefficients. Where these are estimated, the distribution of the estimates of these coefficients is known and stochastic simulation can evaluate the uncertainty due to the margin of error involved in the estimation. Where the parameters of a model are imposed, however, their distribution is unknown and measures of uncertainty cannot be derived. When considering the margin of error around a forecast, the random disturbances are typically more important that the contribution coefficient estimation error. When the uncertainty of policy responses and multipliers is the focus of interest, the random disturbances make no contribution, coefficient error estimation being the only source of uncertainty in the model (Fair, 1984).

Deterministic versus stochastic simulation

> The deterministic solution values do not coincide with the conditional mean of the distribution and are therefore biased.

Ignoring dynamic complications, which are not necessary for this comparison, we write the non-linear model as:

$$f(y_t, z_t, \alpha) = u_t \tag{5.44}$$

and the solution for the endogenous variables, y as:

$$y_t = g(u_t, z_t, \alpha) \tag{5.45}$$

The deterministic solution (which is the normal mode of solution) is obtained by setting the disturbances equal to the expected value of zero. Thus:

$$\hat{y}_t = g(0, z_t, \alpha) \tag{5.46}$$

The first point to note is that this does not coincide with the conditional expectation. This is the same argument that was used earlier to show that the model-consistent solution is not fully rational. In the present case, it implies that the deterministic solution is biased. This arises since the expected value of a non-linear function of a random variable is not in general equal to the non-linear function of the expected value of the variable.

$$E(y_t | z_t, \alpha) = E[g(u_t, z_t, \alpha)] = h(z_t, \alpha)$$

$$E[g(u_t)] \neq g[E(u_t)] = g(0) \tag{5.47}$$

Therefore the deterministic solution has a bias given by:

$$\hat{y}_t - h(z_t, \alpha) \neq 0 \tag{5.48}$$

Since g is not known, nor is h, and so the conditional expectation cannot be calculated directly. It can be estimated as the mean of replicated stochastic simulations. Vectors of random disturbances are generated with the same probability distribution as the model error terms. The model is then solved and the sample mean over all the replications is calculated. So for R vectors of pseudo-random numbers, the estimate is:

$$\hat{y}_t = \frac{1}{R} \sum_{r=1}^{R} g(u_{tr}, z_t, \alpha) \tag{5.49}$$

and the difference $(\hat{y}_t - \bar{y}_t)$ is an estimate of the bias in the deterministic solution, estimated for R replications.

This measure of bias can also be interpreted as a measure of non-linearity. A popular view is that the bias due to non-linearity in large-scale models is small. Fisher and Salmon (1986) criticise the experimental design of many of these studies, however, and find that, in dynamic simulation, the bias can build up as the simulation period is extended. The bias may increase as we move away from initial conditions, which implies that, in general, the bias is base dependent, and is sensitive to the values of the z variables. The size of any bias needs to be interpreted in terms of economic significance, for this is not a matter of statistical significance. The standard error of the conditional mean can be made smaller by increasing the number of replications: thus by increasing the number of replications, we could make any non-zero bias 'statistically significant'.

There are various suggestions for calculating the pseudo-random shocks. The Nagar method (Nagar, 1969) suggests drawing deviates using an estimate of the residual covariance matrix from the historical equation residuals. However, this requires that the matrix of residuals is non-singular, whereas in practice the number of time periods (T) is usually less than the number of equations (N).

The most common method used is the McCarthy method. It employs the equation residuals directly, just using the N equation residuals, essentially drawing weights for a linear combination of residuals. It is possible to allow for autocorrelation and heteroscedasticity in the residuals by filtering these through appropriate transformation procedures (for example, through autoregressive (AR) processes for autocorrelation). In models with forward-looking expectations, it is important to recognise that only the innovation in the AR process is unanticipated, and estimated AR models should be regarded as part of the full model. Both the Nagar and McCarthy methods rely upon a zero-mean historical residual for each equation. Since not all the equation residuals correspond to estimation residuals (some parts of models are not regularly re-estimated), it is necessary to make an adjustment to the residuals to ensure a zero mean. A similar problem arises from the fact that model equations are typically transformed into an equation for the level of each variable, but they may have been estimated in log-linear form. The model equation residuals may therefore not conform with the structural equation residuals. Thus, an equation estimated as:

$$\ln y_t = \alpha \ln z_t + \beta \ln y_{t-1} + u_t \qquad (5.50)$$

may have been rewritten:

$$y_t = \exp(\alpha \ln z_t + \beta \ln y_{t-1}) + v_t \qquad (5.51)$$

Ideally, the model should be recoded in a form that allows the structural residuals to be identified. Fisher and Salmon (1986) show that using the model residuals in place of the structural residuals understates the deterministic bias. Another distributional assumption that may not be met is that of normality, particularly where there are technical equations that have not been estimated, or where an estimated equation includes dummy variables to avoid non-normality, but where these are excluded from the model code.

An alternative method which is sometimes used is the method of Mariano and Brown (1984). This does not rely on an underlying assumption of normality in the disturbances. Instead a sample of the residuals is used directly, replicating the actual historical distribution of residuals.

One of the problems in applying stochastic methods is the number of replications involved, since this is a computationally burdensome task. To reduce the standard error of the sampling estimates, a high number of replications might be needed, yet most exercises have used fewer than 1000 replications. Fisher and Salmon (1986) used 500 replications for the NIESR model and 250 replications for the LBS model. Melliss and Whittaker (1987) used 500 replications on the HMT model, and Hall and Henry (1988) report 1000 replications on the NIESR model. One way of improving the efficiency of the estimates is to adopt the suggestion of Calzolari (1979), pairs of antithetic random numbers. This method uses the principle that the same set of pseudo-random numbers in two situations generally reduces the variability of the difference between the estimates. The Calzolari suggestion is to use the negative of a given drawing of random numbers.

Yet another experimental problem arises from the fact that the model may fail to solve for certain random shocks. Sometimes these may be due to convergence problems that may be solved by adjusting the iterative solution method, but others may arise because endogenous variables take unacceptable values (e.g. negative unemployment). Problems of model failure can become more acute with forward-looking models. If these draws are discarded, the distribution is truncated and the empirical issue is whether this is acceptable or whether new drawings should be made. There is no standard procedure for whether the antithetic should also be discarded if a model failure occurs. One way round the problem is to rescale the input disturbances to prevent numerical failure and to avoid truncating the input distribution.

Stochastic simulation and forward expectations

> The presence of forward expectations in stochastic simulations may require more complicated solution steps, depending on the informational assumptions.

The main issue involved in conducting stochastic exercises with forward-looking models is that a conventional solution along deterministic lines assumes that future random shocks applied to the model are anticipated. It is important to be explicit about the informational assumptions underlying the stochastic exercise. One could assume that agents anticipate the random shock in the current period, but this is rather unrealistic. It is more appropriate to assume that the random shock is unanticipated and only included in economic agents' information set with a one-period lag. The appropriate solution method is then to build up the solution as a series of dynamic steps. The first solution takes lagged values and calculates a forward-consistent solution on the basis of no random shocks (this is equivalent to assuming that the shock is recognised with a lag). The expectations generated from this solution are then used in a second solution which also includes the random shocks. In the next period we use the lagged data from the previous solution to generate a new set of expectations, then apply the random shocks with these expectations – and so on. Thus the solution is stacked up period by period, allowing agents to revise their expectations as more information becomes known. Of course, the last few periods of the solution should be shock free to enable the model to settle on its stable path (the terminal condition problem). The experiment is repeated R times, where R is the number of replications.

The presence of expectational terms in the structural equations complicates the drawing of residuals. Estimates of equation disturbances are the single-equation residuals from the structural equations, and so depend on the unobserved historic values of the expectations variables. One way of dealing with this problem is to use the perfect foresight assumption: that is, to use the actual historical outcome for the variable as a proxy for the expectation. Under rational expectations, agents should make unbiased estimates of the actual outcome with no systematic error, for if they made such an error, it could be exploited to improve the forecast. Hence using perfect foresight to generate the expectations should generate a zero mean, implicitly combining expectations errors with structural disturbances. If explicit expectations mechanisms were available, the two disturbances could be separately identified and the random errors entered separately.

Since the proposed stochastic simulation procedure involves a sequence of solutions, a model failure at any stage invalidates the whole solution and in practice can lead to a very truncated distribution.

The results of stochastic exercises on the earlier versions of the LBS and NIESR models (Wallis *et al.*, 1984) which were backward looking, found standard error bands of around 1 per cent for GDP. More recent estimates by Ireland and Westaway (1990) using a forward looking version of the NIESR model found a standard error of 1 per cent of GDP in the first period, rising to 4.3 per cent after 12 quarters.

Other stochastic issues

So far we have pointed out that the deterministic solution is a biased measure of the conditional expectation, or mean. Emphasis on this criterion arises from its optimality with respect to a quadratic loss function – it is the least squares forecast. But if we use other loss functions, the optimal point forecast may change. One possible alternative is to assume that the loss is proportional to the absolute value of the forecast error. Then the optimal point forecast becomes the median of the probability distribution. Since the random disturbances are usually assumed to have not only a zero mean but also a zero median, the deterministic solution will coincide with the median if the transformation $g(.)$ preserves the median, i.e. provided that:

$$[g(u)]^m = g(u^m) \tag{5.52}$$

where m denotes the median. (We know that this is not true of the mean.) This is satisfied if the transformation is bijective, a condition that is met by models which use the exponential function. Given that most models are log-linear, this might provide a justification for the deterministic method. The practical question is whether the bijectivity condition is met by large-scale models. Hall (1985) presents evidence that the median of the distribution of stochastic simulations either coincides with the deterministic solution or is very close to it.

An even more convincing reason for staying with the deterministic model of solution is that of internal consistency. In a deterministic solution, the identities of the model are automatically satisfied (for example, the components of GDP add up to the total). But this may not be the case in a non-linear model if conditional expectations are used. Particular problems can arise from the relationship between values, volumes and prices. This feature, coupled with the computational burden of stochastic simulation, is a key factor why stochastic methods are not in common use.

Stochastic simulations and policy multipliers

Policy multipliers also should be derived from stochastic simulations, since these are defined as the partial derivatives of the conditional expectation of each endogenous variable with respect to each policy instrument. That is:

$$\Pi_t = \delta h(z_t, \alpha)/\delta z_t \tag{5.53}$$

Since h is non-linear, the multipliers are base dependent. Writing the estimates as the difference between the base and perturbed solution:

$$\bar{\pi}_t = \Delta\bar{y}_t/\Delta z_t \tag{5.54}$$

To reduce the simulation variance, we should use the same pseudo-random disturbances in both solutions. Although what little evidence there is (Fair, 1984) suggests that the bias in policy multiplier is small, this is derived on the basis that the variance–covariance matrix of the coefficients is known.

Empirical exercises using stochastic simulation methods

In this section we review briefly an empirical exercise that has been carried out using stochastic simulations with macroeconometric models. This involves an analysis of the financing of a government expenditure increase (Fisher, Wallis and Whitley, 1985).

> Financing changes in the PSBR – the possibility of instability in bond finance.

Fisher, Wallis and Whitley (1985) used backward-looking models of the UK to explore the possible instability of a bond-financed government spending increase. If instability results, this suggests that it is impossible to conduct a permanently bond-financed deficit in a forward-looking model. The theoretical literature on deficit financing is founded on the work of Christ (1968) and Blinder and Solow (1973). More recently, Whittakker et al. (1986) used a calibrated framework and concluded that fixed money stock rules are less stable than fixed bond stock rules. Fisher et al. (1985) found that deterministic simulations are not particularly informative in concluding whether different forms of deficit finance are stable, since the solutions of the versions of the UK models used did not settle down to a path that could easily be recognised as either

Table 5.4 Stochastic results for alternative financing rules

Model	GDP		Price level	
NIESR:				
Money finance	59	(59)	0.234	(0.17)
Bond finance	75	(73.5)	0.226	(0.20)
LBS:				
Money finance	126	(40)	0.101	(0.078)
Bond finance	132	(61)	0.087	(0.078)
LPL (annual):				
Balanced finance	6672		4.94	
Bond finance	6459		5.55	

Note: Figures in the table are standard deviations; figures in brackets refer to the earlier backward-looking version of the models.

Source: Fisher (1992), Tables 5.1-5.3

unstable or stable. The alternative was to conduct stochastic simulations that examined the variance of output and inflation under different financing rules. Using this approach, one can also examine the dynamic variability of forms of finance. The results presented in Table 5.4 are both for forward-looking versions of the models and for earlier versions that contained backward-looking expectations.

For the NIESR model, the standard deviation of GDP rises under bond finance, but the variability of the price level decreases. Although the output variability is similar on the older, backward-looking version of the model, the price variability is higher. In the case of the LBS model, the variability of output has increased markedly under the forward expectations version of the model. However, output variability under bond finance in the forward-looking version does not increase relatively by as much as under money finance.

Further reading

Fisher (1992)
Cuthbertson, Hall and Taylor (1992)
Hall (1994)

Reference: K F Wallis (1991) in Simulation methods for large-scale macroeconomic models. *Cuardenos Economicos de ICE,* No 48, 11-30.

6 | Forecasting with models

Despite much criticism of the forecasting record, forecasts continue to be in demand. Those in business and elsewhere who require a macroeconomic background to their planning are regular customers for macroeconomic forecasters. At the same time, forecasts can be used to monitor the economy with reference to the government's current economic strategy, and to suggest modifications, either of substance or of tactics. This demand can come from government itself, or from outside bodies or pressure groups which have an interest in influencing policy. Forecasting does not necessarily require a formal model. There are many regular forecasters, especially those sponsored by financial institutions, who do not use a model. Experience shows that their forecasts can be at least as good (or as bad) as model-based forecasts. The easy access to personal computers means that the set-up costs for forecasting are quite small. Our attention here focuses on forecasts produced by macroeconometric models, although we also consider some of the alternatives.

> There is a difference of view as to whether forecasting performance is a good criterion on which to judge models.

Much attention has been given to the forecasting performance of macroeconomic models in the media. For some this is seen as the acid test of models, whereas others regard it as the wrong criterion to apply. In this chapter we review some of these arguments. We then describe how forecasts are constructed using models and methods which might be used to judge between them. As part of this we give information on the relative forecasting ability of the UK models.

> Ex-post forecasts are predictions of the model for some period over which the outcomes are known at the time of prediction; ex-ante forecasts are forecasts with both endogenous and exogenous variable outcomes unknown.

6.1 A framework for analysis

It is important to distinguish between ex-post and ex-ante forecasts. Ex-post forecasts are predictions of the model made over some period for which the data are known; this can be within the sample period on which the model was estimated or outside the sample period. Ex-ante forecasts are forecasts made for some future period where the exogenous variables are unknown and have to be projected, and where the results for the endogenous variables cannot be assessed. This is the mode of operation which is in most people's minds when they refer to forecasting.

The reduced form of the model can be written (using our earlier notation) as:

$$\hat{y}_t = \Pi z_t \qquad\qquad (6.1)$$

The use of a dynamic model to forecast over several periods requires a distinction between exogenous and lagged endogenous variables, and we separate the vector of predetermined variables, z, into exogenous variables and lagged endogenous variables.

$$\hat{y}_t = \Pi_1 y_{t-1} + \Pi_2 x_t + v_t \qquad\qquad (6.2)$$

If we specify the start of the forecast as n, then the one-step ahead forecast is given by:

$$\hat{y}_{n+1} = \Pi_1 y_n + \Pi_2 \hat{x}_{n+1} \qquad\qquad (6.3)$$

where y_n are known and $\hat{x}_{n+1}$ are projected. In a sequence of forecasts up to an horizon h, the forecast for one period enters into the calculation of the next:

$$\hat{y}_{n+j} = \Pi_1 \hat{y}_{n+j-1} + \Pi_2 \hat{x}_{n+j}, j = 2 \ldots h \qquad\qquad (6.4)$$

‖ Most forecasts are made by adjusting the residuals in the model.

In practical forecasting, there are two important departures from this simple model. First, most forecasters do not rely completely on their models to produce forecasts, but adjust them through a process known as 'residual adjustment', 'constant adjustment' or 'add factors'. Although the term 'constant' is often used, there is no requirement that these residuals remain the same over the forecast horizon. Residuals tend to be applied to structural equations rather than to the reduced form of the system. The following equation describes the sequence of adjusted forecasts:

$$y_{n+j}^* = \Pi_1 y_{n+j-1}^* + \Pi_2 \hat{x}_{n+j} + \hat{v}_n, j = 2 \ldots h \qquad\qquad (6.5)$$

The second feature is that there is rarely a complete break, but usually a 'ragged edge' between periods for which data exist and the forecast period for which they do not, for different data are available at different dates and with different delays. In many cases data will not be available for the current period, so that the forecasting exercise begins by forecasting the past. Where the values of some variables are known (a common example is the exchange rate), it is common to exogenise 'temporarily' the variable for which data are available. This is equivalent to deleting the relevant equation. An alternative is to calculate the necessary residual adjustment which generates the known value of the variable, thus retaining the equation (Wallis, 1986). The use of model-consistent expectations does not pose any additional complications for production of ex-ante forecasts, except that the model will need to be solved beyond the forecast horizon to ensure that it is not unduly influenced by terminal conditions. However, forecasters tend not to use forward expectations (especially that of the exchange rate) in their routine forecasting. This is principally because they wish to avoid the feature of sharp changes in contemporaneous variables due to developments in the forecasts some periods away. In addition, solution of models with forward-consistent expectations tends to take considerably longer than standard backward-looking models, and so substantially increases the turn round between forecast runs.

6.2 Components of forecasts

Exogenous assumptions

The forecasting framework shows that an ex-ante forecast requires projections of the exogenous variables. In the single-economy models these can be classified into three main areas: domestic economic policy (tax rates, government spending, monetary policy instruments, etc.); variables describing the world economic environment (world trade, prices, oil prices, etc.); and those variables describing resource variables (technological progress, population, natural resources, etc.). In multicountry models the world economy itself is endogenous.

Forecasts are often be made on unchanged policy assumptions. This is where the current policy stance is assumed to be maintained through the forecast horizon. Alternatively, if the forecast on unchanged policies proves to be unsatisfactory in terms of the government's stated objectives, policy adjustments may be explicitly incorporated. This adjustment can be formalised using reaction functions which purport to describe the authorities' reaction to deviations from their policy objectives.

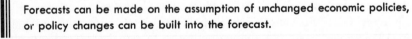

Forecasts can be made on the assumption of unchanged economic policies, or policy changes can be built into the forecast.

Residual adjustments

Residual adjustments are made for a variety of reasons: to take account of model misspecification; to allow for known or expected factors that are not included in the model; or to ensure that 'plausible' or 'consistent' results are obtained.

Most forecasters regularly make residual adjustments to their forecasts. With a well-specified model that is structurally stable, the optimal forecast values of non-autocorrelated equation disturbances are their conditional means of zero (in the absence of any evidence of bias from stochastic simulations). In practice, however, models are usually not well specified and structurally stable, so recent values of the equation residual may be helpful in forecasting later disturbances to the equation. In principle it would be desirable to re-estimate equations routinely to take account of recent data and to adjust for any observed misspecification. However, not only is this a time-consuming task, but often modellers may be reluctant to give full weight to recent data which may be subsequently revised. A more convincing reason why equations are not regularly respecified is that reasons for the breakdown of an equation may take some time to be found. The effort in explaining the behaviour of consumption following financial deregulation in the 1980s and the sharp rise in the savings ratio at the beginning of the 1990s is a case in point, and gave rise to an extensive programme of research.

Where the adjustments are considered to be part of the underlying error process of the model, mechanical rules may be used to project the residuals into the future. Osborn and Teal (1979) suggest several alternative rules. These are given in equation 6.6. The first merely sets the residual in future periods to zero; the second uses a constant based on the last four observations; the third uses an average of the last eight observations; and the final rule is a simple autoregressive rule. In many cases the residuals are used to bring the model back on track at the beginning of the forecast period: that is, the residuals are used to calculate a new intercept term which makes the values of the predicted values from the equation equal to the last known data values.

$$u_{t+j} = 0$$

$$u_{t+j} = \left[\sum_{i=1}^{i=4} u_{t+j-i} \right] \bigg/ 4$$

$$u_{t+j} = \left[\sum_{i=1}^{i=8} u_{t+j-i} \right] \bigg/ 8$$

$$u_{t+j} = \rho_1 u_{t+j-1} + \rho_2 u_{t+j-2} \cdots + \rho_n u_{t+j-n}$$

(6.6)

In addition, there are various social, political and economic factors that may be believed to have an impact during the forecast period, but which are not formally incorporated into the specification of the model. Examples of these might be a dock strike, which may change the behaviour of trade, or evidence from investment intentions surveys. Changes in policy instruments not embodied in the model are another possible rationale for model intervention of this kind (see the discussion on policy analysis in Chapter 7). To the extent that the extraneous information pertains to future events which have only a weak correspondence with historical behaviour or are regarded as one-off events, it is not likely to be practical to respecify the formal model to take account of them, and residual adjustment is the most efficient solution.

The third main reason for including residual adjustments is to allow for the forecaster's judgement to be imposed on the model. The forecaster may have reasons to believe that the forecast is not plausible: for example, an analysis of the liquidity position of firms may suggest that the investment forecast emanating from the model is unduly optimistic. The forecaster can allow for this by including a residual in the investment equation. Extensive use of residual adjustments by the forecaster can mean that the forecast becomes largely a product of the forecaster's judgement and far less a product of the formal macroeconometric model.

> Different reasons for making residual adjustments will also determine the nature of the adjustment.

Different reasons for including a residual adjustment will also influence the form of adjustment. Where residuals are used to correct model misspecification, as in the case of bringing the model back on track, the residual is calculated as in a normal single-equation static context. It may be a constant or vary over time, depending on the forecaster's judgement as to the nature of the misspecification. In a dynamic setting the difference between the unadjusted and the adjusted forecast will increasingly diverge for a constant adjustment, depending on the coefficients of the lagged dependent variables. However, as long as the model is stable, the difference will eventually settle down to a finite limit. For example, if the model is:

$$\tilde{y}_{n+1} = \alpha + \beta y_n + \gamma \hat{x}_{n+1} + \bar{e} \tag{6.7}$$

where e is the residual adjustment, and the unadjusted model is given by:

$$\hat{y}_{n+1} = \alpha + \beta y_n + \gamma \hat{x}_{n+1} \tag{6.8}$$

the corresponding forecasts in period j are:

$$\tilde{y}_{n+j} = \alpha + \beta \tilde{y}_{n+j-1} + \gamma \hat{x}_{n+j} + \bar{e}$$
$$\hat{y}_{n+j} = \alpha + \beta \hat{y}_{n+j-1} + \gamma \hat{x}_{n+j} \tag{6.9}$$

and the difference between the two tends to a finite limit of $\bar{e}/(1 - \beta)$.

If the forecaster has evidence that the parameters have changed, the appropriate residual adjustment is:

$$a_{n+j} = (\hat{\gamma} - \gamma)x_{n+j} \tag{6.10}$$

However, when residuals are used to adjust the value of the relevant endogenous variable to a given value, the residual added to the equation has to be chosen to take account of the equation dynamics, as shown in Chapter 7. For example, if the forecaster wishes to adjust the value of an endogenous variable by an amount d such that:

$$\tilde{y}_{n+1} - \hat{y}_{n+1} = \tilde{y}_{n+j} - \hat{y}_{n+j} = d \tag{6.11}$$

the value of d depends on the dynamics of the model.

Turner (1990) analyses the residuals made by the LBS and NIESR forecasters in autumn 1988 following interviews with the forecasters. He concludes that the forecasters' judgement exerts a strong influence on the forecasts. He finds that the majority of adjustments in this exercise are based on analysis of past single-equation errors, with the most frequently occurring case being where systematic over- or under-predictions are reflected in a simple adjustment to the intercept term in the equation. However, there are also some cases where a more specific judgement is made about the cause of past errors, and in these cases it is quite possible for single-equation errors to be interpreted in different ways by different forecasters, and so to lead to the adoption of different sets of residual adjustments over the forecast. Less frequent is the use of specific adjustments to achieve a certain model outcome.

What is not revealed in Turner's study is the extent to which the forecast is not simply the product of a single run of the model with given exogenous variable projections and assumptions about residuals, but is the result of an iterative process by which the preliminary results are inspected and may lead to subsequent revisions in the adjustments made to the model. Without necessarily attempting to achieve a specific model solution, the forecaster may have some prior views as to what represents a plausible forecast. This may be based on historical experience, on consistency with other evidence (including other forecasts) or on the forecaster's reading of the current economic situation. As well as residual adjustments being changed during the forecasting process, it is also possible that assumptions about policy variables are revised. This might arise if the initial forecast were seen to be divergent from the government's stated policy goals. This change also involves quite a large degree of judgement as to the authorities' future policy response. Less rare is for the model itself to be changed during the forecasting round. Although inspection of past residuals may imply some misspecification of the model, it is unlikely that this can be remedied by simple re-estimation. Econometric modellers prefer to add value to the re-estimation process by considering a reasonably wide range of alternatives, and this precludes a 'quick fix'. Moreover, it is fairly common to spend some time checking the impact of any new specification on the overall properties of the model before it is used seriously. The fact that subsequent data revisions may lead to different conclusions about the nature of misspecification, or about whether there is any misspecification at all, is another consideration weighing against updating the model during the forecasting round.

> Forecasts are the product of the model and the forecaster's judgement; this means that different forecasts can easily arise from the same underlying model, or vice versa.

The fact that the forecast is the product of a model and the forecaster's judgment in a variety of ways suggests that different forecasts can easily arise from the same underlying model or, in contrast, that the same broad forecast may result from models which see the economy working in quite different ways. McNees (1991) shows that forecasts produced in the USA tend to show less divergence than do the underlying models, suggesting that the forecasters' judgement pushes the forecasts towards consensus with other forecasters. A similar conclusion was found by the analysis of UK forecasts described in Wallis *et al.* (1984, 1985).

The arrangements within model-based groups can also mean that the modelling and the forecasting processes are carried out by different individuals or sets of individuals. This can mean that the construction of the model may give less weight to the practical needs of the forecaster than if the modellers themselves were using the model for forecasting. It can also mean that the forecaster may attach less faith to the model, and hence may be more prepared to override it in the forecasting process. Forecasts made by the official institutions such as the Treasury and the Bank of England tend to be made by committee, whereas forecasts made by the independent groups in the UK, such as the LBS, NIESR and OEF, tend to be in the hands of one or two people.

The Bank of England does not publish a forecast. The Treasury is obliged to publish some details as part of the Budget and Autumn statements, but provides no forecast for unemployment. The underlying assumptions are not made public and nor does the Treasury allow independent forecasters access to its detailed forecast assumptions after the event.

6.3 Evaluation of forecasts

The evaluation of past forecasting performance may be a useful input into the forecasting process, and is of interest to outside users who may use it as a guide to which particular forecast(s) to adopt as an input into their own decision making. The fact that the forecasts are rarely based solely on the model means that they cannot be regarded as a model validation test.

Evaluation of forecasts faces the problems of which variables to focus upon, over which time horizon to measure them, and how to distinguish between the role of judgement and model inadequacies.

The forecasters themselves regularly publish accounts of their own performance and contrast this with that of other groups (for example, Britton and Pain, 1992). There have been several independent studies of the performance of different forecasters: in the UK by Ash and Smyth (1973), Holden and Peel (1983, 1986), Wallis *et al.* (1986, 1987), and Wallis and Whitley (1991b); for the USA by McNees (1982, 1986, 1991) and Zarnowitz (1979, 1985). Artis (1988) examines the forecasting performance of the IMF.

In evaluating different forecasts there is the problem of how to judge forecasting performance over more than one economic variable, and over which period to evaluate the forecasts. For example, should the focus of attention be GDP growth over the next six months, over the next year, or over the next three years? Ways in which these problems may be tackled are discussed below, but first we describe some of the formal tests of forecast performance.

Formal forecast tests

> Formal forecast tests are often based on summary statistics, but they face
> the problem that there is no absolute measure of forecast performance
> against which to judge them.

If there are sufficient observations on the forecasts and their outcomes over time, simple summary measures can be constructed, such as the mean absolute error (MAE), and the root mean square error ($RMSE$).

$$MAE = \sum_{i=1}^{n} |y_i - \hat{y}_i|/n \tag{6.12}$$

$$RMSE = \sqrt{\sum_{i=1}^{n} (y_i - \hat{y}_i)^2/n} \tag{6.13}$$

where n is the number of forecasts. However, there is no absolute measure of forecast performance against which to compare these summary statistics.

Three approaches can be taken. We can compare forecast properties against those of the 'optimal' model; compare the model-based forecast with a time-series approach based on the variables' own past behaviour; or compare forecasts across a variety of models and forecasts.

> Three approaches can be used to evaluate forecasts. Their properties can
> be compared against an 'optimal' forecast; they can be compared against
> time-series models; or they can be compared against each other.

An optimal forecast is unbiased and efficient. That is, the forecast error has an expected value of zero and cannot be predicted by any other variable in the information set; all the information has been used fully in the construction of the forecast. A common approach has been to use the forecast realisation regression:

$$A_t = \alpha + \beta F_t + u_t \tag{6.14}$$

where A and F denote actual and forecast values respectively. The joint hypothesis that $\alpha = 0$ and $\beta = 1$ is a test for unbiasedness and is a necessary condition for efficiency, but it is not a sufficient one, since it neglects possible autocorrelation of the forecast error (Granger and Newbold, 1986). Autocorrelated errors indicate that the forecast is not making efficient use of the own-variable information and is therefore inefficient. Holden and Peel (1985), in their assessment of NIESR forecasts, regress past values of the variable on the forecast error to test for efficiency. Thus:

$$e_i = y_i - \hat{y}_i = \beta_1 y_{t-1} + \beta_2 y_{t-2} + \dots \beta_n y_{t-n}$$
$$H_0 : \beta_1 = \beta_2 = \dots \beta_n = 0 \tag{6.15}$$

Britton and Pain (1992) show that information contained in leading indicators could have improved the efficiency of the NIESR forecasts. This result is obtained by regressing the forecast error on leading indicator variables, such as housing starts.

The second approach is to use forecasts based on statistical time-series models to provide a yardstick against which model-based forecasts can be judged. A simple example of such a comparison is the use of the Theil inequality coefficient (U). This is the ratio of the $RMSE$ to the $RMSE$ of a no-change forecast.

$$U = \frac{\sqrt{\sum_{i=1}^{n} (y_i - \hat{y}_i)^2 / n}}{\sqrt{\sum_{i=1}^{n} (y_i - y_{i-1})^2 / n}} \tag{6.16}$$

Other comparisons are with vector autoregressive models (VARs) or Bayesian autoregressive models (BVARs). These are described below. First we note some problems in a formal comparison of time-series methods with model-based forecasts.

Since the data used in the empirical estimation of the two forms are the same, their forecasts, forecast errors and summary measures are not statistically independent (Wallis, 1989). Hence a formal test based on comparison of the two error variances cannot be applied. Second, a univariate time-series model can be regarded as an approximation to the final form of the econometric model, and cannot provide an independent check upon it. Wallis (1989) argues that, since the time-series models emphasise dynamic and stochastic features of the data, comparisons in which they outperform the structural models suggest that the latter are deficient in this respect and so do provide a useful diagnostic check.

This line of reasoning has been applied to multivariate time-series models (VARs). Litterman (1986) has pioneered the use of VARs with a Bayesian modification, and his forecasts are intended as serious forecast attempts in their own right. McNees (1986) suggests that they are among the most accurate for real output, unemployment and investment. Work reported in Wallis et al. (1986, 1987) did not find dominance of VAR forecasts for the UK over the published model forecasts, but once the influence of residual judgement is removed, they are a serious contender to the pure model forecasts (Wallis and Whitley, 1991b). In common with other studies, the accuracy of the VAR forecasts deteriorates as the forecast horizon lengthens. More recently, Artis, Bladen-Hovell and Zang (1992a) have reported on VAR models for the UK which outperform even the published model forecasts. However, Hendry and Clements (1992) criticise the Artis et al. findings on the basis that the VAR models will continue to forecast better than the structural models in periods of structural change, but will fail against the models if the criterion is one of parameter constancy. VARs are usually expressed in differences and this gives them low power to detect misspecification. The more general point made by Hendry and Clements (1992) is that assessment of forecasts by the mean square forecast error criterion is sensitive to the transformation of the variables made (for example, the rate of growth of output against its level).

> Vector autoregressive models can be used to as a check on forecast
> performance of structural models or can be used to produce forecasts in
> their own right.

Much of the stimulus for work using VAR models stems from criticism by Sims (1980) of the methodology of macroeconometric modelling. He argues that the restrictions imposed on the models are incredible. They involve the following:

1. An arbitrary normalisation of each equation. In a simultaneous model, all variables are determined jointly. Sims argues that the consumption function could equally be called an income function.
2. Aggregation problems. Since economic theory is generally developed from partial equilibrium analysis and then aggregated, the restrictions imposed may not be valid.
3. Arbitrary lag lengths. Since economic theory has little to say about dynamic adjustment, the choice of lags is *ad hoc*.
4. Assumptions about expectational variables. Expectations are often modelled in an *ad hoc* fashion and are subject to the Lucas critique.

While the criticisms of Sims retain some force, many regard them as extreme, and not of great practical importance. The expectations argument has lost a great deal of weight since the introduction of rational expectations into macroeconometric models. The normalisation critique is of less force when the degree of simultaneity is not high. In addition, the choice of particular explanatory variables is typically related to a theoretical paradigm and does not preclude simultaneous estimation procedures.

Sims's solution to these difficulties was to estimate unrestricted reduced forms in which all the variables are treated as endogenous. Judgement is involved in choosing which variables are included and in selecting the lag length, depending on the number of observations (so that there are sufficient degrees of freedom to estimate all the coefficients). It is not clear how the variables are to be selected apart from using economic theory, so the idea that VARs are value or judgement free is wrong. It is also necessary to decide upon the form in which the variables are measured (e.g. logs, first differences). The system of equations is:

$$y_{1t} = f(y_{1,t-1}, y_{1,t-2} \cdots y_{1,t-m}, y_{2,t-1}, y_{2,t-2} \cdots y_{2,t-m} \cdots y_{k,t-m})$$

$$y_{2t} = f(y_{1,t-1}, y_{1,t-2}' \cdots y_{1,t-m}, y_{2,t-1}, y_{2,t-2} \cdots y_{2,t-m} \cdots y_{k,t-m}) \qquad (6.17)$$

$$y_{kt} = f(y_{1,t-1}, y_{1,t-2} \cdots y_{1,t-m}, y_{2,t-1}, y_{2,t-2} \cdots y_{2,t-m} \cdots y_{k,t-m})$$

The common lag length is m and the right-hand side variables are the same in each equation. There are no current right-hand side variables, so the model can be estimated by ordinary least squares. The lag length is chosen by using standard F tests to examine whether zero restrictions can be imposed upon higher-order lags. In practice this might mean starting with only one or two lags and then testing whether additional lagged variables are statistically significant.

The main problem with unrestricted VAR modelling is that there will be a large number of parameters in the model. This results in over-fitting the model, and although this produces good within-sample fit, it usually behaves very poorly out of sample. For example, if we have 25 years of quarterly data (100 observations) for a six VAR model with six variables in each equation and a common lag length of 12, we would have 72 lagged variables in each equation and only 28 degrees of freedom, even before constants and dummies are added. This is likely to result in very imprecise coefficient estimates due to multicollinearity.

The Bayesian vector autoregressive model (BVAR) solution to this problem is to use prior ideas about some of the parameters in the model. This was originally discussed by Doan, Litterman and Sims (1984). The prior view for each equation is that it is a random walk with drift, i.e.

$$y_t = y_{t-1} + c + \varepsilon_t \tag{6.18}$$

where c is a constant and ε is a random error term. Other variables and other lags only enter if they contribute to the model. This limits both the number of other variables and the lag length. Another adaptation is to update the coefficients, period by period, using the Kalman filter approach. This enables the model to pick up changes in the underlying processes in the economy. One problem with VARS and BVARS is that they are usually expressed in first differences, and therefore do not embody long-run effects.

A third approach to comparing model-based forecasts is the use of cross-comparisons. Leaving aside for the moment the problem that a comparison of published forecasts over time confuses the contributions of the forecaster and the model (and changes in these contributions over time), one can compare forecasts made at roughly the same time, and therefore based on the same information set. One difficulty referred to above is that the model may contain different degrees of exogeneity. This is not a major problem for the UK models.

Another difficulty is in choosing the set of variables of interest and the time horizon over which they are considered. Implicitly, this involves the specification of a loss function. The use of the mean square error criterion implies a quadratic loss function.

Given the relative freedom of information and the range of alternative criteria, it is not surprising that comparative studies tend to find no unambiguous rankings of forecasts (Zarnowitz, 1979, for the USA; Holden and Peel, 1986 for the UK).

Figure 6.1 shows the forecast performance on growth and Figure 6.2 that on inflation from the main UK forecasters over the 1980s, by plotting their forecast errors on one-year-ahead forecasts. The main impression is that they miss all the major turning points in economic activity (the recession of 1979–81, the boom of 1988 and the recession of 1990–2). The late 1980s boom is under-predicted and forecasters were consistently over-optimistic about output during the recession period of 1990–2. No one forecaster dominates, and there is no evidence of improvement in forecasting performance. There is a tendency to under-estimate inflation. LPL is distinguished by its relative optimism over growth and inflation, in the sense that its forecasts were on average above the growth outturn and below that of inflation.

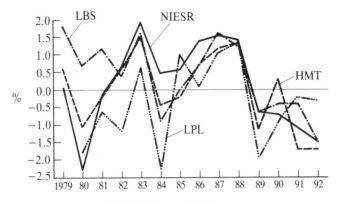

Figure 6.1 GDP growth forecast errors

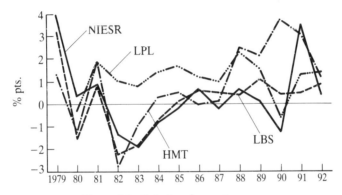

Figure 6.2 Inflation forecast errors

Wallis and Whitley (1991b), using an idea from Ron Smith, consider four key macroeconomic variables from four models over the period 1984–8, using both one- and two-year-ahead forecasts. The root mean square error of forecasts over both horizons is computed for the level and growth of output, the rate of unemployment, and the rate of inflation. (Both the level and growth of output are included to consider the possibility of compensating errors in one or the other over a two-year horizon.) The average *RMSE* is then calculated over the four forecasts and each group's *RMSE* is expressed as a ratio of this average, in order to allow for different degrees of difficulty in forecasting the different variables over this forecast period. These 'relative' *RMSE*s are then plotted in Figure 6.3. A relative *RMSE* greater than unity for a given forecast group indicates that its performance is better than average, and vice versa.

The resulting figure is a tetrahedron with the relative *RMSE*s plotted along each axis. The figure confirms that there is no unambiguous ranking of forecasts. The axes are scaled to give equal weight to each variable. If one tetrahedron lies inside another, that group has superior forecast performance across all the variables, and therefore judgements of relative performance do not depend on the relative weights attached to

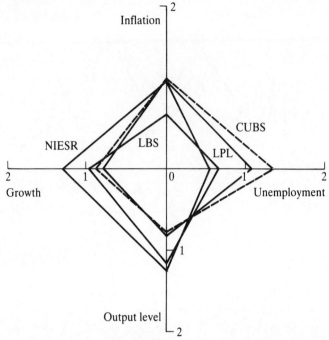

Figure 6.3 Relative root mean square errors of published forecasts: 1984–1988
Source: Wallis and Whitley (1991b)

the economic outcomes. Different relative weights could be depicted graphically by changing the scale of one or more axes. Where the tetrahedra intersect, there is no unambiguous ranking. For example, in the figure LPL is seen to have a better one-year-ahead forecast record on growth than either LBS or NIESR, but does worst in respect of unemployment, and so cannot be considered as superior to the other forecasts unless growth performance is allocated a much higher weight in the loss function than either unemployment or inflation.

If the variables are given equal weight in the loss function, then LPL has the lowest average *RMSE* for the two-year-ahead forecasts, with CUBS ranked second. For the one-year-ahead forecasts, however, it is LBS that performs best, followed by LPL. It is worth noting that good performance in respect of growth does not necessarily correspond with good performance in respect of the level of output. Nor is a relatively good performance on real magnitudes associated with a relatively good ranking in nominal variables such as inflation, suggesting that the forecast trade-offs between these two variables are in error.

The statistical significance of differences in summary statistics such as *RMSEs* cannot be directly tested, as they are not statistically independent. Combining forecasts (Bates and Granger, 1969) is a way of testing forecasts with a view to improving forecast performance. This is based on the encompassing principle and is further developed by Chong and Hendry (1986). Consider a combination of two forecasts:

$$\hat{y}_1 \in M_1$$

$$\hat{y}_2 \in M_2$$

(6.19)

If the combined forecast has an error variance smaller than the first forecast alone, the second forecast appears to offer no further additional information and the first model encompasses the second. Consider the regression equation:

$$y_t = \beta \hat{y}_t^1 + (1 - \beta)\hat{y}_t^2 + u_t$$

(6.20)

and a test of the null hypothesis that $\beta = 1$. Chong and Hendry propose an encompassing test of model 1 by testing the null hypothesis of $\alpha = 0$ in the regression:

$$y_t - \hat{y}_t^1 = \alpha \hat{y}_t^2 + u_t$$

(6.21)

that is, seeing whether the second forecast helps to explain the error in the first forecast. However, the test proposed by Chong and Hendry relies on two assumptions that may not always be satisfied. The first is that the forecast period is outside the estimation period (this is usually true for ex-ante forecasts), but the second condition is more of a problem. This is that the individual forecasts are unbiased and efficient. This strong condition may be relaxed by running the regression to allow for an influence from the forecast values themselves. Thus:

$$y_t - \hat{y}_t^1 = \alpha + (\beta_1 - 1)\hat{y}_t^1 + \beta_2 \hat{y}_t^2 + u_t$$

(6.22)

The coefficient β_2 indicates the extent to which the second model explains the first model's error. Similarly, an encompassing test of the second model is given by the coefficient on β_1.

6.4 Forecast decomposition

As noted above, tests of forecast accuracy combine tests of the model and the forecaster. Wallis and Whitley (1991b) present a method whereby the different elements of a forecast can be distinguished. This rests on the possibility of recomputing the forecasts under different assumptions.

The framework for this decomposition is as follows. Let the published forecast be represented by $f(\hat{x}, a)$ where $\hat{x}$ are the projected values of the exogenous variables, and a is the set of residual adjustments. If we replace the projected exogenous variables, $\hat{x}$, by their actual outcomes, x, we obtain an alternative forecast $f(x, a)$. Comparing this variant forecast with the published forecast gives an estimate of incorrect assumptions about the exogenous variables. Then all residual adjustments are set to zero to give a forecast described as a pure model-based or hands-off ex-post forecast, $f(x, 0)$. The error in this forecast, the 'model error', includes the effects of model misspecification, parameter estimation and random disturbances, together with data errors not accounted for elsewhere. For a given variable, y, the observed error in the published forecast is then decomposed as follows:

Model error $\qquad\qquad\qquad\qquad$ $y - f(x, 0)$

less Contribution
of residual adjustments $\qquad\qquad$ $-[f(x, a) - f(x, 0)]$

plus Contribution
of exogenous variable errors $\qquad$ $+[f(x, a) - f(\hat{x}, a)]$

equals Error in published forecast $\quad$ $y - f(\hat{x}, a)$ $\qquad\qquad\qquad$ (6.23)

An alternative decomposition would measure the role of residual adjustments as $[f(\hat{x}, a) - f(\hat{x}, 0)]$ and that of exogenous variable error as $[f(x, 0) - f(\hat{x}, 0)]$. In a linear model this would give identical results. In the non-linear models used in Wallis and Whitley, the differences were negligible.

This framework sees the role of residual adjustments as offsetting some of the underlying model error, and so improving the quality of the forecast. The results for the LBS, NIESR, LPL and CUBS forecasts analysed in Wallis and Whitley show that, in general, residual adjustments improved the forecast. However, most of the improvement came from the rather mechanical use of constant changes which bring the model back on track, rather than the forecasters' more discretionary adjustments. A priori we would expect forecast performance to improve when the model has the benefit of the correct exogenous information. This was not always the case in the sample investigated in Wallis and Whitley. In several cases the inclusion of correct values of the exogenous variables actually worsened the forecast, suggesting some model misspecification. In principle, forecasters could deliberately incorrectly project the exogenous variables in order to offset model inadequacies elsewhere. However, exogenous variable error tends to be quite common across the models, and the correct projection of these variables adds credibility to the forecast. The perverse role of exogenous variable error, together with the beneficial impact of residual adjustments, leads the published forecasts to outperform the model-based forecasts.

> Evaluating forecasts from forward expectations models requires a two-step procedure to derive the role of expectations; it is not appropriate to substitute actual outcomes for the expectations variables.

The role of forward expectations in forecasts can also be assessed within this framework. Consider a simple linear regression model:

$$y_t = \beta y_{t+1}^e + \gamma x_t + u_t \qquad\qquad\qquad\qquad (6.24)$$

Published model-consistent forecasts then satisfy:

$$\hat{y}_t = \beta \hat{y}_{t+1} + \gamma \hat{x}_t + a_t; \quad t = 1 \ldots h \qquad\qquad\qquad (6.25)$$

conditional on exogenous projections and adjustments, and terminal conditions specified at the horizon, h. There are now two separate influences working. One is the current effect working directly through the contemporaneous exogenous variable, and the other is working through the expectations variable. We can therefore break down the contribution of exogenous variable error into direct and expectational influences. The one-year-ahead and two-year-ahead forecasts satisfy:

$$\hat{y}_{t+1} = \beta\hat{y}_{t+2} + \gamma\hat{x}_{t+1} + q_{t+1}$$
$$\hat{y}_{t+2} = \beta\hat{y}_{t+3} + \gamma\hat{x}_{t+2} + a_{t+2} \tag{6.26}$$

where future expectations depend on further projections of x. The variant forecasts use actual data on x in periods 1 and 2 and are:

$$\hat{y}_{t+1} = \beta\hat{y}_{t+2} + \gamma x_{t+1} + a_{t+1}$$
$$\hat{y}_{t+2} = \beta\hat{y}_{t+3} + \gamma x_{t+2} + a_{t+2} \tag{6.27}$$

where future model-consistent expectations depend on projections of x in subsequent periods obtained from time-series rules. The decomposition into direct and expectational effects is obtained by calculating an intermediate run where future expectations are held fixed, but actual exogenous data are used.

$$y_{t+1}{}^0 = \beta\hat{y}_{t+2} + \gamma x_{t+1} + a_{t+1}$$
$$y_{t+2}{}^0 = \beta\hat{y}_{t+3} + \gamma x_{t+2} + a_{t+2} \tag{6.28}$$

As discussed earlier, there is no role for substituting actual outcomes for the expectations variables, since the best one-step-ahead forecast requires the best estimate of current expectations and this is provided by the model-consistent expectation. The decomposition made by Wallis and Whitley suggests no major role for expectational variables on forecast performance over this period; this may reflect the fact that they have not been extensively used in forecasting as distinct from policy analysis.

6.5 Data revisions

Data revisions can affect forecasts by changing the values of the actual recorded outcomes, by changing the values of the exogenous inputs into the forecast, or by changing the forecaster's perception of the recent performance of the model.

One source of error that is difficult to account for is that due to data revisions. These are quite common in macroeconomic statistics, and revisions can substantially alter the view of the past. They can affect forecast evaluation in three ways. First, they change the values of the endogenous outcomes, and hence estimates of the actual values against which the forecast is compared. Second, they can change the value of exogenous variables and lagged values of the endogenous variables, and hence change the predicted values of the endogenous variables. Finally, they can alter the perception of the forecaster about the current and recent past, and lead to a different choice of residual adjustment. Estimating this possible influence is difficult without having inside knowledge of the forecaster's decision process. In Wallis *et al.* (1986) an attempt is made to evaluate the role of data revision in UK forecast performance by recalculating residual settings on the basis of data revisions. The effects are not found to be large.

6.6 A typical forecasting round

In this section we describe the process of a typical forecasting round. For a more detailed account the reader is referred to Keating (1985a). The UK HM Treasury makes internal forecasts three times a year, and is obliged by the Industry Act 1975 to publish twice a year. These published forecasts correspond with the Budget and the Autumn Statement. Not all details of the forecasts are published, where they might be very sensitive in terms of financial markets (exchange rates and interest rates) or for political reasons (the level of unemployment). At the start of the forecasting round, Treasury ministers are invited to approve the broad policy assumptions of the forecasts, and at the end of the forecasting round, they also approve the final forecasts. The status of the Treasury forecasts is that they are the official view of the government and are the responsibility of ministers based on the advice of their officials. There has been criticism of this approach, which is not always followed by other countries, and calls for a more independent framework for forecasting. As a first response the Treasury has established a group of seven 'wise men', who are economists drawn from academia and the City and who also publish regular forecasts.

The typical outline of forecasting procedures is as follows. The first step in forecasting is usually to collect the latest data on the variables in the model. This is not a simple task. Although much of the data may be directly available from official sources in computer-readable form, other data may require more human effort to extract (for example, the construction of wealth aggregates). Even if the data are easily obtained, two other problems may arise. First, the cautious forecaster will spend some time examining the new data to check whether they are consistent with other information. Second, there is an inevitable lag between collection of data and publication. In the case of national accounts data this can be between five and six months. Publication lags on other data may be far longer (for example, data on stocks of financial or physical assets), and publication lags also differ between different countries. The forecaster attempting to predict the world economy may find that no data are available at all for some countries, or that there are large gaps in the data or other inconsistencies. For example, balance of payments statistics may not have been collected in some countries.

Consequently, the second task of the forecaster is to 'forecast' the recent past in order to assess the current position of the economy. Often there is some partial information available which can be used to construct a picture of the current state of the economy. In large organisations such as HM Treasury, one individual may take responsibility for one sector of the economy and will provide an assessment of its current situation using an amalgam of available information. For example, an assessment of consumer spending patterns might include data on retail trade, consumer confidence surveys, the financial and income position of households, and detailed information on the car market and other consumer durables.

Having assembled data (and estimates of the data) for the recent past, the next task is to assess how well (or badly) these data are explained by the model. This means calculating the residuals of each equation in turn and inspecting them for any systematic pattern.

The next stage is to make projections of the exogenous variables. In single-country models, this involves a projection of the external environment as well as the setting of economic policy. Usually the latter task is conducted in a sequential manner: that is, an initial set of assumptions about policy are made, based on the reading of policy pronouncements by the authorities, and these may be reassessed depending on the outcome of the forecast. There remains a distinction between forecasts based on 'unchanged' policies and those that assume policy will have to adjust to ensure a more favourable outcome. HM Government's own forecasts are closer to the second approach, for the government usually has an incentive to produce forecasts which come closer to meeting their declared objectives, and they are not obliged to make their detailed assumptions known. However, there may be circumstances where the authorities have an incentive to make the economic outlook appear less favourable in order to gain support for radical policy measures.

The final element in the forecasting process is to project the residuals into the future, based on external evidence and the model's recent performance. This is where much of the forecasters' judgement comes into play.

It is now possible to make an initial forecast. The plausibility of this forecast can then be assessed in terms of both its internal consistency and its consistency with other information about the economy, including survey evidence and other forecasts. An iterative process then begins which may lead to the final forecast diverging substantially from the initial one. Many forecasters will have clear priors about products of the forecasts, such as the personal sector savings ratio, productivity growth and the share of investment to GDP, and the forecast may be substantially amended to coincide with these priors. A common way to treat the rational expectations of the exchange rate in forecasts is to assume that the current value of the exchange rate (which is almost instantaneously observed) incorporates all currently known information and hence will only 'jump' if there is additional 'news'. In the absence of 'news', the exchange rate can then be forecast into the future along its UIP path. Recent work has attempted to mimic the forecaster by the use of an expert systems approach (Artis, Moss and Ormrod, 1992b). However, this work has yet to be shown as a genuine alternative.

In the UK Treasury, the forecast which emerges is then subject to the scrutiny of ministers, and in particular the Chancellor of the Exchequer. The forecast is seen as a political view for which the Chancellor takes responsibility. This has meant that the model-based forecasts have been substantially overwritten at times; most notably in respect of the large balance of payments deficit forecast in 1988. Similar considerations often underlie forecasts made by the policy authorities in other countries. The danger with this approach is that 'official' forecasts are always regarded with suspicion and treated as optimistic. Nowhere is this more true than in Japan, where official forecasts often become unbelievable as further information on the economy becomes available.

Reasons for forecast failure

This chapter concludes on a more light-hearted note, but one which reflects some of the problems involved in forecast evaluation. It is based on material collected by Ron Smith, to whom I am grateful for allowing its publication, and it collects together various responses to forecast failure. These are real excuses provided by the forecasters, and most of them relate to evidence given to the Treasury and Civil Service Select Committee on Official Forecasting. Page references are to this publication.

Forecasters' rules

1. Avoid precision. By not giving exact numbers of dates or defining the forecast measures precisely, subsequent comparison with the actual data can be avoided. This is based on the familiar maxim: never give the estimate and the forecast of when it is expected to occur together.

2. Explain that the evaluation is no longer relevant.
   (a) Either the model or the forecaster has changed (or both). 'The Bank model has changed considerably over this period as a result of research, and to reflect major changes in the way the economy operates'. (p. 58).
   (b) The model is not really designed for forecasting, but for some other purpose. 'Thus the idea that the Bank forms a central view of the most likely course of the economy at discrete points which could be compared with other forecasts or the outturn does not properly reflect what the Bank actually does'. (p. 54).

3. Blame the exogenous variables.
   (a) Government policy. This is more difficult for the Treasury.
   (b) Other exogenous events that were clearly unpredictable: for example, the 1986 oil price collapse; the 1990 Iraqi invasion of Kuwait; the changes in eastern Europe in 1989; the 1987 stock market crash; the 1988 UK budget.
   (c) The self-defeating forecast. 'By pointing out the need for action it may provoke changes that render it inaccurate. But it will nevertheless have served its purpose' (Bank of England) (p. 54).

4. Blame the data. Bad data caused the forecast error either by distorting the parameters of the model or by distorting the forecasters' view of the current situation. A strong form is to allege that the forecast is a better guide to the truth

than the official estimates of the actual outcome. 'Furthermore data inaccuracies have been a major and increasing source of actual or apparent forecast error. One cannot be sure that recent forecast "errors" will not be changed as further revisions are made to the national accounts statistics' (Bank of England) (p. 58).

5. Confuse the issue (this is standard professional practice!). There are many possible examples, including that the user selected the wrong variable to look at, or the wrong period, or just got the timing wrong. Jargon is also a useful defence: for example, 'these are integrated processes and after adjustment for a stochastic trend and multiplicative seasonal factors, the error is quite small'.

6. Point out that everyone else made the same mistake. This is commonly used. 'Some explanations for why the Treasury got its forecasts wrong are set out earlier in this memorandum. The same problems seem to have afflicted all forecasters' (Treasury) (p. 19).

6.7   Conclusions

This chapter has reviewed some of the issues involved in producing forecasts with a macroeconometric model, and some of the methods and pitfalls in evaluating forecasts. The general conclusion is that macroeconometric models have not proved particularly successful in forecasting over the last decade, despite the many empirical innovations in their structure. We might ask the question: why forecast with macroeconometric models? Model validation is not the answer, not only because the forecast combines the model and the forecasters' judgement, but also because ex-ante forecasts are not necessarily a proper validation tool. The answer seems to be that there has been no diminution in the demand for forecasts, and that macroeconometric models help organise the forecasting judgement and are useful in constructing economic scenarios. However, many people forecast quite successfully without a full model, or without a model at all. A case for forecasting with models may be made on the grounds that it focuses attention on key empirical issues, and indeed many of the developments described in Chapters 3 and 4 stemmed from forecast failure. The outstanding question is then whether too much resource input goes into forecasting relative to its benefits.

Further reading

Treasury and Civil Service Committee (1991)
Keating (1985a)
Wallis (1989)
Wallis and Whitley (1991b)

7 | Policy analysis

In this chapter we review some of the applications of models in policy analysis.

Although there are alternative approaches to macroeconomic models for forecasting, there is less direct competition for their use in policy analysis. In this chapter we review some of the applications of models to the analysis of policy. We examine how new policies might be analysed with macro models, and the issues involved in using models to analyse the past.

We begin with a summary of the procedures involved in policy analysis, and the relative roles of simulation and optimal control methods. We also discuss the complications involved when models contain forward-consistent expectations.

7.1 The methodology of policy simulations

Policy simulations are relatively straightforward when the policy instrument is included in the model, but need more care when the instrument is not part of the formal statistical model.

The policy instrument is known

We begin with the standard exposition of the standard linear model:

$$By_t + Cz_t = u_t \tag{7.1}$$

which has a reduced form:

$$y_t = \Pi z_t + v_t \tag{7.2}$$

where

200

$$\Pi = -B^{-1}C$$

$$v_t = B^{-1}u_t \tag{7.3}$$

and Π represents the set of policy multipliers.

In policy analysis we need to start with a benchmark against which to compare the results of the policy change. This we call the base run, and it is often equated with a forecast. The base run or control solution is given by:

$$B\hat{y}_t = Cz_t = 0 \tag{7.4}$$

where the error term u has been set equal to its mean value of zero. Replacing the set of exogenous variables z by $z_t + \delta_t$, the revised or perturbed solution is then:

$$B\tilde{y}_t + C(z_t + \delta_t) = 0 \tag{7.5}$$

Consequently, the effect of the policy can be calculated as $\tilde{y}_t - \hat{y}_t$.

In this formulation, δ is a vector of policy changes and can vary over time. Most simulations would use either a step or a growth change in the exogenous policy instrument. For example, it might be assumed that government expenditure is raised by a constant amount relative to the value that it takes in the base or control solution (a step change), or it might be assumed that the growth of government expenditure is permanently higher than in the base simulation (a growth change). Normally we might consider only one policy instrument change at a time, so that only one element of δ is non-zero but, alternatively, changes in more than one instrument at a time gives what is often called a policy scenario. Note that in a linear model the effect of a scenario change (that is, several policy instruments taken together) is the same as the collective result of considering one policy change at a time. Thus any policy scenario can be decomposed into its various elements. The PC ready reckoner program (Macdonald and Turner, 1991) is an empirical application of this 'linear' approach to non-linear models, and is an easy form of access to the UK models.

Given that:

$$B(\tilde{y}_t - \hat{y}_t) + C\delta_t = 0 \tag{7.6}$$

we could solve for δ in order to find the required change in a policy instrument(s) to produce the desired change in the endogenous (target) variables. This is obviously a very crude targeting approach, and we consider below how this relates to the method of optimal control.

The policy instrument is not known

The methodology above assumes that the policy instrument is included as one of the policy instruments on the model. In many cases, however, the policy instrument may not be part of the model, if there is a new policy, or if the policy change is similar but not defined by an included exogenous variable. Let us take the case of a new policy first. If there is no existing policy instrument, one possibility is to augment the model by a residual adjustment:

$$a_t = -C\delta_t \tag{7.7}$$

that is, to use an adjustment which is the product of the policy change and its matrix of coefficients. Typically, the adjustment will be applied to the most relevant structural equation in the model. This will correspond to where the initial impact of the policy is expected to be felt. For example, an adjustment might be applied to the import equation in order to allow for a new policy of quantitative import restrictions. It would be strange to apply an adjustment for this new factor directly to the investment equation, even though investment might be indirectly affected. Although the model is usually simultaneous and the two methods can be made identical, any external evidence is more likely to relate to the direct initial impact on imports.

The major problem here is that the matrix of direct effects (C) is normally unknown. The main problem for simulating a new policy is the derivation of C, since the model itself does not normally provide this. In some cases, however, the existing model can supply the necessary informative. Consider the introduction of a new tax. If a relevant price variable is already included in the model equation, it might be appropriate simply to augment this variable by the size of the tax increase. In many cases this option is not available, and then the model-user has to rely on off-model evidence. This can be in the form of other information: perhaps cross-section or cross-country evidence; or from calibrated or theoretical models. Lack of information may mean that only very crude estimates of the impact of the policy might be possible, but the important factor is that the underlying assumptions are made explicit. In these situations the aim is to provide the model with an estimate of the initial direct effect of the policy. The role of the model is then to calculate the relevant multiplier and feedback effects; it cannot totally assess the policy, since it cannot provide an estimate of the direct effect. This is the responsibility of the model-user. The distinction between giving the model an estimate of the initial effect of the policy and imposing the results of the policy is considered below under the heading of exogenisation. An example of model simulation analysis of this form is the analysis of a marginal employment subsidy (Whitley and Wilson, 1983).

The policy instrument is not specified in sufficient detail

In the absence of explicit policy variables, procedures differ according to whether the structural equation or the reduced form is to be adjusted.

One possibility is that the policy instrument is included in the model and is specified in sufficient detail for it to be directly perturbed, but important features of the transmission mechanism through which the instrument operates are not distinguished. This represents a kind of aggregation problem, in that the policy instrument is a particular component of an aggregate variable whose influence on other variables in the model is different from other components of the aggregate. Turner, Wallis and Whitley (1989) give an example where there is an increase in government investment specifically concentrated on housing. The key issue is whether housing investment, separately identified or not, has a lower marginal import content than other forms of (government) investment. Turner *et al.* show how off-model information, in this case from the input–output table on the average import content of different forms of final expenditure, can be used to adjust the import equation to reflect the lower import content of housing investment. This is done by adjusting the import residual by the difference in C. Formally, we can set this out as follows:

$$\tilde{y}_t = \cdots + c_{11}(z_{1t} + \delta_{1t}) \qquad (7.8)$$

where the variable z is simply perturbed by an amount δ.

If the perturbation applies only to a component of the aggregate, and the variable does not appear elsewhere in the model with differential effects, we can simply scale the size of the shock. Thus:

$$\tilde{y}_t = \cdots + c_{11}(z_{1t} + \delta_{1t}^*)$$
$$\delta_{1t}^* = c_{11}^* \delta_{1t}/c_{11} \qquad (7.9)$$

If, as in this example, the transmission effects differ from the normal effect implied by the model, the original perturbation should be maintained and an allowance to the equation (in this case the import equation) should be made by the residual adjustment to reflect the different impact:

$$a_{1t} = (c_{11} - c_{11}^*)\delta_{1t} \qquad (7.10)$$

This procedure amounts to a structural adjustment of the model to reflect influences not otherwise incorporated. Alternatively, we may wish to adjust the reduced form of the model.

Adjusting the reduced form

The reduced form can be adjusted in a variety of ways: by a type 1 fix; by a type 2 fix; or by exogenisation. These are not always exactly equivalent methods.

The type 1 fix

The type 1 fix works by choosing the appropriate structural residual to achieve the desired result.

In some simulations we way wish to constrain the reduced form rather than the structure. We may, for example, wish to constrain an endogenous variable to have a certain value, and to investigate the impact of this assumption on the rest of the endogenous variables in the system. For example, it may be of interest to know how key policy targets – output, inflation and unemployment – might be affected if the underlying level of consumer spending were higher than in the base solution. This might then be used to judge possible uncertainties in policy setting. Policies which are successful in attaining given policy targets for a given base scenario for the economy may become inappropriate if the underlying conditions are different.

The first case we consider is where we allow the so-called constrained variable to adjust to changes in the other endogenous variables. This is equivalent to assuming a shock to the variable in question, and involves adjusting the residual in the relevant equation. This procedure is known as a type 1 fix.

$$\begin{bmatrix} B_{11} & B_{12} \\ B_{21} & B_{22} \end{bmatrix} \begin{bmatrix} y_{1t} \\ y_{2t} \end{bmatrix} + \begin{bmatrix} c_1 \\ c_2 \end{bmatrix} z_t = \begin{bmatrix} u_{1t} \\ u_{2t} \end{bmatrix} \tag{7.11}$$

We could simply assign a value for the first element of y:

$$y_1 = y_{1t}^* \tag{7.12}$$

we then solve for y_2:

$$y_{2t}^* = -B_{22}^{-1}(B_{21}y_{1t}^* + C_2 z_t) \tag{7.13}$$

This is like treating y_1 as if it were an element of the exogenous variable set, z, and switching out the relevant equation.

The type 1 fix which generates this solution is:

$$a_{1t} = B_{11}y_{1t}^* + B_{12}y_{2t}^* + C_1 z_t \tag{7.14}$$

Using the residual in this way to control y_1 is equivalent to switching out the first block of the model. Both assume that the given value of y_1 can be achieved, and the focus of interest is what happens to y_2.

The switching-out method is called *exogenisation*. It does not reveal how the given value of the first element of y is achieved.

The type 2 fix

|| The type 2 fix works by adjusting some other variable to which the variable of concern is related; it is a crude form of optimal control.

The type 1 fix achieves given value for one of the ys by adjusting the residual on 'its' equation. The type 2 fix adjusts some other variable to which this y variable is related – normally an exogenous variable. It can be regarded as a direct form of targeting. For example, we might consider varying a price variable to achieve a given quantity effect, or interest rates to achieve a given money target. In essence, the type 2 fix is asking how much we need to adjust a given exogenous variable to obtain the desired effect on the endogenous variable of interest. Thus we choose the value of the adjustment, δ, such that:

$$(B_{11} - B_{12}B_{22}^{-1})y_{1t}^* = -(C_1 - B_{12}B_{22}^{-1}C_2)(z_t + \delta_t) \tag{7.15}$$

The change to the exogenous variable influences y_1 directly through C_1 and indirectly through C_2 and B_{12}. For this procedure to work, it requires that the elements of C are non-zero.

The type 2 fix has a single-equation interpretation in that it is similar to inverting the equation to derive the required value of one of the explanatory variables, which produces the desired value of the endogenous variable. It does not, however, imply any change in the classification of exogenous variables.

The solution for the non-targeted variables, y_2, is given by:

$$y_{2t}^* = -B_{22}^{-1}[B_{21}y_{1t}^* + C_2(z_t + \delta_t)] \tag{7.16}$$

Now compare this with the type 1 fix:

$$y_{2t}^* = -B_{22}^{-1}[B_{21}y_{1t}^* + C_2 z_t] \tag{7.17}$$

The difference lies in the absence of the specific policy adjustment in the type 1 fix case. Consequently, if the policy variable adjusted has a direct non-zero influence on the other endogenous variables, the type 1 fix or exogenisation methods will produce a different effect on the other endogenous variables in the system, even though the effect on the endogenous variable of interest, y_1, is the same. Before we compare directly the type 1 fix, type 2 fix and exogenisation methods, we note that exogenisation can play a role in the decomposition of simulation results. By partitioning the system (i.e. closing off certain transmission routes by exogenisation, holding values at their base settings), the relevant contribution of different components of the system can be assessed. Examples of this procedure were given in Chapter 5.

Comparison of the type 1 fix, type 2 fix and exogenisation methods

In order to compare these three commonly used methods of adjusting variables, we select an example where the exchange rate is the desired endogenous variable that we wish to assign. This is particularly relevant to the discussion of exchange rate targeting, as in ERM. The first conclusion is that all three methods give the same result for the exchange rate. The distinction between them is the effects on other endogenous variables.

Let us choose an exchange rate equation which relates the change in the nominal exchange rate to the interest rate differential, relative prices and other influences:

$$e_t = e_{t-1} + (r_t - r_t^*) - (P_t - P_t^*) + RES_t \tag{7.18}$$

The three methods are:

Exogenisation   Fix $e_t - \bar{e}_t$

Type 1 fix   Choose RES_t such that $e_t = \bar{e}_t$

Type 2 fix   Vary r_t such that $e_t = \bar{e}_t$

All three methods give the same effect on e. Now consider the effect on other variables. Let us consider p, the price level. The exogenisation and type 1 methods will give the same result: p will be changed to the extent that there exists a transmission mechanism from e to p elsewhere in the model. However, the type 2 method explicitly changes the interest rate, r, which may also affect p, so the total impact from the type 2 method may be different from the other two methods.

Now assume further that the foreign price level, p^* changes. The exogenisation method has already assigned the value of the exchange rate, and nothing happens except that p^* may influence other variables in the model. In the type 1 fix method, the value of the exchange rate will change by the amount of p^* unless the residual is further changed itself. In the type 2 fix case, the exchange rate remains at its pre-assigned level as in the exogenisation case, but the interest rate also changes and this influences p through the rest of the model as before. The type 1 fix and exogenisation methods do not explain how the exchange rate has attained its given level, whereas the type 2 method is explicit about the scale of required adjustment to policy variables, and also indicates the scale of additional policy changes required if there is a shock to the system.

> Standard simulation analysis can be termed 'what-if' analysis; exogenisation is more like 'if-only', since no adjustment mechanism is specified.

Whereas the standard policy simulation can be regarded as an example of 'what-if' experiment, the exogenisation method in policy analysis is more a case of 'if-only'. The study by Andrews et al. (1984) criticised the HMT study of real wages and employment for this very reason, for it did not explain how real wages might change. Further, the Andrews study showed how the different ways that real wages might be changed (e.g. through a demand or a supply shock) would produce a different direction of reduced-form correlation between real wages and employment. The problem is that both real wages and employment are endogenous variables. Turner, Wallis and Whitley (1989a) also show the sorts of bias that might emerge for exchange rate targeting under the different methods. In this study, results of an oil price shock to the HMT model are examined under a variety of ways of targeting the exchange rate (see Table 7.1).

The standard oil price shock with no exchange rate target shows a rise in GDP and in the price level. With a target exchange rate (set equal to the base solution) the results vary according to how this is achieved. If exchange rate intervention is used, GDP falls initially and then rises, and the price level falls consistently. If interest rates are used, however, the GDP fall is quite marked and permanent, and the price level rises after five years. If, instead, the exchange rate is fixed exogenously, output rises and there is a small fall in the price level. The difference in the effects compared with the interest rate case show how a required rise in the interest rate to maintain the exchange rate target has deflationary effects on the rest of the economy, effects which are ignored by the exogenous exchange rate case. The extent of any bias in the exogenisation procedure therefore depends on the degree of simultaneity in the model. In policy experiments, it is important to specify how a proposed intervention takes place, and to detail the supporting evidence. If this is not done, the outside observer cannot be sure how far the results derive from the model or from the judgemental intervention of the modeller.

Table 7.1 Exchange rate targets: HMT model – responses to a 20% fall in the price of oil

	GDP (%)		Price level (%)		Unemployment (000s)	
	Year 1	Year 5	Year 1	Year 5	Year 1	Year 5
No target	0.16	0.35	0.15	2.23	−4	6
Exchange rate target:						
Intervention	−0.14	0.14	−0.23	−0.33	65	74
Interest rates	−0.39	−0.65	−0.07	0.58	45	139
Exogenous	0.02	0.18	−0.16	−0.03	2	31

Source: Turner, Wallis and Whitley (1989a)

As a further example, Whitley (1989) criticises a study by the Bank of England on inflation (Mackie, Miles and Taylor, 1989) where the real exchange rate was assumed to be fixed at a constant rate over the past without any mechanism specified as to how this result came to be achieved. This is another example of an 'if-only' experiment, and the Bank of England study casts little light on the behaviour of inflation over the 1980s.

Non-linear dynamic models

Although most of the basic issues in policy analysis have been covered by the linear analysis above, there are one or two extra complications which are introduced when we are dealing with non-linear dynamic models.

First, there is the problem of the form of the residual.

$$\ln y_{it} = b \ln y_{jt} + c \ln z_{kt} + u_{it} \tag{7.19}$$

might be a standard log-linear equation, but this may be transformed in the model code to transform the residual into the same units as the endogenous variable. Thus:

$$y_{it} = \exp(b \ln y_{jt} + c \ln z_{kt}) + a_{it} \tag{7.20}$$

It is also possible that the residual is treated as a multiplicative factor, taking values on either side of 1.

A second issue is that of dynamics. If residual adjustment is being used, this needs to take account of dynamics. In a dynamic model, a constant residual may have a cumulative effect, as is discussed in Chapter 6.

$$b(L)y_t + c(L)x_t = u_t$$
$$\tilde{y}_t = -b(L)^{-1}c(L)(x_t + \delta_t) + b(L)^{-1}a_t \tag{7.21}$$

Here the pattern of residuals follows the polynomial in $b(L)$. In the first-order case:

$$b(L) = 1 - b_1 L$$
$$\tilde{y}_t - \hat{y}_t = a_t + b_t a_{t-1} + b_1^2 a_{t-2} + \cdots + b_1^{t-1} a_1 \tag{7.22}$$

To achieve a constant difference, d, where d is given by:

$$\tilde{y}_t = \hat{y}_t = d \qquad (7.23)$$

requires

$$a_1 = d; a_2 = a_3 = \cdots = d(1 - b_1) \qquad (7.24)$$

If $b(1) = 1$, i.e. we have a first difference equation, only the first time period needs to be adjusted by the residual d. The dynamics of the type 2 fix reflect both $b(L)$ and $c(L)$:

$$\Pi(L) = -b(L)^{-1}c(L)$$
$$\Pi(L) = \Pi_0 + \Pi_1 L + \Pi_2 L_2 \qquad (7.25)$$

Problems with the type 2 fix are as follows:

1. The required policy instrument change may be different in the short run to the long run: for example, interest rates may need to rise initially and then fall in order to achieve the required target.
2. The size and frequency of the required policy change may be implausible. The change in the policy instrument may be far larger than from historical experience, and assumptions that tax rates are varied in every quarter, say, might be institutionally unlikely.
3. The type 2 fix procedure only works when there is a contemporaneous effect from policy instrument to endogenous variable. For example, if interest rates only influence money demand with a one-period lag, a type 2 fix cannot be used to model a policy of money targeting.

A more general treatment of the policy target problem is the optimal control approach.

7.2   Optimal control

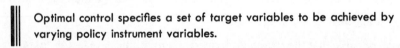

Optimal control specifies a set of target variables to be achieved by varying policy instrument variables.

The application of control theory to problems of macroeconomic policy making has a long history, and recent control theory literature has been concerned with optimal control. The techniques were originally developed in the engineering literature and adapted to economic systems (e.g. Chow, 1975). An objective function is first specified, which is a scalar function of the endogenous (target) variables and policy instruments over the planning period. The optimal control problem is then to find the values of the policy instruments that, together with the resulting predicted values of the endogenous variables, minimise the objective function. The objective function may depend on deviations of actual values from their desired values, and on the path of the policy instruments. Relative weights applied to the target variables reflect the policy-maker's priorities: for example, between inflation and unemployment. The presence of the path of the instrument variables in the objective, or loss, function may reflect institutional constraints, such as the extent to which certain policy instruments can be used, or the desirability of relatively smooth changes in policy instruments. In a linear model, with a quadratic loss function (i.e. one which penalises equally deviations from the target in either direction), optimal control theory gives a control policy in the form of a linear feedback rule for the instruments. In the non-linear case, a time series of policy instrument settings is obtained by numerical methods, conditional on the paths of the exogenous variables.

In a simple one target–one instrument case, a multiperiod quadratic loss function may be written:

$$w = \sum_{t=1}^{T} [k_{1t}(\tilde{y}_t - y_t{}^*)^2 + k_{2t}(\Delta(x_t + \delta_t)^2 + k_{3t}\delta_t{}^2] \tag{7.26}$$

where y^* denotes the target value of the endogenous variable, and x is the base value of the instrument. The k_2 coefficients indicate the relative cost of changing the instruments from one period to the next, and the k_3 coefficients the cost of changing the instruments from their base setting. Where instrument costs are absent, this expression collapses to the type 2 fix, where a minimum loss of zero is obtained by achieving the target in all periods. As noted above, a common difficulty with the type 2 fix approach is the implausibility of the instrument paths which, if not modified, may produce erratic or destabilising influences on other variables.

Much of the classic control theory literature is concerned more with stability and robustness than with narrow ideas of optimality. The aim is to produce linear feedback rules for policy instruments that give acceptable behaviour of the system under control. An example are the proportional, integral and derivative rules introduced by Phillips (1954).

Optimal values can be determined as a linear control rule:

$$z_t = K_t y_{t-1} + h_t \tag{7.27}$$

where K is called the feedback gain in the technical literature.

The same ideas can be related to non-linear models. For example, papers in Britton (1989) attempt to derive explicit feedback rules that approximate the fully optimised solution in large, non-linear models. A further motivation for expressing the policy rule in this form is to obtain simple policy rules which are easy for policy-makers to understand, and hence which have a greater chance of being applied.

Applications of optimal control to large-scale models have been made by Henry, Karakitsos and Savage, (1982) and Wallis et al. (1987), where the main focus has been on deriving inflation-unemployment trade-offs.

Calculating trade-offs by optimal control methods

||| Optimal control methods can be used to calculate trade-offs.

We showed in Chapter 5 how simulation methods could be used to calculate trade-offs between reduced-form variables in a model. We now consider how this can also be done using optimal control methods. The control method is based on the idea that trade-offs can be treated as a menu for policy choice. Optimal control is designed to select the combination of outcomes that maximises welfare, or minimises loss, subject to the relative priorities attached to different outcomes.

Subject to instrument costs, the control solution traces out the feasible solution space (see Figure 7.1). This is equivalent to a production possibility curve (PP), and the choice of relative priorities is equivalent to selecting an indifference curve (such as IC_1). The point of tangency of the indifference curve (e.g. IC_2) with the production possibility curve gives the optimal combination of unemployment and inflation. By changing relative preferences, we change the shape of the indifference curve and hence the point of tangency. By changing relative priority weights, we can then slide the indifference curve around the production possibility frontier and hence trace out the frontier itself.

This method is valid for systems that are feasible and controllable. Controllability relates to the familiar Tinbergen (1952) rule that there must be as many independent effective instruments as there are independent targets. Non-linearity may destroy controllability if non-linear transformations or boundary and ceiling conditions (e.g. non-zero conditions) place limitations on the solution of both endogenous and exogenous variables. (This occurs by reducing the rank of the reduced-form matrix.) Controllability may also be lost as the solution moves some way away from its base: in other words, the multipliers are base dependent.

Trade-offs are calculated by altering the weights within the objective function, following the suggestion of Chow and Megdal (1978):

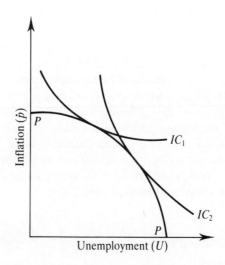

Figure 7.1 Trade-offs and optimal control

$$w(\dot{p}, U; T) = \sum_{t=1}^{T} (a_{1t}(\dot{p}_t - \dot{p}_t^*)^2 + a_{2t}(U_t - U_t^*)^2) \tag{7.28}$$

This corresponds to the minimisation of the loss function above, subject to the constraint of the dynamic model. Introducing costs associated with large and rapid changes in policy instruments gives:

$$w(\dot{p}, U, x; T) = w(\dot{p}, U; T) + \sum_{t=1}^{T} \sum_{k=1}^{K} [b_{kt}(x_{kt} - x_{k,t-1})^2 + c_{kt}(x_{kt} - x_{kt}^*)^2] \tag{7.29}$$

where x_{kt} is the value of the kth instrument in period t, and * denotes its desired or zero-cost value. The b coefficients indicate the cost of changing instruments from one period to the next, and the c coefficients the cost of departing from the base values of the instruments.

There is no unique boundary, however, in the sense that the solution may be sensitive to the choice of instrument variables. In addition, once we allow for instrument costs, the optimal solution may no longer coincide with points on the boundary. Consider a case where we impose very large costs on the departure of the instruments from their base setting (the c coefficients). Then total cost will be minimised with instrument values very close to their own base-run values, giving a solution very close to the original inflation–unemployment values.

Wallis *et al.* (1987) calculate trade-offs for the main UK models using control methods, and these results can be compared with those obtained by standard simulation methods described above. The results for the LBS model are shown in Figure 7.2. The chosen set of instruments are government expenditure and the standard rate of income tax. The optimised trade-off is given by the line AA whereas lines BB and

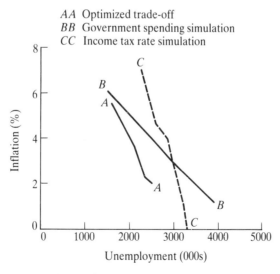

Figure 7.2 Optimised inflation–unemployment trade-offs: LBS model

CC are the results of changes in government expenditure and income taxes separately. The slope of *AA* is clearly a combination of the two instrument slopes shows no great tendency to become vertical over time, suggesting that there was a long-run trade-off in this model.

Results for the HMT model are shown in Figure 7.3. The standard optimised trade-off is calculated by maintaining a constant joint target loss relative to the instruments as the relative priorities between targets are varied. This is shown as *AA*. It has a fairly similar slope to the trade-offs generated by use of the government expenditure simulation (*BB*), but lies to the left of it and so shows a small improvement in both inflation and unemployment. If we reduce instrument costs (i.e. reduce the *c* weights), we shift the trade-off to the left by some 300 000 unemployed (curve *CC*) whereas increasing instrument costs shifts it to the right by some 75 000 unemployed. The curve *CC* actually represents the furthest that instrument costs can be reduced, and is therefore the best estimate of the possibility frontier of the model. Failure to renormalise the weights to obtain a constant total loss can bias the slope of the trade-off. If, for example, only one of the inflation or unemployment weights is varied (as in Henry, Karakitsos and Savage, 1982), the slope shifts to either *FF* (inflation weight only) or *GG* (unemployment weight only). Thus although optimal control is quite useful in deriving trade-offs, the results are quite sensitive to the exact specification of the objective function and the way in which the weights are varied to calculate the trade-off.

Forward expectations and control methods

‖ Models with forward expectations face the problem of time inconsistency.

Models with forward expectations add a further complication for policy analysis under optimal control, since current behaviour may be influenced by anticipations of the policy.

Kydland and Prescott (1977) argue that control theory is no longer applicable once rational expectations are treated as rational. The main force of their criticism is that policies can be time inconsistent: that is, policies which are initially optimal fail to remain so with the passage of time. In particular, there may be an incentive for the policy authorities to renege on previously announced policies. For example, the government may announce a policy of monetary restraint designed to reduce inflation. If expectations are rational and the policy is believed, economic agents will form their current behaviour on the basis of these policies. The government, having achieved its goal of reducing inflationary expectations, is now free in subsequent periods to change its policy towards one of monetary expansion to reduce unemployment, since it can now do this without causing accelerating inflation. Time-inconsistent policies in this sense can be anticipated, however, and announced policies may not be credible unless there is some mechanism that pre-commits the authorities to stick to their announced policies. The literature on this dilemma is surveyed by Blackburn (1987).

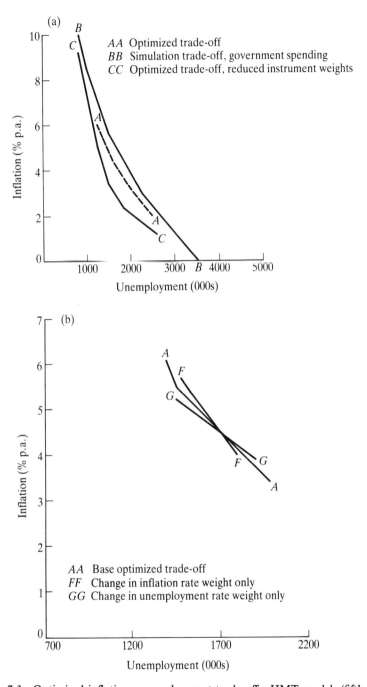

Figure 7.3 Optimised inflation–unemployment trade-offs: HMT model: (fifth year)

Many of the methods used for dealing with this are in the nature of a dynamic game between policy-makers and the private sector. Alternatively, the approach can be applied to international policy co-ordination, where the players in the game are national policy-makers; for examples of this approach, see Holtham and Hughes-Hallett (1992).

Policy formation exercises in models of a single economy usually assume non-cooperative behaviour, and time-inconsistent approaches typically follow the Stack-leberg assumption. This is where one player (set of agents) acts as a leader, anticipating the reactions of the follower to announced policies, and optimises on this basis. This is the case where the model describes the behaviour of economic agents who form expectations on the basis of announced policy, which is taken as given, and the policy-makers then optimise their actual policy. The approach can be fairly easily incorporated into the standard optimisation methods with some modifications.

Essentially, solution requires that the model is solved in consistent expectations mode, optimising on this basis. There are two main complications. First, a consistent expectations solution requires that variables are on a stable trajectory near the terminal date; in this instance, instrument variables should also be stable. This problem can be dealt with by solving the model over a longer time horizon than used for the optimisation. The second complication is that the control algorithm may use derivative-based procedures which assume that current-dated variables are not affected by future policy changes; this is clearly inappropriate in this case. These derivatives have to be calculated in addition, and this is easily done by impulse shocks in the terminal period. It is also possible that there may be a dependence on initial and terminal dates, particularly where there is a distinction between anticipated and unanticipated effects. Hence there may be a need to recompute derivatives for each time period, so that instead of just nx derivative calculations being needed (where nx is the number of instruments), we may need up to $T.nx$ model solutions. Because forward expectations require stability of the solution, there is explicit penalisation of implausible instrument changes near the end of the optimisation period. This has tended to pose problems for models without forward-consistent expectations, for it is always possible to introduce large policy changes at the end of the policy horizon, and these are only automatically penalised by the costs of instrument change.

Time-consistent policies

Time-consistent approaches usually adopt the Nash assumption. Under this approach, each player in the game takes the other's actions as given and an equilibrium exists when neither has an incentive to move, again taking each other's optimal policy as given. In this case, it is now necessary to ensure that expectations are consistent with the optimised policy. The Nash approach might be regarded as more realistic in that economic agents are assumed to understand and correctly anticipate the policy-makers' actions – this is then a time-consistent solution. Fisher (1992) describes some of the solution procedures that might be used in the Nash non-cooperative framework.

The optimisation process works by finding a consistent expectations solution for given policy settings. Forward expectations elements are separated out from the policy optimisation calculations so that time inconsistency is ruled out. Expectations consistency is enforced by searching across time consistent strategies until expectations consistency is achieved. In a single country model the typical economic players are wage-setters and the policy authorities. The relevant steps are as follows:

1. Take an initial set of expectations of wage-setters (perhaps from a consistent expectations base).
2. Solve the policy optimisation problem, treating expectations as fixed to get $\hat{y}$.
3. Check for consistency of expectations. If consistent then stop, otherwise ...
4. Solve for consistent expectations given the optimal instrument setting from 2. Then solve from 2 again.

This can be a time-consuming process, so some short-cuts are useful. These can take the form of incomplete iterations at either step 2 or step 4; alternatively, convergence tests could be restricted to variables of interest. The exact methods used are obviously subject to experimentation. Hall (1985) has attempted to use such an algorithm for a model with a single expectations variable. A further modification that might be useful is to start the solution from the time-inconsistent solution. Alternatively, linearised versions of the models could be used (Barrell et al., 1992), but this always poses the problem of whether non-linearities matter. There is always the potential problem that there may be no time-consistent, expectations-consistent solution.

The algorithm can be extended to cover several policy-makers, and this is particularly appropriate to apply to multicountry models. In this case, step 2 is replaced by a loop where the policy optimisation is solved for each player in turn. The solution is a non-cooperative solution. An alternative is to treat the game as one of co-operation. For example, the policy-makers could agree to stay with their announced policies, and agents behave as if expectations were inconsistent, because they are being compensated in some form. For example, they may be rewarded by a more expansionary economic policy if they agree to lower wage claims. The solution to the problem allows the welfare function to be expressed as the joint welfare function of the two parties. Solution proceeds by:

1. Taking initial expectations variables.
2. Solving the joint optimal control problem for both policy instruments and expectations.

7.3 Policy reaction functions

Policy reaction functions can approximate feedback rules from the optimal control approach; or they can be derived from statistical analysis; or they can be 'plausible' policy rules.

The optimal control approach delivers the required changes to policy instruments consistent with minimising a loss function that contains the relative objectives of the policy-makers. The resultant paths of the policy adjustments may not be easily described, and this has been a problem for those wishing real-world policy-makers to adopt 'optimal' policies. A way forward has been found whereby the policy adjustments are translated into an easy-to-understand set of policy rules. These can then be used to specify how the authorities should react to shocks to the economy that impinge upon their policy objectives. These rules can be forward looking, in the sense that they relate to expected deviations from target, or they can be backward looking and relate to known values of the target variables.

The emphasis of the control approach and derivation of simple policy rules is on prescriptive behaviour: that is, how the authorities should behave 'optimally' in differing circumstances. An alternative approach uses reaction functions to attempt to model the actual policy behaviour of the authorities. These reaction rules may not correspond with optimal behaviour. Reaction functions of this kind can be arrived at in a variety of ways. Attempts can be made to estimate them over some period of history (see Wallis and Whitley, 1992) or to specify them a priori. Reaction functions can be particularly useful when it is inappropriate to keep policy setting fixed, during simulation exercises that involve different economic outcomes. They can also be used to simulate alternative economic policy regimes. For example, Whitley (1992b) describes simulations with multicountry models to illustrate the different economic outcomes under EMS, EMU and floating. In a general sense, policy reaction rules can be thought of as enabling full closure of the model. They typically describe how government spending, tax rates, interest rates and other policy instruments are set. Internal consistency is an important requirement. A good example of this is the government budget constraint, first emphasised by Christ (1968). Here a change in government spending has to be financed by taxes, high-powered money or the issue of bonds either to the domestic non-bank private sector, or to the overseas sector.

Simple consistency in the above sense may be insufficient, however, for it does not guarantee the sustainability of fiscal stance. Here we are concerned with whether an unbalanced deficit can be permanently sustained, and this is the issue illustrated in stochastic analysis of budget financing in Chapter 5. One way of looking at sustainability is to model the development in the stock of government debt to GDP, and this is described in Chapter 8.

The form of finance of any given government deficit is a key assumption in any simulation that has a central role for a change in the budget deficit. It is therefore important that the nature of the underlying policy stance, whether deficit finance or some other form of policy, is explicitly understood when analysing macroeconometric model simulations. The problem with many UK models is that they often embody an implicit assumption that cannot be easily modified. In fact, it is only in the LPL and BE models in the UK that the financing rule for the budget deficit is expressed in a way that money and bond finance can be clearly observed. In the other UK models, interest rates are either fixed (which approximates but is not identical to money finance) or used to target a measure of money supply. The latter is again only an approximation, this time to bond finance.

> Assumptions about the finance of any given budget deficit are key to policy simulation analysis that involves any fiscal change. In historical simulations, it is important to ensure that the overall policy stance is internally consistent.

The form of financing rules and the nature of the underlying policy regime are important issues in counterfactual or historical simulations of the economy, to which we now turn.

The interrelationship of monetary and fiscal policy

In simple *IS-LM* analysis, this is usually represented by a distinction between money and bond finance. Under money finance, any change in fiscal policy is accompanied by a shift in the *LM* curve (accommodating monetary policy) in such a way that the interest rate remains constant. In contrast, under bond finance, the *LM* schedule is held fixed and the interest rate rises, so that a new equilibrium is reached at the intersection of the new *IS* schedule and the original *LM* schedule. These are the mechanisms assumed in the volume edited by Klein (1991), where an attempt is made to estimate the partial slopes of the *IS* and *LM* schedules from simulation analysis. This methodology is described in Chapter 5.

In the simple closed-economy model, a bond-financed expansion is seen to lead to a smaller increase in total output than under money finance. In an open economy, the impact of a fiscal expansion depends critically on the nature of exchange rate adjustment. If there is less than perfect capital mobility, a money-financed increase tends to lower the exchange rate, thus adding to the expansionary effect of the fiscal stimulus, whereas a bond-financed expansion tends to operate in the opposite direction. However, some of the models under consideration in this book do not correspond to this simple paradigm.

The general framework described above can be expressed in terms of the balance sheet of the UK banking sector (see Table 7.2). This implies that the change in sterling M3 is given by the following:

$\Delta£M3 = \Delta$ notes + coin
$+ \Delta$ sterling lending to the UK public and private sector
$+ \Delta$ sterling lending to overseas residents
$+ \Delta$ overseas residents' currency deposits
$- \Delta$ non-deposit liabilities

The PSBR comprises four different components:

1. Current and capital expenditure.
2. Tax revenues.
3. Financial transactions.
4. Interest payments.

Table 7.2   The relationship between assets, liabilities and broad money

Liabilities	Assets
Sterling deposits of UK residents	Sterling lending to the UK private sector
Sterling deposits of overseas residents	Sterling lending to the public sector
Foreign currency deposits	Sterling lending to overseas residents
Non-deposit liabilities	Foreign currency lending

Its financing is expressed as follows:

PSBR = Δ notes and coin
+ sales of public sector debt to the UK non-bank private sector
+ external finance of the public sector
+ Δ sterling lending to the public sector by the banking system

The relationship between changes in the monetary aggregate and the PSBR can therefore be written as:

Δ£M3 = PSBR − gilt sales + Δ bank lending + net external flows −Δ non-deposit liabilities

This relationship makes clear the roles of the two main instruments to control the growth of broad money. First, a reduction in the size of the PSBR is directly associated with a reduction in the growth of broad money. Second, a rise in short-term interest rates will normally increase sales of public sector debt, or restrain the demand for sterling lending. In fiscal shocks that involve an increase in the PSBR, holding the money supply constant corresponds not to a simple definition of bond finance, but rather to monetary targeting through the use of interest rates. Similarly, the alternative policy of holding interest rates constant corresponds only loosely to the term 'money finance'.

Simulation of bond finance usually involves inverting the demand for money function to target a given money aggregate by interest rates. Where an accounting framework such as that above is used, the demand for money function is often implicit. Whereas this framework is applicable to the mainstream UK models, the approach in more monetarist models, such as LPL, is different.

Here, the banking sector is consolidated with that of the monetary authorities and the supply of money is treated as an exogenous variable under the influence of the authorities. The monetary aggregate is then more closely related to high-powered money, so that a money-financed increase can be simulated directly by increasing the monetary base by an amount that corresponds with a public expenditure increase, and bond finance by holding the money base constant so that the PSBR is residually financed. In the mainstream models, bond finance is more correctly defined as money targeting, since interest rates are required to rise to offset the induced monetary expansion arising from the operation of the monetary multiplier between high-powered money and broad money aggregates.

7.4   Counterfactual exercises and historical tracking

Counterfactual simulations consider how the economy might have behaved in the past if some alternative policy or exogenous environment had existed.

Many policy-related simulation exercises with macroeconometric models can be termed prescriptive, in that they relate to discussion of how policy might or should evolve over some future period. Macroeconometric models can also be used to consider how the economy might have behaved over some historical period if some alternative policy had been pursued. This form of simulation is often termed counterfactual, in that it assesses the impact of a different economic environment. Several studies have been carried out on various vintages of the UK models. Artis *et al.* (1984) use the NIESR and HMT models to examine the recession and recovery of 1979–82, a period also assessed in a Bank of England study (1981). Artis, Bladen-Hovell and Ma (1992) use the NIESR model with forward expectations to examine the Labour government of 1974–9, and Wallis and Whitley (1992) also use the forward-looking NIESR model, together with the BE model, to investigate factors underlying the period 1979–84. The 1980s are considered in a further study by the Bank of England (Mackie, Miles and Taylor, 1989), and Matthews and Minford (1987), whereas Savile and Gardiner (1986) investigate the 1970–83 period using a backward-looking version of the NIESR model.

Three principal issues relate to counterfactual experiments of this kind. The first is the setting of policy. The second is the possibility of changes in the policy regime, and hence the impact of the Lucas critique. The third is whether the models can be considered valid for such exercises. We deal with these in turn, but first consider how counterfactual experiments are conducted.

The first step in the counterfactual simulation is to set up a base from which the effects of the alternative (counterfactual) policy can be assessed. This will usually be a simulation where the policy instruments or policy rules are equivalent to those that were actually used over the period in question. The base can then be made consistent with history by adding back single-equation residuals so that the actual values of the endogenous variables are replicated. (The use of adding back single-equation residuals to verify a given model solution is a useful consistency check on the model.) Alternatively, the residuals can be set to zero, as they would in a simulation over the future, and then the counterfactual results compared with this base rather than with the actual values of economic variables over the period, as in the first method. As long as non-linearities are not too serious and the base solution is not too distant from actual historical experience, it should not matter which alternative is used. However, if the base with zero residuals is quite different, the use of contingent policy rules in the counterfactual might lead to different conclusions. In the counterfactual simulation, the policy variables or rules are replaced by other settings that may be derived from some other historical period, or which are simply written down as a plausible alternative. This alternative might represent a set of different policy objectives, or the assignment of different policy instruments to the same set of objectives.

219

The results of the counterfactual policy regime can then be derived by taking the difference in outcomes either from historical values or from base-run settings of the endogenous variables. In exactly the same way that alternative policy settings can be used, so it is also possible to consider additional counterfactual environments: for example, to investigate the effects of a different world economic environment. In this case, one would simulate the model with a different set of exogenous world inputs in the counterfactual run. If both world and policy counterfactuals are used, their effects on the domestic economy can be decomposed into separate contributions (see Wallis and Whitley, 1992). However, the choice of counterfactual setting is not straightforward.

Defining the policy regime

There is a conceptual difference between counterfactual simulations that attempt to assess the different impact on the economy if an alternative policy regime had been adopted in the past, and counterfactual simulations that attempt to derive the role that actual policy played in the evolution of the economy. The former is relatively straightforward and corresponds with the normal form of simulation over some future period. The latter requires comparison of the actual policy regime with some idea of a 'neutral' or 'unchanged' policy regime in the counterfactual. A common assumption used is that tax rates and interest rates are held constant in the neutral policy setting, and that government expenditure grows on trend. In addition, it is often assumed that either the nominal or the real exchange rate is held constant.

This set of assumptions does not guarantee internal consistency, however, partly because this combination cannot be said to have been actually observed over time. Two possible elements of internal inconsistency might be mentioned. First, there is the lack of an explicit examination of the outcome for the government deficit that emerges from the tax rate and spending assumptions. In turn, this raises two further considerations. Is the size of the implied budget deficit plausible, and is the way of funding the deficit sustainable? Is it possible that the funding assumption might imply an accelerating bond or money stock? If the implicit assumption is one of money finance (interest rates are constant), a balanced funding rule is expressly ruled out. The second possible inconsistency relates to the joint assumptions about interest rates and exchange rates, for a constant (nominal) interest rate may not be consistent with the path of the exchange rate that is either assumed or derived from the counterfactual simulation.

These are serious objections to the methodology of assessing economic policy over the past by reference to a neutral policy path. Not only may the results be internally inconsistent, but they may be sensitive to relatively small differences in the neutral policy setting (for example, the trend rate of growth of government spending, the precise choice of the level at which interest rates are held constant). Furthermore, if key variables are exogenised, a potential bias is involved if an instrument by which this is achieved is not made explicit, as discussed in Chapter 5. There is also a problem if some decomposition of the policy contribution is desired.

In the Bank of England study (Mackie, Miles and Taylor, 1989), the real exchange rate was held constant as part of the exercise to estimate the effect of monetary policy on inflation over the period 1978–86. In a standard counterfactual simulation it is possible, subject to non-linearities, to derive the contribution of components of the total either by building up the simulation by successively adding in each separate policy component, or alternatively by starting with the total and subtracting each component in turn. The role of each element is then calculated as the difference between simulations in which it is included and those from which it is absent. The order of calculation should not matter. However, when a variable that is jointly determined by both policy elements is exogenised, the order of calculation does matter for the results. In fact, there is no longer a unique way of separating individual policy contributions. In the exercise conducted by Mackie *et al.*, they start with counterfactual monetary policy and an assumed exogenous real exchange rate and then add the changes in fiscal policy. Now since the real exchange rate is exogenous, fiscal policy can, by definition, have no impact on the exchange rate. The monetary policy contribution is therefore overstated, for if the order of calculation were to be reversed, monetary policy would also have no effect by definition on the real exchange rate.

In order to avoid some of these problems, Wallis and Whitley (1992), in a study with the NIESR and BE models, use policy rules in the counterfactual setting to evaluate the role of Mrs Thatcher's economic policy. These rules are derived partly from reaction functions estimated over an earlier historical period (the 1970s) for interest rates and government spending, and partly from an explicit budget rule which states that the tax rate adjusts to maintain a stable government deficit to GDP ratio. The exchange rate is determined endogenously. The use of policy rules enables them to judge policy as conditional on external events rather than totally fixed. Wallis and Whitley also consider a counterfactual world environment that is derived from a prior use of the GEM multicountry model. Domestic policy is therefore allowed to adjust to a different world environment, so that, for example, domestic interest rates reflect a different outcome for world interest rates as well as domestic policy factors.

Change in the policy regime (the Lucas critique)

A strong argument against the use of macroeconometric models in analysis of history is that they cannot capture changes in behaviour from a change in policy regime. This is popularly known as the Lucas critique. It argues that comparison of non-marginal changes in economic policy is not a legitimate exercise with macroeconometric models, since they are not structurally stable. Much of the force of this argument has been lost with the routine inclusion of rational expectations in macro models. Both Artis, Bladen-Hovell and Yue Ma (1992) and Wallis and Whitley (1992) use the NIESR model with forward-consistent expectations in their assessment of different periods of economic history. Matthews and Minford (1987) also use forward expectations with the LPL model. However, they use static simulation whereas we argue that in counterfactual analysis, a shock may evolve over time and, due to the dynamics of the model, may have effects over a considerable period of time. Hence dynamic simulations are more appropriate. This is in contrast to evaluating the tracking performance of models, where it is argued that static simulation is the appropriate method. Counterfactual exercises with model-consistent expectations require some changes in methodology.

The informational assumptions are a key element in counterfactual experiments under forward-consistent expectations. Usually it is assumed that economic agents have information dated to the previous period, but that they correctly anticipate the rules by which the authorities set policy. Current outcomes for the exogenous variables, and in particular the variables relating to the world economic environment, are not known at the time when agents form their expectations. However, expectations are updated sequentially as information on actual outcomes and exogenous variables become known. In order to form expectations of the exogenous variables other than policy instruments, time-series rules can be used. The simulation is built up as a series of steps.

1. Run a standard model-consistent solution from period t to period $t + n$, using the policy rules in the counterfactual case and using time-series rules for the other exogenous variables.
2. Holding expectations fixed, solve again, replacing the values of the exogenous variables for period t by their actual values. This is also done for the policy variables, i.e. replacing the value determined by the policy rules by actual values. The result is then the counterfactual solution for period t.
3. Using the solution values from 2, solve the model in consistent expectations mode from period $t + 1$ to $t + n$, as in 1 above.
4. Repeat step 2, replacing values at $t + 1$.
5. Continue solving sequentially, updating lagged information until the model is solved for period $t + n$ using information from $t + n - 1$.
6. In order for the results to be insensitive to terminal conditions, the solution period needs to be longer than $t + n$, where this is the period of interest for the historical exercise. This can be done by extending the solution period by one period at a time as the sequential process continues. Alternatively, we could choose the longest solution period necessary and maintain this throughout the sequence of steps.
7. In order to compare the counterfactual simulation, we need a base solution. This is constructed in the same spirit, with the difference that the model is not augmented with the policy rules, but uses time-series rules for policy variables as for other exogenous variables.

This approach treats the unobserved expectations as model consistent, and hence on average correct, in the absence of direct measures of expectations. A possible refinement would be to use an alternative set of policy rules to generate expectations in step 1 – these rules being those believed by agents, but not those actually implemented. It has been suggested that the perfect foresight assumption could be used to derive expectational errors: that is, to replace the expected value of the endogenous variable by its actual outturn. But this merely transfers the expectational error elsewhere.

It also misses the conceptual point that it is a matter not of whether expectations were correct, but of whether they were correctly estimated at the time.

Model adequacy

In order to have confidence in policy results obtained from counterfactual exercises, it is first necessary to have confidence that the model can itself explain history. Various criteria may be used for tests of model adequacy. Pesaran and Smith (1985) provide a useful guide to model evaluation criteria. Some argue that a good ex-ante forecasting performance is a necessary step for a valid model, but others argue that 'good' forecasts can be produced from 'bad' models, that outside sample experience should concentrate on parameter constancy, and that these should be the focus of tests of predictive ability. Within-sample experience is typically evaluated at the individual equation level by batteries of econometric tests, but there is rarely any attempt to test the system performance of the model. Here again there is a conflict of views. Pagan (1989) argues that static simulation is to be preferred to dynamic simulation as a validation of model performance. Hendry (1993) criticises dynamic simulation methods, since they argue that its accuracy depends on the extent to which the model attributes data variance to factors outside the model: that is, on the degree of exogeneity. A model that treats several key variables as exogenous is likely to have a lower root mean square error from dynamic simulation than another model which treats fewer variables as exogenous. Hendry and Richard (1983) argue that exogeneity claims need to be tested – there is a difference between weak and strong exogeneity, the latter concept corresponding to proper independence of the variables in question from other endogenous variables.

Static versus dynamic simulation

As noted above, there is some dispute about whether dynamic or static simulation should be used as a diagnostic tool in model evaluation. A static simulation is one where the solution for the endogenous variables in period, t, depends on the actual data for the previous period, whereas dynamic simulation uses calculated values from the model for the previous period as an input into the solution for the current period.

The argument of Pagan, who uses a linear model, is that if a model is simulated over a period that is the same as that over which it was originally estimated, the reduced-form residuals, which are simply transformations of the original structural residuals, will average zero. Therefore calculating the mean error of the simulation is not helpful as a measure of unbiasedness, since we would expect the mean error to be small. Additionally, he argues that dynamic simulation provides no extra information. The dynamic model errors will just be a correlated transformation of the original structural errors from a linear model. Thus, if the original errors were non-autocorrelated, the dynamic errors will show autocorrelation, and if this were to be judged as evidence of misspecification, it would be misleading. This conclusion has been challenged by Mariano and Brown (1991), who argue that this conclusion is not valid in a non-linear model and that dynamic simulation is a useful diagnostic device.

Evidence from historical tracking

Fisher and Wallis (1990) conduct an historical tracking exercise on the UK models (1987 vintage) over the 1979–88 period using static simulation methods. They show that the system performance of the UK models is quite poor. This suggests that the models may be a poor guide to evaluating alternative historical developments. Systematic errors in tracking can be traced back to errors in the underlying structural equations, which supports the Pagan linear view. The exchange rate equation is found to be an important source of tracking error. Moreover, some of the failure of the models could be traced to areas of the models that are regarded as relatively unimportant. In some cases, the use of imposed technical relations was a source of non-zero mean errors, while in other cases, relatively neglected equations in the model produced systematic model error – for example, the equation that linked manufacturing earnings to whole-economy private earnings in the HMT model.

Fisher and Wallis calculate Theil inequality coefficients for the models. The Theil coefficient is defined as the ratio of the root mean square error of the forecast to the root mean square error of a no-change forecast: that is, the root mean square of the first difference of the relevant variable. For a given variable, a value greater than unity indicates that the one-step-ahead forecast performs less well than a random-walk model. Fisher and Wallis present results for four key variables and six models, and in less than half of the cases the model fits no better than a random walk. The results also show that there is no uniform ranking of the models across the four variables (Table 7.3).

Fisher and Wallis also apply forecast-encompassing tests to the rival models and find that in general there is no encompassing model, each model having something to contribute in explaining the other models' errors. Each model could therefore, in some general sense, be improved by taking account of the properties of the other models. The use of forecast-encompassing tests was described in Chapter 6. Models with forward expectations have to be treated differently in model tracking exercises, the methodology being very similar to that involved in the counterfactual experiments. In fact, the construction of the base solution in the counterfactual exercise is in itself a model

Table 7.3 Theil inequality coefficients for the UK models

Model	Unemployment	Inflation	Exchange rate	Output growth
BE	0.921	0.493	1.826	1.234
HMT	1.996	4.960	1.478	1.390
NIESR	0.880	0.554	3.681	1.123
LBS	1.126	0.950	20.060	0.950
LPL	0.819	2.011	1.654	1.476
CUBS	1.240	0.500	0.531	0.565

Source: Fisher and Wallis (1990), table 2, p. 193.

tracking solution if equation residuals are not added back into the solution. The model is first solved under model-consistent expectations, but with extrapolations of the exogenous variables by time-series rules. Then, in the second stage, expectations are held fixed and the simulation repeated, but with actual current values of the exogenous variables substituted. Since a static simulation is being used, the solution for the subsequent periods merely uses actual data as lagged values. Thus the second step of the solution procedure merely involves a one-period-ahead solution. In an expectational model, current model variables depend on their expected values, and these in turn depend on the future projected values of the exogenous variables. The procedure can be set out as follows:

Step 1 $\hat{y}_t = f(y_t^e)$

$y_t^e = f(\hat{x}_{t+i})$

Step 2 $\tilde{y}_t = f(\hat{y}_t^e, x_t)$ (7.30)

An alternative procedure is to use the perfect foresight assumption so that expectational errors become part of the overall model error.

7.5 Conclusions

In this chapter we have considered the use of models in policy analysis. We have shown how models may be amended in certain ways to accommodate policy changes which are not part of the formal statistical model, but care must be taken to make the auxiliary assumptions explicit, otherwise the validity of the exercise is threatened. The use of the optimal control approach enables instrument changes to be calculated which are consistent with a given welfare function. Once forward-looking behaviour is present, the standard approach needs to be modified to avoid time-inconsistency. In policy analysis, the setting of the overall policy regime can be of critical importance; in particular, it should be internally consistent. In counterfactual analysis, the ability of the model to replicate history is necessary before the model can be taken seriously to evaluate alternative policies.

Reference: K F Wallis (1988) 'Empirical models and macroeconomic policy analysis' in Empirical Macroeconomics for Interdependent Economies in R C Bryant et. al., pp 225-237.

8 | Multicountry models

8.1 Introduction

Greater integration of economic activity internationally and the desire to take interdependencies between economies into account have increased the interest in multicountry models.

There has been a rapid growth in the number of multicountry models in recent years. Artis and Holly (1992) note that this activity reflects an increasing interest in, and concern with, the international transmission of shocks, and the role that increasing interdependencies among countries from growing trade, capital market integration and foreign investment play in reducing the discretion of individual governments. Within Europe, the steady integration of the members of the European Community and increasing awareness of the need for closer co-operation in monetary and fiscal policy have stimulated greater interest in modelling the interdependencies between European countries and the impact and feedbacks from the other major economic blocks in the world economy, principally the USA and Japan. Many of the key economic issues now have important international aspects, so it has become more and more difficult to rely on single-country models to provide the necessary analysis.

The early multicountry models were essentially linked single-country models where the linkages emphasised trade flows, but where the national models were not necessarily based on the same underlying structure. In this chapter we outline some of the key differences between modelling the world economy and modelling a national economy, and we describe how far multicountry modelling has advanced. We assess whether the multicountry model is a serious contender for replacing the standard single-country model for forecasting and policy analysis. One important point to note is that the existing multicountry models are one-good models – this is in contrast to much of international trade theory, which uses the two-good model. There is therefore a whole range of issues which cannot be tackled by the existing empirical models: for example, discriminatory trade policies.

8.2   Modelling the world economy

> Multicountry modellers have to take a judgement as to whether to adopt a
> similar specification across different economies or whether to allow
> institutional characteristics and other specific-country features to dominate.

Size is clearly an important restricting feature in multicountry modelling, limiting the
depth of coverage of each separate economy. It is also not possible, and in many cases
not necessary, to cover each economy to the same degree. The amount of detail is
therefore usually less than for the equivalent single-country model. For example, a
10-country global model would have 1000 equations if it attempted to combine
single-country models of 100 equations each. Most multicountry models attempt to
model at least the G7 economies in reasonable detail, but of course there has to be some
modelling of the rest of the world in order to describe total world trade (see Table 1.2
for a summary of the disaggregation in multicountry models). There is obviously a
substantial difference in the degree of exogeneity between a multicountry model and
national economy models. In the latter, world demand and world prices are usually
exogenous inputs. In the multicountry models, world trade is derived as the sum of
individual imports or exports, and world trade prices are the weighted averages of
individual trade prices, expressed in common currency. World commodity prices, such
as those of food, basic materials and oil, can also no longer be considered as
independent variables, although the degree of simultaneity may not be very strong.

The modelling strategy in a multicountry model has to consider whether the same
structure is imposed on the different economies or whether institutional characteristics
are given a high weight in the construction of the model. The latter alternative may be
characterised by basing the modelling of a particular economy upon the structure(s) of
the relevant national economy model. Project Link is an extreme version of this
approach. The danger here is that the multicountry model may then consist of
components which have quite different theoretical foundations. Most multicountry
models, however, tend to adopt the former strategy: that is, to adopt the same broad
specification for each economy, but allow the empirical estimates of key coefficients to
differ. For example, the specification of the consumption function would include the
same variables in each country, but where some variables are found to be statistically
very insignificant in estimation, they may be excluded from the model. Important
differences may then arise between countries. In addition, the dynamics tend to be
'freely' estimated, so this is also a source of potential difference.

Most multicountry models tend to select model parameters by estimation, but
there are exceptions: for example, the McKibben–Sachs global model (MSG2) is a
calibrated model where parameters are derived from general equilibrium foundations.
Furthermore, the same values of the parameters are imposed across the different
countries in the model. Where data considerations are key to construction of the model,
there is the need to ensure consistency of concept and definitions across economies.
This is not usually a great problem for the OECD economies, but absence of some data
for some economies can prevent the full adoption of identical specifications.

227

> The links between economies in multicountry models are through trade, prices, interest rates and exchange rates, and through flows of factors of production.

Links between countries are potentially of four forms: first, financial variables such as interest rates and exchange rates; second, price levels; third, trade volumes; and fourth, flows of factors (labour and capital).

The increasing integration of international capital markets and the dismantling of exchange controls have increased the opportunities for arbitrage in financial asset markets. This has the implication that interest rates and exchange rates are intrinsically linked, not only within each economy, but also across economies. The operation of the European exchange rate system is an example where interest rates and exchange rates become strongly linked. A useful framework in which to examine some of these mechanisms is the Mundell–Fleming framework.

Multicountry models and the Mundell–Fleming framework

In the traditional Mundell–Fleming analysis, with sticky prices and high capital mobility, a bond-financed fiscal expansion in the home country raises interest rates in the expanding economy and this leads to an appreciation of the exchange rate. This shifts demand towards foreign goods, thereby raising demand abroad. So fiscal policy has a positive effect at home and abroad, although the domestic expansion is moderated by the rise in the exchange rate and interest rates. The domestic fiscal expansion lowers domestic prices through the currency appreciation, but raises prices abroad. If wages are flexible, foreign wages and prices rise in response to the exchange rate change, thus reducing the improvement in competitiveness. Foreign output may fall if the level of competitiveness is unchanged in the long run but world interest rates are higher. This will increase the benefits to domestic output as there is no diversion of domestic demand towards foreign goods. Domestic prices may now rise, however, if higher foreign prices offset the exchange rate appreciation and increase import prices in domestic currency (the results are summarised in Table 8.1).

Now consider a monetary expansion. This lowers domestic interest rates and stimulates domestic demand. The exchange rate falls as lower interest rates cause a potential capital outflow. Domestic output rises as a result of lower interest rates and a lower real exchange rate, but foreign output falls as a result of the real exchange rate appreciation (from the viewpoint of the foreign country). Domestic prices rise and foreign prices fall due to the exchange rate change. This is a beggar-thy-neighbour policy. If wages respond fully to the higher level of prices (full homogeneity), the real exchange rate is unchanged, there is no substitution of demand from foreign goods towards domestic goods, and money neutrality holds.

The transmission effect of changes under a fixed exchange rate regime are highly relevant to the modelling of ERM and EMU regimes. In discussing a fixed exchange rate regime, it is important to specify which country is responsible for pegging the rate;

Table 8.1 Transmission of fiscal and monetary shocks under perfect capital mobility

	Monetary policy				Fiscal policy			
	q	q^*	p	p^*	q	q^*	p	p^*
Floating exchange rate:								
Fixed wages	+	−	+	−	+	+	−	+
Flexible wages	0	0	1	0	+	?	?	+
Fixed exchange rate (home peg):								
Fixed wages	0	0	0	0	+	+	0	0
Flexible wages	0	0	0	0	+	+	+	+
Fixed exchange rate (foreign peg):								
Fixed wages	+	0	+	−	+	0	+	−
Flexible wages	+	+	?	+	+	?	+	+

Notes: q domestic output; q^* foreign output.
      p domestic price level; p^* foreign price level.

this country no longer has an independent monetary policy. Assume first a monetary expansion with the home country pegging the currency. This has no effect on domestic output, since lower interest rates stimulate a capital outflow, which has to be offset by selling foreign currency to maintain the exchange rate. Hence the *LM* curve cannot shift and we obtain the familiar result that monetary policy has no power under a fixed exchange rate regime. If instead the foreign country fixes the peg, a domestic monetary expansion leads to a foreign monetary expansion (and hence a global monetary expansion). This lowers interest rates in both countries and raises output both at home and abroad. If wages are flexible, both prices also rise. Under a fiscal expansion with a domestic peg, there is an accompanying monetary expansion as the interest rate rise leads to a potential capital inflow, which has to be offset by buying foreign currency. This reinforces the output rise, and if wages are fixed, the real exchange rate is constant, so the foreign country also gains from higher demand in the home country. With flexible wages, prices rise in both countries. With a foreign exchange rate peg, there is now a foreign monetary contraction accompanying the domestic fiscal stimulus, and although domestic output and prices rise, the effects on foreign output and prices are ambiguous.

    The next question is to consider how well empirical multicountry models incorporate the Mundell–Fleming mechanisms described above. We exclude MSG2 from this comparison since it is a calibrated model. Although models such as GEM and MULTIMOD contain flexible exchange rates with a high implied degree of capital mobility, many other multicountry models either have *ad hoc* exchange rate mechanisms or treat the exchange rate as fixed. Most models have a high degree of homogeneity in wages and prices. Interest rates affect domestic demand. In turn, however, the Mundell–Fleming model makes some simplifying assumptions. These are as follows:

1. The absence of dynamics.
2. The absence of wealth effects.
3. No intertemporal dimension.
4. No expectations effects.

Dynamics

The introduction of dynamics into the Mundell–Fleming framework introduces a distinction between short- and long-run responses and allows flow and stock equilibrium to be differentiated. The inclusion of dynamic responses is a standard feature of the empirical models, but they do not all have stock variables. Exceptions are MULTIMOD and GEM.

Wealth effects

The inclusion of wealth effects can change some of the standard Mundell–Fleming results, for, as discussed in Chapter 2, the *IS* and *LM* curves can now shift as wealth changes. Wealth effects provide a direct link between the government budget constraint and private sector behaviour. Wealth effects are becoming more important in multicountry models, and currently both GEM and MULTIMOD contain them. However, GEM uses financial wealth, whereas MULTIMOD includes both financial and human wealth. The latter provides an additional intertemporal mechanism.

Intertemporal dimensions

We consider three key intertemporal elements. The first is the government budget deficit and the relationship with the outstanding stock of public sector debt. The second is the balance of payments and the stock of net overseas indebtedness. The third is human wealth.

Consider government borrowing. The principal concern of the theoretical literature (Blanchard and Fischer,1989) is whether current fiscal policy is sustainable in the sense that there is no tendency towards excessive debt accumulation. The key to understanding sustainability comes from the government budget constraint:

$$\Delta B = G + H - T + rB \tag{8.1}$$

This states that the change in nominal debt (B) is equal to government spending (G) plus transfers (H) less taxes (T) plus debt interest (which is the product of nominal interest rates, r, and outstanding debt). This can be restated as the primary deficit ($G + H - T$) plus interest payments. In a growing economy, it is customary to write this expression in terms of ratios of GDP. Hence:

$$\Delta b = g + h - t + (r - \theta)b = d + (r - \theta)b \tag{8.2}$$

where d is the primary deficit, θ is the real rate of growth of output and r is the real ex-post rate of interest. If the real rate of interest (σ) is greater than the real rate of growth (θ), it is necessary to run primary surpluses in order to offset the growing interest burden. Sustainability requires that the debt ratio is stable, and one definition of this is that it tends back to its initial ratio to GDP. The condition for this to occur is that the present discounted value of the ratio of primary deficits exactly offsets the current debt ratio. In other words, a government with outstanding debt must sooner or later run primary surpluses, and these surpluses must be sufficient to satisfy the above condition. This is a fairly strict condition for sustainability, since there seems to be no good reason why one particular level of debt is more sustainable than another. In this case, a weaker condition is that primary surpluses must occur at some point if the debt ratio is to be stabilised. This issue is part of the model closure issue discussed in Chapter 7, and one particular way that fiscal solvency can be imposed is by imposing the rule that taxes adjust to stabilise the budget deficit in the long run. Such rules are included as a standard operating mode in MULTIMOD, and can be optionally used in GEM.

The relationship of the balance of payments to net overseas assets is very similar to that of the government deficit and public sector debt. In this case, net international debt cannot grow indefinitely, and sooner or later governments will have to run trade surpluses so that their present discounted value equals the initial stock of debt. One way that this constraint can be satisfied is by the terminal condition in the exchange rate equation that ensures that net overseas assets return to their equilibrium path (or to one that is parallel to it). GEM has such a condition as a terminal condition for the exchange rate.

The third element is that of human wealth, which depends on the discounted value of future (after-tax) labour income. If consumer spending depends on human wealth, it becomes forward looking and the Mundell–Fleming fiscal results can be overturned (see McKibben and Sachs, 1991), especially if Ricardian equivalence also follows. MULTIMOD includes human wealth and this has a key influence on its simulation properties described below.

Expectations

As our earlier discussion has made clear, the inclusion of rational expectations is readily incorporated into empirical models and these can strongly influence the adjustment to a given shock.

In summary, therefore, we can conclude that the basic Mundell–Fleming framework and its many extensions can and have been reflected in empirical models, although not all the features are present in many of the models.

The treatment of exchange rates

GEM and MULTIMOD have a forward-consistent (rational) determination of exchange rates. This is not a trivial matter for multicountry models. Whereas a single-economy model usually contains only one jumping variable in *the* exchange rate, the multicountry model will have as many jumping variables as there are bilateral exchange rates. Again, internal consistency is an issue – not all exchange rates can appreciate! Usually multicountry models concentrate on exchange rates in the main market economies (the G7). Each individual country's level of competitiveness is measured by the effective exchange rate, which is constructed as a weighted average of all the bilateral rates, the weights being given by trade shares. Of course, there is a multiplicity of bilateral exchange rates, and usually one currency is chosen as numeraire. The dollar often occupies this role, primarily because of it primacy as the currency on which many trade contracts are made. It is also the main currency in which commodities such as oil are traded. Consequently, exchange rate equations would be expressed in terms of the interest rate differential between the relevant domestic rate and the US interest rate.

In forecasting there is the need to ensure that the cross-rates implied by bilateral movements against the dollar are plausible. For example, if the French franc and the German mark both rise against the dollar, should they move the same, so that the franc–mark rate is unchanged, or is the forecast for a relative movement in the franc against the mark? The most common paradigm for modelling the exchange rate is that of UIP, and this would determine the bilateral exchange rates on the basis of relative interest rates. In our example, the franc–dollar exchange rate would move in line with the mark–dollar rate if French exchange rates were equal to German rates.

> Multicountry models have to ensure consistency between single-country outcomes and world aggregates which are the sum of these individual components. In the case of exchange rates, there is the need to ensure plausible behaviour of cross-rates. The UIP condition satisfies this need.

The Mundell–Fleming framework emphasises the interest and exchange rate links, but our discussion above reveals the importance of the transmission of price and wage influences. Whereas the links between asset markets can be considered to determine relative nominal exchange rates and interest rates, the international feedbacks between prices might be said to determine real exchange rates and real interest rates. However, although this is a useful accounting framework, theoretical considerations would lead us to account for differences in real exchange rates and real interest rates by 'real' factors such as productivity, change in factor environments, thrift and so on. A shock which raises the price level in one economy will lower its competitiveness relative to other economies. In a single-country model, one would then concentrate upon the implications for trade and output of the economy experiencing the shock. In the multicountry model, other countries gain in competitiveness, but also, to the extent that the initial shock raises the global level of prices, import prices in other economies may increase. This is an example of how inflation can be 'exported'. The size of this effect will depend on the importance of the shock-experiencing economy in the trading pattern of others, so that, for example, a shock in the USA might be expected to have fairly substantial price effects elsewhere.

The third link between economies in multicountry models is directly through trade volumes. These may be occasioned by changes in competitiveness, as described above, or may arise because an expansion of output in one economy will be expected to increase the demand for imports. These imports correspond to another country's exports. The treatment of exports and imports is different from the national economy models because the model has to ensure consistency between total imports and exports of all countries taken together. A common approach is to determine the import demand of each separate economy or block in the model using fairly standard import functions, where imports are related to a measure of competitiveness, domestic demand, and perhaps an indicator of domestic capacity utilisation, together with various proxies for long-run trends in import penetration. In the developing economies outside the G7, imports are typically related to export earnings, which in turn largely derive from the demand for basic commodities. Imports are then aggregated across all the economies to derive the measure of world trade in the multicountry model. This is translated into export volumes for each country, with export shares being determined by a trade matrix. This sharing-out of world trade can often be quite complex, with weighting by both export markets and main export competitors. Some multicountry models attempt to model trade on a bilateral basis. This entails modelling the import demands of each country by source so that export demands are automatically generated. In practice, this is often more complicated than it sounds (see Allen and Whitley, 1994, for a survey). Whitley (1992a) in a comparison of some of the multicountry models shows that trade links are quantitatively weak for a shock originating from a single-country, but can be important for symmetric shocks.

Finally, we consider possible links through factor flows. The current supply side of the models largely consists of their wage response (see the descriptions below). It is also possible that changes in demand and/or relative prices and costs may lead to movements of labour and capital between economies. One area where some current work is proceeding is in the investigation of links between investment and trade and potential output (and hence growth), which gives a different supply-side perspective. In many of the multicountry and single-country models, trend growth is exogenous, or is determined by a production-function-style framework where there is no connection between trend rates of growth in different economies. Thus the multicountry models are forced to explain the tendency for international growth rates to converge by coincidental developments in individual countries. There are (at least) three ways in which we might consider growth transmission between countries. The first is through trade, the second by the location of investment, and the third through labour force migration.

Consider the trade possibility. Work on bilateral trade by Allen and Whitley (1994) has found some evidence that export performance is improved if one country has a better investment performance than another (and, conversely, import penetration is reduced for the high-investment country). They use cumulated investment as a proxy for technological innovation. Work by Greenhalgh, Taylor and Wilson (1990), using patents data at the industrial level, has shown an association between innovative activity and UK export performance. This is equivalent to an improvement in non-price competitiveness and, in the spirit of the analysis in Chapter 4, can be expected to result in appreciation of the real exchange rate (FEER) and a reduction in the equilibrium unemployment rate (NAIRU), so that potential growth is increased. Some benefits of this increase in trend growth in the innovating country will be felt in other economies as higher growth increases the country's demand for imports. The main question is whether this can be a permanent process, whereby relative growth rates diverge but absolute growth rates are increased, or whether equilibrating forces will be set off. The location decision is one way in which this equilibration might take place.

For many internationally traded goods, the location of production is irrelevant in the eyes of the international consumer. Rather, it is the producers who have locational preferences as they seek optimal ways of locating their production around the world. Bradley and Fitzgerald (1988) have shown how location might be made endogenous using Ireland as an empirical example, and Pain (1993) has constructed a model of direct investment into the UK. In particular, he finds that the location of productive facilities is sensitive to factor prices in both the home (host) and foreign country.

The third possible mechanism is through labour force migration. In a competitive environment where labour is highly mobile, differences in real wages (adjusted for exchange rates) would tend to result in labour force movement so as to equalise these differentials. So far there has been little attempt to incorporate labour force migration into global models, and this principally reflects the view that differences in culture and other barriers make labour force movements relatively unimportant. However, labour force mobility is an important aspect of the design of an integrated Europe.

In multicountry models, it is important to distinguish between symmetric and asymmetric shocks. A symmetric shock is one which affects several economies simultaneously: for example, an increase in oil prices. Asymmetric shocks are those shocks which are country specific, such as a change in productivity, an exogenous shift in cost pressure, or an expansion in demand. Whether a shock is symmetric or not depends on the viewpoint being adopted. For example, a shock to US demand might be regarded as a symmetric shock from the point of view of the European economies, but it is clearly an asymmetric shock from the US perspective. Where symmetric shocks do occur, differences between the reactions of different economies will then largely reflect institutional differences or differences in the characteristics of the different economies. For example, the oil price shock might be expected to have a different impact on the UK, which is an oil producer, than on other European economies. Much of the analysis of the possible European monetary union focuses on whether shocks are symmetric or asymmetric (see Chapter 9).

8.3 Characteristics of the main multicountry models

Table 8.2 gives a brief summary of the main structural characteristics of some of the principal multicountry models. Four of the models are those described in Whitley (1992b); the remaining four are the global version of the LPL model, the US Federal

Table 8.2 Structural characteristics of the multicountry models

	MCM	MULTIMOD	MIMOSA	MSG2	LPL	DIW	GEM	OEF	OECD
Time dimension	Quarterly	Annual	Annual	Annual	Annual	Quarterly	Quarterly	Quarterly	Semi-annual
Features	Keynesian, sticky-wage model	New classical	Neo-Keynesian	CGE	New classical; market clearing	Bilateral trade system	Sticky prices	Sticky prices	Sticky prices
Expectations	Backward	Rational	Implicit	Rational	Rational	Implicit	Rational	Implicit	Implicit
Demand	Interest rates, real income	Wealth (financial and human), real long rate, demographic factors	Real incomes, interest rates, inflation, unemployment	Forward-looking consumption	Expected real returns, wealth (financial)	Interest rates, real income, inflation, unemployment	Real incomes, wealth, interest rates	Real incomes, interest rates, wealth	Real incomes, real interest rates, inflation, unemployment
Supply:									
Production function	Cobb–Douglas: capital labour, materials	Cobb–Douglas	Cobb–Douglas; putty–clay in manufacturing	Cobb–Douglas	Not explicit	Underlying CES	Not explicit	CD in UK only	3-factor/2-stage pf
Employment		Substituted out from production function	Adjustment to desired level given by pf plus hours adjustment	Intertemporal profit maximisation	Not explicit	Output, real wages	Output, real wages	Output, relative factor prices	Adjustment in planned output
Wage formation	Phillips curve	Implicit in reduced-form inflation equation	Phillips curve; productivity, unemployment	Overlapping wage model with hysteresis	Real wages depend on output from trend, long-term real interest rate, but implicit	Phillips curve; unemployment, productivity	Real wages depend on output, productivity	Real wages depend on unemployment, productivity	Phillips curve; unemployment, productivity, terms of trade

Table 8.2 (*continued*)

	MCM	MULTIMOD	MIMOSA	MSG2	LPL	DIW	GEM	OEF	OECD
Price setting	User cost of capital, costs, output	Variable mark-up on costs depending on capacity utilisation	Mark-up on costs and competitiveness	From inverted aggregate supply function	Variable mark-up on costs, but substituted out with wage equation in terms of real exchange rate	Cost mark-up, capacity utilisation	Cost mark-up, capacity utilisation	Cost mark-up, capacity utilisation	Cost mark-up, capacity utilisation
Exchange rate	UIP under adaptive expectations	UIP	Exogenous	UIP	UIP	Exogenous	UIP	Interest rates, current balance, wage costs	Deviations from PPP depend on interest rate differences and net assets
Interest rates	Short-term rates exogenous; term structure for long rates	Short rate equates supply and demand for M0; long rates from arbitrage condition	Reaction functions; inflation, output, exchange rate, foreign rate, current account	Perfect capital mobility	Efficient markets hypothesis	Exogenous	Various rules	Exogenous or money targeting	Exogenous or money targeting
Fical solvency	Tax rule	Tax rule		Tax rule	Financing rule				
Money supply	Endogenous via money demand function	Supply from central bank reaction function	Money demand equations	Money treated as a factor of production	Equilibrium government deficit		Money demand equations	Money demand in UK, US and Japan equations	Money demand equations

Reserve Board multicountry model (MCM), the McKibben and Sachs global model (MSG2) and the IMF's MULTIMOD model. The last two models together with that of LPL are annual and have neo-classical or new classical features, identified by the role of wealth in the determination of expenditure and the use of rational expectations. MULTIMOD is specifically not designed for forecasting. The GEM model also contains wealth effects and has rational expectations, but otherwise tends to be based on the imperfectly competitive paradigm. The size of the country models differs considerably, with LPL having only 153 equations in total, whereas the other models have between 40 and 200 for each major country. There is some variation in the number of industrial countries explained in detail, but there is a tendency to link the rest of the world blocks through trade links only. This means that the interaction of the behaviour of developing countries with those of the industrial countries is very limited; world commodity prices are only linked in a crude way to the rest of the world economy. These other country/regional blocks (for example, LDCs) tend to be represented by a very small number of equations. In the GEM model there are just four or five behavioural equations for each non-OECD block. MULTIMOD has a more extensive treatment. In particular, it emphasises financing constraints, the change in debt being assumed to reflect both expected growth in developing countries' exports (forward looking) and an adjustment that takes the ratio of interest on debt to exports towards an exogenous target level. Those developing countries with a wide margin between their current ratio and its target are constrained to run down net debt through current account surpluses, which means that imports are determined residually. Work by Allen *et al.* (1992) has developed a model of Latin America which can be added to the GEM model and used to illustrate linkages between the North and South, and to explore debt problems in a similar spirit. More details of the treatment and interaction of the other blocks in world models are given below.

 The changes that have taken place in the formerly 'planned' economies raise major problems for multicountry modellers.

A major challenge for the multicountry models is their adaptation to the impact of developments in eastern Europe. Previously, models tended to identify a 'centrally planned economies' block which comprised the eastern European economies together with the former Soviet Union. The feedbacks between the 'planned' sector and the remainder of the world economy were very weak. The changes that have occurred very recently in the Eastern bloc suggest that this assumption may no longer be valid, and raise three main problems. First, there is the problem of data; second, the modelling of transition in these economies; and third, the nature of these economies once adjustment has taken place.

The data problem arises since the statistics in the former planned economies were often of a dubious nature, and inflation adjustment was almost certainly inadequate in the absence of market-based price indices. One of the measures currently being undertaken is to construct more reliable and consistent national accounts, but inevitably this takes time and leaves the model-builder with no time-series data on which to base an empirical model.

Given that these economies are likely to be based more on a market economy, there is then the issue of how rapid this transition is likely to be. Speed of adjustment is dependent on political as well as economic issues, but it is likely to involve the interplay of the Eastern bloc with the existing industrialised block.

The major problem, however, concerns the likely structure of these economies once the bulk of the transition process has been completed. This is an example of a regime change, *par excellence*. One way round the problem may be to use the existing structure of models of the industrialised block, together with 'plausible' parameters, to specify the new state of these economies, in the absence of historical data. Current work of the LBS is using the learning approach to update initial parameter estimates of models of the former Eastern bloc as new data becomes available. This assumes that these economies will eventually transform themselves into carbon copies of the western industrialised economies, an assumption that may be proved to be far off the mark.

Domestic demand

The main endogenous components of domestic demand are consumers' expenditure and fixed investment. Consumption is determined by real incomes and real, or nominal, interest rates in many of the models. Wealth effects appear explicitly in the GEM, MSG2 and OEF models (UK sector only in the latter) alongside income variables, but wealth alone appears in the MULTIMOD and LPL models. In the other models, wealth effects are often proxied by inflation variables, and this can result in different behaviour in simulation analysis (see section 4.1). Some models also include an unemployment variable to capture uncertainty in income and hence in consumption behaviour.

While many models describe their consumption equation as consistent with the permanent income or life-cycle hypothesis (e.g. Edison, Marquez and Tryon, 1987, for MCM), practice does not always support this interpretation. In the case of MCM, lags of actual real income proxy permanent income, so this model tends to be observationally equivalent to the more Keynesian approach which sees consumers as liquidity constrained. It is only the LPL, MSG2 and MULTIMOD models which appear to be genuine examples of the life-cycle approach. This approach can be summarised as follows.

Households are assumed to maximize the discounted utility of current and future consumption, subject to the constraint that the present value of consumption does not exceed initial wealth. The stock of wealth is defined as the sum of the real value of assets held by households plus the present value of the flow of disposable labour income ('human wealth'). Because households face a constant probability of death, λ, and the total population is growing at a rate n, not all future labour income accrues to households. The rate of discount used is the real interest rate plus $\lambda + n$. Human wealth, WH, can then be defined as:

$$WH = \int_{t=0}^{\infty} (Y_t - T_t)e^{-(r+\lambda+n)t} dt \tag{8.3}$$

where $(Y - T)$ is the flow of disposable income. Total wealth is the sum of human and asset wealth (A):

$$W = WH + A \tag{8.4}$$

Utility maximisation implies that current consumption is determined by the real interest rate, the degree of relative risk aversion, the rate of time preference (δ) and the death rate:

$$C = \alpha(r, \sigma, \delta, \lambda)W \tag{8.5}$$

Human wealth, WH, is forward looking, being the discounted value of future income plus the initial stock. The degree of risk aversion, the rate of time preference and the death rate are typically ignored or assigned 'plausible' values. The other elements in total wealth are the real market value of the capital stock (WK), and real financial wealth (money, bonds and net foreign assets). Thus:

$$W = WH + WK + (M + B + NFA)/P \tag{8.6}$$

where M are money balances, B is the stock of domestic government bonds, and NFA are net foreign assets.

If the value of government bonds is not fully offset by the present value of associated future tax liabilities in human wealth, Ricardian equivalence does not hold. This is true for almost all multicountry and single-country models where government bonds constitute net wealth. MULTIMOD (and the MSG model) comes close to the Ricardian proposition, but even then it does not completely hold, since the rate at which consumers discount their expected labour income differs from the rate of interest on government securities. In the life cycle model consumption is assumed to vary exactly in line with wealth so the model can be restated in the form that the consumption–wealth ratio depends on the real interest rate (i.e. consumption is homogeneous of degree one in total wealth. Additional life-cycle features are introduced into the MULTIMOD formulation by demographic variables.

The variety in the treatment of fixed investment is similar to that of single-country models, with derivations based on both profit-maximising and cost-minimising assumptions in the standard way. The OECD model is a little different. Here there is a two-stage process. In the first stage the capital/energy bundle is determined in a vintage framework, and in the outer stage this capital/energy mix is combined with labour in a CES function.

> Multicountry models need to ensure consistency between total world exports and imports in both volume and values. This implies that the two sides of the trade balance have to be modelled with this restriction in mind.

Trade

In most of the models, the import equations are the main source of additions to world trade, with exports being shared out' from the global import total, the share being influenced by competitiveness. The system can be simplified as follows:

$$\sum_{i=1}^{n} M_i = WT \tag{8.7}$$

where WT is the total of world trade calculated as the sum of the imports of the i countries. World trade (WT) is shared out on the basis of the relative export price of country i to the weighted average of competitors' prices.

$$X_i/WT = \alpha_i + \beta_i \ln(p_i/p_c) \tag{8.8}$$

In order for total imports to equal total exports, the relative price elasticities are required to sum to zero, and the intercepts sum to unity.

$$\sum_{i=1}^{n} \beta_i = 0$$

$$\sum_{i=1}^{n} \alpha_i = 1 \tag{8.9}$$

Where time trends are included in the export equations (as in MULTIMOD) and if the above restrictions are not imposed across countries, there is the possibility that global imports do not in fact equal global exports (in practice, a large residual item is also needed to balance the world current account). For consistency to be found, it would be necessary for the time trends in different equations to cancel out exactly. The use of the Almost Ideal Demand System (AIDS) used by Deaton and Muellbauer (1980) guarantees consistency, but applications of this approach have not proved very successful (see Allen and Whitley, 1994). Many of the multicountry models attempt to ensure global consistency by various scaling procedures. Consistency of world trade was a problem in early versions of the GEM model, where the world current balance (which should always be zero) changed in simulations.

As well as ensuring consistency of trade volumes, there is also the need to obtain consistency in terms of prices and hence in trade values. In GEM, export prices of manufactures in the major industrial economies depend on both domestic prices and competitors' prices. This assumes that exporters have some market power and is a common assumption in the multicountry models (although the smaller countries are assumed to follow world pricing). It is possible that some exporters might price differently in different export markets (the pricing to markets hypothesis), but is not generally a feature of the multicountry models, where the usual assumption is that the same export price is relevant for each different export market. In many of the models (e.g. the OECD Interlink model), the world demand variable in the export share equation is weighted to reflect the relevant export market. Thus the size of the export market is calculated by using bilateral trade weights to measure the importance of a particular market and/or a particular competitor. Since the bilateral weights sum to unity, consistency is not lost. This procedure is also often used to measure the relevant competitors' export price.

$$PXG = f(WDPXG, P, RX) \tag{8.10}$$

where $WDPXG$ is a weighted average of competitors' prices, P is the domestic price and RX is the exchange rate, and where PXG is the export price in terms of dollars. Import prices are in turn given by export prices in other countries. Thus:

$$PMG_i = f(PXG_j) \tag{8.11}$$

Total export and import prices depend on manufactured prices and commodity prices:

$$PXA = f(PXG, POIL, PCOMM)$$
$$PMA = f(PMG, POIL, PCOMM) \tag{8.12}$$

where PXA and PMA are the average prices in dollars of imports and exports, $POIL$ is the dollar price of oil, and $PCOMM$ is the dollar price of other commodities. In order to ensure that aggregate import prices for the world economy match aggregate export prices, some scaling adjustment to export prices may be necessary. In MULTIMOD it is import prices which are adjusted.

There is the familiar problem of how to capture the trend increase in import shares which has occurred for most of the OECD economies. The MULTIMOD model uses both a linear and a quadratic time trend to account for this phenomenon (although this raises the consistency problem described above). Imports of goods (or often manufactures) depend on domestic demand or incomes, and relative prices or costs. MULTIMOD uses domestic absorption as the activity variable. In the LDCs and other non-OECD areas, export and import prices are typically given as a weighted average of world commodity prices, and export volumes are determined by an estimated equation containing market-weighted world import growth and the terms of trade. Import volumes are assumed to depend on available foreign exchange.

> The determination of trade in invisible items in terms of asset stocks, which in turn depend on current account deficits, and possibly on exchange rate and stock price revaluations, introduces a further link between countries in a multicountry model.

Further elements of the trade links between countries in the multicountry model can occur through the modelling of the invisibles sector. Consistency between debits and credits is also necessary here, and this may require some scaling adjustment in practice, as for trade in goods. We describe briefly the treatment of invisibles in GEM, since the GEM treatment is fairly typical, and contrast this with one or two of the other models.

GEM distinguishes between non-factor services, returns on assets held overseas, and unrequited transfers. Exports and imports of services are determined by overseas and domestic income and relative prices. Consistency is not guaranteed. Flows of factor service incomes depend on the stocks of overseas assets and liabilities. All assets must correspond with liabilities, so receipts and payments based on them in combination with interest rates should be consistent in simulation experiments. Asset stocks are largely accumulated through the flow of current account deficits or surpluses, but revaluation effects may also change asset stocks.

MULTIMOD merely cumulates asset stocks through accumulated current account deficits/surpluses, but GEM includes revaluation effects. These revaluation effects involve revaluations due both to equity price changes and to exchange rate variations, not only in the home country but in all other countries. These revaluation effects can be very large in practice and can dominate movements in net assets. The final item of the invisible balance is that of transfers. These tend to be lumpy in nature and depend on country-specific factors; hence they are not easily modelled. In most cases they are treated as exogenous.

A rather different treatment is followed by MSG2, where exports and imports are determined directly from the underlying utility functions.

Wages and prices

All the models include a 'core' equation to define domestic prices, which is based on a variable mark-up on unit costs (although this is substituted out with wages in terms of the real exchange rate in the LPL model). There are some differences between models in respect of whether a full set of deflators is modelled so that accounting identities between real and nominal magnitudes hold. Static homogeneity is present in most cases.

Wage equations are the main component of the supply side in the multicountry models, and are broadly based on a bargaining framework (the LPL model adopts the competitive paradigm instead). The main issues which differentiate the models are whether the wage equation is specified in terms of wage inflation or the (real) wage level, and whether productivity, terms of trade and tax effects are included. There is no estimated wage equation in either MULTIMOD or LPL, the assumptions about wage determination being used to substitute out the equations into a reduced form along with price-setting behaviour.

In MULTIMOD there is a reduced-form inflation equation whose determinants are capacity utilisation, expected inflation and the real exchange rate. This can be derived as follows:

1. Assume that there is nominal inertia in wages due to features such as overlapping contracts. Then we write:

$$\Delta w = \alpha(L^d - L^s) + \delta\pi^e + (1 - \delta)\Delta w_{t-1} \qquad (8.13)$$

where L^d and L^s are labour demand and supply respectively, and π^e is expected inflation.

2. Labour demand is derived from the Cobb–Douglas production function such that:

$$L^d = (y - \beta k_{t-1})/(1 - \beta) \qquad (8.14)$$

where β is the capital exponent in the production function.

3. Labour supply depends on exogenous factors and the real consumption wage:

$$L^s = \bar{L} + \gamma(w - p) \tag{8.15}$$

4. The output price (q) is a mark-up over normalised wage costs, the size of the mark-up depending on capacity utilisation (cu).

$$q = w + \bar{L} - \bar{y} + \theta cu \tag{8.16}$$

5. Writing the consumption price in terms of the output and import prices gives:

$$p = \phi q + (1 - \phi)(q^* + e) \tag{8.17}$$

where e is the exchange rate and q^* is the foreign price.

6. This can be rewritten in terms of the real exchange rate:

$$q - p = (1 - \phi)REER \tag{8.18}$$

which implies that a real exchange rate appreciation raises output prices relative to consumer prices. Combining 1 to 6 gives the final reduced form expression for inflation:

$$\Delta q = (1 - \delta)q_{t-1} + [\alpha/(1 - \beta) + \alpha\gamma\theta]cu + \Delta cu - (1 - \delta)\theta\Delta cu_{t-1}$$
$$+ \delta\pi^e - \alpha\gamma(1 - \phi)REER \tag{8.19}$$

The LPL system is similar except that the real exchange rate equation embodies a marginal cost pricing equation together with a real wage equation. This is then inverted to determine real output in terms of the real exchange rate, utilisation and the real long-term rate of interest (proxying the user cost of capital).

The OECD, MIMOSA and DIW models use the Phillips curve approach, as does MCM. The GEM and OEF models use the bargaining approach, which expresses the level of the real wage in terms of unemployment and wage-push variables. GEM uses output instead of unemployment. Most of the models include productivity as one of the determinants of real wages, or wage growth, but they do not all impose the condition that the long-run effect of productivity is unity (GEM is an exception), and this has implications for the form of the NAIRU (see section 4.4). The presence of tax or other wage-push factors in the wage equations is rare, and hence the models do not contain a very rich menu of supply-side variables.

Interest rates and exchange rates

The multicountry models often tend not to have fully fledged financial sectors. This reflects two considerations. First, there is the problem of obtaining consistent data across different countries. Second, full financial sectors tend to increase the size of

models considerably, and may tend to make them somewhat unwieldy to maintain and operate. Some models contain money demand functions
(for example, DIW, GEM and the OECD model), so that interest rates can be determined by money targeting or otherwise used as an exogenous policy variable. Alternatively, policy reaction functions may be used. In MULTIMOD, short-term interest rates equate the demand and supply for M0. In LPL, interest rates and exchange rates are consistent with the efficient markets hypothesis, and this assumption about perfect substitutability is also used by MSG2. Long-term interest rates are usually given by a term structure equation which is based on arbitrage, but in the models with forward-looking expectations (GEM, MULTIMOD, MSG2 and LPL) long rates depend on future short-term rates. This has some importance for fiscal shock simulations, and an example is described in Chapter 9.

Not all the models have an endogenous treatment of exchange rates (for example, DIW and MIMOSA). Otherwise the dominant paradigm is that of UIP, but as in the case of interest rates, UIP is not always applied using future expectations. The OECD formulation is slightly different. Here the expected value of the exchange rate is driven by PPP considerations, and deviations from this are determined by relative interest differentials and the net stock of foreign assets. Where the exchange rate is endogenous, it is usually in the form of the dollar rate. This is convenient when trade prices are denominated in dollars, and requires that competing interest rates are the relevant US rate. Other bilateral exchange rates are left to be determined implicitly in the models. The treatment of exchange rates in an environment where exchange rates are targeted against one another (as in the case of European monetary union) is described in Chapter 9. Effective exchange rates are derived as trade-weighted averages of the individual dollar rates.

MULTIMOD and MSG2 have an explicit mechanism which prevents a debt explosion from a permanent bond-financed increase in government spending. Tax rates are assumed to adjust so as to stabilise the ratio of bonds to GDP. GEM has also been used with a similar debt solvency condition (see Chapter 9).

8.4   Properties of the multicountry models

In this section we describe some of the main features of the multicountry models, as revealed in simulation analysis. The intention is not to make a full comparison of simulation properties, which could change as the models are revised, but to draw out some general conclusions. A discussion of standardised simulations with some of the multicountry models is given in Whitley (1992a).

The basic multipliers of the multicountry models were described in Chapter 3, and this revealed the greater tendency towards crowding out in MULTIMOD and MSG2 than in the other models. In this discussion we remarked upon the importance of the fiscal solvency rule, whereby taxes rose to maintain the budget deficit at its initial level. Evidence of the role of this rule comes when we inspect Figure 8.1, which shows a US fiscal expansion of 1 per cent of GDP with unchanged monetary aggregates for MULTIMOD, MCM, MSG2 and GEM. The GEM simulation reported here assumes

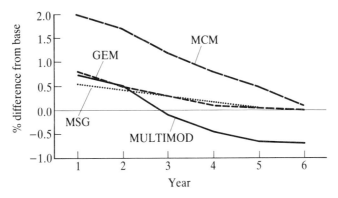

Figure 8.1   US fiscal shock (output response)

that fiscal solvency is in place and produces complete crowding out after six years, unlike the version without the tax rule reported in Chapter 3.

> Trade links are relatively weak in model simulations; more interaction comes from exchange rates and interest rates.

Differences between countries and models

Comparisons of model simulation results tend to show that differences between the models dominate (this conclusion is also apparent from the comparative exercise reported by Bryant *et al.*, 1988). Differences appear to be no more marked than those that arise from comparisons of single-country models. There are some basic differences in approach between some of the models (e.g. MULTIMOD, MSG2 and LPL against the rest), but aside from these models, most of the differences are generally related to different empirical estimates of structural parameters rather than to differences in approach. However, the dominance of the choice of model means that it is difficult to make consistent judgements about different characteristics of different countries. For example, a weaker inflation response in one country than elsewhere may be due to that particular model and might not be repeated if we were to use the results from another model. The results from MSG2 are generic as common parameter estimates are imposed across the various country blocs, and MULTIMOD also has a great deal of symmetry. The exception to the common parameterisation in MSG2 comes from the wage equation, where there are differences in wage dynamics between countries.

Links between countries

The role of trade links between the models is relatively weak. This is partly because a single-country expansion usually only has a small impact on total world demand, but also because the transmission of shocks through competitiveness is modest. An exception is the USA, where a domestic expansion has a more significant effect on world trade. However, the models give very different estimates of the impact of an increase in exogenous expenditure on the US economy itself, and hence consequently differ considerably in their assessment of the potential spillover effects on other economies. The weakness of the inflation transmission under a non-US expansion arises from a combination of two factors. First, domestic inflation responds only very sluggishly to increases in demand, so price competitiveness consequences are muted. Second, competitiveness elasticities in trade equations are also rather small.

In Whitley (1992a) expenditure injections on a single-country basis were compared under the alternative assumptions of trade links and the absence of trade links. The results suggested that simulation differences were minor. One possible exception to this conclusion was revealed in a further comparison of multicountry models under EMU (Whitley, 1992b). Here it was found that, where European interest rates were linked together and determined by a reaction function whose determinants were output and inflation, a strong accelerator response in the DIW model's investment equations caused a synchronised cyclical response, which had major effects on the world aggregates and hence feedbacks on the European economies themselves. This result is suggestive of the conclusion that it is exchange rate and interest rate links that are more powerful in the multicountry models. However, even these links are not immediately apparent in simulations that involve expenditure increases. The basic Mundell–Fleming framework implies that a (bond-financed) fiscal expansion should induce a positive spillover on other economies. Not only does the fiscal expansion raise domestic demand initially and lead to a deterioration in the balance of payments, but it also leads to a rise in interest rates and hence a currency appreciation. This raises foreign income. However, the results reported in Whitley (1992b) show that under a floating exchange rate regime the size of the spillovers is very small, and for most practical purposes a domestic fiscal expansion can be analysed in much the same way as for a single-country expansion.

In MULTIMOD and MSG2, where the domestic demand effects of a US fiscal expansion are only temporary, spillover effects on foreign output are also quite small. But for MULTIMOD they are persistently positive, whereas results for MSG2 show only a temporary positive boost to foreign output which is subsequently reversed.

It is in the operation of monetary policy that the role of financial links becomes more obvious. Where interest rates and exchange rates are interlinked, as in a managed exchange rate system, spillovers can become more important, but still not to the extent of dominating the individual country's response. Moreover, the direction of spillover can be reversed, for interest rates and exchange rates increase in the countries linked to the economy that initiates the policy action. This implies that there is no competitiveness gain due to exchange rate changes, and also domestic demand will be reduced through higher interest rates.

The supply-side response

To the extent that an expenditure simulation can be regarded as an aggregate demand shock, it is possible to infer the shape of the underlying aggregate supply schedule in the models (as discussed in Chapter 5). For example, if the level of output returns to its base level combined with a rise in the price level, we would infer that the aggregate supply schedule was vertical. With sticky wage and price adjustment, we would expect the long-run supply schedule to be steeper than the short-run schedule. In general, reduced-form price–output elasticities in the multicountry models, apart from LPL, MSG2 and MULTIMOD simulations, are small, suggesting that there is some long-run trade-off between prices and output. Simulation periods are generally too short to infer long-run properties, however, since the models have not all settled down following the shock. The finding that the aggregate supply curve is downward sloping in the DIW and MIMOSA models in some of the countries is quite remarkable and has little empirical support in the theoretical literature. This arises because a fiscal expansion lowers unit costs and hence prices.

The finding that, in the absence of exchange rate adjustment, the implied elasticity of the aggregate supply curve is well above zero within the simulation horizon is consistent either with weak supply-side factors in the models or with very protracted adjustment to the long run.

In most cases, a relatively low value of the implied aggregate supply elasticity is associated with a relatively high level of the ratio of the reduced-form response of wages to unemployment. Contributions from factors other than the wage–employment ratio are important in individual cases, but of less value in predicting the overall inflationary impact.

The demand-side reaction implied from an expenditure increase in most of the multicountry models reveals that consumer spending and investment rise, but that exports fall as competitiveness is reduced (if the exchange rate is unchanged or nominal interest rates are constant). There is considerable variation in the consumption and investment responses, however. These differences arise from the use of nominal rather than real interest rates in the expenditure functions, and in some cases the statstically invalid imposition of a long-run elasticity between output and investment, which tends to result in very protracted adjustment. Variations in the consumption response are typically related to whether wealth or inflation is included. The use of wealth tends to produce a permanent reduction in consumption, *ceteris paribus*, where inflation rises, whereas inflation itself tends to generate only a temporary downward shock to consumption. Where housing enters into the definition of wealth, as in the OEF (UK) model, the rise in house prices in the expenditure simulation raises real wealth and hence consumption, as described in Chapter 3.

In the case of MULTIMOD, an initial injection of spending is rapidly crowded out. Impact multipliers are well below unity, and sometimes lower than 0.5. The main factor inducing crowding out is a jump in the nominal exchange rate as interest rates rise (although the tax increases required to stabilise the government deficit are also a factor). The results show a decline in output following a single-country fiscal expansion, as early as three years into the simulation period, and this decline tends to increase in size with no evidence that the long-run equilibrium has been reached after six years. The LPL results of a fiscal expansion are very similar qualitatively to that of the LPL domestic model: that is, a small impact multiplier, a sharp rise in inflation, and a relatively rapid return to equilibrium.

The role of monetary policy

An increase in short-term interest rates in the models tends to lower output in each country that faces the rate increase, and to lower inflation. The main mechanisms which operate are components of final demand. In the case of consumers' expenditure, interest rates may have an effect on spending directly, or through receipts and payments, or through a reduction of personal sector wealth through revaluation effects and through net additions to or reductions from the stock of assets held by the personal sector. In the case of investment, interest rates may appear as part of a cost-of-capital term, and may also influence employment demand directly through a relative factor price effect. In MULTIMOD, MSG2 and LPL, a change in monetary policy is applied by changing the money supply itself. In MULTIMOD, a monetary expansion raises domestic output for four years as the nominal exchange rate fall overshoots its long-run equilibrium and results in a fall in the real exchange rate. Given the exchange rate response, the effects on foreign output are adverse but not particularly large. Money neutrality is not a medium-term property of MCM either, so domestic output rises but foreign output is hardly changed in the first four or five years of the simulation period. Neutrality in the MSG2 model is satisfied within the first five years of the monetary shock, and hence domestic output returns to its base level with hardly any effect at all on foreign output in the interim.

Price homogeneity

Diagnostic simulations where the dollar exchange rate is lowered by 10 per cent in each country in turn, with fixed nominal interest rates in each country, can be interpreted as a test of the homogeneity properties of the model. For full homogeneity of degree one, we would expect to observe an increase of 11.1 per cent in domestic prices and costs (that is, the reciprocal of the exchange rate fall). This test is not valid where the shock applies to more than one economy, for then the effective exchange rate no longer changes in line with the bilateral rate. A more relevant criterion in this case is that the real exchange rate returns to base.

Homogeneity is only present in a small number of country models within a six-year time span. Adjustment lags do not appear to be the explanation for the apparent lack of homogeneity in some cases, for the price level is falling towards the end of the simulation. Lack of homogeneity is quite important for policy analysis with the models, since it implies that nominal shocks can permanently influence real variables. Homogeneity is a necessary condition if output is to be determined by supply in the long run, and these simulations serve to explain why the computed aggregate supply elasticities observed in the government expenditure simulation are so low.

Some comparative issues

Although the models all tend towards similar specifications across the different countries, differences in simulation responses still occur. There appears to be no real consensus across all the multicountry models, with the LPL, MSG2 and MULTI-MOD models giving quite different responses, but the other models do support some general qualitative conclusions. These are as follows.

Fiscal policy does appear to have some limited power to raise real output, but the short-term effects are rather small. However, the conclusion rests heavily on the accompanying monetary policy assumption. Monetary policy, as represented by changes in interest rates, appears to have greater power over output in the medium term than fiscal policy under fixed real interest rates. But there is considerable divergence between the models over the transmission mechanisms involved, and hence in the full-model properties of interest rate changes.

The main transmission links between economies are interest rates and exchange rates rather than trade flows. Consequently, those models which are routinely operated under the assumption of fixed exchange rates and interest rates are unlikely to capture spillover and feedback effects between different countries. Note that there is an important difference between assuming fixed (i.e. exogenous) interest rates and exchange rates, and assuming a fixed link between interest rates and exchange rates in different economies. The latter assumption is likely to increase the size of spillovers (see Chapter 9), since monetary developments in one economy are directly translated to those of the linked economies.

Structural differences between economies might be expected to be more evident for a common external shock, such as a change in the world oil price, but the results do not accord with this expectation. Nor is there any consensus as to whether oil price shocks have a permanent or transitory effect on domestic output. The property that higher inflation results, rather than a step in the price level, is a surprising result.

The sectors of the models which are key to understanding full-model properties are the consumption equation, imports and the wage equation – very similar to the most relevant structural elements in single-country models. The main differences in respect of the consumption equation concern the size of interest rate effects; whether these are nominal or real; and whether inflation or an explicit wealth variable is included. The main differences with respect to imports concern the size of the import activity elasticity, which in turn is related to the treatment of the secular trend in import penetration.

Wage behaviour is fundamental to the supply side of the models. In some models, the level of real wages is explained by excess demand, whereas in others the Phillips curve approach is adopted, which determines the rate of change of wages. The latter approach leaves the equilibrium real wage to be determined elsewhere in the system. There is also considerable diversity in the effect of productivity on wages and, in particular, whether wages adjust fully to productivity changes. Differences in investment equations, although not fundamental to the source of inter-model and inter-country differences, are important in amplifying or modifying any initial disturbance. The size of output elasticity is the critical element here.

Although there are many differences between the multicountry models examined, the extent of diversity does not seem any more pronounced than in comparable exercises between different single-country models, and some are due to policy closure rules. Probably the greatest weakness in the multicountry models is in their modelling of the supply side, but this is not fully developed in the single-country models either. The differences which do emerge in this comparative exercise are informative. Most of the differences observed are the product of particular parameter estimates, or combinations of parameter estimates, and hence are capable of resolution. It is only by understanding how simulation differences arise that it is possible to proceed to use the models in full policy analysis.

Further reading

McKibben and Sachs (1991)
Whitley (1992a)

9 Some empirical exercises with multicountry models

In this chapter we consider two examples of empirical exercises with multicountry models, designed to show features of the models and to illustrate some of the modelling issues that have been discussed in the preceding chapter. The first example is the treatment of EMS and EMU in the models, and the second is the effects of a global deficit reduction package, announced in advance.

9.1 The treatment of EMS and EMU in models

In this section we consider how macroeconometric models can be used to analyse a regime change. We focus on two possible regimes which have received considerable policy attention: the European monetary system and European monetary union.

General modelling issues

The impact of membership of the European exchange rate mechanism (ERM) and possible membership of a full European monetary union (EMU) has received much attention in policy circles and is an obvious candidate for analysis by macroeconometric models. In this section we review the methodological issues raised by these regime changes, and how the models may be used to evaluate the consequences for output and inflation, both for a single country and globally. We shall refer to several published studies as examples, but our intention is not to evaluate these policy regimes, but to consider the relevance of macroeconometric models for this type of analysis.

First, we define the possible regimes. We start with ERM. This we interpret as an agreement to maintain exchange rates within an agreed band. Membership of the European monetary system (EMS) comprises ERM but also involves the removal of controls on capital movements. European monetary union (EMU) involves both monetary and economic union, and we assume that it embodies a common currency and hence permanently locked exchange rates. Note, however, that the common

European currency is still free to move against non-European currencies. A key empirical issue is how the common European monetary policy is determined. The main differences of these regimes from that of floating exchange rates is the loss of exchange rate variation. The issue is whether this makes the economy more or less robust to shocks.

> Discussion of the impact of alternative exchange rate regimes involves the classification of shocks that might occur into symmetric shocks, which hit all economies equally, and asymmetric shocks, which are particular to one economy.

Shocks can be classified into two groups: symmetric shocks, which affect all European economies more or less equally (such as a change in US economic policy, or a change in world oil and commodity prices); and asymmetric shocks, which are shocks which affect particular economies (such as a change in productivity or a labour force change). One form of asymmetric shock of particular interest is domestic policy, for under EMU where monetary policy is in common, and possibly fiscal policy also, there is less scope for such asymmetric shocks.

> Under ERM or EMS the exchange rate is still endogenously determined, but it must be targeted by domestic policies. Under EMU exchange rates are fixed, so any shock automatically impacts on monetary aggregates.

Some of the issues involved in modelling EMS or EMU can be discussed by reference to the modified-UIP treatment of the exchange rate.

$$\rho_1 = \rho_{t+1}{}^e + (r - \pi)_t - (r^* - \pi^*)_t + \gamma\Theta \tag{9.1}$$

where ρ is the real exchange rate (defined as ep/p^*), β is the risk premium and π is the inflation rate. This is a real UIP exchange rate equation.

In the single-country context, the wrong approach is simply to exogenise the nominal exchange rate (appropriately defined) at its parity level. This falls into the same trap as other exogenisation examples described in Chapter 7, namely that no instrument change is specified to ensure that this target is attained. In simple economic terms, this approach would imply that the policy-making authorities could remain free to choose monetary policy, mainly through interest rates, in the fixed exchange rate environment. This is clearly implausible. The main reason why many monetarists do not like ERM or EMS (see, for example, Minford, Rastogi and Hughes-Hallett, 1992) is that it involves the loss of control over monetary policy. This school of thought tends to argue that interest rates should be set in relation to domestic monetary growth, rather than arguing the need to maintain an independently set exchange rate.

A regime such as EMS, where exchange rates are maintained within an agreed band, is different to regimes such as EMU, where exchange rates are permanently locked. In the former case, capital movements can still cause pressure on individual currencies within EMS (as was graphically illustrated by the events of September 1992 and August 1993), so it is not the case that the exchange rate equation is now redundant in the model and can therefore be deleted. Exchange rates are still endogenous, but the authorities are now obliged to follow a policy rule which ensures that the outcome for the exchange rate lies within the desired range. What may be at issue is whether the form of the exchange rate equation remains unchanged in the new regime. We discuss this point below. The EMU regime is different, however. Here currencies are locked together. Shocks to the economy cannot therefore put pressure on exchange rates, but will automatically be translated into variations in foreign net holdings of domestic currency, and hence will influence money aggregates. The assumption that exchange rates are completely fixed under EMU is not completely correct, since the European currencies can still fluctuate against those outside of Europe.

> Use of the interest rate to target the exchange rate under
> backward-looking expectations can be viewed as an example of the type
> 2 fix.

Under EMS there are a variety of ways in which the target exchange rate could be achieved. Fiscal policy could be used, either through changes in expenditure or by changes in taxes. However, monetary policy is usually considered to be more appropriately assigned to the exchange rate. Monetary policy instruments include the use of interest rates and foreign exchange market intervention. Although the latter is used on a day-to-day basis, limits on foreign exchange reserves invariably rule this method out over a sustained period, leaving interest rates as the main policy weapon. If we formally assign the interest rate to target the exchange rate in a model with backward-looking expectations, this is equivalent to the type 2 fix approach. When exercises of this type were conducted on the HMT and BE models (Church *et al.*, 1991), a demand expansion led to complete crowding out after five years due to the powerful impact of interest rates on demand in these models. These results suggest that fiscal policy is impotent in a targeted exchange rate regime. This appears to be inconsistent with the Mundell–Fleming theoretical framework (see Carlin and Soskice, 1990, chapter 13). In the Mundell–Fleming analysis, fiscal policy in a floating exchange rate environment is less potent under perfect capital mobility than under a fixed exchange rate regime, for in the latter case the fiscal expansion is accompanied by a monetary expansion.

What appears to be happening in these models is that the wealth effect associated with the strong impact of interest rates on house prices in these models (identified in Chapter 3) causes the *IS* schedule to shift to the left, so offsetting the original shift. The standard Mundell–Fleming model ignores the role of wealth, but we have reason to believe that the strong effects observed in the HMT and BE models are unrepresentative, and that the impact of wealth is overstated due to the response of house prices. Consequently, the implications for fiscal policy under a targeted exchange rate regime should not be considered as general. Furthermore, the link through implied monetary expansion in the fixed exchange rate case is either weak or absent in these models, thus leading to a deviation of the results from those expected from the Mundell–Fleming framework.

The HMT and BE models contain exchange rate equations which do not correspond with the forward-looking UIP paradigm, and in the HMT model changes in the level of interest rates affect the level, rather than the rate of change, of the exchange rate. Hence interest rate changes are permanent and consequently have a more sustained crowding-out effect on domestic demand and output. The UIP explanation of the exchange rate would require only a temporary change in interest rates to offset any change in the expected depreciation (appreciation) in the exchange rate.

> Targeting the exchange rate in a single-country model with interest rates tends to produce crowding out under a fiscal shock as interest rates rise. The rise in interest rates is temporary in models which adopt the underlying UIP paradigm of exchange rate determination.

The EMU regime, where exchange rates are fixed, would, under the Mundell–Fleming analysis, produce the result that fiscal policy can raise domestic output whereas monetary policy is impotent if the home currency provides the exchange rate peg. However, if the foreign currency is the peg, monetary policy does have the power to raise domestic output. A key criticism of this theoretical framework is the neglect of the supply side. Under a fixed exchange rate regime, an important part of the transmission process of inflation is cut out (in simple theoretical models, the rate of domestic inflation is constrained by world inflation), and hence the supply-side adjustment in models must occur through lower profitability and hence lower domestic output supply, rather than there being an adjustment of demand through higher inflation. There are good reasons to suspect that these profitability influences are largely absent from most macroeconometric models.

> Under EMU supply-side adjustment takes place through changes in profitability, but these influences are largely neglected in models.

Let us now consider four other key aspects of these particular regime changes: the decision to join EMS at parities other than those consistent with equilibrium exchange rates; the role of credibility; possible changes in the risk premium; and possible changes in wage bargaining.

> Other aspects of EMS and EMU which need to be considered are the entry into EMS at non-equilibrium exchange rate levels; the role of credibility; and possible changes in the risk premium and in wage bargaining.

The entry decision

Many of the issues associated with the choice of a non-equilibrium entry level of the exchange rate have been discussed in Chapter 4 under the heading of the FEER (or fundamental equilibrium exchange rate). There is an important distinction between real and nominal exchange rates. Let us assume that entry into EMS takes place at a level of the nominal exchange rate which is equivalent to a real exchange rate higher than the equilibrium level. This will be interpreted by markets as implying an expected real depreciation (assume that the authorities are determined to maintain the nominal rate), so real interest rates will have to rise above competing real interest rates to maintain real interest rate parity. If domestic inflation falls as a result of the 'high' exchange rate, the domestic nominal interest rate consistent with the same real interest rate can fall. To the extent that lower inflation also reduces the real exchange rate towards its equilibrium value, real interest rates may also fall. In modelling terms, nominal interest rates are used to target the exchange rate as above. This is essentially as issue of transition. If the entry into EMU was at a real exchange rate level higher than equilibrium, the consequence would be a loss of output until domestic costs and prices adjusted, but there would be no need to maintain real interest rates above the average European level. Real interest rate equality would emerge only if inflation rates were equalised across the European economies.

Credibility

Much has been made of the credibility argument in association with EMS and EMU exchange rate regimes. Credibility has two aspects. One is the possible reduction in uncertainty that comes from the commitment to maintain the nominal exchange rate within its agreed band. The second is the implication that this commitment brings with it a reduction in inflation, which, with forward-looking expectations, will result in a reduction in wage pressure. The first element is associated with the risk premium in holding different currencies. The modified UIP model presented above allows for two aspects of risk premium.

The first is in terms of the interest differential. If one currency is thought to be riskier than another, interest rates may need to be made correspondingly more attractive to potential holders of the currency. In the context of ERM, which was started in 1979, a reduction in this uncertainty would be reflected in a narrowing of interest differentials, and there is some evidence that this has occurred (see Hall, Robertson and Wickens, 1992). In terms of the UIP equation, this could be associated with the expected exchange rate term. To the extent that the exchange rate commitment is more credible, $e_t^e = e_{t+1} = e_t$, i.e. expectations converge on the current level. This then produces greater convergence of interest rates in the UIP framework. Clearly, this happens under EMU where the future exchange rate is known with certainty. However, even then there is still room for risk between European currencies and non-European currencies. (In modelling terms, this requires that different bilateral rates can be identified.)

The second risk premium element arises from the use of a modified UIP equation where there is a separate explanation of the risk premium, which is in terms of the balance of payments deficit, or stock of net assets. Specifically, those economies with relatively larger current account deficits are more risky. As capital movements become freely mobile internationally, we would expect this element of the risk premium to be reduced, but this would appear to be related to institutional arrangements which facilitate free movement of capital, rather than to issues of credibility. Even with greater capital mobility, however, there is an argument that different assets are not perfect substitutes. Although different government bonds might be considered as perfect substitutes, domestic and foreign private assets might not, due to the different information available to investors on domestic and foreign firms. Returning to the credibility issue itself, we note that the commitment has to be stated and believed by the markets. If there is a risk that the authorities will realign the exchange rate, they may lose their reputation. These arguments are spelt out in depth in Britton (1992).

Wage bargaining

So far we have concentrated on the possible impact of the regime change on interest rates and the exchange rate, using the exchange rate equation itself to focus our arguments. We now consider how the regime change may lead to variations in behaviour in the rest of the economic system. A possible candidate is wage bargaining. If the authorities do succeed in gaining credibility for their exchange rate commitment, and on the assumption that this is seen to promise lower inflation, wage-bargainers may settle now for lower wages than they would have done otherwise. This requires that they have forward-looking expectations of prices. All that occurs is that they revise their expectations rather than change the nature of wage bargaining. In modelling terms, we can interpret this as a change in the value of one of the explanatory variables in the wage equation, the equation itself remaining a valid representation of the wage-setting process. If the model is solved in a forward-looking model, these changes will be automatically picked up. An alternative interpretation of the effects of the regime change, however, is that the wage-bargainers now realise that the authorities are constrained in their freedom to accommodate wage pressures, and that this leads to increased 'realism' in their wage demands. This is more akin to a genuine structural change which might be associated with a different wage response to changes in unemployment, for example, and it is far more difficult to quantify ex-ante.

An intermediate case is where wage-bargainers become more forward looking in their behaviour, perhaps due to greater belief in the stance of the authorities. Unlike the change in structure above, there is no long-run change in real wages but a faster adjustment. Unlike the first example above, however, this does require some respecification of the wage equation.

Some empirical evidence on the role of the labour market, and particularly the behaviour of wages, is provided by Anderton, Barrell and in't Veld (1992). They examine the structural stability of wage equations in the four main European economies, with a view to judging whether the convergence of inflation in Europe can be ascribed to increased credibility of policy, changes in labour market structural characteristics, or merely the loss of monetary control under a fixed exchange rate regime. They find no evidence of structural changes in wage relationships for Germany and the UK (despite the Thatcher reforms). There does appear to be some support for a credibility effect in France, however. In the case of Italy, they find strong evidence of a shift towards more forward-looking behaviour in recent years, which may or may not be related to the presence of EMS. Anderton *et al.* also conduct some simulations on the GEM model, using both a fiscal and an oil price shock under the assumptions of forward-looking and backward-looking behaviour. The forward-expectations variant tends to produce a faster inflation response for a fiscal shock but little difference otherwise, suggesting that the response of the economy to shocks does not depend critically on labour market participants believing policy commitments to reduce inflation.

There are some other aspects of economic behaviour which may be susceptible to the different exchange rate regimes. One of these is trade. Less variation in exchange rates may induce higher trade between economies as a result of increased certainty over the foreign currency price. Changes to reflect this would require modifications to the trade (export and import) equations of the model.

Fiscal solvency

Under the present arrangements for monetary union in Europe, set out in the Maastricht agreement, the participant members must satisfy certain convergence criteria, including exchange rate stability and convergence of inflation rates. The particular requirement that we emphasise here is that of fiscal solvency. Economies must have a government deficit of less than 3 per cent of GDP and a level of gross government debt of less than 60 per cent of GDP. To be able to simulate the EMU regime, models will therefore need to embody fiscal policy adjustment rules which are consistent with this outcome (ignoring the problems of transition from fiscal conditions which are initially out of line with the necessary convergence conditions in the base setting). This requires the addition of a fiscal adjustment rule which relates either expenditure or taxes, or both, to changes in the deficit in model simulations. The debt ratio condition is a little more complicated. This requires an integral control rule (see the example below), but also requires that the model is able to simulate changes in debt interest payments arising from changes in the deficit, and typically requires an explicit model of the public sector.

9.2 Empirical exercises on EMS/EMU

In order to give more flavour to the discussion of modelling regime changes of the EMS and EMU type, we describe some model-based simulation exercises. These are based on multicountry models. It is obvious that a proper comparison of these regimes requires the use of multicountry models, particularly since the transmission of shocks between the member countries is then taken into account. This should become clear from our discussion of the results. We distinguish between exercises based on deterministic simulation methods and those based on stochastic simulation.

Deterministic simulation is concerned with specific single shocks and compares the values of endogenous outcomes under the different policy regimes. The value of the method depends upon the relevance of the selected shocks to those likely to be experienced. Stochastic simulation subjects the models to random shocks, as described in Chapter 5, and therefore produces results in terms of the variability of the endogenous outcomes under the different regimes. It can be used as an indicator of the robustness of the economy in the different regimes, an increase in variability signalling a less robust outcome. The stochastic approach is more general than the deterministic method, but it is more difficult to implement.

Choosing the endogenous outcomes to compare is always an important consideration in model-based simulation exercises. Where more than one outcome is identified, there is then the problem of how to combine them. This can be done either formally, using an explicit welfare function that describes the relative loss associated with each outcome, as in the optimal control case (see Chapter 7), or implicitly, by focusing on one or two selected outcomes. Where the latter is done, output and inflation are typically chosen. Where results are being compared over several economies, the mean tendency as well as the dispersion of the results may be of interest.

> Evaluation of alternative regimes can be undertaken by deterministic or by stochastic simulation methods. The stochastic approach is more general and describes the robustness of the outcomes under different regimes, but is it computationally more difficult to implement.

Stochastic exercises

We begin by describing some of the stochastic studies carried out on multicountry models. These are of interest mainly for the issues that arise rather than for the results *per se*. In fact, different studies tend to come to different conclusions, and we focus on the areas of experimental design that contribute to these differences. These exercises are therefore another good example of how model-based results should not be taken on trust, and how an understanding of the underlying off-model assumptions as well as knowledge of the model itself can be fruitful in appreciating the results.

> The results of stochastic studies depend on the choice of monetary policy, the treatment of expectations, and the treatment of risk premiums and realignments.

We contrast three studies concerned with the evaluation of alternative policy regimes for the European economies, studying the variability of inflation and output. They come to different conclusions. A study by Minford, Rastogi and Hughes-Hallett (1992) uses the LPL global model to show that the EMS regime produces instability. In sharp contrast is the study by the European Commission (1990), which uses the MULTIMOD multicountry model and concludes that EMS reduces average inflation variability but at the cost of increased average output variability. It predicts that moving to EMU would produce improvements in both output and inflation variability for the EMS countries taken together. The third study is that by Masson and Symansky (1992), which is of particular relevance because they use the same MULTIMOD model as the European Commission. Masson and Symansky conclude that EMS is much less a potential source of instability than is implied by Minford *et al.*, but on the other hand they find no strong evidence to support EMU over alternative regimes. Masson and Symansky attempt to explain the differences in the three sets of results in terms of differences in experimental design.

In order to compare alternative exchange rate regimes, some benchmark is necessary. The standard device is to assume that this is a pure floating exchange rate regime and can be represented by the UIP approach. In the study by Minford *et al.*, optimal control methods are employed, and the benchmark case is more accurately described as floating without co operation.

The role of risk premiums

The first issue that Masson and Symansky draw attention to is the treatment of risk premiums. In stochastic simulations, it is typically assumed that historical error terms of the equations represent the relevant probability distribution, and repeated drawings are made from this distribution. The variability is usually calculated relative to a baseline path, which is the model solution with errors set equal to zero.

EMS and EMU may reduce exchange rate risk and hence reduce the role for risk premiums. The problem in these studies is that the risk premiums are not explicitly identified, but are implied from a simple UIP condition. We rewrite the equation as:

$$r = r_g + e^e - e + u \tag{9.2}$$

where r_g is the German interest rate and u is the (unmeasured) risk premium. It might simply be assumed (as the EC Commission does) that EMS and EMU eliminate risk premium shocks. Hence the variability of exchange rates is automatically reduced, and this goes a long way towards reducing inflation variability, depending on how large these shocks are historically. The problem is that the errors in the UIP equation also reflect expectations errors – that is, making a wrong forecast of the exchange rate. The EC Commission actually uses a small partial model to generate expectations compared with the alternative of estimating model-consistent expectations (Minford *et al.*) or using time-series rules (Masson and Symansky). The Masson and Symansky method essentially uses a time-series model for exchange rate expectations that has the property that market forecasts are close to the current rate. The EC method produces quite different forecasts from the current rate, and hence attributes large risk premium errors. This is judged implausible by Masson and Symansky. This contrast reflects the problem of measuring expectations in historical simulations as well as attributing all the exchange rate error to risk premiums.

The second issue raised by Masson and Symansky is the method of averaging variability across the different economies. Minford *et al.* assume that the European welfare function is a simple average of each individual welfare function. For example, if each country's individual function is:

$$L_i = E[q_i^2 + \alpha\pi_i^2] \tag{9.3}$$

where q is output, π inflation and E the mathematical expectation (average) then global welfare (G) is given by:

$$G = L_1 + L_2 \tag{9.4}$$

which implies:

$$G = E[q_1^2 + q_2^2] + \alpha E[\pi_1^2 + \pi_2^2] \tag{9.5}$$

Masson and Symansky argue that the correct measure of inflation variability should be that of the average inflation rate not the average of the individual inflation variability measures, since relative prices should not matter so much in a single-currency area. The relevant measure should then be $E([\pi_1 + \pi_2]/2)^2$. They go on to show that differences in this measure of variability account for some of the findings of the EC Commission on EMU.

Monetary policy

The next issue we consider is that of the form of monetary policy. Under floating exchange rates, monetary policy can be set independently, but this may take the form of monetary targeting, the use of a nominal income target, or an optimal uncoordinated setting for each country independently. Another option, used by the EC Commission, is an interest rate rule which targets inflation and real output. Under EMS, monetary policy has to be used to defend the parity, but given that there are permitted margins of fluctuation, there is some scope for independent action within the band. Minford *et al.* exclude the interest rate rule as unstable, and argue that each exchange rate regime should involve the adoption of the most appropriate form of monetary policy, rather than the establishment of one rule over all regimes. For example, they argue that nominal income targeting may be more favourable to floating relative to EMU, whereas the reverse may hold for fixed money targets.

Under EMS there may be some latitude for monetary policy to be aimed at domestic considerations while the exchange rate is within its permitted band, but the exchange rate has to be defended when it moves close to its limits. In the EC Commission study this is accomplished by use of a strong non-linearity in the interest rate rule. In the floating case, monetary policy is given by:

$$r - r^b = 100[2(\pi - \pi^b) + 0.4(q - q^b)] \tag{9.6}$$

where the superscript b refers to base settings of inflation π and output q.

Under EMS this rule is modified:

$$r - r^b = 200[(e - e^p) + 2.1 \times 10^{18}(e - e^p)^{11}] + 100[2(\pi - \pi^b) + 0.4(q - q^b)]$$

$$(9.7)$$

where e^p is the exchange rate central parity. This particular functional form is chosen to give very strong non-linearity beyond ± 1 per cent deviations.

Minford et al. assume that money is exogenous within the band, but becomes endogenous at the edge of the band. Realignments of the exchange rate occur in the EC Commission study when there is an 8 per cent divergence in the price level from Germany, but the size of the realignment is limited to 4 per cent. Minford assumes that realignments occur when the exchange rate is expected to lie outside of its band next period if flexible, but the parity change is defended in the current period and only takes place with a one-period lag. It is this realignment that causes instability under EMS because realignments occur at discrete intervals after a period when monetary policy has had to be very active in defending the band. Alternative realignment rules such as that of the EC Commission are less unstable.

Deterministic simulations

We now consider the analysis of alternative exchange regimes using deterministic analysis. This is based on the comparative study using five different multicountry models (Whitley,1992b). A set of standard rules for the conduct of monetary and fiscal policy was established, and in the absence of endogenous exchange rate behaviour in all of the models, an approximation to the UIP paradigm was used. Four different policy regimes were analysed:

1. Independent interest rate policy using the same reaction function as the EC Commission study above, together with a floating exchange rate.
2. An EMS where the central parity is held and there are no realignments, with interest rate and exchange rate policy determined by Germany.
3. EMU with interest rates determined using the same interest rate rule as in 1 and 2 above, but where deviations of average European values from their base levels are penalised. Rule 2 can be considered more like an asymmetric EMU than EMS.
4. EMU where fiscal policies are designed to be consistent with long-run fiscal solvency.

These alternative regimes are then considered for two shocks: a rise in government spending (fiscal shock), which is an example of an asymmetric shock; and a world oil price shock, which can be considered as a symmetric shock. The interest rate rule under floating is equivalent to that used by the EC Commission, but allows for partial adjustment because of potential instrument instability.

$$(r_t - r_t^b) = \gamma[100(2(\pi_t - \pi_t^b) + 0.4(\ln y_t - \ln y_t^b))] + (1 - \gamma)[r_{t-1} - r_{t-1}^b] \quad (9.8)$$

where the parameter γ is a damping factor and is chosen to ensure that the mean lags are equivalent across different model periodicities. The rule implies that a 1 per cent rise in inflation generates an increase of 2 percentage points in nominal interest rates eventually.

Under EMS this interest rate reaction function applies only to Germany, and under EMU the inflation and output variables are replaced by average European values.

Under the EMU fiscal solvency case, a government expenditure rule is used which adjusts expenditure so as to move the budget deficit back towards its base level (this does not always cancel out the original spending case in the simulations). The rule is:

$$(G - G^b)/y^b = \beta_i \left[\left(1/12 \sum_{j=0}^{11} GBR_{i,t-j} \right) - 3.0 GDR_{i,t-j} \right] \tag{9.9}$$

where GBR is the ratio of the deficit to GDP and GDR is the ratio of debt. The parameters β are scaling factors which vary across countries to reflect the size of government spending and the units of GDP. The parameter on government debt was chosen empirically.

We now discuss the treatment of the exchange rate. It is not always a simple matter to embody a UIP model of the exchange rate complete with forward expectations in macro models, as the discussion in earlier chapters has revealed. In particular, the model has to have a stable long-run solution. In the comparative exercise there is an attempt to mimic the UIP framework without actually using a formal UIP model. A modified UIP equation for each country of the following form is assumed:

$$e_t = e_{t+1}^e + (r_t - r_t^*) + \eta(CB/GDP)_t \tag{9.10}$$

where CB/GDP is the current account to GDP ratio and the parameter η is chosen to be 0.1. This rule is used to determine the nominal exchange rate under the floating regime for all the countries and to determine the exchange rate for Germany under the EMS regime. For the other countries under EMS it is assumed that interest rates are dependent on the German rate subject to the risk premium. Thus:

$$r_i = r_g - \eta CB/GDP \tag{9.11}$$

In order to approximate the properties of the UIP treatment, it is assumed that the terminal exchange rate is the same as in the base. Then substituting for the expected exchange rate gives:

$$e_0 = e_T + \sum_{t=0}^{T} (r_t - r_t^*) + \sum_{t=0}^{T} \eta A_t \tag{9.12}$$

where e_0 is the exchange rate in the first period and e_T the terminal value. This then gives the initial jump in the exchange rate by the cumulated interest differential and the cumulative risk premium, and is calculated from a simulation where the exchange rate is held fixed. The exchange rate in subsequent periods follows the UIP path and is determined endogenously following the rule:

$$e_t = e_{t-1} - (r_t - r_t^*) - \eta A_t \tag{9.13}$$

for $t = 1 \ldots n$.

In principle, an iterative procedure should be used, for the new exchange rate will change inflation and output and hence imply a different value of the interest rate from that used in the UIP rule. In forward-looking models, the terminal condition is an approximation to the equilibrium path, and the main problem lies in knowing what the appropriate terminal condition should be. We would expect the equation to ensure that the current account is cleared in the long run. The problem is that, under a demand shock, we expect the current account to worsen and interest rates to rise. If inflation and output returned to their base levels, we would expect the rise in interest rates to be temporary, and exchange rate adjustment would be dominated by asset equilibrium considerations. However, in practice, the simulation period is too short for this to occur, so interest rates are still divergent at the end of the five-year simulation period and the exchange rate path is dominated by interest differentials rather than asset equilibrium. Hence the real exchange rate tends to appreciate following a demand shock, and there is no tendency for the current account deficit to be corrected. In principle, this could be done by inflation and wealth effects, but these feedbacks are weak and slow acting. The approximation to UIP is therefore not terribly satisfactory.

One final point of experimental design which might be mentioned is that of the measurement of the risk premium. This should be defined as a relative current balance term, reflecting the riskiness of different assets. This is only of practical importance in the oil price simulation.

The results can be summarised very briefly as follows. In most of the models the direct spillovers from fiscal expansion are small, and hence inflation and output do not vary much in response to a fiscal impulse in another country. Under floating, the exchange rate appreciates. In general, interest rate and exchange rate effects outweigh trade effects. Membership of the ERM gives fiscal authorities more leverage in the UK, France and Italy than under floating, since they are sheltered from the interest rate and exchange rate crowding out that occurs under floating. In contrast, inflation effects are stronger, since the economies can no longer export their inflation through exchange rate appreciation. However, there are negative spillovers resulting from a German fiscal expansion.

Conclusions

This section has focused upon the treatment of EMS and EMU as an example of a regime change in macroeconometric models. It has described methods of analysis which have been used, and has highlighted some of the auxiliary assumptions which are made and shown that they can be of key importance.

9.3 Modelling a deficit reduction package

In this section we consider the use of multicountry models to examine a policy of a phased public sector deficit reduction. This illustrates some of the properties of the multicountry models. Earlier discussions in Chapter 7 and in the context of EMU above have emphasised the issue of sustainability of fiscal policy. The example that we consider below is one where, faced with a deficit which is judged unsustainable, governments announce a phased reduction. A common view is that high deficits, particularly in a global sense, may lead to real interest rates being high in order to supply these extra demands on savings. A policy of reducing deficits may consequently lower real interest rates, and this may have expansionary effects on output and employment. Furthermore, if the deficit reduction policy is announced in advance, financial markets may respond by lowering long-term interest rates before the deficit reduction policy commences.

The empirical issue concerns the extent to which current long-term interest rates are reduced, and how far these can stimulate economic activity and so offset the recessionary impact of higher taxes. In order to model this impact, it is necessary that models contain a forward-looking representation of long-term interest rates. We consider the effects of pre-announced deficit reduction policies on three multicountry models which contain forward-looking features: MULTIMOD, MSG2 and GEM. The MULTIMOD simulation is that reported in the IMF *Economic Outlook* for January 1993; that for MSG2 is reported in McKibben and Sachs (1991); and the GEM simulations correspond to those in the LBS *International Outlook* for June 1993.

In all three cases the reduction in the deficit is equivalent to 1 per cent of US GDP (this is calculated for MULTIMOD by scaling down the published results), and in all three cases the reduction is phased in. In the case of GEM the reduction only begins in the second year of the simulation, but it is assumed to be announced, and hence anticipated, by economic agents at the beginning of the simulation period. In MULTIMOD and MSG2 the deficit reduction actually begins in the first year of the simulation. The exchange rate is also forward looking in the models. The reduction in the deficit spills over into lower short-term interest rates in all three models. GEM and MSG2 assume a fixed monetary base, whereas in MULTIMOD interest rates are determined by a reaction function. Long-term rates are forward looking and depend on future short rates. Hence long-term rates also fall. In the case of GEM this is in advance of any deficit reduction.

The striking feature of the effects on US output of this fiscal reduction package (Figure 9.1) is that there is hardly any fall in demand and output for the MULTIMOD simulation. MSG2 produces an initial boost to US GDP, which becomes a fall, and after five years output is almost back to base. In contrast, the GEM results show a very minor increase in output initially, which turns into a steady reduction in output as the fiscal reductions reduce consumer spending through higher taxes. There is one feature of experimental design which strongly influences the MULTIMOD result, and one economic feature which is highly relevant to explaining the MSG2 and MULTIMOD responses.

The issue of experimental design in MULTIMOD concerns the fact that some variables (the price level and the exchange rate among them) are imposed at their 'new steady state' values in order to obtain expectations beyond the terminal date. This is similar to the LPL methodology of terminal conditions described in Chapter 5, and this

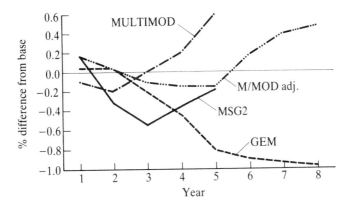

Figure 9.1 Fiscal reduction package – GDP

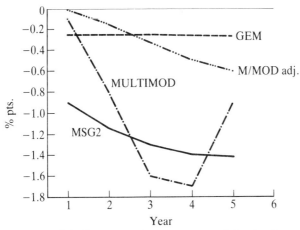

Figure 9.2 Long term interest rates and fiscal cuts

approach runs the risk that the imposition of these terminal conditions may unduly influence the responses of the model in the short term. As an alternative, we present a simulation with MULTIMOD where the terminal conditions are treated in a more standard way, and where the deficit package begins in year 2 of the simulation, but is assumed to be announced in year 1. The results are shown in Figures 9.1 and 9.2 as an adjusted version of MULTIMOD, and these results are quite different. There is an initial increase in output which is reversed in year 3 to become a small fall, and is reversed again in the medium term to become a rise of around 0.4 per cent. A key part of the difference between all four results lies in the reaction of long-term interest rates. Since long-term interest rates fall by far less in GEM than in either of the other two models (Figure 9.2), the appreciation of the currency and the rise in fixed investment are much less, and the tax effects of the deficit reduction dominate. The adjusted version of MULTIMOD shows a very similar interest rate profile to that of MSG2, but with a far smaller decline in interest rates.

The economic feature which dominates the MULTIMOD and MSG2 results is the assumption of near-Ricardian equivalence in the treatment of forward-looking consumption. In the Ricardian world, the tax increases to reduce the deficit have already been anticipated and so do not reduce consumption. Hence there is a very small reduction in private consumption, whereas lower long-term interest rates increase the level of private investment. In addition, lower interest rates cause a depreciation of the exchange rate which stimulates net exports. These effects are all much stronger in MULTIMOD than in MSG2, where consumption is not fully forward looking – hence the temporary reduction in demand in MSG2.

These results give a good illustration of how hidden features of models (in this case the treatment of terminal conditions in MULTIMOD) can dominate model-based results. Also of importance, however, is the basic economic structure of the models, in this case the consumption response. Finally, the relevance of forward expectations is emphasised in situations where policies are pre-announced.

Further reading

Barrell and Whitley (1992)

agents, and that simple analysis using commonsense models has proved more fruitful in the past. Although it is the case that models have come a long way in developing their theoretical credentials in recent years, they still fall well short of the models of macroeconomic theorists. The main problem for the empirical models lies in the fact that they often fail to be consistent with the optimising behaviour of individual agents. However, the many insights available from theory have often failed to be translated into models that have some empirical support when tested empirically on real-world data. Part of the problem lies in the fact that the appropriate data are not available on which to test these models. Macroeconomic modellers have shown in the past that they are prepared to incorporate empirical innovations into their models. A possible criticism is that they have often reacted too rapidly in accepting new developments, and left too little time for the full implications of innovations to be assessed.

Policy relevance

Even if we cannot be persuaded that the models are particularly reliable in explaining past, current or future trends in the economy, they may still have an important role to play in policy analysis. They provide a consistent quantitative framework in which to test alternative policies. However, if the empirical models do not explain the past very well, one is inclined to ask whether one should put much faith in their ability to explain alternative policy prescriptions. Calibrated theory models might then be an attractive alternative to macroeconomic models based on poor theory and inadequate empirical performance. Once more the decision process reflects a question of balance. Empirical models may be less than satisfactory in their ability to explain the past behaviour of the economy, but at least they have some empirical support. On the other hand, the theory models may contain a richer account of behaviour, but may have no evidence of empirical validity. Furthermore, they may fail to have macroeconomic closure, which would make them inappropriate for policy use (for example, they may ignore the feedback from tax revenues to real incomes and the government budget).

Many policy actions are more specific than those routinely incorporated in models, or else are new policies for which there may be no historical precedent. In this strict view, macroeconomic models are certainly inadequate. To some extent this reflects the fact that models have not been used enough in policy design and evaluation. However, it is also the case that models would become unwieldy if all potential policy instruments were to be identified. Future policy innovations may also be different from those in the past. The main problem for macroeconomic models lies with policy changes which are more institutional in nature. These are areas where great care has to be taken in interpreting the model results in order to judge the role of additional assumptions made off-model. It is unlikely that models can be constructed to cope with all conceivable policy actions. They are perhaps best viewed as a framework for investigating the macroeconomic consequences of actions, in which they need augmenting by additional information or evidence. In this book we have emphasised the ways in which models may be augmented and the need for care in the experimental design of policy simulations. Otherwise it is all too easy to obtain apparently conflicting results from what seems to be the same policy experiment on the same model.

Forecast performance

Faith in macroeconometric models has probably diminished in recent years, and this decline is associated with poor forecast performance. One school of thought sees ex-ante forecast ability as the acid test of a model, whereas others argue that it is not a relevant test of validity because poorly specified models can outperform a well-specified model. Examination of ex-ante forecast performance can also be a poor evaluation tool to the extent that forecast errors are 'explained' by poor forecasts of exogenous variables, or if the model is substantially adjusted by the forecasters' judgements. Doubts about the credentials of the models are raised by the common finding that their forecast performance deteriorates when they are supplied with the correct exogenous information, and also that residual adjustments tend to improve forecasts. Macroeconomic models have the advantage that they can explain 'why' certain developments are forecast, and their results are replicable. However, they usually fail to incorporate survey information, and most macroeconomic forecasts predict a gradual return to trend growth of output. This trend is based on historical information, yet medium-term output growth rates appear to change quite frequently, and smooth behaviour is not a characteristic of real-world economies. Models in particular rarely predict the sharp changes in behaviour which are a feature of the real world. There is a strong argument that too many resources are devoted to forecasting, and not enough to model development and use in policy analysis. On the other hand, forecasting failures have proved useful in the past in stimulating new empirical research.

Comparative performance

Our first conclusion is that models differ! We distinguish two types of difference. The first concerns the purpose of the model and whether it is intended for detailed analysis and forecasting, in which case it will tend to be large and quarterly, or whether it is an analytical tool, in which case it is probably small and annual. The second concerns its theoretical underpinnings. With the exception of the LPL (UK and world model) and MULTIMOD (multicountry) models, which are new classical, the other empirical models are very similar in spirit. That is, they are characterised by sluggish adjustment in the short term, so they appear quite Keynesian in this respect, but are more classical in the long run. There are clear differences between them in the length of adjustment to equilibrium and in whether practical features prevent a new equilibrium from being reached following an exogenous shock.

We can identify three crucial areas where structural differences between the models can dominate their simulation properties. These are the consumption equation, where the role of wealth or its absence is of major importance; the wage equation, which is key to understanding the nature of the supply side in the models (and where the distinction between the Phillips curve and the Layard–Nickell bargaining approach separates UK from non-UK models); and the determination of the exchange rate. Although the dominant paradigm here is that of UIP, it is not always applied with forward expectations of the exchange rate, and this causes significant differences in the short-run responses of models. Many of the empirical differences between models in simulation can be traced back to structural differences in respect to single equations, or even to single coefficients, and in principle these can be resolved by comparative econometric testing.

Where models are attempting to explain the same economy, there is only one set of data and so in principle models should converge. However, in practice, modellers innovate and change their models in the face of new evidence or policy problems, so convergence is never attained. Given these facts of life, and the different uses for which models are intended, it is rather optimistic to expect there to be only one model for each economy. In fact, this might be a disadvantage, for it can be argued that a degree of competition encourages modellers to innovate and develop. However, this probably also requires an element of support from public funds (there being a public-good element in models), otherwise the tendency will be to mimic the US experience where models have failed to develop in a commercially funded environment.

If there is to be competition between models, however, this should encourage a wide range of approaches. This occurred in the UK when the LPL, CUBS and Cambridge Growth Project models were supported out of public funds, but reductions in funding have narrowed the range of opinion in the UK rather dramatically. Competition also requires systematic monitoring, comparison and evaluation of the competing models if the relative merits of the different approaches are to be judged. The ESRC Macroeconomic Modelling Bureau at Warwick has fulfilled this role in the UK, but for this to continue also requires support from public funds in order to ensure independence.

10.2 Recent and prospective challenges for the models

Current models

Given that we have observed many structural changes in the mainstream models over the last ten years, we might ask whether this has radically changed their properties. The analysis of Chapter 3 would suggest a negative response to this question, for government expenditure multipliers still tend to be around unity in the short run. Where there have been changes in short-run properties, these have been associated with the introduction of forward-consistent expectations, which has often had the unexpected result of raising the short-term output response for a fiscal shock. Where there have been changes in long-run properties, this reflects a greater concern with the supply-side response, and medium-term multipliers have tended to fall, although not always. However, in many of the models there is no evidence that the model is settling down to a new equilibrium within typical simulation horizons of up to six years.

The various ways of examining the supply side suggests that the aggregate supply schedule only becomes steeper very gradually, and that sluggishness of wage and price behaviour is a key factor. While the basic government expenditure multiplier under money finance seems to have remained relatively constant over the last ten years or so, the interest rate sensitivity of the models has probably increased. The main direction in which the models might be said to have changed is in the inclusion of stock effects, such as in the explanation of consumption by wealth. There is also greater attention to the intertemporal issues, such as the sustainability of government policy actions, which has led some models to close the system by various feedbacks.

It is often in the assumptions about policy and in particular about model closure rules that the characteristics of models change in simulation analysis. This is particularly true of models such as MULTIMOD. Given that these closure rules are rarely based on observed behaviour, their role in model simulation results should be treated with some caution. In particular, assumptions about the dynamic policy responses embodied in these models are arbitrary, but can dominate the behavioural mechanisms in the model. For example, the finding that an increase in government spending is ineffective in raising the level of output for more than a period of one or two years may simply reflect the assumption that taxes are raised to bring the budget back into balance within this period. Yet in practice we observe that governments do run budget deficits for several years at a time without disastrous effects on inflation or interest rates.

Models like MULTIMOD, MSG2 and LPL are constructed in such a way that the economy returns quite rapidly to equilibrium following a shock, and many of the other models also contain equilibrium features. This is a modelling strategy which guarantees certain policy results. Successful policies are those which can shift the position of equilibrium (for example, supply-side policies). Yet real-world problems are often of a disequilibrium nature, and it is not clear that these types of model have much to say about such problems. The presence of equilibrium models such as LPL in the UK has proved to be a strong motivating force for developments in other models, but it is doubtful whether they should be regarded as directly useful for practical policy analysis and forecasting, although they are helpful in providing a stylised reference point.

Rational expectations

Many modellers in the USA saw the introduction of rational expectations or, more strictly, model-consistent expectations as akin to a new classical approach, and consequently refused to incorporate it in their models. UK modellers correctly distinguished between the modelling of expectations and assumptions about market clearing, and had no ideological objections to the rational expectations approach. Even so, it took a new classical model, LPL, to introduce practical rational expectations modelling to the UK. The mainstream UK models found that rational expectations often increased the short-run impact of fiscal policy on output, an unexpected result. The main technical problems of implementing rational expectations have been largely overcome, but it remains a computer-intensive approach, especially in stochastic or control theory applications. In practical terms, the use of rational expectations tends to change the time profile of adjustment in models, but in order to solve these models they have to have a well-defined equilibrium. This has been an important, but unexpected, product of the rational expectations approach, and has encouraged modellers to develop the long run of their models.

Rational expectations does not seem to have improved the ability of the models to explain the past, or to forecast the future (partly since rational expectations are not regularly used in forecasting). Its main benefits have been in policy analysis, where a minimum condition for an economic policy to be successful would appear to be when it is fully understood (Currie, 1985). However, there are doubts about the strong informational assumptions involved in rational expectations approaches, and the recent application of learning methods offers some hope for a more realistic approach.

Competing methodologies

Structural macroeconometric models have the advantage that they can be used for both forecasting and policy analysis, although there are some who argue that model development is often stunted if resources are regularly devoted to forecasting exercises. The two main competing methodologies are VAR models and CGE (or computable general equilibrium) models. VAR models are most often regarded as a serious competitor in forecasting, but recent evidence suggests that a superiority in forecasting does not signify a failure of the structural model. VARs do not lend themselves easily to policy analysis and hence have only limited appeal for those dissatisfied with the structural approach. The alternative of CGE models has the appeal of theoretical depth and can be useful in guidance on issues where there is no previous historical evidence, but its assumptions about parameter estimates remain untested. Furthermore, CGE models tend to have little to say about dynamic adjustment, a key element in the assessment of alternative policy options and often have inadequate model closure. However, CGE models can be of use in either augmenting macroeconometric models or providing a theoretical benchmark against which the structural models can be compared.

Thus there does not appear to be an alternative approach which can be used to replace the all-round capability of the macroeconometric model. Macroeconomic models are here to stay, but their role and use will probably change. In particular, some consolidation of the advantages of the CGE approach with traditional macroeconomic modelling may be a fruitful way forward.

The main issues facing models

The fact that there are no serious contenders to replace macroeconometric models does not mean that they are satisfactory. Far from it, they have many shortcomings, and face several new challenges. Probably some faith in models has been lost because they (or mainly their users) promised too much in the early days. One might now conclude that they find it quite difficult to deal with the sort of structural changes that have taken place in the industrial economies over the last 20 years. There will always be the problem that future changes may cause the same sort of failure, added to which is the perennial problem that the availability and quality of the data rarely match the conceptual needs of the model. There is also the question of whether models need to be become more consistent with theory or with tracking empirical regularities in the economy – there often being a trade-off between the two requirements.

Current issues which may influence the development of models concern aggregation over economic agents, and incomplete markets. Modern microeconomic theory has been concerned with how to aggregate the microeconomic decisions of agents facing transactions costs who adjust infrequently, but by large amounts. Theorists have also focused their attention on explaining how incomplete access to financial markets and the non-tradability of human wealth affect the consumption and portfolio behaviour of consumers. This development supersedes the simple Keynesian consumption function or the certainty-equivalent representations of the permanent income theory. Recent developments in the world economy have also raised the importance of developing the role of financial fragility in business cycles.

We can identify two further areas in which models face a specific challenge: the incorporation of environmental factors and policies to tackle the 'greenhouse effect', and the endogenous explanation of long-run growth. Some work has also begun on the environmental question. This is an example of where existing models can be modified, particularly in their treatment of the energy sector. However, there is a danger if each new modification tends to increase model size and make models unmanageable. A way forward is to see the models as a core to which specific modifications can be made where these are relevant to the policy issue in question. For example, where environmental feedbacks are likely to be minor, this part of the model may be neglected. The endogenous growth literature emphasises the role of innovation and investment and moving away from the simple aggregate production function. Some possible lines of development are discussed in Chapter 8.

10.3 Conclusions and summary

Much of this discussion emphasises the role of models as a tool for thought, and not as a black box. Models will survive, but to apply them usefully and to interpret their findings requires an investment of intellectual effort – they do not provide a short-cut to answering questions about the national or international economy. Probably the main mistake is to see them as simple mechanical devices. In order to use them properly, it is necessary that they are adequate for the desired purpose, and if not, they should be modified without imposing results upon the model that have no supporting evidence.

Models are a tool of applied macroeconomic research, but they are not the only tool. Just as the prudent traveller takes alternative clothes to cope with different weather contingencies, so the analyst of economies needs to consider which 'set of clothes' is best for the purpose in hand. Viewed in this way, different models and different modelling approaches can be seen as complements, and an unbending subservience to one alone is not a sensible strategy (in the analogy of the traveller, a heavy winter coat could spell disaster in a desert climate, as could a light-weight suit in the Arctic). It is not sensible to ask which model is best, or which modelling strategy. To return to our introductory theme, there are different models constructed for different purposes.

There is no absolute best buy, but it is important that consumers of model-based analysis are aware of the particular features of different models and approaches. This book has attempted to give some general guidance, but the reputation of macro-econometric modelling in the future depends on the regular availability of independent expert assessment. The public-good argument can also be extended to the need for some state support for macroeconomic modelling activities. Without this there is the danger that modelling resources will be diverted towards commercial forecasting activities rather than towards academic innovation and useful support for policy analysis. This appears to be recognised in most European countries but less so in the UK and the USA.

APPENDIX I
Structural developments in the UK models

Principal changes in model structure:

	NIESR	LBS	HMT
1983	Wage equation with real-wage target Demand influence on prices Inflation effect via real balances on consumption Real interest rate effect on consumption Relative prices on exchange rate	Real stock of liquid assets on consumption Interest rates in housing investment and stockbuilding equations Real-wage effect on employment Monetary explanation of exchange rate	Demand influence on prices Inflation influence on consumption Real interest rates on housing, investment and consumption Money influence on exchange rate
1984	No change	Financial model introduced, determines exchange rate as market-clearing price together with price of gilts and equities	Relative factor prices on employment and investment Liquidity effects on employment and investment
1985	Forward-consistent expectations, in exchange rate, investment, stocks, employment and narrow money equations Exchange rate equation: real exchange rate depends on real interest differentials and trade balance Real-wage effects on employment Unemployment determined by sectoral employment	Forward-consistent expectations in the financial sector Labour force participation equation Unemployment-benefit effect on earnings	New stockbuilding equations with financial effects

Principal changes in model structure (*continued*)

	NIESR	LBS	HMT
1986	Real financial assets in consumption equation Productivity in wage equation New employment–unemployment relationship Application of Engle–Granger cointegration estimation	Differential-duration unemployment effect on wages	Endogenous labour force New earnings equation based on target real wage/affordable wage bargain Unit labour costs in trade equations Stock of consumer durables depends on inflation-adjusted income, net financial wealth and equity withdrawal Manufacturing stockbuilding equations use expected output based on CBI survey
1987	Financial wealth on consumption Investment no longer depends on expected output	Little change	Some change to price equations, employment and exports
1988	Major changes: Vintage production function Capacity utilisation on imports and prices UIP-style exchange rate equation Layard–Nickell-style wage equation with tax effects New investment and employment equations, with disequilibrium liquidity effects New import equation New consumption equation with explicit credit effects	New supply side with integrated treatment of production, prices and factor demand Imports treated as a residual	Slim model; reduced in size from 1200 to 520 variables Company sector, indirect tax system, domestic financial sector and treatment of North Sea main areas of pruning
1989	No major change	No major change	No major change

Principal changes in model structure (*continued*)

	NIESR	LBS	HMT
1990	No change	UIP exchange rate equation Removal of financial sector Revised consumption equation with housing wealth Productivity effect on wages Revised price equation with faster dynamics	New import equation with specialisation measure
1991	No change	Learning treatment of expectations in exchange rate equation	No major change

10 The relevance of macroeconometric models

In this final chapter we review briefly the main conclusions that we can draw about macroeconometric models and their usefulness in forecasting and policy analysis. We begin by commenting on model evaluation.

10.1 Model evaluation

Models can be evaluated in a variety of ways. They can be judged on their ability to explain past data, their relevance to economic theory, their relevance for policy analysis, their forecasting performance, or their relation to other models.

Consistency with past data

Although econometric techniques for evaluating single equations of small blocks have become quite sophisticated, system methods are rarely used. The main tool of historical validation lies with the so-called tracking performance of the models. The use of dynamic simulation as a diagnostic device has been questioned by Chong and Hendry (1986) and by Pagan (1989), yet it is still regularly used by model-builders. The work by Fisher and Wallis (1990) on the UK models suggests that they may have some deficiencies in their historical performance, and that some of the problems can arise from inadequate attention to the apparently minor equations in the models. However, in the absence of satisfactory absolute validation criteria, it is not possible to conclude that models fail the test of history.

Consistency with theory

Macroeconomic models have been criticised for their poor theory underpinnings, although a contrary view is taken by Summers (1991), who argues that little is gained from sophisticated econometric techniques or theory models based on maximising

APPENDIX II
Model simulation properties

Government expenditure multipliers
(absolute change in GDP divided by absolute change in government spending)

(i) Laury, Lewis and Ormerod (1978) estimates

		Fixed exchange rate		Floating exchange rate	
		Money finance	Bond finance	Money finance	Bond finance
HMT	Q4	1.11	1.09	1.21	1.17
	Q16	1.09	1.10	1.12	0.63
LBS	Q4	1.25	1.25	1.19	1.06
	Q16	1.11	1.22	1.22	1.06
NIESR	Q4	0.84	0.8	0.96	0.90
	Q16	0.49	0.48	0.80	0.89

(ii) Ormerod–Economic Modelling, 1979

		Floating exchange rate	
		Bond finance	Money finance
HMT	Q4	1.11	1.07
	Q16	0.81	0.19
LBS	Q4	n.a	0.85
	Q16	n.a	0.62
NIESR	Q4	n.a.	0.81
	Q16	n.a.	0.24

(iii) Artis, Bladen-Hovell *et al.* – NIER 1984 – floating exchange rate

		Money finance	Bond finance
LBS	Q4	1.18	0.84
	Q16	0.90	0.87
NIESR	Q4	0.88	0.74
	Q16	0.79	0.73

(iv) MMB estimates – floating exchange rate, money finance

	Yr	83	84	85	86	87	88	89	90
HMT	1	1.03	0.97	0.95	0.96	1.02	1.05	0.99	1.06
	4	0.90	0.96						
	5			0.91	1.01	0.84	1.12	1.24	1.33
LBS	1	0.96	0.88	0.97	0.96	0.97	1.15	1.13	0.82
	5	1.15	1.41	1.52	1.53	1.88	2.20	1.65	1.03
NIESR	1	1.21	1.07	0.98	1.29	1.47	1.42	1.77	1.49
	5	1.16	1.28	0.93	1.26	1.83	0.48	0.46	0.98
BE	1				0.90	0.90	0.82	0.99	0.99
	5				1.04	0.96	1.59	1.75	1.47

(v) Bond finance

	Yr	83	84	85	86	87*
HMT	1	0.77	0.88	0.74	0.63	0.75
	4	0.26	−0.14	−0.12	−0.09	−0.16
LBS	1		0.84	0.88	0.90	0.81
	4		0.88	1.18	1.48	1.14
NIESR	1		1.01			1.24
	4		1.07			1.31
BE	1					0.86
	4					0.96

(vi) Price-level effects of money-financed expansion: £2bn increase per annum @ 1990 prices – MMB estimates – floating exchange rate

	Yr	83	84	85	86	87	88	89	90
HMT	1	0.3	0.3	0.2	0.3	0.10	0.14	0.17	0.1
	5	2.4	2.6	3.1	1.7	1.3	2.26	1.94	2.0
LBS	1	−0.13	0.1	0.2	0.1	0.08	0.07	0.08	0
	5	n.a.	2.3	3.4	2.0	1.51	2.12	2.6	0.6
NIESR	1	0	0.6	0.1	0.2	0.21	0.97	1.29	0.9
	5	2.2	5.2	2.4	1.4	1.3	4.22	4.21	2.6
BE	1			0.2		0.06	0.1	0.08	0
	5			0.8		0.41	1.06	1.84	1.0

(vii) Unemployment effects of expenditure increase under money finance – MMB estimates – floating exchange rate (thousands, difference from base)

	Yr	84	85	86	87	88	89	90
HMT	1	n.a.	−119	−117	−73	−81	−77	−80
	5	n.a.	−96	−112	−58	−108	−103	−93
LBS	1	−121	−135	−125	−73	−72	−85	−76
	5	−159	−191	−181	−110	−129	−77	−60
NIESR	1	−159	−52	−79	−52	−45	−36	−32
	5	−206	−27	−139	−97	−70	−58	−55

(viii) Interest rate change: effect of 1 percentage point increase on GDP – MMB estimates – floating exchange rate (% difference from base)

	Yr	85	86	87	88	89	90
HMT	1	0.30	0.35	0.38	0.42	0.45	0.39
	3			0.74	0.98	1.16	1.27
	5	0.65	0.95	0.67	0.82	1.26	1.47
LBS	1	0.35	0.35	0.36	0.37*	0.22	0.34
	3			0.77	0.83*	0.21	0.86
	5	0.4	0.30	0.49	0.55*	−0.12	−0.19
NIESR	1	0.05	0.05	0.67	0.42*	0.50	0.41
	3			1.09	0.58*	0.50	0.40
	5	0.05	0.05	1.13	−0.10*	0.15	−0.01
BE	1			0.24	0.19	0.18	0.19
	3			0.29	0.58	0.90	1.03
	5			−0.27	0.50	1.36	1.36

Note: Years 85, 86 onwards denote the vintage of the model. From 1988 onwards the interst rate shock is temporary for LBS and NIESR.

* narrow money.

References

Adelman, I., and Adelman, F. (1959) 'The dynamic properties of the Klein–Goldberger model', *Econometrica*, 27, 596–625.

Allen, C., and Currie, D. (1990) 'Empirical macroeconomic interactions between North and South', Centre for Economic Forecasting Discussion Paper, 27–90, London: London Business School.

Allen, C. and Whitley, J.D. (1994) 'Modelling bilateral trade', in Hall, S.G. (ed.), *Applied Forecasting Techniques*, Hemel Hempstead: Harvester Wheatsheaf.

Anderton, R. (1991) 'UK exports of manufactures: testing for the effects of non-price competitiveness using stochastic trends and profitability measures', *The Manchester School*, 60, 23–40.

Anderton, R., Barrell, R.J., and in't Veld, J.W. (1992) 'Forward looking wages and the analysis of monetary union', in Barrell, R.J., and Whitley, J.D. (eds) *Macroeconomic Policy Coordination in Europe: The ERM and monetary union*, London: Sage.

Andrews, M.J., Bell, D.N.F., Fisher, P.G., Wallis, K.F., and Whitley, J.D. (1985). 'Models of the UK Economy and the real wage-employment debate, *National Institute Economic Review*, 112, 41–52.

Arrow, K., and Debreu, G. (1954) 'Existence of an equilibrium for a competitive economy', *Econometrica*, 22(3), 265–90.

Artis, M.J. (1982) 'Why do forecasts differ?' paper presented to the Panel of Academic Consultants, no 17, Bank of England.

Artis, M.J. (1988) 'How accurate is the World Economic Outlook? A post mortem on short-term forecasting at the International Monetary Fund', *Staff Studies for the World Economic Outlook*, July, 1–48, Washington, DC: International Monetary Fund.

Artis, M.J., and Green, C.J. (1982) 'Using the Treasury model to measure the impact of fiscal policy 1974–79'. In Artis, M.J., *et al.* (eds.), *Demand Management, Supply Constraints and Inflation*, Manchester: Manchester University Press.

Artis, M.J., and Holly, S. (1992) 'Modelling the world economy: the European perspective', *Journal of Forecasting*, 11, 333–40.

Artis, M.J., Bladen-Hovell, R., and Ma, Y. (1992) 'The measurement of policy effects in a non-causal model: an application to economic policy in the UK 1974–79', mimeo, University of Manchester.

Artis, M.J., Bladen-Hovell, R., and Zang, W. (1992) 'Leading indicators in forecasting', mimeo, University of Manchester.

Artis, M.J., Bladen-Hovell, R., Karakitsos, E., and Dwolatzky, B. (1984) 'The effects of economic policy: 1979–82', *National Institute Economic Review*, 108, 54–67.

Artis, M.J., Moss, S., and Ormerod, P.A. (1992) 'A smart automated macroeconomic forecasting system', mimeo, University of Manchester.

Ash, J.C.K., and Smyth, D.J. (1973) *Forecasting the United Kingdom Economy*, Farnborough: Saxon House.

Ball, J., and Holly, S. (1991) 'Macroeconometric model-building in the United Kingdom', in Bodkin, R.G., Klein, L.R., and Marwah, K. (eds.) *A History of Macroeconometric Model-Building*, Aldershot: Edward Elgar.

Ball, R.J. (ed.) (1973) *The International Linkage of National Economic Models*. Amsterdam: North-Holland.

Ball, R.J., and St Cyr, E.B.A. (1966) 'Short-term employment functions in British manufacturing industry', *Review of Economic Studies*, 33, 179–97.

Ball, R.J., Burns, T., and Laury, J.S.E. (1977) 'The role of the exchange rate changes on balance of payments adjustment: the United Kingdom case', *Economic Journal*, 87, 1–29.

Bank of England (1981) 'Factors underlying the recent recession', papers presented to the Panel of Academic Consultants, no. 15, London: Bank of England.

Barker, T.S. (1985) 'Forecasting the economic recession in the UK 1979–82: a comparison of model based forecasts', *Journal of Forecasting*, 4, 133–51.

Barrell, R.J., and Whitley, J.D. (eds.) (1992) *Macroeconomic Policy Coordination in Europe: The ERM and monetary union*, London: Sage

Barrell, R.J., and Wren-Lewis, S. (1989) 'Fundamental equilibrium exchange rates for the G7', National Institute Discussion Paper, no. 155, London: NIESR.

Barrell, R.J., Caporale, G.M., Hall, S.G., and Garratt, A. (1994) 'Learning about monetary union: an analysis of boundedly rational learning in European labour markets', in Hall, S.G. (ed.), (forthcoming), London: Harvester Wheatsheaf.

Barrell, R.J., Christodoulakis, N., Currie, D.A., Garratt, A., Ireland, J.A., Kemball-Cook, D., Levine, P., and Westaway, P. (1992) 'Policy analysis and model reduction techniques using GEM', in Bryant, R.C, Hooper, P., Mann, C.L., and Tryon, R.W. (eds.), *Evaluating Policy Regimes: New research in empirical macroeconomics*, Washington DC: Brookings Institution.

Bates, J.M., and Granger, C.W.J. (1969) 'The combination of forecasts', *Operational Research Quarterly*, 20, 451–68.

Bean, C.R., Layard, P.R.G., and Nickell, S.J. (1986). 'The rise in unemployment: a multi-country study', *Economica*, 53, S1–22.

Beenstock, M., Warburton, P., Lewington, P., and Dalziel, A. (1986) 'A Macroeconomic model of aggregate supply and demand for the UK', *Economic Modelling*, 3, 242–68.

Biorn, E., Jensen, M., and Reyment, M. (1987) 'KVARTS: a quarterly model of the Norwegian economy', *Economic Modelling*, 4, 77–109.

Blackburn, K. (1987) 'Economic policy evaluation and optimal control theory: a critical review of some recent developments', *Journal of Economic Theory*, 7, 53–65.

Blanchard, O. J., and Fischer, S. (1989) '*Lectures on macroeconomics*', London: MIT Press.

Blanchard, O.J. (1988) 'Comment on Nickell: the supply side and macroeconomic modelling', in Bryant, R.C. *et al.* (eds.), *Empirical Economic for Interdependent Economies*, Washington, DC: Brookings Institution.

Blanchard, O.J. and Kahn, C.M. (1980) 'The solution of linear difference models under rational expectations', *Econometrica*, 48, 1305–11.

References

Blinder, A.S., and Solow, R.M. (1973) 'Does fiscal policy matter?' *Journal of Public Economics*, 2, 319–337.

Bodkin, R.G., Klein, L.R., and Marwah, K. (eds.), (1991) *A History of Macroeconometric Model-Building*, Aldershot: Edward Elgar.

Bradley, J., and Fitzgerald, J. (1988) 'Industrial output and factor input determination in an econometric model of a small open economy', *European Economic Review*, 32, 1227–41.

Brechling, F. (1965) 'The relationship between output and employment in British manufacturing industry', *Review of Economic Studies*, 32, 187–216.

Britton, A.J. (ed.) (1989) *Policymaking with macroeconomic models*, Aldershot: Gower.

Britton, A.J. (1992) 'Exchange rate realignments in the European Monetary System', in Barrell, R.J., and Whitley, J.D. (eds.) (1992) *Macroeconomic Policy Coordination in Europe: The ERM and monetary union*, London: Sage

Britton, A.J., and Pain, N. (1992) *Economic Forecasting in Britain*. National Institute of Economic and Social Research, Report series, No 4.

Bryant, R.C., Henderson, D., Holtham, G., Hooper, P., and Symansky, S. (eds.) (1988) *Empirical Macroeconomics for Interdependent Economies*, Washington, DC: Brookings Institution.

Budd, A., Dicks, G., Holly, S., Keating, G., and Robinson, B. (1984) 'The London Business School econometric model of the UK', *Economic Modelling*, 1, 355–420.

Burns, T. (1986) 'The interpretation and use of economic predictions', *Proceedings of the Royal Statistical Society*, series A, 407, 103–25; reprinted in Mason, J., Mathias, P., and Westcott, J.H. (eds.), *Predictability in Science and Society*, London: Royal Society and British Academy.

Burridge, M., Dhar, S., Mayes, D., Meen, G., Neal, E., Tyrell, N., and Walker, J. (1991) 'Oxford Economic Forecasting's system of models', *Economic Modelling*, 8, 227–413.

Byron, R. (1970) 'Initial attempts in model-building at NIESR', in Hilton, K., and Heathfield, D. (eds.) *An Econometric Study of the United Kingdom*, London: Macmillan.

Calzolari, G. (1979) 'Antithetic variates to estimate the simulation bias in nonlinear models', *Economic Letters*, 4, 323–38.

Carlin, W. and Soskice, D. (1990) 'Macroeconomics and the Wage Bargain, Oxford: Oxford University Press

Chong, Y.Y., and Hendry, D.F. (1986) 'Econometric evaluation of linear macroeconomic models', *Review of Economic Studies*, 53, 671–90.

Chow, G.C. (1975) *Analysis and Control of Dynamic Economic Systems*, New York: John Wiley.

Chow, G.C. (1980) 'Estimation of rational expectations models', *Journal of Economic Dynamics and Control*, 2, 241–55.

Chow, G.C. (1981) *Econometric Analysis by Control Methods*, New York: John Wiley.

Chow, G.C., and Corsi, P. (eds.) (1982) *Evaluating the Reliability of Macroeconomic Models*, New York: John Wiley.

Chow, G.C., and Megdal, S.B. (1978) 'An econometric definition of the inflation–unemployment trade-off', *American Economic Review*, 68, 446–53.

Christ, C.F. (1968) 'A simple macroeconomic model with a government budget constraint', *Journal of Political Economy*, 76, 53–67.

Christensen, A. and Knudsen, D. (1992) 'MONA: a quarterly model of the Danish economy', *Economic Modelling*, 9, 10–74.

Church, K.B. (1992) 'Properties of the fundamental equilibrium exchange rate in models of the UK economy', *National Institute Economic Review*, 141, 62–70.

Church, K.B., Mitchell, P.R., Turner, D.S, Wallis, K.F., and Whitley J. D.(1991) 'Comparative properties of models of the UK economy', *National Institute Economic Review*, 137, 59–74.

Commission of the European Communities (CEC) (1991) 'Quest: a macroeconomic model for the countries of the European Community as part of the world economy', *European Economy*, 47, 51–236, Brussels: EEC.

Courakis, A. (1988) 'Modelling portfolio selection', *Economic Journal*, 98, 619–42.

Coutts, K., Godley, W., and Nordhaus, W. (1978) *Industrial Pricing in the United Kingdom*, Cambridge: Cambridge University Press.

Currie, D.A. (1985) 'Macroeconomic policy design and control theory: a failed partnership?' *Economic Journal*, 5, 31–8.

Currie, D.A. and Hall, S. G. (1994) 'Expectations in empirical macroeconomic models', in Hall, S. (ed.), (forthcoming), London: Harvester Wheatsheaf.

Cuthbertson, K., Hall, S., and Taylor, M.P. (1992) *Applied Econometric Techniques*, London: Harvester Wheatsheaf.

Davidson, J.E.H., Hendry, D.F., Srba, F., and Yeo, S. (1978) 'Econometric modelling of the aggregate time-series relationship between consumers' expenditure and income in the United Kingdom', *Economic Journal*, 88, 661–92.

Deaton, A.S. (1977) 'Involuntary saving through anticipated inflation', *American Economic Review*, 67, 899–910.

Deaton, A.S., and Muellbauer, J. (1980) 'An almost ideal demand system', *American Economic Review*, 70, 312–26.

Dinenis, E., Holly, S., Levine, P., and Smith, P. (1989) 'The London Business School econometric model: some recent developments', *Economic Modelling*, 6, 243–51.

Doan, T., Litterman, R., and Sims, C. (1984) 'Forecasting and conditional projection using realistic prior distributions', *Econometric Reviews*, 3, 1–100

Dornbusch, R. (1976) 'Expectation and Exchange Rate Dynamics', *Journal of Political Economy*, 84, 1161–76

Edison, H., Marquez, J., and Tryon, R. (1987) 'The structure and properties of the Federal Reserve Board Multicountry Model', *Economic Modelling*, 4, 115–36.

European Commission (1990) 'One market, one money: an evaluation of the potential benefits and costs of forming an economic and monetary union', *European Economy*, no. 44.

Fair, R.C. (1979) 'An analysis of a macro-econometric model with rational expectations in the bond and stock markets', *American Economic Review*, 69, 539–52.

Fair, R.C. (1984) *Specification, Estimation and Analysis of Macroeconometric Models*, Harvard, Mass.: Harvard University Press.

Fair, R.C., and Taylor, J.B. (1983) 'Solution and maximum likelihood estimation of dynamic nonlinear rational expectations models', *Econometrica*, 51, 1169–86.

Fase, M.M., Kramer, P., and Boeschoten, W. (1992) 'MORKMON II: the Nederlandische Bank's quarterly model of the Netherlands economy', *Economic Modelling*, 9, 146–204.

Fisher, P.G. (1992) *Rational Expectations in Macroeconomic Models*, London: Kluwer Academic Publishers.

Fisher, P.G., and Hughes-Hallett, A.J. (1987) 'The convergence characteristics of iterative techniques for solving econometric models', *Oxford Bulletin of Economics and Statistics*, 49, 231–44.

Fisher, P.G., and Hughes-Hallett, A.J. (1988) 'An efficient solution strategy for solving dynamic nonlinear rational expectations models', *Journal of Economic Dynamics and Control*, 12, 635–57.

Fisher, P.G., and Salmon, M.H. (1986) 'On evaluating the importance of nonlinearity in large macroeconometric models', *International Economic Review*, 27, 625–46.

Fisher, P.G. and Wallis, K.F. (1990) 'The historical tracking performance of UK macro-economic models, 1979–85', *Economic Modelling*, 20, 179–97.

Fisher, P.G., Holly, S., and Hughes-Hallett, A.J. (1986) 'Efficient solution techniques for dynamic nonlinear rational expectations models', *Journal of Economic Dynamics and Control*, 10, 139–45.

Fisher, P.G., Tanna, S.K., Turner, D.S, Wallis, K.F., and Whitley, J.D. (1988) 'Comparative properties of models of the UK economy', *National Institute Economic Review*, 125, 69–87.

Fisher, P.G., Tanna, S.K., Turner, D.S, Wallis, K.F., and Whitley, J.D. (1989) 'Comparative properties of models of the UK economy' *National Institute Economic Review*, 129, 69–87.

Fisher, P.G., Tanna, S.K., Turner, D.S, Wallis, K.F., and Whitley, J.D. (1990a) 'Econometric evaluation of the exchange rate in models of the UK economy', *Economic Journal*, 100, 1230–44.

Fisher, P.G., Turner, D.S, Wallis, K.F., and Whitley, J.D. (1990b) 'Comparative properties of models of the UK economy', *National Institute Economic Review*, 133, 91–104.

Fisher, P.G., Wallis, K.F. and Whitley, J.D. (1985) 'Financing rules and output variability: evidence from UK macroeconomic models', ESRC Macroeconomic Modelling Bureau Discussion Paper 7, University of Warwick.

Flemming, J. (1976) *Inflation*, Oxford: Oxford University Press.

Ford, R., and Poret, P. (1990) 'Business investment: recent performance and some implications for policy', *OECD Economic Studies*, 16, 79–132.

Friedman, M. (1968) 'The role of monetary policy', *American Economic Review*, 58, 1–17.

Gilbert, C.L. (1989) 'LSE and the British approach to time series econometrics', *Oxford Economic Papers*, 41, 108–28.

Granger, C.W.J. (1981) 'Some properties of time series data and their use in econometric model specification', *Journal of Econometrics*, 16, 251–76.

Granger, C.W.J., and Newbold, P. (1986) *Forecasting Economic Time series*, (2nd edn), New York: Academic Press.

Green, R.J., Hickman, B.G., Howrey, E.P., Hymans, S.H. and Donihue, M.R. (1988) 'The IS–LM curves of three econometric models', in Bryant, R.C. *et al.* (eds.), *Empirical Macroeconomics for Interdependent Economies*, Washington, DC: Brookings Institution.

Greenhalgh, C., Taylor, P., and Wilson, R. (1990) 'Innovation and export volumes and prices: a disaggregated study', *CEPR Discussion Paper*, no. 4–87.

Grunberg, E., and Modigliani, F. (1954) 'The predictability of social events', *Journal of Political Economy*, 62, 465–78.

Gurney, A. (1988) 'The exchange rate, interest rates, and the current balance in a forward looking model', *National Institute Economic Review*, 125, 40–45.

Gurney, A. (1990) 'Fiscal policy simulations using forward looking exchange rates in GEM', *National Institute Economic Review*, 131, 47–50.

Hall, R.E. (1978) 'Stochastic implications of the life cycle permanent hypothesis', *Journal of Political Economy*, 86, 971–87.

Hall, S.G. (1984) 'Confidence intervals', *National Institute Economic Review*, 33–7.

Hall, S.G. (1985) 'On the solution of large economic models with consistent expectations', *Bulletin of Economic Research*, 37, 157–61.

Hall, S.G. (1986) 'An investigation of time consistency and optimal policy formulation in the presence of rational expectations', *Journal of Economic Dynamics and Control*, 10, 323–6.

Hall, S.G. (ed.) (1994) *Applied Economic Forecasting Techniques*, Hemel Hempstead: Harvester Wheatsheaf.

Hall, S.G., and Garratt, A. (1992) 'Model consistent learning and regime switching', LBS Discussion Paper, 02–92, London: London Business School.

Hall, S.G. and Garratt, A., Barrell, R.J., Gurney, A., and in't Veld, J.W. (1992) 'The real exchange rate, fiscal policy and the role of wealth: an analysis of equilibrium in a monetary union', *Journal of Forecasting*, 1, 361–88.

Hall, S.G., and Henry, S.G.B. (1985) 'Rational expectations in an econometric model: NIESR model 8', *National Institute Economic Review*, 114, 58–68.

Hall, S.G. and Henry, S.G.B. (1986) 'A dynamic econometric model of the UK with rational expectations', *Journal of Economic Dynamics and Control*, 10, 219–33.

Hall, S.G., and Henry, S.G.B. (1988) *Macroeconomic Modelling*, Amsterdam: North-Holland

Hall, S.G., Robertson, D., and Wickens, M. (1992) 'Measuring convergence of the EC economies', *The Manchester School* (supplement), 60, 99–111.

Harnett, I., and Patterson, K. (1989) 'An analysis of changes in the structural and simulation properties of the Bank of England quarterly model of the UK economy', *Economic Modelling*, 6, 20–55.

Hayashi, F. (1982) 'Tobin's marginal q and average q: a neoclassical interpretation', *Econometrica*, 50, 213–24.

Hendry, D.H., and von Ungern-Sternberg, T. (1981) 'Liquidity and inflation effects on consumers' expenditure', in Deaton, A.S. (ed.), *Essays in the Theory and Measurement of Consumer Behaviour*, Cambridge: Cambridge University Press.

Hendry, D.H. (1980) 'Econometrics: alchemy or science?' *Economica*, 47, 387–406.

Hendry, D.H. (1993) *Lectures in Econometric Methodology*, Oxford: Oxford University Press.

Hendry, D.H., and Clements, M. (1992) 'Towards a theory of economic forecasting', mimeo, Institute of Economics and Statistics, Oxford.

Hendry, D.H., and Mizon, G.E. (1992) 'Evaluating dynamic econometric models by encompassing the VAR', in Phillips, P.C.B., and Hall, V.B. (eds), *Models, Methods, and Applications of Econometrics*, London: Basil Blackwell.

Hendry, D.H., and Richard, J.-F. (1983) 'The econometric analysis of economic time series', *Statistical Review*, 51, 111–63.

Henry, S.G.B., Karakitsos, E., and Savage, D. (1982) 'On the derivation of the "efficient" Phillips curve', *The Manchester School*, 50, 151–77.

Hickman, B.G. (1988) 'The US economy and the international transmission mechanism', in Bryant, R.C., *et al.* (eds.), *Empirical Macroeconomics for Interdependent Economies*, Washington, DC: Brookings Institution.

Hickman, B.G. (1991) 'Project link and multicountry modelling', in Bodkin, R.G., Klein, L.R., and Marwah, K. (eds.) *A History of Macroeconometric Model-Building*, Aldershot: Edward Elgar.

Higgins, C.I. (1987) 'Discussion on modelling', conference on macroeconomic modelling, Centre for Economic Policy Research, Australian National University.

Higgins, C.I. (1988) 'Empirical analysis and intergovernmental policy consultation', in Bryant, R.C., *et al.* (eds.) *Empirical Macroeconomics for Interdependent Economies*, Washington, DC: Brookings Institution.

Holden, K., and Peel, D.A. (1983) 'Forecasts and expectations: some evidence for the U.K., *Journal of Forecasting*, 2, 51–8.

Holden, K., and Peel, D.A. (1985) 'An evaluation of quarterly National Institute forecasts', *Journal of Forecasting*, 4, 227–34.

References

Holden, K., and Peel, D.A. (1986) 'An empirical investigation of combinations of economic forecasts', *Journal of Forecasting*, 5, 229.

Holly, S. (1991) 'Economic models and economic forecasting: Ptolemaic or Copernican', *LBS Economic Outlook*, 15, June, 32–8.

Holly, S., and Corker, R. (1984) 'Optimal feedback and feedforward stabilisation of exchange rates, money, prices and output under rational expectations', in Hughes Hallett, A.J. (ed.), *Applied Decision Analysis and Economic Behaviour*, Lancaster: Martinus Nijhoff.

Holly, S., and Hughes-Hallett, A.J. (1989) *Control, Expectations and Uncertainty: Problems in the design of economic policy*, Cambridge: Cambridge University Press.

Holly, S., and Wade, K. (1989) 'UK exports of manufactures: the role of supply side factors', CEF Discussion Paper, 14–89, London: London Business School.

Holly, S., Rustem, B., and Zarrop, M.B. (eds.) (1979) *Optimal Control for Econometric Models*, London: Macmillan.

Holly, S. and Zarrop, M.B. (1983) 'On optimality and time consistency when expectations are rational', *European Economic Review*, 20, 23–40.

Holtham, G., and Hughes-Hallett, A.J. (1992) 'Policy cooperation under uncertainty: the case for some disagreement', *American Economic Review*, 82, 1043–51.

Horton, G. (1984) 'Modelling the world economy', Government Economic Service Working Paper, 73.

Ireland, J., and Westaway, P. (1990) 'Stochastic simulation and forecast uncertainty in a forward looking model', National Institute Discussion Paper, 183.

Isard, P. (1988) 'Exchange rate modelling: an assessment of alternative approaches', in Bryant, R.C. *et al.* (eds.), *Empirical Macroeconomics for Interdependent Economies*, Washington, DC: Brookings Institution.

Joyce, M., and Wren-Lewis, S. (1991) 'The role of the exchange rate and capacity utilisation in convergence of the NAIRU' *Economic Journal*, 101, 497–507.

Keating, G. (1985a) 'Fooling all the people: LBS forecast release', vol. 9, no. 11, London: London Business School.

Keating, G. (1985b) *The Production and Use of Economic Forecasts*, London: Methuen.

Kelly, C.M. (1985) 'A cautionary note on the interpretation of long-run equilibrium solutions in conventional macro models', *Economic Journal*, 95, 1078–86.

Kelly, C.M., and Owen, D. (1985) 'Factor prices in the Treasury model', Government Economic Service Working Paper, 83.

Klein, L.R. (ed.) (1991) *Comparative Performance of US Econometric Models*, Oxford: Oxford University Press.

Kuh, E., Neese, J., and Hollinger, P. (1985) *Structural Sensitivity in Econometric Models*, New York: John Wiley.

Kydland, F.E., and Prescott, E.C. (1977) 'Rules rather than discretion: the inconsistency of optimal plans', *Journal of Political Economy*, 85, 473–91.

Lahti, A., and Viren, M. (1988) 'Examining the role of expectations in a macroeconomic model: some results with the Finnish QMED model', *Economic Modelling*, 5, 347–53.

Landesmann, M., and Snell, A. (1989) 'The consequences of Mrs Thatcher for UK manufacturing exports', *Economic Journal*, 99, 1–27.

Laury, J.S.E., Lewis, G.R., and Ormerod, P.A. (1978) 'Properties of macroeconomic models of the UK economy: a comparative study', *National Institute Economic Review*, 83, 52–72

Layard, P.R.G., and Nickell, S.J. (1985) 'The causes of British unemployment, *National Institute Economic Review*, 111, 62–85.

Layard, P.R.G., and Nickell, S.J. (1986) 'Unemployment in Britain', *Economica* (supplement), S3, S121–S169.

Layard, P.R.G., Nickell, S.J., and Jackman, R.A. (1991) *Unemployment: Macroeconomic performance and the labour market*, Oxford: Oxford University Press.

Levačić, R., and Rebman, A. (1982) *An Introduction to Keynesian and Neo-classical Controversies*, London: Macmillan.

Lipton, D., Poterba, J., Sachs, J., and Summers, L. (1982) 'Multiple shooting in rational expectations models', *Econometrica*, 50, 1329–33.

Litterman, R.B. (1986) 'Forecasting with Bayesian vector autoregressions: five years of experience', *Journal of Business and Economic Statistics*, 4, 25–38.

Lucas, R.E. (1976) 'Econometric policy evaluation: a critique', in Brunner, K., and Meltzer, A.H. (eds.), *The Phillips Curve and Labour Markets*, supplement to the *Journal of Monetary Economics*.

Lucas, R.E., and Sargent, T.J. (1978) 'After Keynesian macroeconomics', in *After the Phillips Curve: Persistence of high inflation and high unemployment*, Conference series no. 19, Federal Reserve Bank of Boston.

McCarthy, M.D. (1972) 'Some notes on the generation of pseudo-structural errors for use in stochastic simulation studies', appendix to Evans, Klein and Saito in Hickman, B.G. (ed.), *Econometric Models of Cyclical Behaviour*, New York: Columbia University Press.

Macdonald, G., and Turner, D.S. (1989) 'A ready reckoner program for macroeconomics teaching', *Oxford Bulletin of Economics and Statistics*, 51, 193–211.

Macdonald, G., and Turner, D.S. (1991) 'The PC-Ready Reckoner Program', *Economic and Financial Computing*, 1, 115–209.

McKibben, W. and Sachs, J.D. (1991) *Global Linkages: Macroeconomic interdependence and cooperation in the world economy*, Washington, DC: Brookings Institution.

Mackie, D., Miles, D., and Taylor, C. (1989) 'The impact of monetary policy on inflation: modelling the UK experience 1978–86', in Britton, A. (ed.), *Policy-Making with Macroeconomic Models*, Aldershot: Gower

McNees, S.K. (1982) 'The role of macroeconometric models in forecasting and policy analysis in the United States', *Journal of Forecasting*, 1, 37–48.

McNees, S.K. (1986) 'Forecasting accuracy of alternative techniques: a comparison of US macroeconomic forecasts', *Journal of Business and Economic Statistics*, 4, 5–23.

McNees, S.K. (1991) 'Comparing macroeconomic model forecasts under common assumptions', in Klein, L.R. (ed.), *Comparative Performance of US Econometric Models*, Oxford: Oxford University Press.

Mariano, R.S., and Brown, B.W. (1984) Residual based procedures for prediction and estimation in nonlinear simultaneous systems', *Econometrica*, 52, 321–43.

Mariano, R.S., and Brown, B.W. (1991) 'Stochastic simulation tests of nonlinear econometric models', in Klein. L.R. (ed.), *Comparative Performance of US Econometric Models*, Oxford: Oxford University Press.

Masson, P., Symansky, S., and Meredith, G. (1990) 'MULTIMOD Mark II: a revised and extended model', Occasional Paper 71, Washington, DC: IMF.

Masson, P., and Symansky, S. (1992) 'Evaluating the EMS and EMU using stochastic simulations: some issues', in Barrell, R.J., and Whitley, J.D. (eds.) *Macroeconomic Policy Coordination in Europe: The ERM and monetary union*, London: Sage

Matthews, K.G.P., and Minford, A.P.L. (1987) 'Mrs Thatcher's economic policies, 1979–1987', *Economic Policy*, 5, 57–101.

References

Meese, R.A and Rogoff, K. (1983) 'Empirical exchange rate models of the seventies: do they fit out of sample?' *Journal of International Economics*, 14, 3–24.

Melliss, C.L. (1986) 'HM Treasury macroeconomic model 1986', *Economic Modelling*, 5, 237–259.

Melliss, C.L., and Whittakker, R. (1987) 'Stochastic simulations with the Treasury model', Government Economic Service Working Paper, no.95.

Minford, A.P.L. (1984) 'Response to Nickell', *Economic Journal*, 94, 954–59.

Minford, A.P.L., Agenor, P., and Nowell, E. (1986) 'A new classical econometric model of the world economy', *Economic Modelling*, 3, 154–74.

Minford, A.P.L., Marwaha, S.S, Matthews, K.G.P., and Sprague, A. (1984) 'The Liverpool macroeconomic model of the United Kingdom', *Economic Modelling*, 1, 24–62.

Minford, A.P.L., Rastogi, A., and Hughes-Hallett, A.H. (1992) 'ERM and EMU: survival, costs and prospects', in Barrell, R.J., and Whitley, J.D. (eds.), *Macroeconomic Policy Coordination in Europe: The ERM and monetary union*, London: Sage

Moghadam, R., and Wren-Lewis, S. (1989) 'Are wages forward looking?' LSE Centre for Economics, Discussion Paper 375.

Murphy, C. (1988) 'An overview of the Murphy model', *Australian Economic Papers*, 27 (supplement), 175–99.

Muth, J.F. (1961) 'Rational expectations and the theory of price movements', *Econometrica*, 29, 315–35.

Nagar, A.L. (1969) 'Stochastic simulation of the Brookings econometric model', in Duesenberry, J.S., Fromm, G., Klein, L.R., and Kuh E. (eds.), *The Brookings Model: Some further results*, Amsterdam: North-Holland

Nickell, S.J. (1984a) 'The modelling of wages and employment', in Hendry, D.F., and Wallis, K.F. (eds.), *Econometrics and Quantitative Economics*, Oxford: Basil Blackwell.

Nickell.S.J. (1984b) 'A review of *Unemployment: Case and Cure* by Minford, A.P.L. with Davies, D., Peel, M. and Sprague, A.', *Economic Journal*, 94, 946–53.

Nickell, S.J. (1988) 'The supply side and macroeconomic modelling', in Bryant, R.C., *et al.* (eds.) *Empirical Economics for Interdependent Economies*, Washington, DC: Brookings Institution.

Ormerod, P.A. (ed.) (1978) *Economic Modelling*, London: Heinemann

Osborn, D., and Teal, F. (1979) 'An assessment and comparison of two NIESR econometric model forecasts', *National Institute Economic Review*, 88, 60–82.

Oulton, N. (1989) 'Productivity growth and manufacturing, 1963–85: the role of new investment and scrapping', *National Institute Economic Review*, 127, 64–75.

Pagan, A. (1989) 'On the role of simulation in the statistical evaluation of econometric models', *Journal of Econometrics*, 40, 125–39.

Pain, N. (1993) 'An econometric analysis of foreign direct investment in the United Kingdom', *Scottish Journal of Political Economy*, 40, 1–23.

Patterson, K., Harnett, I., Robinson, G., and Ryding, J. (1987) 'The Bank of England quarterly model of the UK economy', *Economic Modelling*, 4, 348–529.

Pesaran, M.H., and Evans, R.A. (1984) 'Inflation, capital gains and UK personal savings 1953–81', *Economic Journal*, 94, 237–57.

Pesaran, M.H., and Smith, R. P. (1985) 'Evaluation of macroeconometric models', *Economic Modelling*, 2, 25–134

Phillips, A.W. (1954) 'Stabilisation policy in a closed economy', *Economic Journal*, 64, 290–323.

Phillips, A.W. (1958) 'The relationship between unemployment and the rate of change of money wage rates in the UK 1861–1957', *Economica*, 25, 283–99.

Richardson, P. (1988) 'The structure and simulation properties of OECD's Interlink model', *OECD Economic Studies*, 10, Paris: OECD.

Romer, P. (1986) 'Increasing returns and long run growth', *Journal of Political Economy*, 94, 1002–37.

Salter, W. (1959) 'Internal and external balance: role of price and expenditure effects', *Economic Review*, 35, 226–36.

Sargan, J.D. (1964) 'Wages and prices in the United Kingdom: A study in econometric methodology', in Hart, P.E., Mills, G., and Whitaker, J.K. (eds) *Econometric Analysis for National Economic Planning*, 22–54, London: Butterworth. Reprinted in Hendry, D.F. and Wallis, K.F. (eds) (1984) *Econometrics and Quantitative Economics*, 275–314, Oxford: Basil Blackwell.

Sargan, J.D. (1975) Discussion on misspecification', in Renton, G.A. (ed.), *Modelling the Economy*, London: Heinemann.

Sargent, T.J. (1978) 'Estimation of dynamic labor demand schedules under rational expectations', *Journal of Political Economy*, 86, 1009–44.

Sargent, T.J., and Wallace, N. (1976) 'Rational expectations and the theory of economic policy', *Journal of Monetary Economics*, 2, 169 83.

Savile, I.D., and Gardiner, K.L. (1986) 'Stagflation in the UK since 1970: a model-based explanation', *National Institute Economic Review*, 117, 52–69.

Shoven, J., and Whalley, J. (1984) 'Applied general equilibrium models of taxation and international trade: an introduction and survey', *Journal of Economic Literature*, 22, 1007–51.

Sims, C.A. (1980) 'Macroeconomics and reality', *Econometrica*, 48, 1–48.

Smith, R.P. (1990) 'The Warwick ESRC Macroeconomic Modelling Bureau: an assessment', *International Journal of Forecasting*, 6, 301–9.

Smith, R.P. (1994) 'The macro-modelling industry: structure, conduct and performance', in Hall, S.G. (ed.), (forthcoming), London: Harvester Wheatsheaf.

Spencer, P.D. (1984) 'The effect of oil discoveries on the British economy: theoretical ambiguities and the consistent expectations simulation approach', *Economic Journal*, 94, 633–44.

Spencer, P.D. (1985) 'Bounded shooting: a method for solving large nonlinear econometric models under the assumption of rational expectations', *Oxford Bulletin of Economics and Statistics*, 47, 79–82.

Stewart, M.B., and Wallis, K.F. (1981) *Introductory Econometrics*, Oxford: Basil Blackwell

Summers, L.H. (1991) 'The scientific illusion in empirical macroeconomics', in Hylleberg, S., and Paldam, M. (eds), *New Approaches to Empirical Macroeconomics*, 1–20, Oxford: Basil Blackwell.

Surrey, M.J.C. (1971) 'The analysis and forecasting of the British economy', NIESR Occasional Paper, XXV, London: NIESR

Swan, T. (1960) 'Economic control in a dependent economy', *Economic Record*, 36, 51–66.

Taylor, J.B. (1977) 'Conditions for unique solutions in stochastic macroeconomic models with rational expectations', *Econometrica*, 45, 1377–87.

Taylor, J.B. (1979a) 'Estimation and control of a macroeconomic model with rational expectations', *Econometrica*, 47, 1267–86.

Taylor, J.B. (1979b) 'Staggered wage-setting in a macro model', *American Economic Review*, 69, 108–13.

Theil, H. (1964) *Optimal Decision Rules for Government and Industry*, Amsterdam: North-Holland.

Theil, H. (1966) *Applied Economic Forecasting*, Amsterdam: North-Holland.

Thirlwall, A. (1980) *Balance of Payments Theory and the United Kingdom Experience*, London: Macmillan.

Tinbergen, J. (1952) *On the theory of economic policy*, Amsterdam: North-Holland.

Tinsley, P. (1971) 'A variable adjustment model of labour demand', *International Economic Review*, 12, 282–316.

Treasury and Civil Service Committee (1991) Memoranda on Official Economic Forecast, House of Commons, Session 1990–1, 532–i, London: HMSO.

Turner, D.S. (1990) 'The role of judgement in macroeconomic forecasting', *Journal of Forecasting*, 9, 315–45.

Turner, D.S. (1991a) 'The determinants of the NAIRU response in simulations on the Treasury model', *Oxford Bulletin of Economic and Statistics*, 53, 225–42.

Turner, D.S. (1991b) 'Does the UK face a balance of payments constraint?' in Christodoulakis, N. (ed.), *Dynamic Modelling and Control of National Economies*, Oxford: Pergamon.

Turner, D.S., and Whitley, J.D. (1991) 'The importance of the distinction between long- and short-term employment in UK macroeconometric models', *Applied Economics*, 4, 317–44

Turner, D.S., Wallis, K.F., and Whitley, J.D. (1989a) 'Using macroeconometric models to evaluate policy proposals', in Britton, A. (ed.), *Policymaking with Macroeconomic Models*, Aldershot: Gower

Turner, D.S., Wallis, K.F., and Whitley, J.D. (1989b) 'Differences in the properties of large-scale macroeconometric models: the role of labour market specifications', *Journal of Applied Econometrics*, 4, 317–44.

van den Berg, P.J., Gelauff, G.M., and Okker, V.R. (1988) 'The FREIA–KOMPAS model for the Netherlands: a quarterly macroeconomic model for the short and medium term', *Economic Modelling*, 5, 170–236.

Wallis, K.F. (1980) 'Econometric implications of the rational expectations hypothesis', *Econometrica*, 48, 49–72.

Wallis, K.F. (1986) 'Forecasting with an econometric model: the "ragged edge" problem', *Journal of Forecasting*, 5, 1–14.

Wallis, K.F. (1989) 'Macroeconomic forecasting: a survey', *Economic Journal*, 99, 28–61.

Wallis, K.F., and Whitley, J.D. (1987) 'Long-run properties of large-scale macroeconometric models', *Annales d'Economie et de Statistique*, 6/7, 207–24.

Wallis, K.F., and Whitley, J.D. (1991a) 'Large-scale econometric models of national economies', *Scandinavian Journal of Economics*, 93, 283–314; reprinted in Hylleberg, S., and Paldam, M. (eds.) *New Approaches to Empirical Macroeconomics*, Oxford: Blackwell

Wallis, K.F., and Whitley, J.D. (1991b) 'Sources of error in forecasts and expectations: UK economic models, 1984–88', *Journal of Forecasting*, 10, 231–53.

Wallis, K.F., and Whitley, J.D. (1992) 'Counterfactual analysis with macroeconometric models: the UK economy 1979–84', ESRC Macroeconomic Modelling Bureau Discussion Paper 29, Warwick: ESRC Macroeconomic Modelling Bureau.

Wallis, K.F., Andrews, M.J., Bell, D.N.F., Fisher, P.G., and Whitley, J.D. (1984) *Models of the UK Economy: A Review by the ESRC Macroeconomic Modelling Bureau*, Oxford: Oxford University Press.

Wallis, K.F., Andrews, M.J., Bell, D.N.F., Fisher, P.G., and Whitley, J.D. (1985) *Models of the UK Economy: A second review by the ESRC Macroeconomic Modelling Bureau*, Oxford: Oxford University Press.

Wallis, K.F., Andrews, M.J., Fisher, P.G., Longbottom, J.A., and Whitley, J.D. (1986) *Models of the UK Economy: A third review by the ESRC Macroeconomic Modelling Bureau*, Oxford: Oxford University Press.

Wallis, K.F., Fisher, P.G., Longbottom, J.A., Turner, D.S., and Whitley, J.D. (1987) *Models of the UK Economy: A fourth review by the ESRC Macroeconomic Modelling Bureau*, Oxford: Oxford University Press.

Westaway, P. (1992) 'A forward looking approach to learning in macroeconomic models', *National Institute Economic Review*, 140, 86–97.

Whitley, J.D. (1989) 'Comment on Mackie *et al.*, "The impact of monetary policy on inflation: modelling the UK experience 1978–86"', in Britton, A. (ed.), *Policy-Making with Macroeconomic Models*, Aldershot: Gower

Whitley, J.D. (1992a) 'Comparative simulation analysis of the European multicountry models', *Journal of Forecasting*, 11, 423–58.

Whitley, J.D. (1992b) 'Aspects of monetary union: model-based simulation results', in Barrell, R.J. and Whitley, J.D. (eds.) *Macroeconomic policy coordination in Europe: The ERM and monetary union*, Sage: London.

Whitley, J.D. (1992c) 'Comparative properties of the Nordic models', in Bergmann, L., and Olsen, Ø. (eds.), *Economic Modelling in the Nordic Countries*, Amsterdam: North-Holland

Whitley, J.D., and Wilson, R.A. (1983) 'The macroeconomic merits of a marginal employment subsidy', *Economic Journal*, 93, 862–80.

Whitley, J.D., and Wilson, R.A. (1988) 'Hours reduction with large-scale macroeconometric models: conflict between theory and empirical application', in Hart, R.A. (ed.) *Employment, Unemployment and Labor Utilisation*, London: Unwin Hyman.

Whitley, J.D., Bray, J., Hall, S., Meen, G., and Westaway, P. (1992), 'UK policies, non-price competitiveness and convergence to an EMU', ESRC Macroeconomic Modelling Bureau Discussion Paper 28, Warwick: ESRC Macroeconomic Modelling Bureau.

Whittakker, R., Wren-Lewis, S., Blackburn, K., and Currie, D.A. (1986) 'Alternative financial policy rules in an open economy under rational and adaptive expectations', *Economic Journal*, 96, 680–95.

Williamson, J. (1983) *The Open Economy and the World Economy*, New York: Harper and Row.

Wren-Lewis, S. (1988) 'Supply, liquidity and credit: a new version of the Institute's domestic econometric macromodel', *National Institute Economic Review*, 126, 32–43.

Wren-Lewis, S. (1992a) 'On the analytical foundations of the Fundamental Equilibrium Exchange Rate', in Hargreaves, C.P. (ed.), *Macroeconomic Modelling of the Long Run*, Aldershot: Edward Elgar

Wren-Lewis, S. (1992b) 'Between the short run and the long run: vintages and the NAIRU', in Hargreaves, C. (ed), *Macroeconomic Modelling of the long run*, Edward Elgar.

Wren-Lewis, S., Westaway, P., Soteri, S., and Barrell, R. (1991) 'Evaluating the UK's choice of entry rate into the ERM', *The Manchester School*, 59, 1–22.

Zarnovitz, V. (1979) 'An analysis of annual and multiperiod quarterly forecasts of aggregate income, output and the price level', *Journal of Business*, 52, 1–33.

Zarnovitz, V. (1985) 'Rational expectations and macroeconomic forecasts', *Journal of Business and Economic Statistics*, 3, 293–311

Index